This Book

presented to the

CHURCH LIBRARY IN MEMORY OF

Marvin Hardin

BY

Mr. & Mrs. Husky Forbes

Code 4386-23, No. 3, Broadman Supplies, Nashville, Tenn. Printed in USA

With loving gratitude to my father,
Dr. Jack MacArthur, who gave me the legacy of
loving books and challenged me by his example
to make use of commentaries

THE MACARTHUR NEW TESTAMENT COMMENTARY
HEBREWS

John MacArthur Jr.

MOODY PRESS/CHICAGO

Library of Congress Cataloging in Publication Data

MacArthur, John F.
  Hebrews: an expository commentary.

  (The MacArthur New Testament commentary)
  Bibliography.
  Includes index.
  1. Bible. N.T. Hebrews—Commentaries. I. Bible.
N.T. Hebrews. II. Title. III. Series: MacArthur,
John F. MacArthur New Testament Commentary.
BS2775.3.M27 1983   227'.87077   83-17450
ISBN 0-8024-0753-6

3 4 5 6 7 Printing/RR/Year 87 86 85

Printed in the United States of America

Contents

Preface

It continues to be a rich and rewarding divine communion for me to preach expositionally through the New Testament. My goal is always to have deep fellowship with the Lord in the understanding of His Word, and out of that experience to explain to His people what a passage means. In the words of Nehemiah 8:8, I strive "to give the sense" of it so they may truly hear God speak and, in so doing, may respond to Him.

Obviously, God's people need to understand Him, which demands knowing His Word of truth (2 Tim. 2:15) and allowing that Word to dwell in us richly (Col. 3:16). The dominant thrust of my ministry, therefore, is to help make God's living Word alive to His people. It is a refreshing adventure.

This New Testament commentary series reflects this objective of explaining and applying Scripture. Some commentaries are primarily linguistic, others are mostly theological, and some are mainly homiletical. This one is basically explanatory, or expository. It is not linguistically technical, but deals with linguistics when this seems helpful to proper interpretation. It is not theologically expansive, but focuses on the major doctrines in each text and on how they relate to the whole of Scripture. It is not primarily homiletical, though each unit of thought is generally treated as one chapter, with a clear outline and logical flow of thought. Most truths are illustrated and applied with other Scripture. After establishing the context of a passage, I have tried to follow closely the writer's development and reasoning.

My prayer is that each reader will fully understand what the Holy Spirit is saying through this part of His Word, so that His revelation may lodge in the minds of believers and bring greater obedience and faithfulness—to the glory of our great God.

Introduction

     I have titled this study of the book of Hebrews, "The Preeminence of Jesus Christ." Jesus Christ is superior to and preeminent over everyone and everything.

     The first three verses provide a fitting introduction. But before we look at these, we need some background as a foundation for our study. Studying Hebrews is a thrilling adventure. Part of that adventure is due to the difficulty of the book. It is a book that has many, many deep truths that are difficult to grasp and that demand diligent and faithful study. There are things here that are beyond understanding apart from complete reliance on God's Spirit and sincere commitment to understand His Word.

     My former Old Testament professor, Dr. Charles L. Feinberg, often said that you cannot understand the book of Hebrews unless you understand the book of Leviticus, because the book of Hebrews is based upon the principles of the Levitical priesthood. But don't worry about your lack of understanding of Leviticus. By the time we get through Hebrews, you should have a pretty good grasp of Leviticus as well. It would be a definite advantage, however, if, on your own, you began to familiarize yourself with Leviticus. It contains the ceremonial symbols for which Hebrews presents the realities.

Authorship

This epistle was written by an unknown author. Some say it was by Paul, some say by Apollos, some say by Peter, some say by this, that, or another person. Due to differences in style, vocabulary, and pattern of personal reference in the epistles known to be his, I do not believe it was written by Paul. We know it was written by an inspired believer to a suffering, persecuted group of Jews somewhere in the East, outside of Israel. As to the exact human authorship, I stand with one of the great teachers of the early church by the name of Origen, who said simply, "No one knows." How fitting, since the book's purpose is to exalt Christ. Throughout this study we will refer to the fact that it was written, as was all Scripture, by the Holy Spirit—whom we do know.

Audience

There are no references to Gentiles in the book. Problems between Gentiles and Jews in the church are not mentioned or reflected here, indicating almost certainly that the congregation being addressed was strictly Jewish. To these suffering Jewish believers—and some unbelievers—are revealed the merits of the Lord Jesus Christ and the New Covenant, in contrast to the Old Covenant, under which they had so long lived and worshiped.

We do not know the exact location of this group of Hebrews. They were perhaps somewhere near Greece. We do know that this community had been evangelized by apostles and prophets (2:3-4). By prophets, of course, is meant New Testament prophets (Eph. 2:20). Evidently this church had been founded fairly soon after Christ's ascension. By the time the letter was written, a small congregation of believers already existed there.

Also addressed in the letter are unbelievers, who evidently were a part of this Jewish community. Unlike many Jews in Palestine, these had never had opportunity to meet Jesus. Anything they may have known about Him was secondhand (Heb. 2:3-4). They of course had no New Testament writings, as such, as a testimony, for it had not yet been brought together. Whatever they knew of Christ and His gospel they knew from believing neighbors, or perhaps directly from the mouth of an apostle or prophet.

The letter had to have been written after Christ's ascension, which was about A.D. 30, and before the destruction of Jerusalem in A.D. 70, since the Temple must still have been standing. I believe it was probably written close to 70, perhaps as early as 65. We know that there were not any apostolic missionaries from Jerusalem until at least seven years after the church there had been founded. Likely it was some time later that they would have reached this Jewish community, perhaps many miles away. And, after they had been reached, the believers would had to have had a certain amount of time to have been taught, as reflected in the letter itself.

> For though by this time you ought to be teachers, you have need again for some one to teach you the elementary principles of the oracles of God, and you have come to need milk and not solid food. (5:12)

He says, in other words, "You've had enough time to become mature, but you are not."

We must understand that three basic groups of people are in view throughout this epistle. If one does not keep these groups in mind, the book becomes very confusing. If, for example, as some have said, it was written exclusively to Christians, extreme problems arise in interpreting a number of passages which could hardly apply to believers. And because it so frequently addresses believers, it could not have been written primarily to unbelievers either. So it must have been written to include both. In fact three basic groups in this Jewish community are addressed. Here is the critical basis for understanding the epistle; and here is where people often get mixed up, especially in interpreting chapters 6 and 10.

GROUP I: HEBREW CHRISTIANS

First of all, there was in this Jewish community a congregation of true believers in the Lord Jesus Christ. They had come out of Judaism, in which they had been born and raised. Now they were born again. They had received Jesus Christ as their personal Messiah and Savior. They had become His followers. The frequent result was tremendous hostility from their own people—ostracism from their families, persecution and suffering of many sorts, though not yet martyrdom (10:32-34; 12:4). They suffered greatly, persecuted not only by their fellow Jews, but also perhaps by Gentiles.

They should have anticipated as much and have been mature enough to deal with it. But they had not and they were not. They lacked full confidence in the gospel, and consequently in their Lord. They were in danger of going back into the standards and patterns of Judaism—not of losing their salvation but of confusing the gospel with Jewish ceremony and legalism and of thereby weakening their faith and testimony. They could not bring themselves to accept the clear-cut distinction between the gospel, the New Covenant in Christ, and the forms, ceremonies, patterns, and methods of Judaism. They were still hung up, for example, on the Temple ritual and worship. That is why the Spirit talks to them so much about the new priesthood and the new Temple and the new sacrifice and the new sanctuary, all of which are better than the old ones.

They had gone beyond Judaism in receiving Jesus Christ but, understandably, they were tempted to hang on to many of the Judaistic habits that had been so much a part of their lives. When their friends and their countrymen began to persecute them in earnest, the pressure led them to hold even tighter to some of the old Jewish traditions. They felt they had to keep a foothold in their old and familiar relationships. It was hard to make a clean break.

With all that pressure, together with their weak faith and spiritual ignorance, they were in great danger of mixing the new with the old. They were in great danger of coming up with a ritualistic, ceremonial, legalistic Christianity. They were a whole congregation of "weaker brothers" (cf. Rom. 14:2; 1 Cor. 8:9), who were still calling "unclean" what the Lord had sanctified (Mark 7:19; Acts 10:15; Rom. 14:12; 1 Tim. 4:1-5).

The Holy Spirit directed this letter to them to strengthen their faith in the New Covenant, to show them that they did not need the old Temple (which in a few years would be completely destroyed by Titus Vespasian anyway, showing that God had brought an end to that economy; cf. Luke 21:5-6). They did not need the old Aaronic-Levitical priesthood. They did not need the old day-in, day-out, day-in, day-out sacrifices. They did not need the ceremonies. They had a new and better covenant with a new and better priesthood, a new and better sanctuary, and a new and better sacrifice. The pictures and symbols were to give way to the reality.

The book of Hebrews was written to give confidence to these floundering believers. The Lord was speaking to Christians and telling them to hold to the better covenant and the better priesthood, and not go back into the patterns of Judaism, either to that priesthood or to that assemblage. They must steadfastly and exclusively live in, and live out, their new relationship in Christ.

GROUP II: HEBREW NON-CHRISTIANS WHO ARE INTELLECTUALLY CONVINCED

We have all met people who have heard the truth of Jesus Christ and who are intellectually convinced that He is indeed who He claimed to be, and yet are not willing to make a commitment of faith in Him.

In the group of Hebrews to whom this epistle was written, there were such non-Christians, as there are in many groups today. It is likely that every church group since Pentecost has had people in it who have been convinced that Jesus is the Christ but who have never committed themselves to Him.

These Hebrew non-Christians, intellectually convinced but spiritually uncommitted, are the object of some of the things that the writer has to say. They believed that Jesus was the Messiah, the Christ, spoken of in the Jewish Scriptures (what we now call the Old Testament), but they had not been willing to receive Him personally as their Savior and Lord. Why? Perhaps, like those described by John, they believed in Him, but they loved the approval of men more than the approval of God (John 12:42-43). They were not willing to make the sacrifice required. And so they are exhorted by the Holy Spirit to go all the way to saving faith; to go all the way to commitment to the lordship of Christ.

In chapter 2 is one of the special statements to this group of the intellectually convinced but spiritually uncommitted.

> For this reason we must pay much closer attention to what we have heard, lest we drift away from it. For if the word spoken through angels proved unalterable, and every transgression and disobedience received a just recompense, how shall we escape if we neglect so great a salvation? (2:1-3a)

They were at the point of acknowledging but not of committing. They were guilty of the great sin of neglecting to do what one is intellectually convinced is right. The truth of the gospel had even been confirmed to them by the apostles, with all the miracles and gifts of the Holy Spirit (v. 4).

In chapter six this group is addressed again.

> For in the case of those who have once been enlightened and have tasted of the heavenly gift and have been made partakers of the Holy Spirit, and have tasted the good word of God and the powers of the age to come, and then have fallen away, it is impossible to renew them again to repentance, since they again crucify to themselves the Son of God, and put Him to open shame. (6:4-6)

Here is a warning to the merely intellectually convinced not to stop where he is. If he stops after having received full revelation, and especially after he is convinced of the truth of the revelation, he has only one way to go. If, when a man is totally convinced that Jesus Christ is who He claimed to be, he then refuses to believe, this man is without excuse and without hope—because, though convinced of the truth of the gospel, he still will not put his trust in it. He is here warned that there is nothing else God can do.

What is the greatest sin that a man can commit? The sin of rejecting Christ.

> For if we go on sinning willfully after receiving the knowledge of the truth, there no longer remains a sacrifice for sins. (10:26)

If a man has heard the gospel, understands it, and is intellectually convinced of its truth, but then willfully rejects Christ, what more can God do? Nothing! All God can now promise this man is "a certain terrifying expectation of judgment, and the fury of a fire which will consume the adversaries" (v. 27).

The warning continues:

> How much severer punishment do you think he will deserve who has trampled under foot the Son of God, and has regarded as unclean the blood of the covenant by which he was sanctified, and has insulted the Spirit of grace? (10:29)

When you know the truth of the gospel and reject it, the consequences are terrible and permanent.

In chapter twelve, verse fifteen, is still another warning.

> See to it that no one comes short of the grace of God; that no root of bitterness springing up causes trouble, and by it many be defiled; that there be no immoral or godless person like Esau, who sold his own birthright for a single meal. For you know that even afterwards, when he desired to inherit the blessing, he was rejected, for he found no place for repentance, though he sought for it with tears. (12:15-17)

This is the tragedy of being too late—with no one to blame but ourselves.

These are controversial passages, and we will deal with them in detail at the proper places.

GROUP III: HEBREW NON-CHRISTIANS WHO WERE NOT CONVINCED

Not only does the Holy Spirit in this book speak to Christians in order to strengthen their faith and to the intellectually convinced in order to push them over the line to saving faith, but He also speaks to those who have not believed at all, to those who may not yet be convinced of any part of the gospel. He seeks to show them clearly that Jesus is in fact who He claimed to be, and this truth is the main thrust of chapter nine.

For example, in 9:11 He says:

> But when Christ appeared as a high priest of the good things to come, He entered through the greater and more perfect tabernacle, not made with hands, that is to say, not of this creation. (9:11)

And He goes on to explain Christ's new priesthood:

> How much more will the blood of Christ, who through the eternal Spirit offered Himself without blemish to God, cleanse your conscience from dead works to

serve the living God? And for this reason He is the mediator of a new covenant, in order that since a death has taken place for the redemption of the transgressions that were committed under the first covenant, those who have been called may receive the promise of the eternal inheritance. . . . And inasmuch as it is appointed for men to die once and after this comes judgment, so Christ also, having been offered once to bear the sins of many shall appear a second time for salvation without reference to sin, to those who eagerly await Him. (9:14-15, 27-28)

These messages speak directly to unbelievers, not to Christians and not to those who are already convinced of the gospel intellectually. They are given to those who first need to know who Christ really is.

These, then, are the three groups in view in the epistle. The key to interpreting any part of Hebrews is to understand which group is being addressed. If we do not understand that, we are bound to confuse issues. For example, the Spirit is surely not saying to believers, "It is appointed for men to die once and after this comes judgment" (9:27). We must always understand what group it is to whom He speaks. As we study the book of Hebrews, we will relate each text to one of the three groups.

The primary message is addressed to believers. Periodically there are interspersed warnings to the two unbelieving groups. In a masterful way, in a way that could only be divine, the Holy Spirit speaks to all three. He meets every one of their particular needs and their specific questions in this one supernatural masterpiece.

In Hebrews there is confidence and assurance for the Christian. There is warning to the intellectually convinced that he must receive Christ or his knowledge will damn him. Finally, there is a convincing presentation to the unbelieving Jew who is not even intellectually persuaded that he should believe in Jesus Christ. To these three groups Hebrews is a presentation of Christ, the Messiah, the Author of a New Covenant greater than the one God had made in the Old Testament. The old one was not bad or wrong; it was God-given and therefore good. But it was incomplete and preliminary. It set the stage for the new.

A THEMATIC OUTLINE OF THE BOOK

As we have stated, the overall theme is the superiority, or the preeminence, of Christ. He is better than anything that was before. He is better than any Old Testament person; He is better than any Old Testament institution; He is better than any Old Testament ritual; He is better than any Old Testament sacrifice; He is better than anyone and everything else. This general outline of the book of Hebrews shows the basic pattern of presenting the superiority of Jesus Christ. We will loosely follow this pattern as we study.

The letter begins with the general superiority of Christ to everyone and everything, a kind of a summary of the whole epistle in the first three verses. Next comes the superiority of Christ to angels, then the superiority of Christ to Moses, the superiority of Christ to Joshua, the superiority of Christ to Aaron and his priesthood, the superiority of Christ to the Old Covenant, the superiority of Christ's sacrifice to old sacrifices, the superiority of Christ's faithful people to all the faithless, and the superiority of Christ's testimony to that of any other. This brief outline gives us the flow of the book, which, above all else, teaches the total, complete, and absolute superiority of Jesus Christ.

A Few Background Observations

NO JEW COULD SEE GOD AND LIVE

Before we begin looking at particular passages and verses, let me suggest a couple of footnotes. To the Jew it had always been a dangerous thing to approach God. "No man can see Me and live" (Ex. 33:20). On the great Day of Atonement (Yom Kippur), which occurred one time a year and which many Jews today still keep to one degree or another—at that time and that time alone could the High Priest enter into the Holy of Holies, where the Shekinah Glory dwelt, where God was uniquely present. They could not see God, they could not behold God. They could not even approach Him except on this one day a year—and only one person, the high priest, could do this. And he had to go in and get out quickly. He could not linger there lest he put Israel in terror of judgment.

Since there was naturally no personal nearness to God, there had to be some basis for communion between God and Israel. So God established a covenant. In this covenant God, in His grace, and in His sovereign initiative, offered to Israel a special relationship with Himself. In a unique way He would be their God and they would be His people to reach the world. They would have special access to Him if they obeyed His law. To break His law was sin, and sin interrupted their access to Him. Since there was always sin, access was always being interrupted.

THE OLD SACRIFICES

So God instituted a system of sacrifices as outward acts of inner repentance. Through the Levitical priesthood, sacrifices were made to symbolize atonement for sin, in order that the barrier might be taken down and there might be access to God. It worked something like this: God gave His covenant, which included His law, and thereby offered the people access to Him. Man sinned, the law was broken, and the barrier went up again. Another repentant act of sacrifice was then made so that the barrier would be dropped and the relationship reestablished.

We naturally wonder how often they had to make sacrifices. The answer is incessantly—hour after hour, day after day, month after month, year after year. They never stopped. Besides this, the priests themselves were sinners. They had to make sacrifices for their own sins before they could make sacrifices for the sins of the people. And so the barrier went up and down, up and down, up and down. This in itself proved the ineffectiveness of the system. It was a losing battle against sin and the barrier it erects. And besides this, the whole system never removed sin fully and finally. It only covered it up.

What man needed was a Perfect Priest and a Perfect Sacrifice to open the way once and for all—a sacrifice that was not just a picture and that did not deal just with one sin at a time, over and over again, but one that took it all away once and for all. That, says the writer of Hebrews, is exactly what Jesus was and what He did.

THE NEW SACRIFICE

Jesus Christ came as the Mediator of a better covenant because it is one that does not have to be repeated every hour, or even every month or year. Christ comes as the mediator of a better covenant because His sacrifice once and for all removes every sin ever committed. Christ comes as the mediator of a better covenant because He is a priest who does not need to make any sacrifices for Himself. He is totally perfect, the Perfect Priest and the Perfect Sacrifice. Jesus Christ, in His own sacrifice—His sacrifice of Himself—showed the perfection that eliminated sin.

> By this will we have been sanctified through the offering of the body of Jesus Christ once for all. (10:10)

Sanctified here means "made pure," and the emphasis is: ". . . through the offering of the body of Jesus Christ ONCE." That is something wonderfully new in the sacrificial system—one sacrifice, once offered. That is indeed a wonderfully better covenant.

> But He, having offered one sacrifice for sins for all time, sat down at the right hand of God. (10:12)

That is something no priest could ever do. There were not even any seats where the sacrifices were made in the Tabernacle or the Temple. The priests had to keep making sacrifices; their task was never finished. Jesus made His sacrifice and "sat down." It was finished. It was done.

"For by one offering He has perfected for all time those who are sanctified" (10:14).

BETTER PRIEST, BETTER SACRIFICE

Thus there is a better priest making a better sacrifice. This is a central message of the book of Hebrews. To the believing Jew the Spirit says, "Continue to have confidence in this Priest and this sacrifice." To the one intellectually convinced He says, "Receive this Priest and accept the sacrifice He made. You are on the borderline of decision; don't fall into perdition when you are only a step away." And to the unconvinced He says, "Look at Jesus Christ. See how much better He is than the Levitical priests and how much better His one sacrifice is than all of their innumerable sacrifices. Receive Him."

The Spirit is saying, "All of your lives you Jews have been looking for the Perfect Priest. You've been looking for the Perfect Final Sacrifice. I present Him to you—Jesus Christ."

DIFFICULTIES FOR JEWISH CHRISTIANS

Keep in mind that the idea of a new covenant was not easy for Jews to accept. Even after they accepted the new, it was hard for them to make a clean break with the old. The Gentiles did not have that problem, of course, since they had never been a part of the old. They had long before lost any real knowledge of the true God, and in consequence were worshiping idols—some of them primitive and some of them sophisticated—but all of them idols (see Rom. 1:21-25).

But the Jews had always had a divine religion. For centuries they had known a divinely appointed place of worship and a divinely revealed way of worshiping. God Himself had established their religion. One might effectively say, when witnessing to a Gentile, "Here is the truth." But when you went to a Jew and said, "Here is the truth," he would likely say, "I already know the truth." When you countered, "But this truth is from the one true God," he would respond, "So is the truth that I have."

It was not an easy thing for a Jew to forsake completely all his heritage, especially when he knew that much of it, at least, was God-given. Even after a Jew received the Lord Jesus Christ this was difficult. He had a traditional desire to retain some of the forms and ceremonies that had been a part of his life since earliest childhood. Part of the purpose of the book of Hebrews, therefore, was to confront that born-again Jew with the fact that he could, and should, let go of all his Judaistic trappings. But since the Temple was still standing and the priests still ministered in it, this was especially hard to do. Letting go became easier after the Temple was destroyed in A.D. 70.

When you consider the intense persecution Jewish Christians were going through at this time, it is easy to appreciate the difficulties and temptations they faced. The high priest Ananias was especially hard and unrelenting. He had all Christian Jews automatically banished from the holy places. That was tough. All their lives they had had access to these sacred places. Now they could have no part in the God-ordained services. They were now considered unclean. They could not go to the synagogue, much less the Temple; they could not offer any sacrifices; they could not communicate with the priests. They could have nothing to do with their own people. They were cut off from their own society. For clinging to Jesus as the Messiah, they were banished from almost every sacred thing they had ever known. Though in God's eyes they were the only true Jews (Rom. 2:28-29), they were considered by fellow Jews to be worse than Gentiles.

Many Jewish Christians were beginning to say to themselves, "This is rough. We received the gospel and believed it. But it's hard to break with our old religion and with our own people and the traditions we have always held and to face persecution. It is hard for us not to doubt that Jesus is the Messiah." Such doubts were a great problem for them, because they were spiritually infantile.

Throughout Hebrews these immature, but beloved, Christians are told to keep their confidence in Christ, the mediator of a better covenant and their new Great High Priest. They are reminded that they were losing nothing for which they were not getting something infinitely better. They had been deprived of an earthly temple but they were going to get a heavenly one. They had been deprived of an earthly priesthood but they now had a heavenly Priest. They had been deprived of the old pattern of sacrifices but now they had one final sacrifice.

BETTER EVERYTHING

In this epistle, contrast reigns. Everything presented is presented as better: a better hope, a better testament, a better promise, a better sacrifice, a better substance, a better country, a better resurrection, a better everything. Jesus Christ is presented here as the supreme Best. And we are presented as being in Him and as dwelling in a completely new dimension—the heavenlies. We read of the heavenly Christ, the heavenly calling, the heavenly gift, the heavenly country, the heavenly Jerusalem, and of our names being written in the heavenlies. Everything is new. Everything is better. We don't need the old.

Now the point in what has been said is this: we have such a high priest, who has taken His seat at the right hand of the throne of the Majesty in the heavens. (8:1)

Here is the whole summary of Hebrews in one sentence. Ours is the High Priest of high priests, and He is seated. His work is done, completely finished for all time and for us.

The Superiority of Christ (1:1-2)

God, after He spoke long ago to the fathers in the prophets in many portions and in many ways, in these last days has spoken to us in His Son, whom He appointed heir of all things, through whom also He made the world. (1:1-2)

The writer does not delay in getting to his point. He makes it in the first three verses. These verses are very simple. They tell us Christ is superior to everyone and everything. The three primary features of His superiority are: preparation, presentation, and preeminence. Keep in mind that all through the book Christ is presented as being better than the best of everyone and everything that was before Him—absolutely better than anything the Old Testament, the Old Covenant, provided.

THE PREPARATION FOR CHRIST

God, after He spoke long ago to the fathers in the prophets in many portions and in many ways. (1:1)

Here is an indication of how God wrote the Old Testament. Its purpose was to prepare for the coming of Christ. Whether by prophecy or type or principle or commandment or whatever, it made preparation for Christ.

The senses of man, marvelous as they are, are incapable of reaching beyond the natural world. For us to know anything about God, He must tell us. We could never know God if He did not speak to us. Thus, in the Old Testament, the writer reminds us, "God . . . spoke."

MAN'S WAYS TO GOD

Man lives in a natural "box," which encloses him within its walls of time and space. Outside of this box is the supernatural, and somewhere deep inside himself man knows it is out there. But in himself he does not know anything certain about it. So someone comes along and says, "We must find out about the supernatural, the world 'out there.'" And a new religion is born. Those who become interested run over to the edge of the box, get out their imaginative mental chisels and start trying to chip a hole in the edge of the box—through which they can crawl, or at least peer, out and discover the secrets of the other world.

That, figuratively, is what always happens. The Buddhist says that when you have worked and thought yourself into Nirvana, all of a sudden you are out of the box. You have transcended the natural and have found your way into the supernatural. The Muslim says basically the same thing, though in different words. So do all the other religions—Zoroastrianism, Hinduism, Confucianism, or whatever it may be. These are all attempts by man to escape from the natural to the supernatural, to get out of the box. But the problem is, he cannot get himself out.

GOD'S WAY TO MAN

By definition, natural man cannot escape into the supernatural. We cannot go into a religious phone booth and change into a superman. We cannot in ourselves or by ourselves transcend our natural existence. If we are to know anything about God, it will not be by escaping, or climbing, or thinking, or working our way to Him; it will only be by His coming to us, His speaking to us. We cannot, by ourselves, understand God any more than an insect we may hold in our hand can understand us. Nor can we condescend to its level, or communicate with it if we could. But God can condescend to our level and He can communicate with us. And He has.

God became a man Himself and entered our box to tell us about Himself, more fully and completely than He was able to do even through His prophets. This not only was divine revelation, but personal divine revelation of the most literal and perfect and wonderful sort. All of man's religions reflect his attempts to make his way out of the box. The message of Christianity, however, is that "the Son of Man has come to seek and to save that which was lost" (Luke 19:10).

When God burst into the box, He did it in human form, and the name of that human form is Jesus Christ. That is the difference between Christianity and every other religion in the world. That is why it is so foolish for people to say, "It doesn't make any difference what you believe or what religion you follow." It makes every difference. Every religion is but man's attempt to discover God. Christianity is God bursting into man's world and showing and telling man what He is like. Because man by himself is incapable of identifying, comprehending, or understanding God at all, God had to invade the world of man and speak to him about Himself. Initially, He told us He would be coming.

BY THE PROPHETS: MANY WAYS

This He did through the words of the Old Testament. He used men as instruments, but was Himself behind them, enlightening and energizing them. The deists teach that God started the world going and then went away, leaving it to run by itself. But God is not detached from His creation; He is not uninvolved in our world. The true and living God, unlike the false gods of man's making, is not dumb or indifferent. The God of Scripture, unlike the impersonal "First Cause" of some philosophers, is not silent. He speaks. He first spoke in the Old Testament, which is not a collection of the wisdom of ancient men but is the voice of God.

Now notice how God spoke: "in many portions and in many ways." The writer uses a play on words in the original language: "God, *polumerōs* and *polutropōs*. . ." These two Greek words are interesting. They mean, respectively, "in many portions" (as of books) and "in many different manners." There are many books in the Old Testament—thirty-nine of them. In all those **many portions** (*polumerōs*) and in **many ways** (*polutropōs*) God spoke to men. Sometimes it was in a vision, sometimes by a parable, sometimes through a type or a symbol. There were many different ways in which God spoke in the Old Testament. But it is always God speaking. Even the words spoken by men and angels are included because He wants us to know them.

Men were used—their minds were used and their personalities were used—but they were totally controlled by the Spirit of God. Every word they wrote was the word that God decided they should write and delighted in their writing.

Many ways includes many literary ways. Some of the Old Testament is narrative. Some of it is poetry, in beautiful Hebrew meter. The "many ways" also includes many types of content. Some is law; some is prophecy; some is doctrinal; some is ethical and moral; some is warning; some is encouragement; and so on. But it is all God speaking.

PROGRESSIVE REVELATION

TRUE BUT INCOMPLETE

Yet, beautiful and important and authoritative as it is, the Old Testament is fragmentary and incomplete. It was delivered over the course of some 1500 years by some forty-plus writers—in many different pieces, each with its own truths. It began to build and grow, truth upon truth. It was what we call progressive revelation. Genesis gives some truth, and Exodus gives some more. The truth builds and builds and builds. In the Old Testament God was pleased, for that time, to dispense His gracious truth to the Jews by the mouths of His prophets—in many different ways, developing His revelation progressively from lesser to greater degrees of light. The revelation did not build from error to truth but from incomplete truth to more complete truth. And it remained incomplete until the New Testament was finished.

Divine revelation, then, going from the Old Testament to the New Testament, is progressive revelation. It progressed from promise to fulfillment. The Old Testament is promise; the New Testament is fulfillment. Jesus Christ said, "Do not think that I came to abolish the Law or the Prophets," that is, the Old Testament, ". . . but to fulfill" (Matt. 5:17). His revelation progressed from promise to fulfillment. In fact, the Old Testament itself clearly indicates that the men of faith who wrote it were trusting in a promise they had not yet understood. They trusted in a promise that was yet to be fulfilled.

Let me give a few supporting verses. Hebrews 11 speaks about many of the great saints of the Old Testament. "And all these, having gained approval through their faith, did not receive what was promised" (v. 39). In other words, they never saw the fulfillment of promise. They foresaw what was going to happen without seeing it fully realized. Peter tells us that the Old Testament prophets did not understand all of what they wrote. 'As to this salvation, the prophets who prophesied of the grace that would come to you made careful search and inquiry, seeking to know what person or time the Spirit of Christ within them was indicating as He predicted the sufferings of Christ and the glories to follow. It was revealed to them that they were not serving themselves, but you, in these things which now have been announced to you through those who preached the gospel to you" (1 Pet. 1:10-12).

We must, of course, clearly understand that the Old Testament was not in any way erroneous. But there was in it a development, of spiritual light and of moral standards, until God's truth was refined and finalized in the New Testament. The distinction is not in the validity of the revelation—its rightness or wrongness—but in the completeness of it and the time of it. Just as children are first taught letters, then words, and then sentences, so God gave His revelation. It began with the "picture book" of types and ceremonies and prophecies and progressed to final completion in Jesus Christ and His New Testament.

FROM GOD, THROUGH HIS MESSENGERS

Now the picture is set for us. Long ago God spoke to "the fathers," the Old Testament people, our spiritual ancestors—also our physical ancestors if we are Jewish. He even spoke to some of our Gentile predecessors. He spoke to them by the prophets, His messengers. A prophet is one who speaks to men for God; a priest is one who speaks to God for men. The priest takes man's problems to God; the prophet takes God's message to men. Both, if they are true, are commissioned by God, but their ministries are quite different. The book of Hebrews has a great deal to say about priests, but its opening verse speaks of prophets. The Holy Spirit establishes the divine authorship of the Old Testament, its accuracy and its authority, through the fact that it was given to and delivered by God's prophets.

Throughout the New Testament this truth is affirmed. Peter, for example, tells us that "no prophecy was every made by an act of human will, but men moved by the Holy Spirit spoke from God" (2 Pet. 1:21). "Prophecy" in that text refers to the Old Testament. No human writer of the Old Testament wrote of his own will, but only as he was directed by the Holy Spirit.

Paul also tells us that "all Scripture is inspired by God and profitable for teaching, for reproof, for correction, for training in righteousness" (2 Tim. 3:16). All Scripture is given by inspiration of God. The *American Standard Version* reads, "Every scripture inspired of God is also profitable," implying that not all Scripture is inspired. But all Scripture is fully, not simply in part, inspired by God. God has not hidden His Word within man's words, leaving His creatures to their own devices in deciding which is which. The Old Testament is only a part of God's truth, but it is not partially His truth. It is not His complete truth, but it is completely His truth. It is God's revelation, His progressive revelation preparing His people for the coming of His Son, Jesus Christ.

BY THE SON: ONE WAY

In these last days [God] has spoken to us in His Son, whom He ap-

pointed heir of all things, through whom also He made the world.
(1:2)

God's full, perfect revelation awaited the coming of His Son. God, who used to speak in many different ways through many different people, has finally spoken in one way, through one Person, His Son Jesus Christ.

The whole New Testament is centered around Christ. The gospels tell His story, the epistles comment on it, and the Revelation tells of its culmination. From beginning to end the New Testament is Christ. No prophet had been given God's whole truth. The Old Testament was given to many men, in bits and pieces and fragments. Jesus not only brought, but was, God's full and final Revelation.

COMING IN THESE LAST DAYS

There are several ways to interpret the phrase, **in these last days.** It could refer to the last days of revelation. It could mean that this is the final revelation in Christ, there being nothing else to add to it. Or it could mean that in the last days of revelation it came through God's Son. But I think the writer is making a messianic reference. The phrase "the last days" was very familiar to the Jews of that day and had a distinctive meaning. Whenever a Jew saw or heard these words he immediately had messianic thoughts, because the scriptural promise was that in the last days Messiah would come (Jer. 33:14-16; Mic. 5:1-4; Zech. 9:9, 16). Since this letter was written first of all to Jews, we will interpret the phrase in that context.

The woman at the well, though a Samaritan, told Jesus, "I know that the Messiah is coming (He who is called Christ); when that One comes, He will declare all things to us" (John 4:25). She knew that when Messiah arrived, He would unfold the full and final revelation of God, as indeed He did.

The writer, then, is saying, "In these promised Last Days Messiah (Christ) has come and has spoken the final revelation of God." Jesus came in these last days. Unfortunately, Messiah's own people rejected Him and His revelation, and so the fulfillment of all of the promises of the last days has yet to be fully realized.

TRUE AND COMPLETE

The Old Testament had been given in pieces. To Noah was revealed the quarter of the world from which Messiah would come. To Micah, the town where He would be born. To Daniel, the time of His birth. To Malachi, the forerunner who would come before Him. To Jonah, His resurrection was typified. Every one of those pieces of revelation was true and accurate; and each one related to the others in some way or another. And each one in some way or another pointed to the Messiah, the Christ. But only in Jesus Christ Himself was everything brought together and made whole. In Him the revelation was full and complete.

Since the revelation is complete, to add anything to the New Testament is blasphemous. To add to it The Book of Mormon, or Science and Health, or anything else that claims to be revelation from God is blasphemous. "God has in these last days finalized His revelation in His Son." It was finished. The end of the book of Revelation warns that if we add anything to it, its plagues will be added to us, and that if we take anything away from it, our part in the tree of life and the holy city will be taken away from us (Rev. 22:18-19).

In the first verse and a half of Hebrews, the Holy Spirit establishes the preeminence of Jesus Christ over all the Old Testament, over its message, its methods, and its messengers. It was just what those Jews, believing and nonbelieving, needed to hear.

And so is established the priority of Jesus Christ. He is greater than the prophets. He is greater than any revelation in the Old Testament, for He is the embodiment of all that truth, and more. God has fully expressed Himself in Christ.

The Preeminence
of Christ (1:2-3)

In these last days [God] has spoken to us in His Son, whom He appointed heir of all things, through whom also He made the world. And He is the radiance of His glory and the exact representation of His nature, and upholds all things by the word of His power. When He had made purification of sins, He sat down at the right hand of the Majesty on high. (1:2-3)

Someone has said that Jesus Christ came from the bosom of the Father to the bosom of a woman. He put on humanity that we might put on divinity. He became Son of Man that we might become sons of God. He was born contrary to the laws of nature, lived in poverty, was reared in obscurity, and only once crossed the boundary of the land in which He was born—and that in His childhood. He had no wealth or influence and had neither training nor education in the world's schools. His relatives were inconspicuous and uninfluencial. In infancy He startled a king. In boyhood He puzzled the learned doctors. In manhood He ruled the course of nature. He walked upon the billows and hushed the sea to sleep. He healed the multitudes without medicine and made no charge for His services. He never wrote a book and yet all the libraries of the world could not hold the books about Him. He never wrote a song, yet He has furnished the theme for more songs than all songwriters together. He never founded a college, yet all the schools together cannot boast of as many students as He has. He never practiced medicine and yet He has healed more broken hearts than all the doctors have healed broken bodies. This Jesus Christ is the star of astronomy, the rock of geology, the lion and the lamb of zoology, the harmonizer of all discords, and the healer of all diseases. Throughout history great men have come and gone, yet He lives on. Herod could not kill Him. Satan could not seduce Him. Death could not destroy Him and the grave could not hold Him.

FULFILLMENT OF PROMISES

The Old Testament tells us in at least two places (Jer. 23:18, 22 and Amos 3:7) that the prophets were let in on the secrets of God. Yet at times they wrote those secrets without understanding them (1 Pet. 1:10-11). In Jesus Christ they are both fulfilled and understood. He is God's final word. "For as many as may be the promises of God, in Him they are yes; wherefore also by Him is our Amen to the glory of God through us" (2 Cor. 1:20). Every promise of God resolves itself in Christ. All the promises become yes—verified and fulfilled. Jesus Christ is the supreme and the final revelation.

In these last days. The last days are days of fulfillment. In the Old Testament the Jew saw the last days as the time when all the promises would be fulfilled. In these days Messiah would come and the Kingdom would come and salvation would come and Israel would no longer be under bondage. In the last days promises would stop and fulfillments begin. That is exactly what Jesus came to do. He came to fulfill the promises. Even though the millennial, earthly aspect of the promised Kingdom is yet future, the age of kingdom fulfillment began when Jesus arrived, and it will not finally be completed until we enter into the eternal heavens. The Old Testament age of promise ended when Jesus arrived.

Has spoken to us in His Son. Jesus Christ is the revelation of God climaxed. God fully expressed Himself in His Son. That affirms Christ as being more than just human. It makes Him infinitely superior to any created being, for He is God manifest in the flesh. He is the final and last revelation of God, in whom all God's promises are fulfilled.

We have looked at the preparation for Christ and the presentation of Christ. Now we will look at His preeminence. In this brief but potent section (1:2-3) the Holy Spirit exalts Christ as the full and final expression of God—superior to and exalted above anyone or anything. In these verses we see Christ as the end of all things (Heir), the beginning of all things (Creator), and the middle of all things (Sustainer and Purifier).

When the question is brought up as to who Jesus Christ really was, some people will say He was a good teacher, some will say He was a religious fanatic, some will say He was a fake, and some will claim He was a criminal, a phantom, or a political revolutionary. Others are likely to believe that He was the highest form of humankind, who had a spark of divinity which He fanned into flame—a spark, they claim, that all of us have but seldom fan. There are countless human explanations as to who Jesus was. In this chapter we are going to look at what God says about who Jesus was, and *is*. In just half of verse 2 and in verse 3 is a sevenfold presentation of the excellencies of Jesus Christ. In all these excellencies He is clearly much more than a man.

HIS HEIRSHIP

Jesus' first excellency mentioned here is His heirship: **In these last days [God] has spoken to us in His Son, whom He appointed heir of all things.** If Jesus is the Son of God, then He is the heir of all that God possesses. Everything that exists will find its true meaning only when it comes under the final control of Jesus Christ.

Even the Psalms predicted that He would one day be the heir to all that God possesses. "But as for Me, I have installed My King upon Zion, My holy mountain. I will surely tell of the decree of the Lord: He said to Me, 'Thou art My Son, today I have begotten Thee' " (Ps. 2:6-7). Again we read, " 'Ask of Me, and I will surely give the nations as Thine inheritance, and the very ends of the earth as Thy possession. Thou shalt break them with a rod of iron, Thou shalt shatter them like earthenware' " (Ps. 2:8-9). And still again, " 'I also shall make him My first-born, the highest of the kings of the earth' " (Ps. 89:27). "First-born" does not mean that Christ did not exist before He was born as Jesus in Bethlehem. It is not primarily a chronological term at all, but has to do with legal rights—especially those of inheritance and authority (which will be discussed in more detail in chapter 3). God's destined kingdom will in the last days be given finally and eternally to Jesus Christ.

Paul explains that all things not only were created *by* Christ but *for* Him (Col. 1:16) and that "from Him and through Him and to Him are all things. To Him be the glory forever. Amen" (Rom. 11:36). Everything that exists exists for Jesus Christ. What truth better proves His equality with God?

In Revelation 5, God is pictured sitting on a throne, with a scroll in His hand. "And I saw in the right hand of Him who sat on the throne a book written inside and on the back, sealed up with seven seals" (v. 1). The scroll is the title deed to the earth and all that is in it. It is the deed for the Heir, the One who has the right to take the earth. In New Testament times Roman law required that a will had to be sealed seven times, to protect it from tampering. As you rolled it up, you sealed it every turn or so for seven times. The seals were not to be broken until after the person whose will it was had died.

John continues his vision: "And I saw a strong angel proclaiming with a loud voice, 'Who is worthy to open the book and to break its seals?'" (v. 2). Who, the angel wondered, is the rightful heir to the earth? Who has the right to possess it? "And no one in heaven, or on the earth, or under the earth, was able to open the book, or to look into it" (v. 3). Perplexed and saddened, John "began to weep greatly, because no one was found worthy to open the book, or to look into it; and one of the elders said to me, 'Stop weeping; behold, the Lion that is from the tribe of Judah, the Root of David, has overcome so as to open the book and its seven seals'" (vv. 4-5). As he continued to watch, he "saw between the throne (with the four living creatures) and the elders a Lamb standing, as if slain, having seven horns and seven eyes, which are the seven Spirits of God sent out into all the earth" (v. 6). Jesus Christ, the Lamb, came and took the scroll out of the right hand of God. Why? Because He, and He alone, had a right to take it. He is Heir to the earth.

Chapter 6 of Revelation begins the description of the Tribulation, the first step in Christ's taking back the earth, which is rightfully His. One by one Christ unrolls the seals. As each seal is broken, He takes further possession and control of His inheritance. Finally, "the seventh angel sounded; and there arose loud voices in heaven, saying, 'The kingdom of the world has become the kingdom of our Lord, and of His Christ; and He will reign forever and ever'" (11:15). When He unrolls the seventh seal and the seventh trumpet blows, the earth is His.

In his first sermon, at Pentecost, Peter told his Jewish audience, "Therefore let all the house of Israel know for certain that God has made Him both Lord and Christ—this Jesus whom you crucified" (Acts 2:36). This carpenter who died nailed to a cross is, in fact, the King of kings and Lord of lords. He will rule the world. Satan knew this truth when he approached Jesus in the wilderness and tempted Him to take control of the world in the wrong way, by bowing down to Satan. As the temporary usurper of God's rule over the earth, Satan continually tries every means of preventing the true Heir from receiving His inheritance.

When Christ first came to earth He became poor for our sakes, that we, through His poverty, might be made rich. He had nothing for Himself. He had "nowhere to lay His head" (Luke 9:58). Even His clothes were taken from Him when He died. He was buried in a grave that belonged to someone else. But when Christ comes to earth again, He will completely and eternally inherit all things. And, wonder of wonders, because we have trusted in Him, we are to be "fellow heirs with Christ" (Rom. 8:16-17). When we enter into His eternal kingdom we will jointly possess all that He possesses. We will not be joint

Christs or joint Lords, but we will be joint heirs. His marvelous inheritance will be ours as well.

SOME STILL REJECT HIM

Amazingly, though Christ is the Heir of all God possesses, and though He offers to share His inheritance with anyone who will trust in Him, some still reject Him. Many rejected God as He revealed Himself in the Old Testament. Now God has perfectly revealed Himself in the New Testament of His Son, and people continue to reject Him.

Jesus illustrated this tragedy in a parable.

> There was a landowner who planted a vineyard and put a wall around it and dug a wine press in it, and built a tower, and rented it out to vine-growers, and went on a journey. And when the harvest time approached, he sent his slaves to the vine-growers to receive his produce. And the vine-growers took his slaves and beat one, and killed another, and stoned a third. Again he sent another group of slaves larger than the first; and they did the same thing to them. But afterward he sent his son to them, saying, "They will respect my son." But when the vine-growers saw the son, they said among themselves, "This is the heir; come, let us kill him, and seize his inheritance." And they took him, and threw him out of the vineyard, and killed him. Therefore when the owner of the vineyard comes, what will he do to those vine-growers? They said to Him, "He will bring those wretches to a wretched end, and will rent out the vineyard to other vine-growers, who will pay him the proceeds at the proper seasons." Jesus said to them, "Did you never read in the Scriptures, 'The stone which the builders rejected, this became the chief corner stone; this came about from the Lord, and it is marvelous in our eyes'? Therefore I say to you, the kingdom of God will be taken away from you, and be given to a nation producing the fruit of it. And he who falls on this stone will be broken to pieces; but on whomever it falls, it will scatter him like dust." (Matt. 21:33-44)

That parable needs no explanation.

To willfully reject Jesus Christ brings on the utter damnation and destruction of a vengeful God. To Israel that parable says, "Since what you have done was so blatant, not only rejecting and killing the prophets but rejecting and killing the Son, the promise has been taken away from you and given to a new nation, the church." Israel was set aside until the time of her restoration.

HIS CREATORSHIP

The second excellency of Christ mentioned in Hebrews 1 is His creatorship: **through whom also He made the world.** Christ is the agent through whom God created the world. "All things came into being by Him, and apart from Him nothing came into being that has come into being" (John 1:3). One of the greatest proofs of Jesus' divinity is His ability to create. Except for His complete sinlessness, His total righteousness, nothing more sets Him apart from us than His creatorship. Ability to create belongs to God alone and the fact that Jesus creates indicates that He is God. He created everything material and everything spiritual. Though man has stained His work with sin, Christ originally made it good, and the very creation itself longs to be restored to what it was in the beginning (Rom. 8:22).

The common Greek word for **world** is *kosmos*, but that is not the word used in Hebrews 1:2. The word here is *aiōnas*, which does not mean the material world but "the ages," as it is often translated. Jesus Christ is responsible not only for the physical earth; He is also responsible for creating time, space, energy, and matter. Christ created the whole universe and everything that makes it function, and He did it all without effort.

Sir John Echols, nobel laureate in neurophysiology, said in Chicago in January, 1968, that the odds against the right combination of circumstances occurring to have evolved intelligent life on earth are about 400 thousand trillion trillion trillion trillion to one. Then, after admitting its great improbability, he went on to say that he believed that such did occur but could never happen again on any planet or in any other solar system! His strange logic illustrates the dilemma of humanistic science. If you do not recognize a Creator you have quite a problem explaining how this marvelous, intricate, immeasurable universe came into being.

Yet thousands upon thousands, probably millions, of men somehow believe that man emerged out of some primeval slime. The wondrous creature of man just evolved—that wondrous creature whose heart beats 800 million times in a normal lifetime and pumps enough blood to fill a string of tank cars running from Boston to New York; that same man whose tiny cubic half-inch section of brain cells contains all the memories of a lifetime; that same man whose ear transfers sound waves from air to liquid without losing any sound. He is thought to be a cosmic accident!

A. K. Morrison, another brilliant scientist, tells us that conditions for life on earth demand so many billions of minute interrelated circumstances appearing simultaneously, in the same infinitesimal moment, that such a prospect becomes beyond belief and beyond possibility.

Consider the vastness of our universe. If you could somehow put 1.2 million earths inside the sun, you would have room left for 4.3 million moons. The sun is 865,000 miles in diameter and is 93 million miles from the earth. Our next nearest star, Alpha Centauri, is 5 times larger than our sun. The moon is only 211,463 miles away and you could walk to it in 27 years. A ray of light travels at 186 thousand miles per second, so a beam of light would reach the moon in only 1-1/2 seconds. If we could travel at that speed, it would take 2 minutes and 18 seconds to reach Venus, 4-1/2 minutes to reach Mercury, 1 hour and 11 seconds to reach Saturn, and so on. To reach Pluto, 2.7 billion miles from earth, would take nearly 4 hours. Having gotten that far, we would still be well inside our own solar system. The North Star is four hundred billion miles away, but is still nearby in relation even to known space. The star Betelgeuse is 880 quadrillion miles (880 followed by fifteen zeroes) from us. It has a diameter of 250 million miles, which is greater than that of the earth's orbit.

Where did it all come from? Who conceived it? Who made it? It cannot be an accident. Somebody had to make it, and the Bible tells us the Maker was Jesus Christ.

His Radiance

Third, we see Christ's radiance, the brightness of the glory of God. **And He is the radiance of His glory. Radiance** (*apaugasma*, "to send forth light") represents Jesus as the manifestation of God. He expresses God to us. No one can see God; no one ever will. The only radiance that reaches us from God is mediated to us from Jesus Christ. Just as the rays of the sun light and warm the earth, so Jesus Christ is the glorious light of God shining into the hearts of men. Just as the sun was never without and cannot be separated from its brightness, so God was never without and cannot be separated from the glory of Christ. Never was God without Him or He without God, and never in any way can He be separated from God. Yet the brightness of the sun is not the sun. Neither is Christ God in that sense. He is fully and absolutely God, yet is a distinct Person.

We would never be able to see or enjoy God's light if we did not have Jesus to look at. Standing one day before the Temple, Jesus said, "I am the light of the world; he who follows Me shall not walk in the darkness, but shall have the light of life" (John 8:12). Jesus Christ is the **radiance** of God's **glory,** and He can transmit that light into your life and my life, so that we, in turn, can radiate the glory of God. We live in a dark world. There is the darkness of injustice, of failure, privation, separation, disease, death, and of much else. There is the moral darkness of men blinded by their godless appetites and passions. Into this dark world God sent His glorious Light. Without the Son of God, there is only darkness.

The great tragedy, of course, is that most men do not want even to see, much less accept and live in, God's light. Paul explains that "the god of this world has blinded the minds of the unbelieving, that they might not see the light of the gospel of the glory of Christ, who is the image of God" (2 Cor. 4:4). God sent His light in the Person of Jesus Christ, that man might behold, accept, and radiate that light. But Satan has moved through this world to blind the minds of men and prevent the light of the glorious gospel from shining on them.

Those, however, who receive His light can say, "For God, who said, 'Light shall shine out of darkness,' is the One who has shone in our hearts to give the light of the knowledge of the glory of God in the face of Christ" (2 Cor. 4:6). That is what happens when God comes into your life.

The hymn writer said, "Come to the light. 'Tis shining for thee. / Sweetly the light has dawned upon me." What a wonderful thing to realize that Jesus Christ, who is the full expression of God in human history, can come into our lives and give us light to see and to know God. His light, in fact, gives us life itself, spiritual life. And, His light gives us purpose, meaning, happiness, peace, joy, fellowship, everything—for all eternity.

HIS BEING

Christ's next excellency is His being. **And He is the radiance of His glory and the exact representation of His nature.** Jesus Christ is the express image of God. Christ not only was God manifest, He was God in substance.

Exact representation translates the Greek term used for the impression made by a die or stamp on a seal. The design on the die is reproduced on the wax. Jesus Christ is the reproduction of God. He is the perfect, personal imprint of God in time and space. Colossians 1:15 gives a similar illustration of this incomprehensible truth: "He is the image of the invisible God." The word "image" here is *eikōn*, from which we get *icon*. *Eikōn* means a precise copy, an exact reproduction, as in a fine sculpture or portrait. To call Christ the *Eikōn* of God means He is the exact reproduction of God. "For in Him all the fulness of Deity dwells in bodily form" (Col. 2:9).

HIS ADMINISTRATION

Also in Hebrews 1:3 is given the fifth of Christ's excellencies, His administration, or sustenance. He **upholds all things by the word of His power.** Christ not only made all things and will someday inherit all things, but He holds them all together in the meanwhile. The Greek word for **upholds** means "to support, to maintain," and it is used here in the present tense, implying continuous action. Everything in the universe is sustained right now by Jesus Christ.

We base our entire lives on the continuance, the constancy, of laws. When something such as an earthquake comes along and disrupts the normal condition or operation of things even a little, the consequences are often disastrous. Can you imagine what would happen if Jesus Christ relinquished His sustaining power over the laws of the universe? We would go out of existence. If He suspended the law of gravity only for a brief moment, we would all perish, in unimaginable ways.

If the physical laws varied, we would have an unbelievable mess. We could not exist. What we ate could turn to poison. We could not stay on the earth; we would drift out into space. We would get flooded by the oceans periodically. Countless other horrible things would happen, many of which we could not even guess.

Consider, for example, what instant destruction would happen if the earth's rotation slowed down just a little. The sun has a surface temperature of 12,000 degrees Fahrenheit. If it were any closer to us we would burn up; if it were any farther away we would freeze. Our globe is tilted on an exact angle of 23 degrees, providing us with four seasons. If it were not so tilted, vapors from the oceans would move north and south and develop into monstrous continents of ice. If the moon did not retain its exact distance from the earth the ocean tides would inundate the land completely, twice a day. After the first flooding, of course, the others would not matter as far as we would be concerned. If the ocean floors were merely a few feet deeper than they are, the carbon dioxide and oxygen balance of the earth's atmosphere would be completely upset, and no animal or plant life could exist. If the atmosphere did not remain at its present density, but thinned out even a little, many of the meteors which now harmlessly burn up when they hit the atmosphere would constantly bombard us. We would have to live underground or in meteor-proof buildings.

How does the universe stay in this kind of fantastically delicate balance? Jesus Christ sustains and monitors all its movements and interworkings. Christ, the preeminent Power, maintains it all.

Things do not happen in our universe by accident. They did not happen that way in the beginning. They are not going to happen that way in the end, and they are not happening that way now. Jesus Christ is sustaining the universe. He is Himself the principle of cohesion. He is not like the deist's "watchmaker" creator, who made the world, set it in motion, and has not bothered with it since. The universe is a cosmos instead of chaos, an ordered and reliable system instead of an erratic and unpredictable muddle, only because Jesus Christ upholds it.

Scientists who discover great and amazing truths are doing nothing but discovering a few of the laws that Jesus Christ designed and uses to control the world. No scientist or mathematician, no astronomer or nuclear physicist, could do anything without the upholding power of Jesus Christ. The whole universe hangs on the arm of Jesus. His unsearchable wisdom and boundless power are manifested in governing the universe. And He does it by the word of His power, without effort. The key to the creation story in Genesis is in two words, "God said." God spoke and it happened.

When I think about Christ's power to uphold the universe, that truth goes right to my heart. We read in Philippians 1:6 the wonderful promise, "For I am confident of this very thing, that He who began a good work in you will perfect it until the day of Christ Jesus." When Christ begins a work in your heart, He holds onto it and sustains it all the way through. We can imagine Jude's excitement when he wrote, "Now to Him who is able to keep you from stumbling, and to make you stand in the presence of His glory blameless with great joy, to the only God our Savior, through Jesus Christ our Lord, be glory, majesty, dominion and authority, before all time and now and forever. Amen" (Jude 24-25). When your life is given to Jesus Christ, He holds it and sustains it and one day will take it into God's very presence. A life, just as a universe, that is not sustained by Christ is chaos.

HIS SACRIFICE

The sixth excellency of Christ is His sacrifice: **When He had made purification of sins.** What a tremendous statement!

The Bible says the wages of sin is death. Jesus Christ went to the cross, died our deserved death for us, and thereby took the penalty for our sin on Himself. If we will accept His death and believe that He died for us, He will free us from the penalty of sin and purify us from the stain of sin.

It was a wondrous work when Jesus Christ created the world. It is wondrous that He sustains the world. But a greater work than making and upholding the world is that of purging men of sin. In Hebrews 7:27 we are told that Jesus "does not need daily, like those high priests, to offer up sacrifices, first for His own sins, and then for the sins of the people, because this He did once for all when He offered up Himself." In the Old Testament the priests had to make sacrifice after sacrifice, for themselves and for the people. Jesus made but one sacrifice. He not only was the Priest, but also the Sacrifice. And because His sacrifice was pure, He can purify our sins—something that all the Old Testament sacrifices together could not do.

> And not through the blood of goats and calves, but through His own blood, He entered the holy place once for all, having obtained eternal redemption. For if the blood of goats and bulls and the ashes of a heifer sprinkling those who have been defiled, sanctify for the cleansing of the flesh, how much more will the blood of Christ, who through the eternal Spirit offered Himself without blemish to God, cleanse your conscience from dead works to serve the living God? . . . but now

once at the consummation of the ages He has been manifested to put away sin by the sacrifice of Himself. (Heb. 9:12-14, 26*b*)

Jesus Christ dealt with the sin problem once and for all. It had to be done. We could not communicate with God or enter into fellowship with Him unless sin was dealt with. So Christ went to the cross and bore the penalty of sin for all who would accept His sacrifice, believe in Him, and receive Him. Sin was purged, wiped out.

This truth must have seemed especially remarkable to those to whom the book of Hebrews was first written. The cross was a stumbling block to Jews, but the writer does not apologize for it. Instead, he shows it to be one of the seven excellent glories of Christ. His words are as straightforward as those of Peter: "[You know] that you were not redeemed with perishable things like silver or gold from your futile way of life inherited from your forefathers, but with precious blood, as of a lamb unblemished and spotless, the blood of Christ" (1 Pet. 1:18-19).

We are all sinners. And either we pay the penalty for our own sin, which is eternal death, or we accept Jesus Christ's payment for it in sacrificing Himself, for which we receive eternal life. If the desire of our heart is to receive Him as Savior, to believe in and to accept His sacrifice, our sins are washed away at that point. The Bible says that without the shedding of blood there is no forgiveness for sin (Heb. 9:22) and that "the blood of Jesus His Son cleanses us from all sin" (1 John 1:7). Jesus came as the perfect Sacrifice. The man whose sins are forgiven has them forgiven only because of Jesus Christ. But the blood of Jesus Christ will never be applied to us unless by faith we receive Him into our lives.

Yet again, there are people who reject Him! Hebrews 10:26 warns, "For if we go on sinning willfully after receiving the knowledge of the truth, there no longer remains a sacrifice for sins." If we reject Jesus Christ there is nothing in the universe that can take away our sin, and we will die in it. Jesus said to such persons, "[You] shall die in your sin; where I am going you can never come" (John 8:21).

HIS EXALTATION

The last of Christ's excellencies mentioned in this passage is His exaltation. **He sat down at the right hand of the Majesty on high.** The **Majesty on high** is God. The **right hand** is the power side. Jesus took His place at the right hand of God. The marvelous thing about this statement is that Jesus, the perfect High Priest, **sat down.** This is in great contrast to the priestly procedure under the Old Covenant. There were no seats in the Tabernacle or the Temple sanctuaries. The priest had no place to sit because God knew it would never be appropriate for him to sit. His responsibility was to sacrifice, sacrifice, sacrifice, over and over again. So the priests offered sacrifices daily—and never sat down. But Jesus offered one sacrifice, and said, "It is finished." He then went and sat down with the Father. It was done. What could not be accomplished under the Old Covenant, even after centuries of sacrifices, was accomplished once by Jesus Christ for all time.

Jesus' sitting down at His Father's right hand signifies at least four things. They are, briefly:

First, He sat down as a sign of honor, "that every tongue should confess that Jesus Christ is Lord, to the glory of God the Father" (Phil. 2:11). To be seated at the right hand of the Father is honor indeed.

Second, He sat down as a sign of authority. "[He] is at the right hand of God, having gone into heaven, after angels and authorities and powers had been subjected to Him" (1 Pet. 3:22). He sat down as a ruler.

Third, He sat down to rest. His work was done. "But He, having offered one sacrifice for sins for all time, sat down at the right hand of God" (Heb. 10:12).

Fourth, He sat down to intercede for us. "Christ Jesus is He who died, yes, rather who was raised, who is at the right hand of God, who also intercedes for us" (Rom. 8:34). He is seated at the right hand of the Father making intercession for all of us who belong to Him.

Here we have God's portrait of Jesus Christ. We have seen the preeminent Christ in all His offices. We have seen Him as prophet, the final spokesman for God. We have seen Him as priest, atoning and interceding. We have seen Him as King, controlling, sustaining, and seated on a throne. This is our Lord Jesus Christ.

A man who says that Jesus Christ is anything less than this is a fool and makes God out a liar. God says that His Son is preeminent in all things.

What does this mean to us? It means everything. To reject Him is to be shut out from His presence into an eternal hell. But to receive Jesus Christ is to enter into all that He is and has. There are no other choices.

Jesus Christ Superior to Angels
(1:4-14)

3

Having become as much better than the angels, as He has inherited a more excellent name than they. For to which of the angels did He ever say, "Thou art My Son, today I have begotten Thee"? And again, "I will be a Father to Him, and He shall be a Son to Me"? And when He again brings the first-born into the world, He says, "And let all the angels of God worship Him." And of the angels He says, "Who makes His angels winds, and His ministers a flame of fire." But of the Son He says, "Thy throne, O God, is forever and ever, and the righteous scepter is the scepter of His kingdom. Thou hast loved righteousness and hated lawlessness; therefore God, Thy God, hath anointed Thee with the oil of gladness above Thy companions." And, "Thou, LORD, in the beginning didst lay the foundation of the earth, and the heavens are the works of Thy hands; they will perish, but Thou remainest; and they all will become old as a garment, and as a mantle Thou wilt roll them up; as a garment they will also be changed. But Thou art the same, and Thy years will not come to an end." But to which of the angels has He ever said, "Sit at My right hand, until I make Thine enemies a footstool for Thy feet"? Are they not all ministering spirits, sent out to render service for the sake of those who will inherit salvation? (1:4-14)

In this chapter we are going to be dealing with meat as opposed to milk. I cannot remember a passage on which I have spent more time. To some extent, it is like an iceberg. You can see the top clearly enough, but it may not appear too impressive or meaningful. We will be looking below the surface of this passage into its deep truths. In that sense, verses 4 through 14 are not easy to understand. If, even in a small measure, I can help make these truths more understandable, I have succeeded in what I asked God to help me do.

Keep in mind that the book of Hebrews is written to Jewish people, primarily to Jewish believers but also to Jewish unbelievers. Both groups are pressed with the truth that the New Covenant is better than the Old—that Jesus Christ is the better Priest, and the better Mediator, and that He is the final Priest and the final Sacrifice at the same time. Throughout the book we have comparisons between the New Covenant and the Old Covenant and between Jesus Christ and everyone else, to show that Jesus is superior in every way.

In the first three verses Jesus is shown as superior to everything and everyone. After unfolding all of the human "everyones" Christ is superior to, the Holy Spirit teaches us that Jesus Christ is also superior to angels.

Man is a wonderful and amazing creation—certainly higher than the plants and the animals, even the most complex animals. He is higher than any other material creation. But there are created beings even higher than man—the angels. Hebrews 2:9 tells us that when Jesus became a man He was "made for a little while lower than the angels." After the fall of the rebellious angels under Lucifer the angels remaining in heaven were no longer subject to sin. They are holy, powerful, and wise. They do not have the infirmities that men have. They are specially created spirit beings, made by God before He made man. They were, in fact, watching in the heavens when God created the world. They were of a higher order than man, at least higher than fallen man.

The Bible speaks a great deal of angels. There are 108 direct references to angels in the Old Testament and 165 in the New. The primary purpose of their creation was to render special worship and service to God.

WHAT ANGELS ARE AND DO

Angels are spirit beings and do not have flesh and bones. But they do have bodies. We are told in 1 Corinthians 15:40 that there are both terrestrial and celestial bodies. That is, some are suitable for earth and some are suitable for heaven. Whatever heavenly form angels have, they are capable of appearing in human form. In fact, in Hebrews 13:2 we are warned to be careful how we treat strangers, since we might be entertaining "angels without knowing it."

Angels may also appear in other forms. Speaking of an angel at Christ's resurrection, Matthew reports that "his appearance was like lightning, and his garment as white as snow; and the guards shook for fear of him, and became like dead men" (Matt. 28:3-4). This angel appeared in dazzling, brilliant glory.

Angels are highly intelligent and have emotions. They rejoice, for example, when a sinner is saved (Luke 15:10). Angels can speak to men, as recorded many places in Scripture. The apostle Paul says, "Though we, or an angel from heaven, should preach to you a gospel contrary to that which we have preached to you" (Gal. 1:8).

Angels do not marry and are unable to procreate (Matt. 22:28-30). In light of Colossians 1:16-17, it seems that they all were created simultaneously. The Bible makes no mention of any angels being added to those of the original creation. God made them all at once, each with a unique identity.

Angels are not subject to death. Scripture nowhere indicates that they die or can be annihilated. A third of them fell (Rev. 12:4), but they still exist as demonic spirit beings. Each is a direct, permanent creation of God and stands in personal relationship to his Creator. Their number, therefore, neither increases by procreation or by additional creation nor decreases by death or by annihilation.

Angels were all created before man, and are therefore countless ages older than men and evidently number in the trillions. Even after hosts of them fell with Satan, numberless holy angels were left. In his vision of the Ancient of Days, Daniel saw "thousands upon thousands" attending Him and "myriads upon myriads" standing before Him (Dan. 7:10). In his vision from Patmos, John also speaks of a vast heavenly multitude that included angels. "And the number of them was myriads of myriads, and thousands of thousands" (Rev. 5:11).

According to Mark 13:32 and Jude 6 the unfallen angels live in all of the heavens. The heaven where God resides in a special way is called the third heaven; the second heaven is the spatial, infinite heaven; and the first heaven is around the earth. Today we hear many theories and fanciful stories about extraterrestrial life. Though they are not of the kinds portrayed on TV and in the movies, special beings do indeed inhabit other parts of the universe. They are angels.

Angels are highly organized and are divided into ranks, in what is doubtlessly a very complex organization. The various ranks apparently have supervisory responsibilities over thrones, dominions, principalities, powers, authorities, and such. Among the special classes of angels are cherubim, seraphim, and those described simply as living creatures.

They are more powerful than men, and men must call on divine power to deal with fallen angels. We are told in Ephesians 6:10, 12 to "be strong in the Lord, and in the strength of His might. . . . For our struggle is not against flesh and blood. . . ." but against angels—fallen angels.

Angels can move and act with incredible speed. Sometimes they are pictured with wings, suggesting fast travel. Some angels have names: Michael, Gabriel, Lucifer. Michael is the head of the armies of heaven and Gabriel is called "the mighty one." Lucifer is the name Satan had before he fell.

Angels minister to God and do His bidding. They are both spectators and participants in His mighty works, both redemptive and judgmental. They ministered to Christ in His humiliation. At the conclusion of His temptation angels came and ministered to Him. They also minister to God's redeemed by watching over the church—assisting God in answering prayer, delivering from danger, giving encouragement, and protecting children. They also minister to the unsaved, by announcing and inflicting judgment.

JEWISH VIEWS OF ANGELS

Because of the Talmudic writings and popular rabbinical interpretations and ideas, the Jewish people at the time this epistle was written had begun to embellish the basic Old Testament teachings about angels. The writer of Hebrews, therefore, was writing not only against the backdrop of true biblical teaching but also against that of common Jewish misconceptions.

Most Jews believed that angels were very important to the Old Covenant. They esteemed these creatures as the highest beings next to God. They believed that God was surrounded by angels and that angels were the instruments of bringing His word to men and of working out His will in the universe. Angels were thought to be ethereal creatures made of fiery substance like blazing light, who did not eat or drink or procreate.

Many believed that angels acted as God's senate or council and that He did nothing without consulting them—that, for example, the "Us" in "Let Us make man in Our image" (Gen. 1:26) refers to this angelic council.

Some Jews believed that a group of angels objected to the creation of man and were immediately annihilated and that others objected to the giving of the Law and attacked Moses on his way up Mount Sinai. Many names for angels were coined. The supposed "presence angels," who stayed in the presence of God at all times, were given such names as Raphael, Yuriel, Phanuel, Gabriel, and Michael. El was a name for God and was used as the ending for each of the angels' names.

They believed two hundred angels controlled the movements of the stars and that one very special angel, the calendar angel, controlled the never-ending succession of days, months, and years. A mighty angel took care of the seas, while others superintended the frost, dew, rain, snow, hail, thunder, and lightning. Still others were wardens of hell and torturers of the damned. There were even recording angels who wrote down every word men spoke. There was an angel of death and, on the other hand, a guardian angel for every nation and even every child. Angels were so numerous that one rabbi claimed that every blade of grass had its angel.

Many Jews believed that the Old Covenant was brought to them from God by angels. This, above all else, exalted the angels in the minds of the children of Israel. They believed that angels were the mediators of their covenant with God, that angels continually ministered God's blessings to them.

Stephen's sermon indicting Israel alludes to this basic belief.

> You men who are stiff-necked and uncircumcised in heart and ears are always resisting the Holy Spirit; you are doing just as your fathers did. Which one of the prophets did your fathers not persecute? And they killed those who had previously announced the coming of the Righteous One, whose betrayers and murderers you have now become; you who received the law as ordained by angels, and yet did not keep it. (Acts 7:51-53)

Now look at Galatians 3:19: "Why the Law then? It was added because of transgressions, having been ordained through angels by the agency of a mediator, until the seed should come to whom the promise had been made."

The Old Covenant was brought to man and maintained by angelic mediation. The Jews knew this, and consequently had the highest regard for angels. Some respected angels to such a degree that they actually worshiped them. Gnosticism (see chapter 1) involved, among other things, the worship of angels. It even reduced Jesus Christ to an angel. The Colossian church had been flirting with Gnosticism and Paul warned them, "Let no one keep defrauding you of your prize by delighting in self-abasement and the worship of the angels" (Col. 2:18).

So, to the Jewish mind angels were extremely exalted, immeasurably important. If the writer of Hebrews, therefore, was to persuade his fellow Jews that Christ is the Mediator of a better covenant than that given through Moses, he would have to show, among other things, that Christ is better than angels—the thrust of 1:4-14. Christ must be shown to be better than the bearers and mediators of the Old Covenant—namely, the angels. Seven Old Testament passages are used to establish this truth.

These quotations in the book of Hebrews vary slightly from the

Old Testament texts from which they are taken. The reason is that, by the time this letter was written, many Jews used a Greek translation of the Old Testament, called the Septuagint. It is from the Septuagint that the quotations in Hebrews are taken. One reason we do not believe Paul wrote this epistle is that, in the writings known definitely to be his, he quotes more from the Hebrew text than from the Septuagint.

If the writer had tried to prove from Christian writings that Christ is a better mediator, his Jewish readers would have said, "We don't accept these writings as Scripture, as being from God." So he wisely and deftly replies, in effect, "Open up your own Scriptures and I'll show you from them that Christ is a better mediator and that the New Covenant is better than the Old." His argument is powerful and irresistible.

Before we go further, it would be well to point out that a number of cults and other unorthodox religious organizations deny the deity of Christ on the basis of the King James translation ("being made") in verse 4, taking this to mean that Jesus was created. But the Greek word here is not *poieō*, "to make or create," but *ginomai*, "to become"—the meaning which most modern translations make clear. Jesus Christ always existed, but He became better than the angels in His exaltation, implying that at one time He had been lower than the angels—the truth that Hebrews 2:9 makes clear. But the reference in 1:4 is to His incarnation as God's Son. As the Son He became lower than the angels. But because of His faithfulness, obedience, and the wonderful work He accomplished as a Son, He was exalted again above the angels, as He had been before. This time, however, He was exalted as the Son. Christ technically did not become the Son of God until He was incarnated. Christ was not the Son of God in eternity past—He was God as the second Person in the Godhead. He became identified as the Son, and as the Son was exalted above the angels. So He became better than the angels again—though for a while He had been lower. We will go into that truth in detail.

This marvelous section shows that Jesus was better than the angels in five ways—in His title, His worship, His nature, His existence, and His destiny. These are the points of the message the Holy Spirit has given us on the text, **having become as much better than the angels.**

GREATER BECAUSE OF TITLE

Having become as much better than the angels, as He has inherited a more excellent name than they. For to which of the angels did He ever say, "Thou are My Son, today I have begotten Thee"? And again, "I will be a Father to Him, and He shall be a Son to Me"? (1:4-5)

Jesus Christ is better than angels first of all because He has a better title, **a more excellent name.** To what angel had God ever said, **"Thou art My Son, today I have begotten Thee"**? The answer is none. Of no angel had God said, **"I will be a Father to Him, and He shall be a Son to Me."** The angels had always been but ministers and messengers. Only Christ is the Son. The angels are created servants. Though the uncreated Christ came to earth as a servant—indeed as the supreme Servant—He also became the Son. He has therefore obtained a far more excellent name or title than they.

Our culture does not put much stock in the meaning of names. Except for nicknames, there is usually no intended connection between a child's personality and the meaning of his name (which seldom is even known). But in biblical times God often chose specific names that related to the character or some other aspect of a person's life.

The writer of Hebrews was well aware of this when he asked the rhetorical question, **"To which of the angels did [God] ever say, 'Thou art My Son, today I have begotten Thee'?** [Ps. 2:7] **And again, 'I will be a Father to Him, and He shall be a Son to Me' "**? [2 Sam. 7:14]. The quotation from 2 Samuel refers, of course, to David's greater Son (cf. Luke 1:32; John 7:42; Rev. 5:5; and others). No single angel had ever been called a son of God. As with Christians, angels collectively are called "sons of God" or "children of God," in the sense that God created them and that, in some ways, they reflect Him. But in Scripture no individual angel is called "son of God." Nor to any angel had God ever said, **"Today I have begotten Thee,"** because angels were not related to God in any such way.

As was noted, **Son** is an incarnational title of Christ. Though His sonship was anticipated in the Old Testament (Prov. 30:4), He did not become a Son until He was begotten into time. Prior to time and His incarnation He was eternal God with God. The term **Son** has only to do with Jesus Christ in His incarnation. It is only an analogy to say that God is Father and Jesus is Son—God's way of helping us understand the essential relationship between the the first and second Persons of the Trinity.

It is the awesome truth of Christ's becoming God's incarnate Son that this passage in Hebrews presents to its Jewish readers. The Bible nowhere speaks of the eternal sonship of Christ. When His eternity is spoken of in Hebrews 1:8, God says to the Son, **"Thy throne, O God, is forever and ever."** When talking about Christ's eternity, the title "God" is used; only when talking about His incarnation is He called "Son."

That brings up a question. Did not Christ always have a better name? Why does it say, **He has inherited a more excellent name than they?** Did He not always have **a more excellent name?** Yes, but He obtained another one. He was always God, but He became **Son.** He had not always had the title of Son. That is His incarnation title. Eternally He is God, but only from His incarnation has He been Son.

This is an extremely important point, one requiring much study to understand. The truth is not easy to follow through Scripture. But it is a truth that will come powerfully to our aid when someone comes to our door and says, "Since Jesus is the Son of God, he is obviously eternally inferior to God the Father. Jesus, therefore, is not God; he is less than God. He is only a *son*."

Christ was *not* Son until His incarnation. Before that He was eternal God. It is therefore incorrect to say the Jesus Christ is eternally inferior to God because He goes under the title of Son. He is no "eternal son" always subservient to God, always less than God, always under God. Sonship is an analogy to help us understand Christ's essential relationship and willing submission to the Father for the sake of our redemption. As already mentioned, the **today** of verse 5 shows that His sonship began in a point of time, not in eternity. His life as Son began in this world.

The quotation in verse 5 from 2 Samuel 7:14 (**I will be a Father to Him, and He shall be a Son to Me**) emphasizes the future—since the words quoted were originally written hundreds of years before Jesus' birth. In John 1:1-3, where Christ's eternity and creatorship are being presented, He is not called the Son but the Word. A few verses later we read that "the Word became flesh" (John 1:14). Christ is not referred to as Son by John until He is made flesh. So there is no justification for saying that Jesus Christ is eternally subservient to God or less than God.

THE SON THROUGH THE VIRGIN BIRTH

There are two basic events in relation to which Jesus Christ is Son—His virgin birth and His resurrection. He was not a son until He was born into this world through the virgin birth. In describing one of the predictions of this birth Luke says, "And the angel answered and said to her, 'The Holy Spirit will come upon you, and the power of the Most High will overshadow you; and for that reason the holy offspring shall be called the Son of God'" (Luke 1:35). Even at that time, less than a year before His birth, His sonship was referred to as future. "He *will* be great, and *will* be called the Son of the Most High" (v. 32). The sonship of Christ is inextricably connected with His incarnation.

> And the Holy Spirit descended upon Him in bodily form like a dove, and a voice came out of heaven, "Thou art My beloved Son, in Thee I am well-pleased." (Luke 3:22)

Only after Christ's incarnation did God say, "This is My Son."

THE SON THROUGH THE RESURRECTION

His sonship came to full bloom in His resurrection. He is the Son not only because He was virgin-born into humanity, but also because He was begotten again from the dead. Just as you and I become sons of God in the fullest sense not by being born once but by being born twice, so Jesus Christ became Son in the fullest sense by being born not once but twice. This deep truth Paul makes clear in the book of Romans:

> Concerning His Son, who was born of a descendant of David according to the flesh, who was declared the Son of God with power by the resurrection from the dead, according to the spirit of holiness, Jesus Christ our Lord. (Rom. 1:3-4)

He became a Son at birth; He was declared to be a Son in resurrection. The fullness of His sonship comes in His twice birth.

Acts 13:33 ties this truth to the same Psalm, and even to the same verse (2:7), as does the writer to the Hebrews, relating the quotation to the resurrection: "God has fulfilled this promise to our children in that He raised up Jesus, as it is also written in the second Psalm, 'Thou art My Son; today I have begotten Thee.'" Jesus is Son in resurrection as as well as in birth. It is His *human* title, and we should never get trapped in the heretical idea that Jesus Christ is eternally subservient to God. He *became* the Son for our sake—setting aside what was rightfully His, humbling Himself, and emptying Himself (Phil. 2:6-8).

Angels are indeed excellent creatures—the most excellent of all creatures. Therefore if Christ has **a more excellent name than they,** He must have the *most* excellent name. And He does—Son. So says the writer of Hebrews to the Jews, arguing from their own Scriptures.

GREATER BECAUSE WORSHIPED

And when He again brings the first-born into the world, He says, "And let all the angels of God worship Him." (1:6)

Jesus Christ is not only greater than angels because He is God's Son but also because He is worshiped. Even though Christ humbled Himself, even though He was made for a time lower than the angels, the angels are to worship Him. If angels are to worship Him, He must therefore be greater than they. And if He is greater than they, His covenant is greater than the one they brought—the New Covenant is greater than the Old, and Christianity is greater than Judaism.

And let all the angels of God worship Him is a quotation from Psalm 97:7. The psalmist predicted that all the angels were to worship the Lord's Christ. Jews should not have been surprised at the point being made here in Hebrews. The truth, in fact the very words, come right out of their own Scriptures. Far from matching the incarnate Son in glory, angels are commanded to worship Him.

But did not angels always worship Christ? Yes, they had worshiped Him throughout all the time of their existence; but prior to His incarnation, they worshiped Him as God. Now they are also to worship Him as Son, in His incarnate character. This Son who became a man is higher than angels. He is the very God that the angels had always worshiped. It is an absolute sin and violation of the most basic of God's laws to worship anyone but God. So if God Himself says that the angels are to worship the Son, then the Son must be God! In His incarnate Person, even as in His eternal Person, Christ is to be worshiped.

THE CHIEF ONE

In this passage Christ is called the **first-born.** Here again, many sects and cults claim a prooftext to show that Jesus is a created being. "Look! He's first-born! You see? He was born like all the rest of us!" A related supposed prooftext is Colossians 1:15, "And He is the image of the invisible God, the first-born of all creation." But "first-born" (*prōtotokos*) has nothing to do with time. It refers to position. It is not a description but a title, meaning "the chief one." The concept was associated with first-born because the oldest son usually was heir to the father's entire estate.

The first son to be born was not always the "first-born." Esau, for instance, was older than Jacob, but Jacob was the first-born, the *prōtotokos.* Genesis 49:3 gives a good description of first-born: "Reuben, you are my first-born; my might and the beginning of my strength, preeminent in dignity and preeminent in power." Might, strength, dignity, and power—these describe the meaning of first-born. It is not a time word; it is a right-to-rule word, an authority word. And Jesus Christ is the supreme First-born, the supreme *Prōtotokos,* the supreme right-to-rule Son. These passages, therefore, do not refer to Christ's birth as such, but to His sovereignty.

"He is also head of the body, the church; and He is the beginning, the first-born from the dead" (Col. 1:18). Jesus was "the first-born from the dead." Had anybody been resurrected before Jesus? Yes. Lazarus, the other people that Jesus raised during His earthly ministry, all the Old Testament saints who came alive at the crucifixion—all these and others had been raised from the dead before Jesus! The term, therefore, obviously does not refer to time. As first-born, Jesus is the most honored One, the most dignified One, the highest One, the most powerful One. Of all those who have been resurrected, He is far and above the greatest.

The Meaning of "Again"

The word **again** in Hebrews 1:6 has caused commentators a great deal of difficulty. Before we can understand **again** we need to look at another key word in the passage: **world. And when He again brings the first-born into the world, He says, "And let all the angels of God worship Him."** The more common Greek word for world (*kosmos,* "the universe") is not used here, but rather *oikoumenē* ("the inhabited earth"). Christ was not the first to be born in the earth, but is the **first-born**—the chief One, the most honored One—who came to an already-inhabited earth, where millions had been born before Him.

The word order of the King James ("And again, when he bringeth in the first begotten into the world") has added to the confusion in interpreting verse 6. As reflected in most modern translations, the Greek word order is "And when He again brings." So in verse 6 **again** refers to God's bringing His firstborn into the world another time. When is this "again" going to happen? The only possible answer is at the Second Coming. God already brought Him once as Son, and He is going to bring Him as Son again—in blazing glory!

It is only at the Second Coming that the fullness of the prophecy, **And let all the angels of God worship Him,** will come to pass. At the present time angels do not understand the whole picture well enough to give the Son full worship. The Old Testament prophets had similar difficulty understanding the full meaning of what they had written. They were inspired by the Holy Spirit but in many cases did not fully understand the messages they were given, "seeking to know what person or time the Spirit of Christ within them was indicating as He predicted the sufferings of Christ and the glories to follow" (1 Pet. 1:11).

In the next verse the apostle explains that "It was revealed to them that they were not serving themselves, but you, in these things which now have been announced to you through those who preached the gospel to you by the Holy Spirit sent from heaven" (1 Pet. 1:12). They were looking to see the things that would not be understood until Christ came, the gospel was preached, and the Holy Spirit was manifested. In fact these are mysteries into which the angels still "long to look" (v. 12*b*). They do not understand it all yet. Perhaps the "presence angels" around the throne do, but the vast angelic hosts evidently are not yet able to discern everything. Angels have remarkable intelligence but are not omniscient. When God again brings His first-born into the world He will say to them, in effect, "Now you have the full picture, and your worship can be full and complete."

> And I looked, and I heard the voice of many angels around the throne and the living creatures and the elders; and the number of them was myriads of myriads,

and thousands of thousands, saying with a loud voice, "Worthy is the Lamb that was slain to receive power and riches and wisdom and might and honor and glory and blessing." (Rev. 5:11-12)

Here is angelic worship! Christ is getting ready to come again and to take the earth for Himself. In 5:1 the Father is pictured with the title deed to the earth (the little scroll), and those around the throne are saying, "Who is worthy to open the book and to break its seals?" (v. 2). John is crying because there is no one to open the scroll, and suddenly one of the elders says, "Stop weeping; behold, the Lion that is from the tribe of Judah, the Root of David, has overcome so as to open the book and its seven seals" (v. 5). Jesus Christ, the Lamb, then takes the scroll. As He is about to unroll the judgments and take possession of the earth, the angels say, "It's all clear now!" And countless millions of them, from all over heaven, burst forth in praise, joined by all other creatures of the universe:

And every created thing which is in heaven and on the earth and under the earth and on the sea, and all things in them, I heard saying, "To Him who sits on the throne, and to the Lamb, be blessing and honor and glory and dominion forever and ever." And the four living creatures kept saying, "Amen." And the elders fell down and worshiped. (Rev. 5:13-14)

This speaks of His Second Coming, where He will be revealed in His full glory as **Son**—as *Prōtotokos*, the **first-born.** The angels finally will see it all then, as they see Him come as King of kings and Lord of lords.

GREATER BECAUSE OF SUPERIOR NATURE

And of the angels He says, "Who makes His angels winds, and His ministers a flame of fire." (1:7)

Jesus is also superior to angels because of His nature. In verse 7 the Holy Spirit shows the basic difference between the nature of angels and that of the Son. The Greek for **makes** is *poieō* ("to create" or "to make"). Since Christ created the angels (Col. 1:16), He is obviously superior to them. Not only were they created by Him, but they are His possession, **His angels.** They are His created servants, His **ministers,** His **winds** and **flame of fire.**

THE FATHER'S CLAIM OF JESUS' DEITY

But of the Son He says, "Thy throne, O God, is forever and ever". (1:8*a*)

The first part of verse 8 expands on the difference between Christ's nature and that of angels. Here is one of the most amazing and important statements in all of Scripture: Jesus is God eternal! Those who say Jesus was just a man, or just one of many angels, or one of many prophets of God, or was but a subgod of some sort are lying and bringing upon themselves the anathema, the curse, of God. Jesus is no less than God. The Father says to the Son, **Thy throne, O God, is forever and ever.** God the Father acknowledges God the Son. I believe this verse gives the clearest, most powerful, emphatic, and irrefutable proof of the deity of Christ in the Bible—from the Father Himself.

JESUS' OWN CLAIM TO DEITY

The Father's testimony about the Son corresponds to the Son's testimony about Himself. Throughout His ministry Jesus claimed equality with God. "For this cause therefore the Jews were seeking all the more to kill Him, because He not only was breaking the Sabbath, but also was calling God His own Father, making Himself equal with God" (John 5:18). When He said, "I and the Father are one" (John 10:30), the Jewish leaders well understood His claim. In light of who they thought He was, a mere man, their reaction was to be expected. "For a good work we do not stone You, but for blasphemy; and because You, being a man, make Yourself out to be God" (v. 33).

THE APOSTLES' CLAIM OF JESUS' DEITY

Talking about Israel and all their blessings, Paul wrote, "whose are the fathers, and from whom is the Christ according to the flesh, who is over all, God blessed forever. Amen" (Rom. 9:5). The Greek text more accurately reads, "God who is over all, blessed forever." The claim is that Jesus Christ is God. In 1 Timothy 3:16 the same apostle writes, "And by common confession great is the mystery of godliness: He who was revealed in the flesh, was vindicated in the Spirit, beheld by angels, proclaimed among the nations, believed on in the world, taken up in glory." Still again Paul declares, ". . . looking for the blessed hope and the appearing of the glory of our great God and Savior, Christ Jesus" (Titus 2:13).

In his first letter, John says, "And we know that the Son of God has come, and has given us understanding, in order that we might know Him who is true, and we are in Him who is true, in His Son Jesus Christ.

This is the true God and eternal life" (1 John 5:20). Throughout the New Testament the claim is unequivocal: Jesus Christ is God.

LOVER OF RIGHTEOUSNESS

In Hebrews 1:8 we continue reading, **"Thy throne, O God, is forever and ever, and the righteous scepter is the scepter of His kingdom."** Jesus Christ has an eternal **throne,** from which He rules eternity as God and King. He is the eternal King, with an eternal kingdom, and an eternal **scepter** of righteousness.

Thou hast loved righteousness and hated lawlessness; therefore God, Thy God, hath anointed Thee with the oil of gladness above Thy companions. (1:9)

This verse reveals both Jesus' actions and His motives. He not only acted in righteousness, He **loved righteousness.** How often do we do what we know is God's will, but do so without joy, in unwilling condescension? Jesus, however, *loved* righteousness. "Every good thing bestowed and every perfect gift is from above, coming down from the Father of lights, with whom there is no variation, or shifting shadow" (James 1:17). That is true righteousness. It never varies from what is true, just, good. "And this is the message we have heard from Him and announce to you, that God is light, and in Him there is no darkness at all" (1 John 1:5). God never varies; His motives, His actions, His character never vary. He is total light. He is total righteousness. Displayed in everything Jesus did was His love for righteousness. Even more than the psalmist could He say, "O how I love Thy law! It is my meditation all the day" (Ps. 119:97).

Because Christ loves righteousness, He hates **lawlessness.** If you love God's right standards, you will hate wrong standards. These two convictions are inseparable. One cannot exist without the other. You cannot truthfully say, "I love righteousness, but I also like sin." When there is true love for God, there will be total love for righteousness and total hatred for sin. Jesus hated sin just as surely as He loved righteousness. You see it in His temptation. You see it in His cleansing the Temple. You see it in His death on the cross. And the more we become conformed to our Lord, the more we are going to find that we, too, love righteousness and hate sin. By our attitudes toward righteousness and toward sin, we can tell how close we are to being conformed to Christ.

In Hebrews 1:9 is the most direct statement of Jesus' superiority to angels: **Therefore God, Thy God, hath anointed Thee with the oil of gladness above Thy companions.** Some commentators believe **companions** refers to men. But angels, not men, are being discussed in the passage. The Greek word simply connotes an association, nothing more. The point being made here is that Jesus Christ is greater than angels, who are His associates, His heavenly companions. But they are only messengers of God. Christ, too, is a messenger of God, but much more than a messenger and therefore much greater than they. He is exalted, **anointed,** above all others.

In his sermon in Cornelius' house, Peter tells of God's anointing of Jesus of Nazareth (Acts 10:38). God had anointed Him and ordained Him. Psalm 2:2 and other places in the Old Testament anticipate this anointing. Messiah is a transliteration of the Hebrew word for "Anointed One." Christ is a transliteration of the Greek word meaning the same thing. In other words, Jesus' supreme title (Messiah, or Christ) means "the Anointed One." Jesus was God's Anointed. When did this happen? I believe Jesus was officially *anointed* as king when He went to heaven after His resurrection. At that time the Father exalted Him and gave Him a name above every name (Eph. 1:20-22). He *assumed* His kingship at His ascension. Although He has not yet brought all of His kingdom together, someday soon He will.

Jesus' nature (that is, His deity), like His title and His being worshiped, show His superiority to angels.

GREATER BECAUSE OF SUPERIOR EXISTENCE

Thou, Lord, in the beginning didst lay the foundation of the earth, and the heavens are the works of Thy hands; they will perish, but Thou remainest; and they all will become old as a garment. And as a mantle Thou wilt roll them up; as a garment they will also be changed. But Thou art the same, and Thy years will not come to an end. (1:10-12)

The fourth way in which Jesus is superior to angels is in His existence. In this quotation from Psalm 102 the Holy Spirit reveals that Christ is better than angels because He exists eternally. If Jesus was in the beginning to create, He must have existed before the beginning and therefore be without beginning. "In the beginning was the Word" (John 1:1).

Just as you would roll up and throw away an old, worn-out **garment** when you are done with it, Jesus one day will discard the heavens and the earth. One day "the elements will be destroyed with intense heat, and the earth and its works will be burned up" (2 Pet. 3:10). "And the sky was split apart like a scroll when it is rolled up; and every mountain and island were moved out of their places" (Rev. 6:14). During the Tribulation, as if the heavens were to be stretched to the limit and the corners then cut, they will roll up just like a scroll. The stars are going to fall, come crashing down to earth, and every island and mountain will move out of its place. The whole world will fall apart.

The things that we can see and feel seem so permanent. Like the people Peter warned, we are tempted to think that "all continues just as it was from the beginning of creation" (2 Pet. 3:4). But all these are going to perish, and the Lord is going to create a new heaven and a new earth. The creation will be changed, but not the Creator. "Thy years will not come to an end." Christ is eternal. He is immutable; He never changes. "Jesus Christ is the same yesterday and today, yes and forever" (Heb. 13:8).

Men come and go. Worlds come and go. Stars come and go. Angels were subjected to decay, as their fall proves. But Christ never changes, is never subject to change, is never subject to alteration. He is eternally the same. He is therefore superior to angels in title, in worship, in nature, in existence, and finally in destiny.

GREATER BECAUSE OF SUPERIOR DESTINY

But to which of the angels has He ever said, "Sit at My right hand, until I make Thine enemies a footstool for Thy feet"? Are they not all ministering spirits, sent out to render service for the sake of those who will inherit salvation? (1:13-14)

Here, within only the first chapter, is the seventh Old Testament quotation, from Psalm 110:1. It climaxes the teaching of the full superiority of Christ to angels.

First we see the destiny of Christ, and then that of angels. No angel has ever been promised a place at God's right hand. Only the Son will sit here. The destiny of Jesus Christ is that ultimately everything in the universe will be subject to Him. "At the name of Jesus every knee [will] bow, of those who are in heaven, and on earth, and under the earth" (Phil. 2:10). Jesus Christ, in God's plan, is destined to be the ruler of the universe and everything that inhabits it. "Then comes the end, when He delivers up the kingdom to the God and Father, when He has abolished all rule and all authority and power. For He must reign until He has put all His enemies under His feet. . . . And when all things are subjected to Him, then the Son Himself also will be subjected to the One who subjected all things to Him, that God may be all in all" (1 Cor. 15:24-25, 28). He is subordinate to the Father, but only in the relationship of Son. The son of a king may be the equal of his father in every attribute of his nature, though be officially subject to his father. So the eternal Son is equally divine, though He is officially in subjection. And under His feet are placed all the kingdoms and authorities and powers of the world. When does that happen? At His Second Coming, when He comes in glory.

Revelation 19:15-16 gives a vivid picture of His next coming: "And from His mouth comes a sharp sword, so that with it He may smite the nations; and He will rule them with a rod of iron; and He treads the wine press of the fierce wrath of God, the Almighty. And on His robe and on His thigh He has a name written, 'KING OF KINGS, AND LORD OF LORDS.' " The destiny of Jesus Christ is eternal reign over the new heavens and the new earth.

Notice the destiny of God's angels: **Are they not all ministering spirits, sent out to render service for the sake of those who will inherit salvation?.** Jesus' destiny is to reign. The angels' destiny is to serve forever those who are heirs of salvation. What a wonderful, awesome prospect for Christians! In addition to being forever in God's presence, our destiny is to be served by angels forever.

Elisha and his servant were once menaced by the king of Syria and had no way to defend themselves. "Now when the attendant of the man of God had risen early and gone out, behold, an army with horses and chariots was circling the city. And his servant said to him, 'Alas, my master! What shall we do?' So he answered, 'Do not fear, for those who are with us are more than those who are with them.' Then Elisha prayed and said, 'O Lord, I pray, open his eyes that he may see.' And the Lord opened the servant's eyes, and he saw; and behold, the mountain was full of horses and chariots of fire all around Elisha" (2 Kings 6:15-17). Who were riding the horses and chariots? Angels. Angels protect and deliver the believer, the saint, from temporal danger. Angels rescued Lot and his family, snatching them out of Sodom. Angels got down into the den with Daniel and stopped the lions' mouths. What a marvelous, comforting truth to know that angels minister to us! Their destiny is to continue to minister to us throughout eternity. But Jesus' destiny is to reign. He is therefore immeasurably superior to the angels.

So we find that the Son of God is superior to angels in every way, with each of His superiorities having been described in the Old Testament. Jesus is Messiah. He is God in the flesh. He is the Mediator of a New Covenant, a covenant better than the Old.

In this brief fourteen-verse chapter, we see the deity of Jesus Christ established by divine names. He is called Son, Lord, and God. By divine works He creates, sustains, governs, redeems, and purges sin. By divine worth He is the one to be worshiped by the angels and all other creatures in the universe. By divine attributes He is omniscient, omnipotent, unchanging, and eternal. In all these ways the superiority of Jesus Christ is proclaimed.

Why are these truths so important? The next passage gives the answer. "For this reason we must pay much closer attention to what we have heard, lest we drift away from it. For if the word spoken through angels proved unalterable, and every transgression and disobedience received a just recompense, how shall we escape if we neglect so great a salvation?" (Heb. 2:1-3). If God expected such a positive response to the law, which came through the angels, what response does He expect concerning the gospel, which came through Jesus Christ?

The Tragedy of Neglecting Salvation
(2:1-4)

For this reason we must pay much closer attention to what we have heard, lest we drift away from it. For if the word spoken through angels proved unalterable, and every transgression and disobedience received a just recompense, how shall we escape if we neglect so great a salvation? After it was at the first spoken through the Lord, it was confirmed to us by those who heard, God also bearing witness with them, both by signs and wonders and by various miracles and by gifts of the Holy Spirit according to His own will. (2:1-4)

Hell is undoubtedly full of people who were never actively opposed to Jesus Christ, but who simply neglected the gospel. Such people are in view in these four verses. They know the truth and even believe the truth, in the sense that they acknowledge its truthfulness, its rightness. They are well aware of the good news of salvation provided in Jesus Christ, but are not willing to commit their lives to Him. So they drift past the call of God into eternal damnation. This tragedy makes these verses extremely important and urgent.

Right Teaching Demands Response

Into the middle of his treatise on angels, the writer interjects an invitation. He applies directly to the readers what he has been saying about Christ—that Christ is superior to everything and everyone, that He is the exalted One, that He alone can purge sin, that He is God, that He is the Creator, and that He is worthy of worship. He gives a personal invitation to his readers and hearers to respond to what they have learned. You might say that doctrine here breaks into invitation.

An effective teacher must do much more than simply present biblical facts. He must also warn, exhort, invite. By the time the writer of Hebrews gets to 2:1 he is impassioned. He cares about the salvation of his hearers. He is not satisfied simply with setting out doctrine and then going on his way. He longs for his readers to respond positively to what he says. He not only wants Christ to be seen and exalted, but also to be accepted. A teacher may know a lot of truth, but if he does not have compassionate concern for how people react to this truth, he is not a worthy teacher. God's Word demands response, and a faithful teacher of the Word teaches for response.

The apostle Paul was like this. Great theologian that he was, with a masterful grasp of philosophy and logic, he still was impassioned. In Romans 9:1-3 (after eight powerful chapters explaining the gospel), Paul breaks into an outburst of concern: "I am telling the truth in Christ, I am not lying, my conscience bearing me witness in the Holy Spirit, that I have great sorrow and unceasing grief in my heart. For I could wish that I myself were accursed, separated from Christ for the sake of my brethren, my kinsmen according to the flesh."

Paul had a holy obsession that all people, especially his Jewish kinsmen, come to Christ. "Brethren, my heart's desire and my prayer to God for them is for their salvation" (Rom. 10:1). Here is the character of a true teacher. He is interested in more than just academics, more than just information and pedagogy. He has a compassionate concern for how people respond to what they hear. "For though I am free from all men, I have made myself a slave to all, that I might win the more. And to the Jews I became as a Jew, that I might win Jews; to those who are under the Law, as under the Law, though not being myself under the Law, that I might win those who are under the Law; to those who are without law, as without law, though not being without the law of God but under the law of Christ, that I might win those who are without law. To the weak I became weak, that I might win the weak; I have become all things to all men, that I may by all means save some. And I do all things for the sake of the gospel" (1 Cor. 9:19-23).

Despite the rejection of His own people, their hardness of heart, and their history of persecuting God's messengers, Jesus nevertheless ached for their salvation. "O Jerusalem, Jerusalem, who kills the prophets and stones those who are sent to her! How often I wanted to gather your children together, the way a hen gathers her chicks under her wings, and you were unwilling" (Matt. 23:37). On another ocassion he told His Jewish listeners, "You search the Scriptures, because you think that in them you have eternal life; and it is these that bear witness of Me; and you are unwilling to come to Me, that you may have life" (John 5:39-40). He had a compassionate concern that His hearers respond. Faithful teaching always demands a response.

In Hebrews 13:22 the entire letter is referred to as a "word of exhortation." It therefore requires a response. So as the writer's heart is warmed by his treatise on the superiority of Christ to angels, he inserts a moving invitation. As all good invitations, it includes both exhortation and warning—what to do and what happens if you do not do it.

The opening verses of Hebrews 2 contain the first of five major warnings interspersed throughout the book—often, as here, in the middle of a discourse on one of the superiorities of Christ. It is as if the writer could only go so far without stopping to make an appeal: "Now what are you going to do about this?" We can know all the truth there is to know about Jesus Christ and yet go to hell if we never make Him our own—by being made His own.

WARNING TO THE INTELLECTUALLY CONVINCED

How shall we escape if we neglect so great a salvation? After it was at the first spoken through the Lord, it was confirmed to us by those who heard. (2:3)

To whom is the warning directed? It cannot be to Christians. They can never be in danger of neglecting **salvation**—in the sense of not receiving it—since they already have it. They can neglect growth and discipleship, but they cannot neglect salvation. Nor can the warning be to those who have never heard the gospel, because they cannot neglect what they do not even know exists. The warning must therefore be directed to non-Christians, specifically Jews, who are intellectually convinced of the gospel but who fail to receive it for themselves.

But if the warning is to unbelievers, why does the writer speak of "we" and "us"? Does he include himself among the intellectually convinced but uncommitted? Is the author saying that he himself is not a Christian? No. The "us" is the us of nationality or of all those who have heard the truth. The author's willingness to identify himself with his readers does not mean he is in the same spiritual condition as they are.

He seems simply to be saying, "All of us who have heard the gospel ought to accept it."

We have all met people who say, "Yes, I believe that Christ is the Savior and that I need Him, but I'm not ready to make that commitment yet." Perhaps your husband, your wife, your brother, or a good friend is like that. They come to church and hear and hear and hear the Word of God. They know it is true and they know they need it, but they are not willing to commit themselves and personally accept Jesus Christ. They have all the facts but will not make a commitment. They are like the man who believes a boat will hold him, but who will not get into it.

We believe this warning is to those who have heard the gospel, know the facts about Jesus Christ, know that He died for them, that He desires to forgive their sins, that He can give them new life, but are not willing to confess Him as Lord and Savior. This surely is the most tragic category of people in existence.

I will never forget the lady who came into my office one day, informed me she was a prostitute, and said, "I need help; I'm desperate." After presenting the claims of Christ to her, I said, "Would you like to confess Jesus Christ as your Lord?" "Yes," she replied, "I've had it." She was at the bottom and knew it. So she prayed a prayer and seemingly invited Christ into her life. I said, "Now, I want you to do something. Do you have your little book with you that has the names of all your contacts?" When she replied that she did, I suggested, "Let's take a match and burn it right now." Looking surprised, she responded, "What do you mean?" "Just what I said," I explained. "If you really met Jesus Christ as your Lord, if you really accepted His forgiveness and are going to live for Him, let's burn that book and celebrate your new birth right now and just praise the Lord." "But it's worth a lot of money, a lot of money," she objected. I said, "I am sure it is." Putting the book back in her purse and looking me in the eye, she said, "I don't want to burn my book. I guess I really don't want Jesus, do I?" And she left.

When she counted the cost, she realized she was not ready. I do not know what happened to that dear girl. My heart aches for her and I often think about her. I know that she knew the facts of the gospel and believed them; but she was not willing to make the sacrifice—even though what she refused to give up was worth nothing and what she could have had in Jesus Christ was everything.

There are many such people. They know the truth, they stand on the edge of the right decision, but they never make it. They just drift. And they are the ones to whom this passage in Hebrews is speaking. The purpose of these four verses is to give such persons a powerful shove toward Jesus Christ.

The message, of course, is not restricted to Jewish nonbelievers. It is for anyone who is on the edge of decision for Christ, but who—because of self-will, sin, fear of persecution from his family and friends, or any other reason—says no to Christ and continues to neglect Him. A man is a fool, a fool beyond fools, an eternal tragedy, when he neglects to decide for Jesus Christ.

THREE REASONS TO RECEIVE CHRIST

We are given three great reasons to receive salvation: the character of Christ, the certainty of judgment, and the confirmation of God.

THE CHARACTER OF CHRIST

For this reason we must pay much closer attention to what we have heard, lest we drift away from it. (2:1)

But what, you may ask, does that statement have to do with the character of Christ? **For this reason** is equivalent to "therefore." The first reason we should pay attention is given in chapter 1. It is Jesus Christ. He is called the Son and Heir of all things and the Creator of the world (1:2). He is the radiance of the glory of God, the exact representation of the divine nature, the sustainer of the universe, the purifier from sin, and the One who sits at the right hand of the Majesty on high (v. 3). He is worshiped and served by angels (vv. 4-7). He is anointed above all others, the Lord of creation, the unchangeable, everlasting God (vv. 8-12).

This is who Christ is. Who could possibly reject Him? What kind of person could reject that kind of Christ—the Christ who came into the world as God incarnate, died on a cross to forgive our sins, paid our penalty, showed us divine love, and offers to introduce us to God and give us blessing and joy beyond imagination?

Jesus was God's voice. Jesus was God in the world, and to reject Him is to reject God. To reject God is to reject the reason for our existence. Because of the magnificence of the Person of Christ, a man is a fool to reject the salvation He offers. I do not understand how a person can know who Christ is, admit that the gospel is true, and still not commit his life to Him. What an incomprehensible mystery—and tragedy!

A look at some of the Greek words in 2:1 will help in understanding all four of the opening verses. The two key words are *prosechō* ("to give attention to") and *pararheō* ("to let slip"). With its modifier, *prosechō* is translated **pay much closer attention to** and is emphatic. In other words, on the basis of who Chirst is, we must give careful attention to what we have heard about Him. We cannot hear these things and let them just slide through our minds. The word *pararheō* translates here as

drift away from and can have several meanings. It can be used of something flowing or slipping past, as of a ring slipping off a finger. It can be used of something slipping down and getting caught in a difficult place. It is used of something which carelessly has been allowed to slip away.

But both of these words also have nautical connotations. *Prosechō* means to moor a ship, to tie it up. *Pararheō* can be used of a ship that has been allowed to drift past the harbor because a sailor forgot to attend to the steerage or to properly chart the wind, tides, and current.

With these meanings in mind, the verse could be translated, "Therefore, we must the more eagerly secure our lives to the things which we have been taught, lest the ship of life drift past the harbor of salvation and be lost forever." The illustration is both graphic and appropriate. Most people do not go headlong and intentionally into hell. They drift into it. Most people do not deliberately, in a moment, turn their backs on God or curse Him. Most people just slowly, almost imperceptibly slip past the harbor of salvation out to eternal destruction.

One writer, building on Shakespeare, put it this way, "There is a tide in the affairs of men which, taken at its ebb, leads to victory; neglected, the shores of time are strewn with the wreckage." How true. The picture is not of an ignorant sailor, or a wantonly rebellious sailor, but of a careless sailor. We had better take all the more heed, therefore, lest, unintentionally and unexpectedly, we one day find ourselves having forever drifted past the harbor of salvation.

We must be sure to understand that it is not the gospel that slips, as the King James seems to imply. That is not the meaning at all. The Greek and most modern translations make it clear that it is inattentive men who slip. The Word will never drift from us. The danger is our drifting from it. The harbor of salvation is absolutely secure. It is Jesus Christ, who never moves, never changes, and is always available to anyone who wants the protection and security of His righteousness.

By the time the letter to the Hebrews was written, countless Jews had heard the gospel, many directly from an apostle. Many, no doubt, were favorably impressed with the message, even intrigued by it. They heard it and perhaps pondered it. But most did not accept it. Jesus' warning in Luke 9:44, "Let these words sink into your ears," can apply to the entire gospel. It must get inside of us and make a change in our lives. It is not enough just to hear it. That is only the beginning, as we are reminded in Proverbs: "My son, give attention to my words; incline your ear to my sayings. Do not let them depart from your sight; keep them in the midst of your heart. For they are life to those who find them, and health to all their whole body" (4:20-22). When you hear the Word of God, make it yours. Do not drift past it, for that is the most dangerous thing you can do.

One cannot help wondering how many thousands of people in

hell were close to salvation, how many thousands were close to being safely moored and anchored, only to drift away forever by their failure to receive what they heard and, in many cases, actually believed. Drifting is so quiet, so easy, but so damning. All you need to do to go to hell is do nothing. It is extremely difficult to understand how anyone who has seen the character of Jesus Christ can ever reject Him. As a Christian who lives everyday with Jesus Christ and experiences Him in my life, it is the greatest mystery to me that people do not rush to Him and everything He has for them.

And so the hearer is urged to respond because of the character of the incomparable Jesus Christ.

I often think of a story that I read about the English explorer, William Edward Parry, who took a crew to the Arctic Ocean. They wanted to go farther north to continue their chartings, so they calculated their location by the stars and started a very difficult and treacherous march north. They walked hour upon hour, and finally, totally exhausted, they stopped. Taking their bearings again from the stars, they discovered that they were farther south than they had been when they started. They had been walking on an ice floe that was moving south faster than they were walking north. I wonder how many people think their good deeds, their merits, and their religiousness are taking them step by step to God, when in fact they are moving away from Him faster than they are supposedly walking toward Him. That is the tragedy of it. They awake one day to find, like Parry's crew, that all the time they have been moving in the wrong direction.

A person should never be satisfied with religious feelings, with coming to church, with being married to a Christian spouse, or with church activities. He will be drifting into a hell unless he has made a personal commitment to the Lord and Savior, Jesus Christ.

THE CERTAINTY OF JUDGMENT

The second important reason for accepting Christ is the certainty of judgment for those who do not do so. Verses 2 and 3 tell us of the inevitability of such punishment:

For if the word spoken through angels proved unalterable, and every transgression and disobedience received a just recompense, how shall we escape if we neglect so great a salvation? After it was at the first spoken through the Lord, it was confirmed to us by those who heard. (2:2-3)

The Greek here for **if** assumes a fulfilled condition, not a possibility. The meaning in context is that the word spoken by angels was absolute and steadfast. The phrase could be translated, "For in view of the fact that the word spoken through angels . . ."

Why is Old Testament law, particularly the Ten Commandments, so connected with angels? Why does the writer emphasize that angels mediated the Old Covenant? He does so because the angels were instrumental in bringing the Ten Commandments, as is clear from several passages.

Psalm 68:17 gives us a clue: "The chariots of God are myriads, thousands upon thousands; the Lord is among them as at Sinai, in holiness." At Sinai, where Moses was given the law, the Lord was accompanied by a host of angels. Moses himself reports that "The Lord came from Sinai, and dawned on them from Seir; He shone forth from Mount Paran, and He came from the midst of ten thousand holy ones; at His right hand there was flashing lightning for them" (Deut. 33:2). We believe this indicates that angels were involved in bringing the law.

Acts 7:38 mentions specifically that at least one angel was with Moses at Sinai: "This is the one who was in the congregation in the wilderness together with the angel who was speaking to him on Mount Sinai, and who was with our fathers." A few verses later we are told of "the law as ordained by angels" (v. 53).

Both the Old and New Testaments tell us that angels were at Sinai and were instrumental in bringing the law. And if you broke that law, that law broke you. There was no out. If a person committed adultery, worshiped false gods, or blasphemed God, he was stoned. The law was inviolable; punishment for breaking it was sure and certain. As our text says, **every transgression and disobedience received a just recompense.** The law punished every sin. And that punishment was fair.

Two words are used here for sin: **transgression** (*parabasis*) and **disobedience** (*parakoē*). Transgression means to step across the line, as a willful act. It is an overt sin of commission—of intentionally doing something we know to be wrong. Disobedience, however, carries the idea of imperfect hearing, but not like that of a deaf man, who cannot help not hearing. Disobedience deliberately shuts its ears to the commands, warnings, and invitations of God. It is a sin of neglect, of omission—doing nothing when we should do something. One is active sin, the other is passive, but both are willful and both are serious.

Look at Leviticus 24:14-16.

> Bring the one who has cursed outside the camp, and let all who heard him lay their hands on his head; then let all the congregation stone him. And you shall speak to the sons of Israel, saying, "If anyone curses his God, then he shall bear his sin. Moreover, the one who blasphemes the name of the Lord shall surely be put to death; all the congregation shall certainly stone him. The alien as well as the native, when he blasphemes the Name, shall be put to death."

That seems severe, but God wanted to make sure that all false prophets and blasphemers were dealt with immediately in order to maintain the spiritual and moral purity of His people.

Now look at Numbers 15:30-36.

"But the person who does anything defiantly, whether he is native or an alien, that one is blaspheming the Lord; and that person shall be cut off from among his people. Because he has despised the word of the Lord and has broken His commandment, that person shall be completely cut off; his guilt shall be on him." Now while the sons of Israel were in the wilderness, they found a man gathering wood on the sabbath day. And those who found him gathering wood brought him to Moses and Aaron, and to all the congregation; and they put him in custody because it had not been declared what should be done to him. Then the Lord said to Moses, "The man shall surely be put to death; all the congregation shall stone him with stones outside the camp."

You ask, "Put to death for picking up sticks on the Sabbath?" Yes, because he deliberately defied the law of God (cf. James 2:10).

The inviolable law that God set was strong. In Jude 5 we read, "Now I desire to remind you, though you know all things once for all, that the Lord, after saving a people out of the land of Egypt, subsequently destroyed those who did not believe." That is severe judgment on unbelievers.

Now notice the word **just** in Heb. 2:2. God is often accused of being unjust when His punishment seems to us to be out of proportion to the wrong committed. But God, by His very nature, cannot be unjust. Under the Old Covenant He punished severely those who were determined to live without Him and to defy Him. He removed them from among His people for the sake of those who were pure and holy and wanted to live for Him. His judgment on the people of Israel was severe because they knew better.

Punishment is always related to light. The more light we have, the more severe our punishment. Jesus was clear about this.

Then He began to reproach the cities in which most of His miracles were done, because they did not repent. "Woe to you, Chorazin! Woe to you, Bethsaida! For if the miracles had occurred in Tyre and Sidon which occurred in you, they would have repented long ago in sackcloth and ashes. Nevertheless I say to you, it shall be more tolerable for Tyre and Sidon in the day of judgment, than for you. And you, Capernaum, will not be exalted to heaven, will you? You shall descend to Hades; for if the miracles had occurred in Sodom which occurred in you, it would have remained to this day. Nevertheless I say to you that it shall be more tolerable for the land of Sodom in the day of judgment, than for you." (Matt. 11:20-24)

The principle is this: the more you know, the greater the punishment for not abiding by what you know. Tyre and Sidon were terribly guilty of unbelief and disobedience, and throughout Scripture Sodom and Gomorrah typify gross ungodliness and immorality. But none of these were as guilty as Capernaum or Bethsaida or Chorazin, because these three not only had the light of the Old Testament, but the very light of God's Messiah Himself.

Mark records a similar teaching of our Lord: "Beware of the scribes who like to walk around in long robes, and like respectful greetings in the market places, and chief seats in the synagogues, and places of honor at banquets, who devour widows' houses, and for appearance's sake offer long prayers; these will receive greater condemnation" (12:38-40).

Hell is a very real place. In the New Testament it is called a place of eternal fire (Matt. 25:41), where the worm does not die and the fire is not quenched (Mark 9:43-44). It is called a lake of fire which burns with brimstone (Rev. 19:20), a bottomless pit or abyss (Rev. 9:11; 11:7; and others), outer darkness where there is continual weeping and gnashing of teeth (Matt. 22:13), and black darkness (Jude 13).

There are degrees of punishment in hell. The hottest places belong to those who have rejected the most light. Listen to Jesus' own words: "And that slave who knew his master's will and did not get ready or act in accord with his will, shall receive many lashes, but the one who did not know it, and committed deeds worthy of a flogging, will receive but few. And from everyone who has been given much shall much be required; and to whom they entrusted much, of him they will ask all the more" (Luke 12:47). The Lord is talking about judgment, and His point is simple: the greater the light, the greater the accountability.

This truth is given as clearly as possible in the book we are now studying. "Anyone who has set aside the Law of Moses dies without mercy.... How much severer punishment do you think he will deserve who has trampled under foot the Son of God, and has regarded as unclean the blood of the covenant by which he was sanctified, and has insulted the Spirit of grace?" (Heb. 10:28-29). The person who knows and understands and believes the gospel, but drifts away from it, will experience the severest punishment there is. So certainty of judgment should be a powerful motivation for accepting Christ.

THE CONFIRMATION OF GOD

How shall we escape if we neglect so great a salvation? After it was at the first spoken through the Lord, it was confirmed to us by those who heard, God also bearing witness with them, both by signs and

wonders and by various miracles and by gifts of the Holy Spirit according to His own will. (2:3-4)

The third important reason for accepting Christ is the confirmation of God. The gospel was first given by Christ and was then confirmed by the apostles who had heard Him in person. Even more importantly, however, it was confirmed by God Himself bearing witness.

When Jesus preached the gospel, He also did some things that made it even more believable. He said, "Though you do not believe Me, believe the works, that you may know and understand that the Father is in Me, and I in the Father" (John 10:38). When He claimed to be God and then did things that only God could do, He confirmed His divinity and, consequently, the truth of His message. On the Day of Pentecost Peter reminded his hearers that "Jesus the Nazarene [was] a man attested to you by God with miracles and wonders and signs" (Acts 2:22).

God gave similar confirming signs through the apostles, the first preachers of the gospel after Christ Himself. Many of their listeners no doubt said, "Why should we believe them? What proof do we have that their message is from God? There have always been a lot of false teachers around. How can we know that these are true?" So God bore His apostles witness by giving them the ability to do the same things that Jesus had done—signs, wonders, and miracles. And they did indeed perform astounding miracles. They raised the dead and healed many diseases and afflictions, and through these wonderful works God confirmed their ministry. To argue with an apostle about the gospel, therefore, was to argue with God. Their preaching and teaching was divine truth, substantiated by miraculous works.

As if this confirmation were not enough, God also gave the apostles special **gifts of the Holy Spirit according to His own will. According to His own will** seems to be inserted here partly to keep us from getting confused about the source of certain spiritual gifts (cf. 1 Cor. 12:11, 18, 28).

Dr. Earl Radmacher, president of Western Conservative Baptist Seminary, once told me of his receiving a pamphlet in the mail that gave the steps necessary to get the Holy Spirit. First you were to say two phrases, "Praise the Lord" and "Hallelujah," three times faster than normal for a period of ten minutes. If you did that long enough you would lapse into a strange language and then get the Holy Spirit. That is as ridiculous as it is blasphemous. Gifts of the Spirit are according to His own will, not our efforts.

The primary point at the end of verse 4 is that the apostles' gifts of the Holy Spirit were additional confirmation by God of their message and ministry. The gifts mentioned in Hebrews 2:4 were miraculous gifts, not promised to believers in general. Romans 12 and 1 Corinthians 12-14 representatively illustrate the nonmiraculous spiritual gifts that were not limited to the apostles.

In Acts 14:3 we read that Paul and Barnabas "spent a long time there [Iconium] speaking boldly with reliance upon the Lord, who was bearing witness to the word of His grace, granting that signs and wonders be done by their hands." Paul explained to the Roman Christians, "In the power of signs and wonders, in the power of the Spirit; so that from Jerusalem and round about as far as Illyricum I have fully preached the gospel of Christ" (Rom. 15:19). As an apostle he had the gift to do these miracles. In another letter he says, "The signs of a true apostle were performed among you with all perseverance, by signs and wonders and miracles" (2 Cor. 12:12). These special works, therefore, belonged exclusively to the apostolic age. They were not to last indefinitely, and they are not for today.

What were these gifts specifically? I believe there were four—healing, miracles, tongues, and interpretation of tongues. These gifts all ceased with the apostolic era. They have no need to exist today because there is no such need to confirm the gospel.

Even in New Testament times these confirmations were given solely for the benefit of unbelievers. "So then tongues are for a sign, not to those who believe, but to unbelievers" (1 Cor. 14:22). When God's written Word was completed, the other confirmations ceased. If someone comes along today and says, "Thus says the Lord," how do you know he is genuine? You check what he says against Scripture. Benjamin Warfield, the great Bible scholar, said, "These miraculous gifts were part of the credentials of the apostles as the authoritative agents of God in founding the church. Their function thus confirmed them distinctively in the apostolic church, and they necessarily passed away with it."

Thus, the three great reasons why a man should not neglect the gospel of salvation are: the character of Christ, the certainty of judgment, and the confirmation of God. God has attested to this gospel with signs, wonders, miracles, and special spiritual gifts; but now He attests to it in the miracle and authority of His written Word.

Let it not be said of you that you neglected Jesus Christ. History tells us that failure to shoot a rocket at the precise time of night caused the fall of Antwerp, and Holland's deliverance was delayed for twenty years. Only three hours neglect cost Napoleon the battle of Waterloo. Neglect of Christ's salvation will cost you eternal blessing, eternal joy, and will bring you damning judgment and eternal punishment. Do not drift past God's grace.

Recovery of Man's Lost Destiny (2:5-9)

5

For He did not subject to angels the world to come, concerning which we are speaking. But one has testified somewhere, saying, "What is man, that Thou rememberest him? Or the son of man, that Thou art concerned about him? Thou hast made him for a little while lower than the angels; Thou hast crowned him with glory and honor, and hast appointed him over the works of Thy hands; Thou hast put all things in subjection under his feet." For in subjecting all things to him, He left nothing that is not subject to him. But now we do not yet see all things subjected to him. But we do see Him who has been made for a little while lower than the angels, namely, Jesus, because of the suffering of death crowned with glory and honor, that by the grace of God He might taste death for everyone. (2:5-9)

After his urgent appeal in 2:1-4 for men not to neglect salvation, the writer briefly returns to his discussion of angels—as an introduction to his teaching about man's destiny. First, he presents another amazing truth about the angels' rank or position in relation to Christ: **For He did not subject to angels the world to come, concerning which we are speaking.** God alone will be Sovereign of the world to come, another indication of His superiority to angels. If angels are next below God, and Jesus is superior to angels, Jesus is obviously God.

In addition to continuing the argument about the superiority of Christ above angels, this passage deals with man's destiny. Man today is lost, totally lost. In losing his right relationship to God, he also lost the meaning of his existence. These verses teach us what man's intended destiny is, how and why it was lost, and how it can be recovered in the exalted Savior.

MAN'S DESTINY REVEALED BY GOD

First, we see man's destiny revealed by God. **For He did not subject to angels the world to come, concerning which we are speaking.** God never intended to give angels rule over the world to come. Rather, angels are to minister to those who will be heirs of salvation (1:14). In the world to come, angels will be servants, not rulers.

Subject translates the Greek *hupotassō*, primarily a term that referred to arranging soldiers in order under a commander. It also came to be used for any system of administration. God will not turn over the administration of the world to come to angels. This will be the great and glorious world, the world of perfection. Whoever reigns in that world will be glorious indeed. But it will not be angels. Their present superiority over men is temporary.

The Greek word translated **world** in verse 5 is not the general term *kosmos,* which means "system," or *aiōn,* meaning "the ages." The word used here is very specific; it is *oikoumenē,* "the inhabited earth." There will be, therefore, an inhabited earth to come. Amillennialists maintain that there is no future earthly kingdom. But this verse plainly says that such an earth *is* to come. It cannot be referring to this present earth, because it is going to be significantly changed (Zech. 14:9-11). Many signs, in fact, seem to indicate that the change is near.

There must, therefore, be another inhabited earth to come. What is it? It is the great millennial Kingdom. The earth itself will be different and all its inhabitants will be different. The animals will be different, and some of the people will be different—redeemed and glorified (cf. Isa. 11:35). But the point being made in verse 5 is simply that this new world will not be ruled by angels.

To get the whole issue in perspective, however, we should understand that this present world, our present inhabited earth, *is* ruled by angels. The chief fallen angel is Satan, who is also prince of this world (John 12:31; 14:30). We also know from Ephesians that this world is under tremendous demonic influence. Demons are fallen angels and they are called rulers, powers, world forces of darkness, and spiritual forces of wickedness (Eph. 6:12). Not only do Satan and his fallen angels have some rule in this world, but even the holy angels now have a kind of sovereignty. Daniel 10 tells of Michael and another holy angel fighting against powerful fallen angels who were influencing the rulers of Persia and Greece. The rule of this earth, therefore, is now in the hands of both fallen and holy angels. Needless to say, this "joint" rulership involves extreme conflict.

Man, however, was created as the king of the earth, and in God's final destiny for him, man will one day be the sovereign that his Creator designed him to be. So it makes no sense to argue that Christ cannot be better than angels because He became a man, for man is lower than the angels only **for a little while.** He will one day again be above them and will, in fact, even judge the angels who have fallen (1 Cor. 6:3).

But one has testified somewhere, saying, "What is man, that Thou rememberest him? Or the son of man, that Thou art concerned about him? Thou hast made him for a little while lower than the angels; Thou hast crowned him with glory and honor, and hast appointed him over the works of Thy hands; Thou hast put all things in subjection under his feet." (2:6-8)

The writer's saying, **But one has testified somewhere** does not indicate that he was either ignorant or forgetful of Scripture. He obviously knew the passage well, since he quotes it perfectly (from the Septuagint, the Greek version of the Old Testament). And Psalm 8, from which he quotes, names David as its composer. Throughout the book of Hebrews, however, no human author is mentioned by name. The writer is so concerned that his Jewish readers understand who really wrote the Old Testament that he ascribes it to no one but God. It is the voice of the Holy Spirit that concerns him; the human author is incidental.

These quoted verses from Psalm 8 refer to mankind, not to the Messiah, who is not mentioned in the Hebrews passage until verse 9. In verses 6-8 we see God's planned destiny for mankind in general. Again the writer beautifully makes his point by using the Old Testament.

David had wondered, "God, you've done this. But why? What is man that you have done so much for him?" When we look at the vast, seemingly endless universe and then think about the little dot that we call earth in the middle of it all, we, too, cannot but ask, "What is man? What right do we have to be so much in the mind of God?" The psalmist goes on to answer his own question. "Thou hast made him for a little while lower than the angels, . . . crowned him with glory and honor, . . . appointed him over the works of Thy hands, . . . put all things in subjection under his feet." God made man to be king. Such is man's destiny.

No doubt both David and the writer of Hebrews were thinking of the first chapter of Genesis.

Then God said, "Let Us make man in Our image, according to Our likeness; and let them rule over the fish of the sea and over the birds of the sky and over the cattle and over all the earth, and over every creeping thing that creeps on the earth." And God created man in His own image, in the image of God He created him; male and female He created them. And God blessed them; and God said to them, "Be fruitful and multiply, and fill the earth, and subdue it; and rule over the fish of the sea and over the birds of the sky, and over every living thing that moves on the earth." Then God said, "Behold, I have given you every plant yielding seed that is on the surface of all the earth, and every tree which has fruit yielding seed; it shall be food for you; and to every beast of the earth and to every bird of the sky and to every thing that moves on the earth which has life, I have given every green plant for food"; and it was so. And God saw all that He had made, and behold, it was very good. (Gen. 1:26-31)

Let us look at Hebrews 2:6-8 part by part. **What is man ... or the son of man?** Some take **the son of man** as a reference to Christ, but I think it is simply a parallel to **man.** "Son of man" is often used in the Old Testament to mean mankind. Several times, for example, Ezekiel is called "the son of man," indicating only that he was a human being, a part of mankind.

The word **concerned** in Greek has to do with looking toward someone with a view to benefiting him. It is much more than simply a wish or desire for the person's welfare. It involves active caring. The word is used twice in Luke 1 to describe God's visiting His people Israel to redeem them (vv. 68, 78). The King James text of Hebrews 2:6, in fact, uses "visitest." God has an involved, active concern for humanity.

Thou hast made him for a little while lower than the angels. When God created man, He made him in one way lower than angels. It is not that he is lower than angels spiritually, or is less loved by God. Nor is he lower than angels in importance to God. Man is lower than angels only in that he is physical and they are spiritual. What does this mean? Just this: angels are heavenly creatures, while man is earth-bound. Obviously this is a limiting and major difference, and man is therefore now of a lower rank. But there is a time limit for this inferiority. The present chain of command is temporary. God has a destiny for man that will elevate him to king, when he will be on at least an equal basis with angels.

Man is confined to the earth and to relatively nearby space. Angels, on the other hand, are not confined to the spiritual. They are able to come to earth at will, and have supernatural power and strength that even sinless man did not have. Not only that, but man's only direct communion with God has been that which he had with Jesus while He was on earth. Angels have continual access to the throne of God. Angels are spirit beings; man is made out of the dust of the earth. After Satan rebelled, the faithful angels were secured in holiness forever; after Adam rebelled, all men were cursed with him. In Adam, all died (1 Cor. 15:22). At the time of the creation, angels were perfect; man was only innocent. Even in his innocence, man had the choice to sin. Still more importantly, angels were never subject to death as man was. God's first words to Adam in the garden of Eden were, "From any tree of the garden you may eat freely; but from the tree of the knowledge of good and evil you shall not eat, for in the day that you eat from it you shall surely die" (Gen. 2:16-17).

In the coming new earth, things will be much different. Then "the saints of the Highest One will receive the kingdom and possess the kingdom forever, for all ages to come. . . . Then the sovereignty, the dominion, and the greatness of all the kingdoms under the whole heaven will be given to the people of the saints of the Highest One; His kingdom will be an everlasting kingdom, and all the dominions will serve and obey Him" (Dan. 7:18, 27). Redeemed men not only will inherit a perfect kingdom but an eternal kingdom, in which they, not angels, will rule. Revelation 3:21 says believers will sit with Christ on His throne and rule with Him. Ephesians 1:20 says He will reign over principalities and powers, that is, angels. Therefore if Christ reigns over angels in the kingdom and we sit on His throne with Him, we, too, will reign over angels. Only **for a little while** are men **lower than the angels.** The whole earth will be redeemed and man will be crowned in Christ. That is the promise for the future.

Now notice the second half of Hebrews 2:7, **Thou hast crowned him with glory and honor, and hast appointed him over the works of Thy hands. Crown** is *stephanos,* the crown of honor. When God made Adam pure and innocent, He gave him honor and glory. Someday, He will restore it.

"Thou hast put all things in subjection under his feet." For in subjecting all things to him, He left nothing that is not subject to him. (2:8*a*)

The king's throne was always elevated, and everyone who came into his presence bowed down before him and sometimes even kissed his feet. His subjects, therefore, were often spoken of as being under his feet. When man is one day given the right to rule the earth, all God's creation will be put under man's feet. That is the revelation of man's destiny.

MAN'S DESTINY RESTRICTED BY SIN

But now we do not yet see all things subjected to him. (2:8*b*)

Something drastic happened. Man's revealed destiny was restricted by Adam's and Eve's sin. To Eve God said, "I will greatly multiply your pain in childbirth, in pain you shall bring forth children; yet your desire shall be for your husband, and he shall rule over you" (Gen. 3:16). The pain of childbirth and the subjection of a wife to her husband are direct results of the Fall. To Adam God said, "Because you have listened to the voice of your wife, and have eaten from the tree about which I command-ed you, saying, 'You shall not eat from it'; cursed is the ground because of you; in toil you shall eat of it all the days of your life. Both thorns and thistles it shall grow for you; and you shall eat the plants of the field; by the sweat of your face you shall eat bread, till you return to the ground, because from it you were taken; for you are dust, and to dust you shall return" (3:17-19). Then man was put out of the garden. "Then the Lord God said, 'Behold, the man has become like one of Us, knowing good and evil; and now, lest he stretch out his hand, and take also from the tree of life, and eat, and live forever'—therefore the Lord God sent him out from the garden of Eden, to cultivate the ground from which he was taken" (3:22-23). When Adam sinned, the earth was corrupted and he immedi-ately lost his kingdom and his crown.

Because all mankind fell in Adam, because he lost his kingdom and his crown, we do not now see the earth subject to man. The earth originally was subject to man, and it supplied all his needs without his having to do anything. He had only to accept and enjoy the earth as it provided for him. Then, tempted by Satan, man sinned, and his tempter usurped the crown. There you see the change in the chain of command. Man fell to the bottom, and the earth, under the evil one, now rules man. If you pay much attention to ecology, you know that we do not rule this world; it rules us. With all our modern technology, we must constantly fight against the earth for our survival.

What else happened to Adam after he had sinned? First, there was murder within his own family. Then there was polygamy. In the next few chapters of Genesis we read of death. By the time we come to chapter 6, God is sending a flood to destroy all mankind but one family. Man indeed had lost his crown. The prince of the earth, of the system of the world, now is Satan. "The whole world lies in the power of the evil one" (1 John 5:19). He rules the cursed earth, which in turn rules sinful man. When man lost his crown, he also lost mastery of himself as well as of the earth. He was totally sinful and became a slave to sin.

Not only that, but the animal kingdom was now subservient to man only out of fear, no longer out of affection. Much of the animal kingdom was no longer able to be tamed at all. The ground originally produced good things naturally and abundantly for man to have for the taking. Now it produces thorns, weeds, and other harmful things natural-ly and abundantly. Whatever good things man now gets from the earth come only by tiresome effort. Extremes of heat and cold, poisonous plants and reptiles, earthquakes, tornadoes, floods, hurricanes, disease, war—all these were released upon man after the Fall. Virtually everything God had given for man's good and blessing became his enemy, and man has been fighting a losing battle ever since. For millennia, he himself has been dying. Now he is finding out that the earth is dying with him.

Amazingly, the earth itself knows its condition. "For the anxious longing of the creation waits eagerly for the revealing of the sons of God. For the creation was subjected to futility, not of its own will, but because of Him who subjected it" (Rom. 8:19-20). God subjected the earth to this curse in order that man might continually have trouble. Man had to know that God was aware of his sin, and he had to suffer the consequences, in part, by fighting against the very earth that was designed to be his servant. But when the new kingdom begins, "the creation itself also will be set free from its slavery to corruption into the freedom of the glory of the children of God. For we know that the whole creation groans and suffers the pains of childbirth together until now" (vv. 21-22). The earth, aware of its curse that came with Adam's fall, is groaning for the day that the sons of God are manifest in the kingdom, for the earth knows that it, too, will be liberated from corruption.

In the meantime, man is subject to the earth. He plants but he is not sure who will reap. He builds cities and houses and dams and monuments—but they are all subject to destruction by lightning or earthquake or flood or fire or erosion or simply aging. Man lives in jeopardy every hour. Just at the height of professional achievement, his brain may develop a tumor, and he becomes an imbecile. Just at the brink of athletic fame, he may be injured and become a helpless paralytic. He fights himself, he fights his fellowman, and he fights his earth. Every day we read and hear of the distress of nations, of the impossibility of agreement between statesmen in a world that languishes in political and social conflict—not to mention economic hardship, health hazards, and military threats. We hear the whine of pain from dumb animals and even see the struggle of trees and crops against disease and insects. Our many hospitals, doctors, medicines, pesticides, insurance companies, fire and police departments, funeral homes—all bear testimony to the cursed earth.

No wonder the creation groans. But God did not intend it to be this way; and it will continue this way only for a little while, in God's timetable. Someday, in the world to come, when the kingdom comes, hospitals will be closed, doctors will be out of business, and the ravenous nature of wild animals (and of human beings) will be changed. The crops and the trees will no longer be infested. The game of politics will be over and wars will cease. Man—redeemed man—will reign. "And they will hammer their swords into plowshares, and their spears into pruning hooks. Nation will not lift up sword against nation, and never again will they learn war" (Isa. 2:4). A day is coming when, in the wonderful plan of God, the dominion that man lost will be given to him again. God's redeemed ones, His children, will never again be subject to death. They will be like the angels (Luke 20:36). In the kingdom they will, in fact, reign over the angels.

MAN'S DESTINY RECOVERED BY CHRIST

But we do see Him who has been made for a little while lower than the angels, namely, Jesus, because of the suffering of death crowned with glory and honor, that by the grace of God He might taste death for everyone. (Heb. 2:9)

That brings us to the third point. Man's revealed destiny, restricted by sin, has been recovered by Christ.

The ultimate curse of man's lost destiny is death. Warning Adam about the tree of the knowledge of good and evil, God said, "For in the day that you eat from it you shall surely die" (Gen. 2:17). The cross conquered the curse. The kingdom will be restored and man will be given the crown again.

But how can it happen? If we are all sinners, how can we become sinless? The only payment for sin is death. "For the wages of sin is death" (Rom. 6:23). The only way man can ever be a king again is to have the curse removed. The only way the curse can be removed is for the penalty to be paid. If man is to be restored to reign as a king, he must die—and be resurrected a new man with sovereign qualities.

But we still ask, "How?" We know, even without God's revelation, that we could not do this ourselves. Paul explains. Speaking of Christ, he writes:

> For if we have become united with Him in the likeness of His death, certainly we shall be also in the likeness of His resurrection, knowing this, that our old self was crucified with Him, that our body of sin might be done away with, that we should no longer be slaves to sin; for he who has died is freed from sin. Now if we have died with Christ, we believe that we shall also live with Him, knowing that Christ, having been raised from the dead, is never to die again; death no longer is master over Him. For the death that He died, He died to sin, once for all; but the life that He lives, He lives to God. Even so consider yourselves to be dead to sin, but alive to God in Christ Jesus. (Rom. 6:5-11)

I died years ago. I am perfectly healthy now, but I died a long time ago. I died the death that Paul describes in Galatians: "I have been crucified with Christ" (2:20). The moment that I put my faith in Jesus Christ, at that moment I was identified with Christ. I died with Him on the cross. For John MacArthur the curse is removed. I am now a king. I have not inherited my dominion yet, but the crown has been restored. And for every one of you who knows and loves Jesus Christ, the moment you received Him, you were identified with Him. You were crucified with Him and were buried with Him, and He has raised you up to a new life. It is life with the curse removed.

In Christ we are kings. We do not have our kingdom yet, but it is certain to be ours. To the saints of the Most High belongs the kingdom. Our old bodies are going to fall off someday, but we are not going to die. Our bodies will die, but even they will one day be resurrected in a new and eternal form. We will be immediately liberated to go into the presence of Jesus. Or, if He comes again before that happens to us, He will take us with Him into the kingdom.

To accomplish this great work on our behalf, Jesus had to become a man. He Himself had to be made **for a little while lower than the angels.** To regain man's dominion He had to taste death for man. If a man dies for his own sin, he is doomed forever to hell. But Christ came to die for us, because in His dying He could conquer death.

> And they sang a new song, saying, "Worthy art Thou to take the book, and to break its seals; for Thou wast slain, and didst purchase for God with Thy blood men from every tribe and tongue and people and nation. And Thou has made them to be a kingdom and priests to our God; and they will reign upon the earth." (Rev. 5:9-10)

As you and I identify ourselves with Jesus Christ in His death, as we receive Him as Savior, the curse is removed, and we become joint heirs with Him in the eternal kingdom.

Obviously, if we are going to reign on earth as kings, there will have to be a kingdom.

> And I saw thrones, and they sat upon them, and judgment was given to them. And I saw the souls of those who had been beheaded because of the testimony of Jesus and because of the word of God, and those who had not worshiped the beast or his image, and had not received the mark upon their forehead and upon their hand; and they came to life and reigned with Christ for a thousand years. (Rev. 20:4)

Who will be on those thrones? We who are the kings. We will be kings with our great King, the King of kings. The Redeemer King will rule with His redeemed saints over the redeemed earth.

Man will be changed:

> Now it will come about that in the last days, the mountain of the house of the Lord will be established as the chief of the mountains, and will be raised above the hills; and all the nations will stream to it. And many peoples will come and say, "Come, let us go up to the mountain of the Lord, to the house of the God of

Jacob; that He may teach us concerning His ways, and that we may walk in His paths." For the law will go forth from Zion, and the word of the Lord from Jerusalem. And He will judge between the nations, and will render decisions for many peoples; and they will hammer their swords into plowshares, and their spears into pruning hooks. Nation will not lift up sword against nation, and never again will they learn war. (Isa. 2:2-4)

The animals will be changed:

And the wolf will dwell with the lamb, and the leopard will lie down with the kid, and the calf and the young lion and the fatling together; and a little boy will lead them. . . . And the nursing child will play by the hole of the cobra, and the weaned child will put his hand on the viper's den. They will not hurt or destroy in all My holy mountain, for the earth will be full of the knowledge of the Lord as the waters cover the sea. (Isa. 2:2-4; 11:6, 8-9)

Even the plants will be changed:

The wilderness and the desert will be glad, and the Arabah will rejoice and blossom; like the crocus it will blossom profusely and rejoice with rejoicing and shout of joy. (Isa. 35:1-2)

Christ tasted death for you and for me. He did it to recover our lost destiny. If you have been groping around, trying to figure out why you exist, I hope you know the reason now. There is no reason for us to be slaves. There is no reason for us to be paupers. There is only reason for us to be kings.

Men today still ask, "What is man?" The idolator and the animist says, "Man is inferior to birds and animals, even to creeping things, stones, and sticks." And he bows down and worships the snake. The materialist says, "Man is obviously higher than any of the other animals, but he is still only the product of chance, the result of evolutionary natural selection." Most people believe such ideas or ones equally as foolish. But God says, "Man was created to be king of the earth. Only for a little time he has been made lower than the angels." Someday he will sit on the throne of Jesus Christ and reign with Him in His kingdom.

I trust that you will be there reigning with Christ.

Our Perfect Savior
(2:9-18)

But we do see Him who has been made for a little while lower than the angels, namely, Jesus, because of the suffering of death crowned with glory and honor, that by the grace of God He might taste death for everyone. For it was fitting for Him, for whom are all things, and through whom are all things, in bringing many sons to glory, to perfect the author of their salvation through sufferings. For both He who sanctifies and those who are sanctified are all from one Father; for which reason He is not ashamed to call them brethren, saying, "I will proclaim Thy name to My brethren, in the midst of the congregation I will sing Thy praise." And again, "I will put My trust in Him." And again, "Behold, I and the children whom God has given Me." Since then the children share in flesh and blood, He Himself likewise also partook of the same, that through death He might render powerless him who had the power of death, that is, the devil; and might deliver those who through fear of death were subject to slavery all their lives. For assuredly He does not give help to angels, but He gives help to the descendant of Abraham. Therefore, He had to be made like His brethren in all things, that He might become a merciful and faithful high priest in things pertaining to God, to make propitiation for the sins of the people. For since He Himself was tempted in that which He has suffered, He is able to come to the aid of those who are tempted. (2:9-18)

A newspaper article some years ago hailed the arrival of the "Son of God" into the world. This proclaimed savior, called the son of God by his followers, was a thirteen-year-old guru. He took his place in a long line of would-be messiahs, would-be sons of God, would-be saviors of one sort or another. He joined the ranks of men like Theudas, who tried to split the waters of the Jordan River and failed, and of Simon Magus, who tried to prove himself the son of God by flying, unsuccessfully, from a building— right down to modern saviors such as Hitler and Father Divine. Some of these were more influential and longer-remembered than others, but all failed utterly to live up to their claims. And none could ever atone for sin.

As we study these verses, which continue to show Christ greater than angels, we find ourselves drawn to the perfections of our Savior. And I pray that those who have not received Jesus Christ might be irresistibly drawn to Him as He is seen in His great beauty.

There is only one real Savior, only one perfect Savior. He is Jesus Christ. "And there is salvation in no one else; for there is no other name under heaven that has been given among men, by which we must be saved" (Acts 4:12). How is it that we know that Jesus Christ is, in fact, the perfect and only Savior? Why should we believe that? What qualifies Him? The answer is given beautifully and completely in Hebrews 2:9-18.

BORN TO DIE

But we do see Him who has been made for a little while lower than the angels, namely, Jesus, because of the suffering of death crowned with glory and honor, that by the grace of God He might taste death for everyone. (2:9)

Jews could not comprehend the idea that God would become man. Even less could they understand how, having become man, He could die. How could the anointed of God, the Messiah, be the victim of death? Consequently, wherever the gospel was preached to Jews, as in Acts 17, it was necessary to explain why Christ had to suffer and die (vv. 2-3). The cross was a serious stumbling block to them. Jewish converts even had difficulty with this issue. How could Jesus be greater than angels if angels never die? How could He be a Savior if He Himself were killed? These were lingering questions.

Christ was made **for a little while lower than the angels** so that He could become a man. He became a man so that He could die. He came to die because His death, and only His death, could accomplish man's salvation. Those tiny hands fashioned by the Holy Spirit in Mary's womb were made to take two great nails. Those little feet were made to climb a hill and be nailed to a cross. That sacred head was made to wear a crown of thorns, and that tender body wrapped in swaddling clothes was made to be pierced by a spear. For this Christ came to earth. His death was the furthest thing from an accident. And, despite the malignant evil that crucified Him, His death was the furthest thing from a tragedy. It was God's ultimate plan for His Son and His ultimate gift for mankind.

God created man in innocence and gave him dominion over the earth. Man sinned and immediately lost his dominion. Jesus Christ came to die to remove the curse so that man could regain dominion; thus His death was the most purposeful in all history. He came to restore the crown to man. But the crown could not be restored until the curse was removed. If He was to remove the curse on man He had to take the place of man by becoming a man Himself. And though, for this purpose, He became lower than angels, He accomplished what no angel ever could have accomplished.

There were actually five accomplishments in this one. Through His death, Jesus Christ became our Substitute, our salvation Author, our Sanctifier, our Satan-Conquerer, and our Sympathizer—the perfect Savior.

OUR SUBSTITUTE

He died **that by the grace of God He might taste death for everyone.** He died in your place and in my place; He became our Substitute. No truth is more basic to the gospel. Here is the first and foremost reason for the incarnation: He who is above angels becoming for a little while lower than angels so that He might suffer death on behalf of everyone. Let me briefly rehearse the simple profundity of the gospel.

Ezekiel warned that "the soul who sins will die" (Ezek. 18:4). The same truth is explicit in the New Testament: "The wages of sin is death" (Rom. 6:23). Sin brings death, inevitably and without exception. Left to his own resources, therefore, man has no prospect but death. But God has another prospect—a Substitute to take the punishment of man on Himself, to die in man's place. That was His design in sending the second Person of the Trinity. Christ humbled Himself, came to earth, and died in our place. Yet this is the doctrine that liberal theology has always found the most repugnant. Its self-sufficient man-centeredness will not allow a substitute. Jesus' death can be a beautiful and inspiring example of dying for a cause, of the true martyr; but no one, it insists, can take our place.

In Scripture, however, there is no gospel, no good news, apart from the substitutionary death of Jesus Christ. Apart from His dying, we have no escape from death. Hebrews 2:9 makes that clear.

THE RECIPIENTS OF HIS HUMILIATION

The very heart of the redemption story is God becoming man in order to substitute for man's death and therefore free man for life with Himself. That is the simplicity of the gospel. It is staggering to realize that the Creator of angels, the Head of angels, the Lord of the angelic hosts, the One worshiped by angels should, for our sakes, for a little time, become **lower than the angels.** That is supreme humility; and it was experienced in our behalf.

THE EXTENT OF HIS HUMILIATION

We see the extent of Christ's humiliation in His death. Angels cannot die; but Jesus came to die. He went so far beneath angels that He did something that they could never do. His death was not easy or costless. It was a suffering death. Christ's exit from the land of the living was not calm and peaceful, but was accompanied by outward torture and inner agony. The death He tasted was the curse of sin. What Jesus felt while dying on the cross was the total agony of every soul in hell for all eternity put together, suffered in a few hours. All the punishment for all the sin of all time—that was the depth of His death. He was guilty of no sin, yet He suffered for all sin.

THE PURPOSE OF HIS HUMILIATION

God sent His Son, and His Son willingly came, to die to redeem man. "But when the fulness of the time came, God sent forth His Son, born of a woman, born under the Law, in order that He might redeem those who were under the Law" (Gal. 4:4-5). Jesus Christ in His death purposed to die as a substitute **for everyone.** And it is only by the Son tasting death as a man for man that we are free from death. Historically, kings have had someone taste their food to protect them from possible poisoning. The cup of poison that belonged to us was drained to the dregs by Jesus Christ. He substituted His own death for ours and released us to live with God.

THE MOTIVE OF HIS HUMILIATION

That by the grace of God He might taste death for everyone. What moved Jesus Christ to suffer for us? It was grace—free, loving kindness. What we did not deserve (salvation) we received, and what we deserved (death) we did not receive. That is grace. And what prompts grace? Love. Love—unbounded love—prompted Christ's gracious work on our behalf. Solely on the basis of His own love Jesus died. Not primarily by the hands of men or by the work of Satan, but by the determined plan and foreknowledge of God He died for our sins. "No one has taken [My life] away from Me, but I lay it down on My own initiative" (John 10:18). The Son's love was one with the Father's love. "In this is love, not that we loved God, but that He loved us and sent His Son to be the propitiation for our sins" (1 John 4:10).

THE RESULT OF HIS HUMILIATION

The result of Christ's humiliation was His exaltation. After He accomplished the work of His substitutionary death, He was **crowned with glory and honor,** exalted to the right hand of the Father. There He sits on a throne from which He reigns and will reign forever. He did not glorify Himself. "No one takes the honor to himself, but receives it when he is called by God, even as Aaron was. So also Christ did not glorify Himself so as to become a high priest, but He who said to Him, 'Thou art My Son, today I have begotten Thee' " (Heb. 5:4-5). He has been seated "far above all rule and authority and power and dominion, and every name that is named, not only in this age, but also in the one to come" (Eph. 1:21), and at His name every knee in heaven, earth, and under the earth will one day bow (Phil. 2:10).

So, the writer says to his Jewish readers, and to all others who may be skeptical or scandalized: "We do not apologize for the cross; we do not shove it under the rug, for the cross not only saves us but magnifies the Lord. Far from being anything of which we are ashamed, Christ's humiliation and death are what we glory in." He is our great Substitute, whom we will thank and praise throughout all eternity.

OUR SALVATION AUTHOR

For it was fitting for Him, for whom are all things, and through whom are all things, in bringing many sons to glory, to perfect the author of their salvation through sufferings. (2:10)

The phrase **it was fitting for Him, for whom are all things, and through whom are all things** refers primarily to God the Father, though it obviously refers to the Son as well. **It was fitting** means that what God did through Jesus Christ was consistent with His character. It was consistent with God's wisdom. The cross was a masterpiece of wisdom. God solved the problem which no human or angelic mind could have solved. What He did was also consistent with His holiness, for God showed on the cross His hatred for sin. It was consistent with His power, being the greatest display of power ever manifested. Christ endured for a few hours what will take an eternity for unrepentant sinners to endure. It was consistent with His love, in that He loved the world so much that He gave His only Son for its redemption. Finally, what He did was consistent with His grace, because Christ's sacrifice was substitutionary. The work of salvation was totally consistent with God's nature. It was entirely fitting for Him to have done what He did.

What was fitting for the Father was equally fitting for the Son. Christ's suffering humiliation for the sake of man's salvation was consistent with His loving and gracious nature. Though all things were both **for** Him and **through** Him, He became for a little while lower than the angels in order to bring **many sons to glory** and become the perfect **author of their salvation through sufferings.** Here is the second perfection that His humiliation accomplished—Author of salvation. Jesus had to become a man and He had to suffer and die in order to be the perfect provider of salvation.

The Greek word for **author** is *archēgos,* literally, a "pioneer" or "leader." In Acts 3:15 and 5:31 the term, used both times of Christ, is translated "Prince." It always refers to someone who involves others in his endeavor. For example, it is used of a man who starts and heads a family, into which others are born or married. It is used of a man who founds a city, in which others come to live. It was commonly used of a pioneer who blazed a trail for others to follow. The *archēgos* never stood at the rear giving orders. He was always out front, leading and setting the example. As the supreme Archegos, Christ does not stand at the rear giving orders. He is always before us, as perfect Leader and perfect Example.

He lived for us the pattern of perfect obedience. "Although He was a Son, He learned obedience from the things which He suffered. And having been made perfect, He became to all those who obey Him the source of eternal salvation" (Heb. 5:8-9). By His own obedience He set the perfect pattern for us. He also set us the the pattern for suffering. "For you have been called for this purpose, since Christ also suffered for you, leaving you an example for you to follow in His steps" (1 Pet. 2:21).

For most people, life becomes most anxious and dreadful at the point of death. That is the point beyond which we cannot go a single step by ourselves. But the Author of our salvation promises us that "because I live, you shall live also" (John 14:19). The world's ultimate question is: "Has anyone ever cheated death?"—to which the Bible replies: "Yes, Jesus Christ." The second most important question is: "If He did, did He leave the way open for me?"—to which the Bible also replies, "Yes." He did leave the way open. All we have to do is put our hand in His hand and He will lead us from one side of death to the other. When we accept Him as our Savior, we can say with the apostle Paul, "O death, where is your victory? O death, where is your sting?" (1 Cor. 15:55).

As the great Pioneer of redemption, He blazed the trail through death and resurrection. He said, "I am the resurrection and the life; he who believes in Me shall live even if he dies, and everyone who lives and believes in Me shall never die" (John 11:25-26). God made Christ for a little while lower than the angels so that He could come down to us, be our Archegos—our spiritual Pioneer and Example—and bring us to the Father.

OUR SANCTIFIER

For both He who sanctifies and those who are sanctified are all from one Father; for which reason He is not ashamed to call them brethren, saying, "I will proclaim Thy name to My brethren, in the midst of the congregation I will sing Thy praise." And again, "I will put My trust in Him." And again, "Behold, I and the children whom God has given Me." (2:11-13)

In addition to becoming our Substitute and Author of salvation, He became our Sanctifier, the One who makes us holy. From our own perspective and experience, of course, it is difficult to think of ourselves as holy. Sin is too much with us. In thought and practice we are far from holy. But in the new nature we are perfectly holy. Before God, those who are in His Son are holy. We may not act holy, but we are holy—just as a child who often does not act like his father or please his father is still his father's child. We are holy in the sense that before God the righteousness of Christ has been applied and imputed in our behalf. "We have been sanctifed through the offering of the body of Jesus Christ once for all" (Heb. 10:10). We were made holy through His sacrifice, and have become **those who are sanctified.**

Christ has removed the possibility of positional sinfulness. "For by one offering He has perfected for all time those who are sanctified" (Heb. 10:14). We are therefore as pure positionally as God is pure, as righteous positionally as Christ is righteous, and we are entitled to be called a brother of Jesus Christ because we now share in His righteousness. Such are the wonder and kindness of God's grace. "He made Him who knew no sin to be sin on our behalf, that we might become the righteousness of God in Him" (2 Cor. 5:21).

The Sanctifier and the sanctified now have **one Father,** and the Sanctifier **is not ashamed to call** the sanctified His brothers. What an overwhelming truth! How humbling to have the Son of God call us brothers and not to be ashamed of it. Conquering sin through His death, He broke sin's mastery over us and placed His eternal righteousness on us. We are "fellow heirs with Christ" (Rom. 8:17) because His holiness is now our holiness. His righteousness not only makes us holy but makes us His brothers. This is the only way a person can become a brother of Christ, and therefore a child of God. We are not born into the divine family, only reborn into it.

The practical experience of a Christian's life, of course, includes sin; but the positional reality of his new nature is holiness. "In Him [we] have been made complete" (Col. 2:10), positionally and in nature perfect. The basic, overriding purpose of our lives now is to become in practice what we are in that new perfection and position. Now that we are Christ's brothers, God's children, we should live like it.

Can you imagine God's being happy to be called the God of you? Yet He is—not because of who you are in yourself, but because of who you are in Christ. The writer of Hebrews says of believers later in the epistle, "But as it is, they desire a better country, that is a heavenly one. Therefore God is not ashamed to be called their God; for He has prepared a city for them" (Heb. 11:16). When we realize that Jesus is not ashamed to call us brothers and that God is not ashamed to say, "I am their God," it should thrill our hearts. And it should make us all the more conscious that it is in the righteousness of Jesus Christ that we stand and not in our own, which at best is "like a filthy garment" (Isa. 64:6). Yet how strange and sad that, though God is never ashamed to call us His, we are so often ashamed to call Him ours. How often are we honestly able to say with Paul, "I am not ashamed of the gospel"?

BROTHERHOOD BEGAN AFTER THE CROSS

The Lord Jesus never called His people brothers on the other side of the cross. Before Calvary He called them disciples or friends or sheep, but never brothers. Why? Because they could not truly be brothers until after the cross, when their sin was paid for and His righteousness was imputed to them. Only then did they become spiritual brothers of the Lord. As soon as Jesus was risen from the dead, He said to Mary, "Go to My brethren." For the first time He called His disciples brothers.

And again, "I will put My trust in Him." And again, "Behold, I and the children whom God has given Me." (2:13)

Jesus, when He was in this world, learned the obedience of faith, and thereby became the perfect Savior. Even the Old Testament revealed that Christ would put His trust in the Father. In the same passage it was also revealed that His brothers would do the same: **Behold, I and the children whom God has given Me.** Jesus Christ is not our Brother because of our common nature, since He is divine and we are human. For the same reason He is not our Brother because of common wisdom or power. He is our Brother because of common righteousness and common faith in the Father.

What a wonderful thing to realize that when we are called to walk by faith, to submit ourselves to God and to live in total dependence on Him, we are called to follow the path that Jesus walked. That is exactly what He did. "The Son can do nothing of Himself, unless it is something He sees the Father doing; for whatever the Father does, these things the Son also does in like manner" (John 5:19). Brotherhood with Jesus means that we possess His righteousness and that we walk by faith as He did.

OUR SATAN-CONQUEROR

Since then the children share in flesh and blood, He Himself likewise also partook of the same, that through death He might render power-less him who had the power of death, that is, the devil; and might deliver those who through fear of death were subject to slavery all their lives. (2:14-15)

Share is from the Greek *koinōnia*, meaning to have fellowship, communion, or partnership. It involves having something in common with others. All human beings have **flesh and blood.** In this we are all alike. It is our common nature. But **partook** is from a very different word, *metechō*, which has to do with taking hold of something that is not naturally one's own kind. We by nature are flesh and blood; Christ was not. Yet He willingly took hold of something which did not naturally belong to Him. He added to Himself our nature in order that He might die in our place, and that we might take hold of the divine nature that did not belong to us (cf. 2 Pet. 1:4).

Obviously Satan's power over us had to be broken in order for us to be brought to God. Satan's primary power over man and supreme weapon against him is death. Sin, of course, gives Satan his power over us; but the power itself is death.

So in this regard, why did Christ become man? Why did He die? **That through death He might render powerless him who had the power of death, that is, the devil.** The only way to destroy Satan was to rob him of his weapon, **death**—physical death, spiritual death, eternal death. Satan knew that God required death for us because of sin. Death had become the most certain fact of life. Satan knew that men, if they remained as they were, would die and go out of God's presence into hell forever. Satan wants to hold onto men until they die, because once they are dead the opportunity for salvation is gone forever. Men cannot escape after death. So God had to wrest from Satan the power of death. And for just that purpose Jesus came.

If you have a more powerful weapon than your enemy, his weapon becomes useless. You cannot fight against a machine gun with a bow and arrow. Satan's weapon is extremely powerful. But God has a weapon even more powerful—eternal life—and with it Jesus destroyed death. The way to eternal life is through resurrection, but the way to resurrection is through death. So Jesus had to experience death before He could be resurrected and thereby give us life. Jesus' dying destroyed death. How? He went into death, through death, and came out on the other side, thereby conquering it. Then He could say, "Because I live, you shall live also" (John 14:19). The resurrection of Jesus Christ provides the believer with eternal life. It is the only thing that could ever have done it. Death is the power of Satan's dominion, and when Jesus shattered Satan's power He also shattered his dominion.

And might deliver those who through fear of death were subject to slavery all their lives. (2:15)

The thing that terrifies people more than anything else is death. It is a horrible fear, the king of terrors. But when we receive Jesus Christ, death holds no more fear. We have been released from bondage to the fear of death, and, instead, actually look forward to it. We say with Paul, "For to me, to live is Christ, and to die is gain" (Phil. 1:21) and "O death, where is your victory? O death, where is your sting?" (1 Cor. 15:55). Death no longer holds any fear, for it simply releases us into the presence of our Lord. Why? Because we have placed our hands into the hands of the Conqueror of death, and He will lead us into one side of the grave and out the other. He never could have done it if He had not become **for a little while lower than the angels.**

OUR SYMPATHIZER

For assuredly He does not give help to angels, but He gives help to the descendant of Abraham. Therefore, He had to be made like His brethren in all things, that He might become a merciful and faithful high priest in things pertaining to God, to make propitiation for the sins of the people. For since He Himself was tempted in that which He has suffered, He is able to come to the aid of those who are tempted. (2:16-18)

Christ did not come to redeem angels but men. So He took on Himself the form of Abraham's descendants and became a Jew. "How odd of God to choose the Jews," someone has quipped. We wonder why He chose them and not some other race or nation on whom to show His special favor. But if He had chosen some other group, we would ask the same question about them. He simply chose them in His sovereign will out of love. "The Lord did not set His love on you nor choose you because you were more in number than any of the peoples, for you were the fewest of all peoples, but because the Lord loved you and kept the oath which He swore to your forefathers" (Deut. 7:7-8).

Again the writer answers the question, "If Jesus is God, why did He become a man?" He came to substitute for men, to reconcile men to God, to fit them for God's presence and to destroy death. But beyond that He also came to help the reconciled when they are **tempted.** He wanted to feel everything we feel so that He could be a merciful and understanding, as well as a faithful, **high priest.** He came not only to save us but to sympathize with us.

In his letters to Timothy, Paul gave words of counsel and encouragement to his young friend about many things—his health, his critics, his moral and spiritual welfare. But all of his counsel could perhaps be summed up in these words in the second letter: "Remember Jesus Christ, risen from the dead, descendant of David" (2 Tim. 2:8). Paul was saying, in effect, "Remember Jesus Christ in His humanity, Timothy. Remember that, wherever you may go, He has been there before you. You can get down on your knees when the going gets tough and you can pray, 'Lord, You know what You went through when You were here. I'm going through it now.' And He will say, 'Yes, I know.' "

When you have a problem, it is wonderful to be able to talk with the divine One who has already experienced it and come through successfully. Other people may be understanding, but they cannot fully understand. Jesus came to identify with us, to experience what we experience. "For we do not have a high priest who cannot sympathize with our weaknesses, but one who has been tempted in all things as we are, yet without sin" (Heb. 4:15). He became our Sympathizer, **a merciful and faithful high priest.** He was hungry, He was thirsty, He was overcome with fatigue, He slept, He was taught, He grew, He loved, He was astonished, He was glad, He was angry, He was indignant, He was sarcastic, He was grieved, He was troubled, He was overcome by future events, He exercised faith, He read the Scriptures, He prayed, He sighed in His heart when He saw another man in illness, and He cried when His heart ached.

Jesus felt everything we will ever feel—and more. For example, He felt temptation to a degree that we could not possibly experience. Most of us never know the full degree of resistible temptation, simply because we usually succumb long before that degree is reached. But since Jesus never sinned, He took the full measure of every temptation that came to Him. And He was victorious in every trial.

Why did He go through that? He did it so that He could become a **merciful and faithful high priest** who could **sympathize with our weaknesses** and who could **come to the aid of those who are tempted.** Ours is not a cosmic God, powerful and holy, but indifferent. He knows where we hurt, where we are weak, and where we are tempted. He is the God we can go to not only for salvation but for sympathy.

This is our Savior. The perfect Savior. Our Substitute, our salvation Author, our Sanctifier, our Satan-Conqueror, and our Sympathizer. What a Savior He is. There is no other.

Jesus Greater than Moses (3:1-6)

7

Therefore, holy brethren, partakers of a heavenly calling, consider Jesus, the Apostle and High Priest of our confession. He was faithful to Him who appointed Him, as Moses also was in all His house. For He has been counted worthy of more glory than Moses, by just so much as the builder of the house has more honor than the house. For every house is built by someone, but the builder of all things is God. Now Moses was faithful in all His house as a servant, for a testimony of those things which were to be spoken later; but Christ was faithful as a Son over His house whose house we are, if we hold fast our confidence and the boast of our hope firm until the end. (3:1-6)

After having seen the exalted supremacy of Jesus, who is better than the prophets and the angels, we are now shown how He is better than Moses, the one through whom the first covenant came.

THE GREATNESS OF MOSES

These first six verses present the doctrine on which the exhortation of the rest of the chapter is built. In order to understand the exhortation, we need to understand the premise; and to understand the premise, we need to review what the Jews of that day thought about Moses. To appreciate how, why, and to what extent Jesus is better than Moses, we need to see how important Moses was even before this. Even before this, we need to ask why it is necessary to prove that Jesus is better than Moses?

Moses was esteemed by the Jews far above any other Jew who ever lived. God had miraculously protected him as a baby and personally provided for his burial. Between those two points in his life are miracle after miracle after miracle. He was the man to whom God spoke face to face. He had seen the very glory of God and, in fact, even had this glory reflected in his own face for a brief while. After he came down from Sinai, "The skin of his face shone because of his speaking with Him" (Ex. 34:29). He was the one who led Israel out of Egypt. As Paul stresses in Romans 2, Jews had great confidence in the law. The Old Testament commandments and rituals were their supreme priorities, and to them Moses and the law were synonymous. The New Testament often refers to the commands of God as the "law of Moses" (Luke 2:22; Acts 13:39; and others). Moses not only brought the Ten Commandments but he also wrote the entire Pentateuch, which lays out the Levitical and other laws that governed everything the Jews did. Moses gave the plans for the Tabernacle and the Ark of the Covenant.

Some Jews believed that Moses was greater than angels. God spoke to the prophets in visions, but to Moses He spoke face to face. He spoke to him in a burning bush. He spoke to him out of heaven. He spoke to him on Sinai and wrote the commandments with a finger of fire. He was, above all others, God's man.

Yet, in this passage of Hebrews the Holy Spirit calls on Jewish readers, especially, to look at Jesus. Moses was indeed great; but Jesus is far greater. Jesus is shown to be superior to Moses in office, in work, and in person. In His office, He is the Apostle and High Priest. In His work, He is the Builder of the house. In His Person, He is the Son.

JESUS' SUPERIOR OFFICE: AS APOSTLE AND HIGH PRIEST

Therefore, holy brethren, partakers of a heavenly calling, consider Jesus, the Apostle and High Priest of our confession. (Heb. 3:1)

The Holy Spirit was speaking directly to Christian Jews who were looking at Jesus with one eye but glancing back to Judaism with the other. The word **therefore** always refers back to something previous. "On the basis of what I've just said," the writer is saying, "**consider Jesus.**" The term **consider** (*katanoeō*) implies attention and continuous observation. The idea is, "Put your mind on Jesus and let it remain there, that you may understand who He is and what He wills."

His recovering of man's lost destiny, His humbling Himself and becoming our Substitute, our Author of salvation, our Sanctifier, our Satan-Conqueror, and our Sympathizer—all these more than qualify Him for the most serious consideration possible. Jesus is the supreme **Apostle,** the Sent-One from God, and the perfect **High Priest.** He is powerful, sympathetic, merciful, faithful, saving, reconciling, protective, helpful, brotherly. On the basis of who He is and what He has done, every person should consider Him. Every person should focus on the absolute sufficiency of Jesus and drop everything else. We have a new **High Priest** and a new Sent-One from God. He is all anyone will ever need. What an amazing message.

HOLY BRETHREN ARE FELLOW BELIEVERS

As believers, we are brothers with Christ because we are identified with Him, as adopted children of the heavenly Father. Many people studying the book of Hebrews have assumed, therefore, that it must have been written exclusively to Christians, since the readers are so often addressed as "brethren." But Scripture recognizes types of brotherhood other than spiritual. Both Peter (Acts 2:29) and Paul (Acts 13:38), for example, addressed unbelieving fellow Jews as "brethren." But **holy brethren** refers to fellow Christians, to those who are true brothers. This particular passage is written to Christians, holy Jewish brothers in Christ. "For both He who sanctifies and those who are sanctified are all from one Father; for which reason He is not ashamed to call them brethren" (Heb. 2:11). These were spiritual brothers, sanctified, set apart, and made holy in Christ.

This section is written to **partakers of a heavenly calling,** who desired a heavenly country (11:16), and who had come to the heavenly Jerusalem (12:22). All of these blessings show the superiority of Christianity to Judaism. Judaism was an earthly calling with an earthly inheritance. Christianity is a spiritual and heavenly calling with a spiritual and heavenly inheritance. It is, therefore, far superior.

Paul said, "I press on toward the goal for the prize of the upward call of God in Christ Jesus. . . . For our citizenship is in heaven, from which also we eagerly wait for a Savior, the Lord Jesus Christ" (Phil. 3:14, 20). Our true home is in heaven and we live spiritually right now in heavenly places (Eph. 1:3; 2:6). As true believers we are brothers of Jesus by position and are thereby holy. We are only strangers and pilgrims on earth. Our bodies are in this world but we do not really belong here.

The writer is saying to his Christian Jewish readers, "You are citizens of the heavenlies, so why don't you let go of the earthly things? Why do you want to hang on to the earthly rituals, the earthly symbols, when you have the heavenly reality?" As Christians we do not need religious ritual because we have spiritual reality. Jesus said that *now*—that is, since He has come—anyone who wants to worship the Father truly, must do so in spirit and in truth, not in rituals and ceremonies (John 4:23). There is no place in biblical Christianity for externalism because Christians have continual access to spiritual reality.

All of us, at times, are tempted to think that our works and our religious trappings are all-important. Even when we know better, we often feel most comfortable and "religious" in traditional, familiar worship settings and when we perform certain religious acts or good deeds that we believe are particularly pleasing to God. We know and accept God's free grace complete in Christ, but we hang on to some form of artificial legalism rather than live a positive, Christ-controlled, Spirit-energized life. Considering and experiencing Christ's sufficiency should shatter all legalistic efforts, whether Judaistic or any other kind.

For Christians to hang on to earthly religious trappings not only is unnecessary and pointless but also spiritually harmful. To do so keeps us from experiencing the fullness of our new relationship with God and from being able to follow Him as faithfully as we ought. These things are barriers, not means, to blessing. Since believers share in the righteous nature of Christ and in His heavenly calling, they live in a heavenly existence. They ought to concentrate on that heavenly existence, not the earthly. It is not just the unsaved who need to **consider Jesus.** Believers also, no matter how mature, need to consider Him in everything they do.

KEEP YOUR EYES ON CHRIST

Why do we need to keep considering Christ, when as Christians we are already in Him and identified with Him? Simply because all of us are far from fully discovering all of His glories, all of His beauties, all that He is. So the Spirit says to us, as to those early believers, "Gaze on Jesus. Keep gazing on Him and don't look around at all the rituals and all the problems and all the persecutions. Keep considering Jesus. You don't need anything else. He is sufficient for everything. Now that you have the supreme Reality, keep your attention on Him."

There may have been a greater Christian than Paul, but I cannot imagine who he could have been. Yet this great apostle said that his greatest desire was to "know Him, and the power of His resurrection and the fellowship of His sufferings, being conformed to His death; . . . Not that I have already obtained it, or have already become perfect, but I press on in order that I may lay hold of that for which also I was laid hold of by Christ Jesus" (Phil. 3:10, 12). Even Paul had not plumbed the full depths of Christ.

The reason so many Christians are weak and worried is that they do not keep considering Christ, and so His full strength and comfort and guidance are not theirs. The Holy Spirit continually says to every believer, "**Consider Jesus.**" When life gets rough and problems seem to have no solution and everything goes bad and disappointment and depression become "normal" and temptations seem impossible to resist—put your gaze on Jesus and keep it there intently until He begins to unfold before your very eyes in all His glorious power.

Jesus said, "Learn from Me" (Matt. 11:29). He did not say, "Learn *about* Me" but "Learn *from* Me." Do you really enjoy your Christian life? Do you get up in the morning and say, "Lord, I just can't wait to see what You're going to do today?" Do you go through the day and say, "Lord, Your fellowship and Your presence are thrilling?" Do you enjoy Jesus Christ? Do you sometimes want to stand up and shout? You ought to enjoy Him like that. But many Christians do not enjoy Jesus. They appear to be miserable and unhappy, and they do not know anything about His joy. They may think the only thing the Lord does for us is to give an occasional rebuke. They see Him this way because they do not walk with Him day by day. They do not know Him richly and deeply and intimately. They need to consider Jesus and learn from Him.

When I was in college, I used to pay fifty cents to go through the back door of the orchestra hall in Los Angeles. I would go up into the balcony with two or three books and sit there and listen to a whole concert by myself while I did homework. I listened to Bartok and Moussorgsky and other great composers. As I listened, I began to gain an appreciation for the masters. To anyone who says he does not appreciate great music or great art, I would say, "My friend, go to the orchestra hall and the art museum and stay there until you enjoy it." You have to learn to love the masters. You have to learn to recognize and enjoy great beauty and genius.

If you want to enjoy Jesus you have to stay with Him until you learn to enjoy Him. Stay there until your Christian life is one thrill after another. Until every waking moment of every day is joy upon joy upon joy. Consider Him. Focus your attention on Him.

When Timothy was still a young man, he began to have stomach trouble. Paul advised him to take some wine (1 Tim. 5:23). Among other things, he was being criticized by some of the Ephesian Christians. He became discouraged and was hurting. In his second letter to his young son in the faith, Paul tells Timothy to keep going, to be like a good soldier, a well-trained athlete, a hard-working farmer (2 Tim. 2:3-6). But his most important counsel was, "Remember Jesus Christ, risen from the dead, descendant of David, according to my gospel" (2:8). There are many practical things, such as taking medicine when we are sick, that Christians can and should do. But when we face spiritual problems, serious problems, insurmountable problems, the really worthwhile prescription is "Remember Jesus Christ. Gaze on Him. Learn from Him."

In Hebrews 12:1-2, the writer says, "Therefore, since we have so great a cloud of witnesses surrounding us, let us also lay aside every encumbrance, and the sin which so easily entangles us, and let us run with endurance the race that is set before us, fixing our eyes on Jesus, the author and perfecter of faith." If we are going to run the Christian race, we must look at Jesus.

I ran the 100- and 220-yard dashes in college. We learned very soon that you cannot run while watching your feet. You look straight ahead. When we ran sprints we set our eyes on the tape, and we kept our eyes on it until the finish. Looking at the tape helped motivate the desire to win and it kept us going in the right direction. It also kept our attention off ourselves and those running next to us. When we are running in the Christian race, we must get our eyes off our feet, get them off ourselves, and off those around us. We look to Jesus, the Author and the Finisher of our faith. We look at Him and then we are able to run. Looking at Him we know why we are running and where we are running, and have the power and the joy to keep on running.

CHRIST AN APOSTLE

Jesus is to be considered as **the Apostle and High Priest of our confession.** The fact that He is both of these is the first way in which He is superior to **Moses.** Though he was never called such in Scripture, Moses could be considered an Old Testament apostle in the basic sense of the word. *Apostolos* means "sent one" and was a title often used for official ambassadors. In this sense Moses was God's apostle, His sent-one to bring His people the law and the covenant. But Jesus was both **Apostle and High Priest.** Though Moses could be considered a type of apostle, he was not a priest at all, much less high priest. Jesus is superior to Moses in office because He has two offices, whereas Moses had only one.

Even in the office of apostle, Jesus is superior—first of all because He brought a better covenant, and second, because He was Himself the sacrifice that made the better covenant effective. Jesus is the supreme **Apostle,** the supreme Sent-One from God.

What are the characteristics of an apostle or an ambassador? First, he has the rights and the power and the authority of the ruler who sends him. Jesus came in the power of God, with all of God's grace, all of God's love, all of God's mercy, all of God's justice, and all of God's power. Second, an ambassador speaks completely on behalf of the one who sent him. Jesus said, "I did not speak on My own initiative, but the Father Himself who sent Me has given Me commandment, what to say, and what to speak" (John 12:49; cf. 8:28, 38). Jesus was the perfect Ambassador, the perfect Apostle sent from God.

CHRIST THE HIGH PRIEST

Jesus is also our great **High Priest.** But since His role as High Priest is dealt with in such detail in Hebrews 4 and 5, we will not elaborate on it here. Suffice it to say that He is the supreme Priest, the supreme Mediator, between God and man. He not only is the Sent-One from God with all God's power, speaking with God's voice, but He is the One who brings man and God together. Thus He brings God to man and man to God.

JESUS' SUPERIOR WORKS: AS BUILDER

He was faithful to Him who appointed Him, as Moses also was in all His house. For He has been counted worthy of more glory than Moses, by just so much as the builder of the house has more honor than the house. For every house is built by someone, but the builder of all things is God. (3:2-4)

Here is a brief comparison of the work of Jesus with that of Moses. Keep in mind that it is hard for Gentiles to understand the affection Jews have always had for Moses. He was a great man, a man of God who stood head and shoulders above all other men. Almost everything of importance connected with God is, in the Jew's mind, connected with Moses. This subject, therefore, is dealt with very carefully by the Holy Spirit in this passage. His wisdom is marvelous. Before showing Jesus' superiority to Moses, He points up the resemblance of the two. Before talking about their differences, He talks about their similarities.

Moses was faithful. The Old Testament confirms that testimony. "My servant Moses . . . is faithful in all My household; with him I speak mouth to mouth" (Num. 12:7-8). He carried out God's plan. He came out of Egypt into the wilderness. God refined him. It took forty years for God to make Moses usable; then, for forty more years, God used him. God's servant faithfully took the children of Israel out of Egypt. When he got to the Red Sea he believed God's promise of deliverance and faithfully led his people through the parted waters. He was faithful in the wilderness. Several times he faltered, as he had long before in Egypt when he slew the Egyptian. For example, he struck the rock instead of speaking to it as God had commanded. But for the most part Moses was faithful. And it is his faithfulness that the Holy Spirit here emphasizes.

Just as Moses was faithful to the One who appointed him, so was

Jesus—only much more so. As God's supreme Apostle, God's supreme Sent-One, Jesus was completely faithful to the Father. "He who speaks from himself seeks his own glory; but He who is seeking the glory of the one who sent Him, He is true, and there is no unrighteousness in Him" (John 7:18). In other words, Jesus was saying, "You can tell I am a true Apostle because I do not seek My own glory. I seek only the glory of the One who sent Me." From childhood He had always been about His Father's business. "And He who sent Me is with Me; He has not left Me alone, for I always do the things that are pleasing to Him. . . . I glorified Thee on the earth, having accomplished the work which Thou hast given Me to do. And now, glorify Thou Me together with Thyself, Father, with the glory which I had with Thee before the world was" (John 8:29; 17:4-5).

Jesus always did the Father's will. He was **faithful.** *Faithful* is such a wonderful word. The chief qualification for an apostle, as with a disciple, is faithfulness. "If I do not do the works of My Father," Jesus said, "do not believe Me" (John 10:37). The Father had said to Jesus, "I am sending You to earth as a man and here is the work you are to do." Jesus came to earth and He accomplished the work, without question and without hesitation.

TRUSTWORTHY IN HIS HOUSE

House is from the Greek *oikos,* meaning "household," and refers to people, not a building or dwelling. Old Testament believers—Israelites in particular, but also proselytes—were God's household. Moses was a trustworthy steward in that household. "In this case, moreover, it is required of stewards that one be found trustworthy" (1 Cor. 4:2). A steward does not own the house, he simply manages it for the owner. God owned the house of Israel; Moses was simply its manager for a while. He was in charge of dispensing to the people of Israel the truths, commandments, requirements, and promises God had committed to his trust. In this he proved trustworthy.

Christ was also **faithful** in *His* **house,** the church. "So then you are no longer strangers and aliens, but you are fellow citizens with the saints, and are of God's household" (Eph. 2:19). "And coming to Him as to a living stone, rejected by men, but choice and precious in the sight of God, you also, as living stones, are being built up as a spiritual house" (1 Pet. 2:4-5). We are the new household and Jesus is the One who cares for us. Just as believers under the Old Testament are called the house of Moses, believers under the New Testament are called the house of Christ. And as Moses was faithful to an earthly household, Jesus is faithful to the heavenly household. Jesus could say to His Father at the end of His life, "I glorified Thee on the earth, having accomplished the work which Thou hast given Me to do" (John 17:4). He said, in effect, "I told the household all that You instructed Me to tell them and did for them all that you instructed Me to do." He was perfectly **faithful to Him who appointed Him.**

All Christians are stewards in God's house, though in a lesser sense, of course. We all, for example, have spiritual gifts. We have them as sacred trusts; they are not ours. If we are unfaithful in administering our spiritual gifts, we are unfaithful stewards. Some of us have been given special responsibilities to witness, specifically to the people in our community that God has placed around us. Some have been unfaithful stewards of this trust. Others of us have been given positions of teaching or instructing and have been unfaithful in studying diligently, faithfully, and sacrificially. These, too, are unfaithful stewards. The Christian life is a sacred trust given to us by God, and it demands our faithfulness. One of the greatest thrills a Christian can hope for is that of hearing his Lord say at the end of his life, "As I was faithful to the Father, so you have been faithful to Me." We have not begun to discover what God can do through us if we are willing to be faithful.

For He has been counted worthy of more glory than Moses, by just so much as the builder of the house has more honor than the house. For every house is built by someone, but the builder of all things is God. (3:3-4)

Moses was faithful, but he was a part of the house. Jesus made the house. That is the difference, the great difference. Jesus created Israel. "All things came into being by Him, and apart from Him nothing came into being that has come into being" (John 1:3; cf. Heb. 1). Moses was only a member of the household which Jesus built. Jesus created Israel; Jesus created the church. Since God built, or created, all things, Jesus obviously is God.

Before any of us became Christians, and thereby parts of Christ's house, the church, someone introduced us to the gospel. That person was responsible in a human sense for part of God's house—just as we are responsible for part of the house when we lead others to Christ. But on the divine side, God alone creates the house and continues building it as new believers are added. Human witnesses are but the instruments He uses. He is the Builder. The Builder is greater than any of His tools. Moses was part of the house of Israel and an instrument God used in building it. To hold on to the forms of Judaism or to its greatest leader is to hold on only to the symbol of reality or to an instrument of reality. To hold on to Jesus is to hold on to reality itself.

JESUS' SUPERIOR PERSON: AS SON

Now Moses was faithful in all His house as a servant, for a testimony of those things which were to be spoken later; but Christ was faithful as a Son over His house whose house we are, if we hold fast our confidence and the boast of our hope firm until the end. (3:5-6)

Here is the climax. In this passage we see that Moses is by person **a servant,** while Jesus is by person a **Son.** There is a great difference between a servant and a son. "And the slave does not remain in the house forever; the son does remain forever" (John 8:35). Servants come and go; sons are sons for life. Moses was a servant, and he conducted himself as a servant. The Greek word used in Hebrews 3:5 for **servant** is *therapōn,* and is a term of dignity and freedom, not of servility. It is only used this once in the New Testament, and suggests that, even as the highest-ranking servant, Moses was still a servant. He was a faithful, obedient, ministering, caring servant—a good steward of God. In Exodus 35 to 40 there are twenty-two references to Moses' faithfulness to God. Exodus 40 alone refers eight times to Moses' obedience in everything God commanded of him. But he was not a son.

TO ACCEPT MOSES IS TO ACCEPT JESUS

Moses' faithfulness had an important and special reason: to be **a testimony of those things which were to be spoken later.** Judaism did not understand then, and does not understand now, that Moses was faithful primarily as a testimony to things which were yet to come in Christ. Judaism without Christ, the Old Testament without the New Testament, is incomplete. It is the shadow without the substance. "For the Law, since it has only a shadow of the good things to come and not the very form of things, can never by the same sacrifices year by year, which they offer continually, make perfect those who draw near" (Heb. 10:1). It was the shadow of the perfect substance that was to come; and if you reject the substance, the shadow is worthless. On the other hand, if a person truly accepted the shadow, he would also accept the substance when it became known. "For if you believed Moses, you would believe Me; for he wrote of Me" (John 5:46).

"But Christ was faithful as a Son over His house whose house we are" (Heb. 3:6). The church building we worship in is not the Lord's house. *We* are the Lord's house. His house is not a building but believers. "In whom you also are being built together into a dwelling of God in the Spirit" (Eph. 2:22). "But in case I am delayed, I write so that you may know how one ought to conduct himself in the household of God, which is the church of the living God" (1 Tim. 3:15). Moses was a servant in someone else's house. Jesus is a Son over His own house, His own people.

THE MARK OF TRUE BELIEVERS

How can we know that we are really God's house? By holding **fast our confidence and the boast of our hope firm until the end.** This does not mean, as many have misinterpreted, that we are saved if we hang on until the end. We can neither save ourselves nor keep ourselves saved. The meaning is simply that continuance is the proof of reality. We can tell if we are really the house of God because we stay there. The one who falls away never belonged in the first place (cf. 1 John 2:19). Apparently there were many Jews who had fallen away, and it is because of them that the writer of Hebrews gives these words, which both warn and encourage. Some were convinced of the gospel and were on the edge of commitment, but kept falling away. Some, no doubt, had even made an outward profession of faith. But in both cases they fell away from the church, proving they were never a part of it. The true saints persevered, and their perseverance was evidence of their salvation. "If you abide in My word," Jesus said, "then you are truly disciples of Mine" (John 8:31). One of the clearest truths of the New Testament is that the Lord keeps those who belong to Him. "And this is the will of Him who sent Me, that of all that He has given Me I lose nothing, but raise it up on the last day" (John 6:39). Jesus has never lost anyone and will never lose anyone from His household.

This passage says two important things to us. First, we should be sure we are real Christians. "Test yourselves to see if you are in the faith; examine yourselves!" (2 Cor. 13:5). Second, when we know we are in Christ, we should keep our eyes on Him. He is all we need. We are complete in Him.

Do Not Harden Your Hearts (3:7-19)

Therefore, just as the Holy Spirit says, "Today if you hear His voice, do not harden your hearts as when they provoked Me, as in the day of trial in the wilderness, where your fathers tried Me by testing Me, and saw My works for forty years. Therefore I was angry with this generation, and said, 'They always go astray in their heart; and they did not know My ways'; as I swore in My wrath, 'They shall not enter My rest.'" Take care, brethren, lest there should be in any one of you an evil, unbelieving heart, in falling away from the living God. But encourage one another day after day, as long as it is still called "Today," lest any one of you be hardened by the deceitfulness of sin. For we have become partakers of Christ, if we hold fast the beginning of our assurance firm until the end; while it is said, "Today if you hear His voice, do not harden your hearts, as when they provoked Me." For who provoked Him when they had heard? Indeed, did not all those who came out of Egypt led by Moses? And with whom was He angry for forty years? Was it not with those who sinned, whose bodies fell in the wilderness? And to whom did He swear that they should not enter His rest, but to those who were disobedient? And so we see that they were not able to enter because of unbelief. (3:7-19)

From Genesis to Revelation the Bible is full of warning signs from God, meant to deter men from sin and thereby keep them from His wrath. The Old Testament tells us that God has no pleasure in the death of the wicked (Ezek. 33:11), and the New Testament tells us that He does not wish for anyone to perish but wants everyone to repent (2 Pet. 3:9). God did not create man to be doomed to hell, and throughout His Word He continually warns him of the dangers and penalty of sin.

Hebrews 3:7-19 is one of these warnings. The Holy Spirit seems to be giving a supernatural push to anyone on the edge of accepting Jesus Christ. Many people intellectually accept the gospel. They believe its message, but never commit themselves to the One whom that gospel proclaims. They do not repent of their sins and turn wholeheartedly to Him as Savior and Lord. It is no favor to God—and no benefit to us—to like, to admire, to praise His gospel, without accepting and obeying it. To know the truth and not accept it brings worse judgment than never to have known it at all.

The warning here is to those who know the gospel, who affirm its truth, but who, because of love of sin or fear of persecution or whatever it may be, have not committed themselves to the truth they know is real. It is as if there were a fire in a hotel and they are on the tenth floor. Because there is a net below, the firemen are yelling, "Jump." But they do not jump. They hesitate. They are well aware of the danger and they know the net is their only way of escape; but they do not act on what they know is true and necessary. They are concerned about saving some of their possessions, or perhaps they think that somehow they can find another way out. They may be afraid of being hurt from the fall. Some might even be concerned about how they would look while jumping— afraid of embarrassment. But the point is this: simply knowing about the danger and knowing about the way out of it will not save them. If they do not jump they will die. When your very life is at stake, nothing else should matter.

The writer of Hebrews, under the Spirit's leading, has a great concern for his fellow Jews who are in this predicament. They have heard the gospel, some of them from the mouth of an apostle, but for various reasons they hold back from commitment. Some, apparently, had made a profession of faith or had given some statement of confidence in Christ, but were beginning to fall back. When they started getting ridiculed by their friends, they began to waver and hesitate. They were not willing to throw their whole weight on Jesus, and as a result they became apostate. Knowing the truth, they willingly and intentionally turned away from it.

To enforce the warning, the Spirit uses an Old Testament story very familiar to Jews. Moses has just been mentioned, and it is from the time of this greatest of Old Testament leaders that the story comes. It falls into four parts: the illustration of Israel; the invitation to take heed; the instruction to exhort one another; and the issue of unbelief.

THE ILLUSTRATION OF ISRAEL

One of the best ways to begin a sermon is to give an illustration. Once you have the people's attention, you go to the Scripture to affirm your point. That is what the Spirit of God does here. In this case the illustration itself is from Scripture. Hebrews 3:7-11 is a quotation of Psalm 95:7-11. The passage quoted was written probably in the time of David, but it speaks about the time of Moses. It is a moving example of the problem many Jews faced in the time of the early church. It describes Israel's disobedience and rejection of God in the Exodus wanderings.

The psalmist used this story to warn his people against disbelief. A thousand years later the writer of Hebrews used it for the same purpose. Nearly two thousand more years later the warning is still valid.

The Holy Spirit here says to the Hebrews who are on the edge of decision but have never made a commitment, "Don't harden your hearts, hear today and do today what God wants you to do. Don't do what the children of Israel did even after they had seen proof of God's power and care for forty years. They continued not to believe in Him. Don't do that."

PROOF OF THE BIBLE'S INSPIRATION

Therefore, just as the Holy Spirit says, "Today if you hear His voice." (3:7)

Here is one of the clearest testimonies in Scripture to its own divine inspiration. The writer of Hebrews is saying that the **Holy Spirit** was the author of Psalm 95, from which Hebrews 3:7b-11 is quoted. Inspiration is the Holy Spirit's speaking through the minds of God's human instruments. What the psalmist said was not his own opinion or his own choice of words. When he wrote these words the Holy Spirit was speaking. That is divine inspiration. Those are the words of the Spirit of God, who is the true Author of Scripture. "For no prophecy was ever made by an act of human will, but men moved by the Holy Spirit spoke from God" (2 Pet. 1:21). The Holy Spirit was involved in the writing of every word of Scripture. That is why it is sin in the first degree, and opens the floodgates to every kind of heresy possible, to deny the absolute verbal inspiration of Scripture. God originated the autographs, the first copies, to the very word.

The basic warning from the psalm ("Today if you hear His voice, do not harden your hearts") is used three times in Hebrews 3 (vv. 7-8, 13, 15) and once in chapter 4 (v. 7). **Today,** of course, indicates urgency. It means "now," not necessarily a 24-hour period. It refers to the period of grace, which sometimes may be less than 24 hours. In other words, it refers to the present moment. If you know the truth of Jesus Christ, if you know the gospel of Jesus Christ, do not do what Israel did when she knew God's truth and saw His revelation. It is so foolish and dangerous to harden your heart. You never know how long you will have to decide. "For He says, 'At the acceptable time I listened to you, and on the day of salvation I helped you'; behold, now is 'the acceptable time,' behold, now is 'the day of salvation' " (2 Cor. 6:2). God's time for salvation is always *now.*

In his earlier ministry D.L. Moody often would end his message with, "Go home and think about what I've said." One night in Chicago he told the people to do this and to come back the next night ready to make a decision. That night the Chicago fire broke out, and some who had been in his congregation died. That was the last time he told anyone to think over the claims of Christ and make a decision later. No one knows if he will have a tomorrow in which to decide. **Today** signifies the present time of grace. Men today, as in the time of Moody and in the time of Hebrews and in the time of David and in the time of Moses, never know how long that time of grace for them will be.

Listening to God and obeying Him are matters of will. So is hardening the heart to Him, as Israel did. Paul warns that our hearts, or consciences, can become seared and insensitive, as skin does when it is badly burned (1 Tim. 4:2). The scar tissue that replaces the skin has very little feeling.

When I was in college I was thrown out of a car that was going about 75 miles an hour. I slid some 100 yards on my back and suffered third-degree burns from the friction. The resulting scar tissue is now insensitive.

Something very much like this happens to a conscience that is repeatedly disregarded. "Today" lasts only as long as there is opportunity to decide—and as long as the conscience is sensitive to God. When a person's "today" is over, it is then too late. His heart gets harder every time he says no to Jesus Christ or to any part of His truth or will. When the heart is soft, when the conscience is sensitive, when the intellect is convinced about Christ—that is the time to decide, when one is still pliable and responsive. Otherwise he will eventually become spiritually hard, stubborn, and insensitive. The gospel will no longer have any appeal.

Do not harden your hearts as when they provoked Me, as in the day of trial in the wilderness. (3:8)

Israel had been in Egypt for more than 400 years, the last 200 years or so as slaves. Afraid that the Hebrews would become a threat, the Egyptians tried to weaken them and deplete their numbers by hard, oppressive labor in building cities and perhaps even pyramids. They were overworked, underfed, and regularly beaten. As both punishment and as an inducement to let His people leave this land, God afflicted the Egyptians with a series of ten plagues, the last and worst of which caused the death of all their firstborn. At this, Pharaoh pleaded with the Israelites to leave, which they hurriedly did under Moses' leadership. By the time they reached the Red Sea, Pharaoh had changed his mind and had led his troops to bring them back. God performed another miracle, allowing His people to travel through the parted waters, which afterward engulfed and drowned the pursuing army of Egypt.

After they arrived for the **trial in the wilderness,** God continued to bless them with miracles—travel direction by pillars of cloud and of fire (for night travel) and provision of food and good water. After each blessing they were satisfied only for a brief time. They soon started again to complain and to doubt God. They became the classic illustration of unbelief in the face of overwhelming evidence. God had clearly and miraculously revealed Himself; they knew He had revealed Himself; they knew what He expected them to do; and they saw evidence after evidence of His power and His blessing. But they never really believed. Just as the Egyptians quickly got over their fear of God, the Israelites quickly got over their trust of Him. They would not commit themselves to Him in faith. As a result, they had to wander and wander and wander—until all of the ungrateful, untrusting, unbelieving generation had died. For some forty years they wandered around in circles in a barren, desolate, and oppressive land—because of their unbelief.

Where your fathers tried Me by testing Me, and saw My works for forty years. (3:9)

Unbelief never has enough proof. Asking for more proof is simply a pretext, an excuse, a delaying tactic. The people of Israel kept testing God, and the **day of trial** lasted forty years. "Then all the congregation of the sons of Israel journeyed by stages from the wilderness of Sin, according to the command of the Lord, and camped at Rephidim, and there was no water for the people to drink. Therefore the people quarreled with Moses and said, 'Give us water that we may drink.' And Moses said to them, 'Why do you quarrel with me? Why do you test the Lord?' " (Ex. 17:1-2). They were not trusting God for water in faith; they were demanding water from God as their due and as a test to see if He really could and would provide it. Their real purpose is spelled out a few verses later: "They tested the Lord, saying, 'Is the Lord among us, or not?' "

(17:7). God had been providing for them all along; they had abundant evidence of His power and care. But they would not put their full trust in God, so they kept saying, in effect, "God, just do this one more thing for us so we'll know you're real." But when He protected them again or provided for them again, they still did not believe. "Don't be like these people," pleads the writer of Hebrews. "Don't make excuses for not believing; don't harden your hearts to God like they did—or you will lose your opportunity like they did."

God had released the Israelites from Egypt by awesome, miraculous plagues. Just as miraculously He brought them through the Red Sea and destroyed their pursuers. Without fail He had provided manna to feed them and the pillars of cloud and fire to guide them. But they still asked, "Is God among us?" Nothing is more illogical or unreasonable than unbelief. It refuses to accept the most overwhelming evidence—simply because unbelief does not *want* to believe. As Jesus made clear in the parable of the rich man and Lazarus, no evidence is sufficient for the person who does not want to believe. "If they do not listen to Moses and the Prophets, neither will they be persuaded if someone rises from the dead" (Luke 16:31). The person, on the other hand, who *wants* to believe trusts God despite any evidence that may seem to be lacking. He says, "I do believe; help my unbelief" (Mark 9:24).

Most people do not need more proof that God is real or that Jesus is His Son and the Savior. They need to hate and repent of their sin and to commit themselves to Him. A God who is continually tested will never be accepted. The one who tests God today does so for the same reason as did the Israelites in Moses day—to put Him off, because they love their sin, their own way, their own plans too much to give them up for God's.

Therefore I was angry with this generation, and said, "They always go astray in their heart; and they did not know My ways"; as I swore in My wrath, 'They shall not enter My rest.' " (3:10-11)

The word **angry** does not mean simply unhappy or disappointed. It means vexed, wrought up, incensed. God was extremely angry with Israel's sin. The people kept it up, kept it up, and kept it up. The Septuagint of this passage could be rendered, "God loathed them." He rejected and repudiated them. Why? Because they always **went astray in their heart; and they did not know My ways.**

As the Israelites finally neared the Promised Land, God commanded them to send out twelve men to spy it out before they entered. The majority report was extremely negative and pessimistic. They saw the enemy as giants and themselves as "grasshoppers." The minority report, by Caleb and Joshua, was optimistic—not because they underestimated the power of the enemy but because they knew the power of the Lord to be greater. The people believed the majority report and immediately began to grumble and complain to Moses and Aaron. As punishment, God said, "Surely all the men who have seen My glory and My signs, which I performed in Egypt and in the wilderness, yet have put Me to the test these ten times and have not listened to My voice, shall by no means see the land which I swore to their fathers, nor shall any of those who spurned Me see it" (Num. 14:22-23). They had more than enough evidence to believe that He could lead them safely into the land of milk and honey, but they would not believe Him and they were not allowed to enter. The **rest** was Canaan, where the toil of wandering would end. As we shall see in the next chapter, it is a symbol of salvation.

That is when today is over. You can stand on the verge of receiving Jesus Christ for a long time, toying with the idea and thinking, "God, prove Yourself some more. I'm not sure. I'm not quite ready yet." And one day He will say, "You've had enough evidence; it's over now. It is no longer today; it is tomorrow. You will never see My promised land."

If Israel had more than enough evidence to trust God in Moses' day, how much more do we have today? We have the evidence that Jesus Christ the Son of God died on a cross, rose again the third day, and lives and saves men. The evidence is in, the evidence is secure. Christ, the only begotten Son of the Father, has manifested God. He has declared Him, He has displayed His love, He has displayed His grace, He has sent the Holy Spirit. We do not need a Moses. In addition to all the historical evidence, we have the third Person of the Trinity to reveal Christ. Unbelief in the face of such overwhelming evidence is tragic indeed—and without excuse.

Even the generation that entered the land never knew God's rest in the true sense. The first thing God commanded them to do was to exterminate the godless and unbelievably wicked Canaanites. God was going to use His people as a tool of judgment. The Canaanites were so pagan and evil that they buried live babies in jars in the walls of every building they built. They were such a grossly immoral and godless people that God wanted them wiped off the face of the earth. But instead of exterminating the Canaanites, the Israelites moved in with them. Consequently, except for a few hundred years under their own judges and kings, the Israelites were exploited, exiled, and ruled by a succession of Gentile conquerors. In A.D. 70 their Temple was destroyed and they have since been scattered across the world. Only in our own day has God begun to gather them back to a homeland. Israel's final rest will come only in the Kingdom that His Son will build when He returns again.

THE INVITATION: TAKE HEED

Take care, brethren, lest there should be in any one of you an evil, unbelieving heart, in falling away from the living God. (3:12)

Based on the illustration of Israel's unbelief in the wilderness, an appeal is made to the readers of Hebrews not to follow this example. It is a warning against rejecting truth that is known. The judgment of the wilderness days fell on those who rejected God's Word through Moses, and the warning here is to those who reject God's Word in Christ. **Brethren** is not a reference to Christians, as is "holy brethren" in 3:1. It refers to racial brothers, unbelieving Jews, as the term does throughout the book of Acts.

The greatest sin in the world is unbelief. It is the greatest offense against God and brings the greatest harm to ourselves. These readers were informed about the gospel. Many, perhaps, professed to be Christians. None considered himself to be actively, aggressively against Christ; but they all were against Him. No matter how close a person may be to accepting Jesus Christ as Savior, if he never comes to Him, he still has an evil, **unbelieving heart.** His punishment will be all the more severe because of his knowledge of the living God. If such "have fallen away, it is impossible to renew them again to repentance" (Heb. 6:6). When you have heard the truth of Jesus Christ, when you have acknowledged that it is the truth, and then turn your back and walk away from Him, there is nothing God can do. Once you have heard the gospel and understood its claims, and then say no to Jesus Christ, you have fallen away. You have become apostate.

The Holy Spirit is saying to everyone who hears the gospel: "Respond to Jesus while your heart is still warmed and softened by His truth, while it is still sensitive. Respond to His sweet love and His call of grace. Wait too long and you will find your heart getting hard and insensitive. The decision will become harder and harder as your heart becomes harder and harder. If you continue to follow your evil, unbelieving heart rather than the gospel, you will forever depart from the living God, and forfeit salvation rest.

Turning away from Jesus Christ is not rejecting a religion. Turning away from Jesus Christ is much more than rejecting historical, traditional Christianity. Turning away from Jesus Christ is turning away from the living God. It is turning away from life itself.

THE INSTRUCTION: EXHORT ONE ANOTHER DAILY

But encourage one another day after day, as long as it is still called "Today," lest any one of you be hardened by the deceitfulness of sin. (3:13)

Encourage is from the Greek *parakaleō*, a form of the word used by Jesus of the Holy Spirit in John 14:16. The root meaning has to do with coming alongside to give help. The writer is saying to the believers among those to whom he is writing, "Get along side each other and help each other." They are especially urged to help their unbelieving Jewish brethren by encouraging them not to harden their hearts but to accept Jesus as the Messiah.

Deceitfulness means "trickery" or "strategem." Sin is tricky; it seldom appears as it really is. It always masks itself. It lies and deceives (cf. Rom. 7:11). When a person becomes spiritually hardened, he rarely is aware of it. He can hear the gospel of Jesus Christ time and time again and not respond. My father often used the well-known expression, "The same sun that melts the wax hardens the clay." If your heart is not melted in faith, it will be hardened in unbelief.

The old nature constantly suggests that sin is not as bad and that trust in Christ is not as important as the Bible says. Becoming a Christian seems too costly, too demanding, too restrictive, too drab and unexciting—and, above all, unnecessary. From one's own perspective, he does not seem so wicked. "I take care of my family, I am a helpful neighbor and a good citizen. I'm not perfect, of course, but I'm not evil, either. My life has room for improvement, but it doesn't need 'saving.' " So the thinking goes. This is what the sin nature deceitfully tells men about their need for salvation.

God's assessment is quite different. "But My righteous one shall live by faith; and if he shrinks back, My soul has no pleasure in him. But we are not of those who shrink back to destruction, but of those who have faith to the preserving of the soul" (Heb. 10:38-39). There we have it. You stand on the edge of decision, a decision which you cannot escape. Either you believe to the saving of your soul or you fall back to damnation.

CONTINUANCE IS PROOF OF SALVATION

For we have become partakers of Christ, if we hold fast the beginning of our assurance firm until the end. (3:14)

If we really believe the gospel, if we have committed our life to Jesus Christ, then at the end of the day, the end of the year, the end of life, our commitment will still stand. The greatest proof of salvation is continuance in the Christian life. The true believer stays with Christ. "If you abide in My word," Jesus said, "then you are truly disciples of Mine" (John 8:31). When someone departs from the gospel, backs away from the faith, we can only conclude that this person never believed. "They went out from us, but they were not really of us; for if they had been of us, they would have remained with us; but they went out, in order that it might be shown that they all are not of us" (1 John 2:19). Staying with the Lord marks the difference between possession and profession.

THE ISSUE: UNBELIEF

While it is said, "Today if you hear His voice, do not harden your hearts, as when they provoked Me." For who provoked Him when they had heard? Indeed, did not all those who came out of Egypt led by Moses? And with whom was He angry for forty years? Was it not with those who sinned, whose bodies fell in the wilderness? And to whom did He swear that they should not enter His rest, but to those who were disobedient? And so we see that they were not able to enter because of unbelief. (3:15-19)

The appeal to turn to the Lord without delay is repeated again. God had become angry with **all those who came out of Egypt** who would not believe, and in anger He refused them His rest in the Promised Land. The writer pleads with his readers not to follow that example and suffer that fate. The disobedience of **unbelief** forfeits blessing and brings judgment.

The illustration and invitation and instruction are worthless apart from belief in that to which they all point. God has great blessings prepared. He wants to pour out these riches on us, not only in this life but throughout all eternity. There is one thing required—faith. **They were not able to enter because of unbelief** (cf. Prov. 29:1; Jude 5).

Many say, "I can't believe. I have a pragmatic, empirical mind that has to see the facts, weigh all the evidence." But everyone lives by faith. We live by faith when we go into a restaurant and eat the food without questioning its safety. When driving down the highway, we are not in constant fear that around the next bend the road will lead us into a river where there is no bridge. We trust the people who made the highways and the people who have traveled over them before us. We live by faith almost constantly. If we can put our faith in the highway department and the people who prepare our food, we surely can put our faith in the God of the universe. Not to trust in Him is fatal.

Entering God's Rest
(4:1-13)

9

Therefore, let us fear lest, while a promise remains of entering His rest, any one of you should seem to have come short of it. For indeed we have had good news preached to us, just as they also; but the word they heard did not profit them, because it was not united by faith in those who heard. For we who have believed enter that rest, just as He has said, "As I swore in My wrath, they shall not enter My rest," although His works were finished from the foundation of the world. For He has thus said somewhere concerning the seventh day, "And God rested on the seventh day from all His works"; and again in this passage, "They shall not enter My rest." Since therefore it remains for some to enter it, and those who formerly had good news preached to them failed to enter because of disobedience, He again fixes a certain day, "Today," saying through David after so long a time just as has been said before, "Today if you hear His voice, do not harden your hearts." For if Joshua had given them rest, He would not have spoken of another day after that. There remains therefore a Sabbath rest for the people of God. For the one who has entered His rest has himself also rested from his works, as God did from His. Let us therefore be diligent to enter that rest, lest anyone fall through following the same example of disobedience. For the word of God is living and active and sharper than any two-edged sword, and piercing as far as the division of soul and spirit, of both joints and marrow, and able to judge the thoughts and intentions of the heart. And there is no creature hidden from His sight but all things are open and laid bare to the eyes of Him with whom we have to do. (4:1-13)

Hebrews 4 continues the warning to informed but unresponsive Jews that began in 3:7. These Jews not only knew the basic truths of the gospel but had even renounced Judaism. Still they did not trust in Christ. The warning, of course, applies to anyone who is hesitating in committing himself fully to Jesus Christ, and can be summarized: "**Do not harden your hearts** like Israel did in the wilderness." The Israelites had left Egypt, but they often longed to go back. They refused to trust the Lord completely and, oppressive and disappointing as it was, the old life still had an appeal. They halted at the crucial point of decision. Consequently, they were not allowed to enter the Promised Land and into God's **rest**. So it is with many who are drawn to Jesus Christ. Unbelief forfeits rest— that is the writer's thought.

THE MEANING OF REST

The English **rest** and the Greek word (*katapausis*) that it translates here have similar meanings. The basic idea is that of ceasing from work or from any kind of action. You stop doing what you are doing. Action, labor, or exertion is over. Applied to God's rest, it means no more self-effort as far as salvation is concerned. It means the end of trying to please God by our feeble, fleshly works. God's perfect rest is a rest in free grace.

Rest also means freedom from whatever worries or disturbs you. Some people cannot rest mentally and emotionally because they are so easily annoyed. Every little nuisance upsets them and they always feel hassled. Rest does not mean freedom from all nuisances and hassles; it means freedom from being so easily bothered by them. It means to be inwardly quiet, composed, peaceful. To enter God's rest means to be at peace with God, to possess the perfect peace He gives. It means to be free from guilt and even unnecessary feelings of guilt. It means freedom from worry about sin, because sin is forgiven. God's rest is the end of legalistic works and the experience of peace in the total forgiveness of God.

Rest can mean to lie down, be settled, fixed, secure. There is no more shifting about in frustration from one thing to another, no more running in circles. In God's rest we are forever established in Christ. We are freed from running from philosophy to philosophy, from religion to religion, from life-style to life-style. We are freed from being tossed about by every doctrinal wind, every idea or fad, that blows our way. In Christ, we are established, rooted, grounded, unmoveable. That is the Christian's rest.

Rest involves remaining confident, keeping trust. In other words, to rest in something or someone means to maintain our confidence in it or him. To enter God's rest, therefore, means to enjoy the perfect, unshakeable confidence of salvation in our Lord. We have no more reason to fear. We have absolute trust and confidence in God's power and care.

Rest also means to lean on. To enter into God's rest means that for the remainder of our lives and for all eternity we can lean on God. We can be sure that He will never fail to support us. In the new relationship with God, we can depend on Him for everything and in everything—for support, for health, for strength, for all we need. It is a relationship in which we are confident and secure that we have committed our life to God and that He holds it in perfect, eternal love. It is a relationship that involves being settled and fixed. No more floating around. We know whom we have believed and we stand in Him.

The rest spoken of in Hebrews 3 and 4 includes all of these meanings. It is full, blessed, sweet, satisfying, peaceful. It is what God offers every person in Christ. It is the rest pictured and illustrated in the Canaan rest that Israel never understood and never entered into because of unbelief. And just as Israel never entered Canaan rest because of unbelief, so soul after soul since that time, and even before, has missed God's salvation rest because of unbelief.

Two other dimensions of spiritual rest will not be found in a dictionary—the Kingdom rest of the Millennium and the eternal rest of heaven. These are the ultimate expressions of the new relationship to God in Christ, the relationship that takes care of us in this life, in the Kingdom, and in heaven forever.

Hebrews 4:1-13 takes us more deeply into this truth by teaching four things about God's rest: its availability, its elements, its nature, and its urgency.

THE AVAILABILITY OF REST

Therefore, let us fear lest, while a promise remains of entering His rest, any one of you should seem to have come short of it. (4:1)

Therefore refers, of course, to Israel's unbelief and consequent failure to enter God's Canaan rest. As illustrated by her experience, not trusting in God is something to be feared. Jesus warned, "Do not fear those who kill the body, but are unable to kill the soul; but rather fear

Him who is able to destroy both soul and body in hell" (Matt. 10:28). Only God has the power to commit a person to hell. If He is not believed, He is the One, the only One, to be feared.

The Christian has no need to **fear** in the sense meant here. "Do not be afraid, little flock," Jesus said, "for your Father has chosen gladly to give you the kingdom" (Luke 12:32). The only kind of fear a Christian should have is that of reverential awe (1 Pet. 2:17; Rev. 14:7; and others). This is the fear of respect and honor, not the fear of condemnation or fear in the sense of terror, of which this text speaks.

But to be lost and face eternal separation from God is cause for the most extreme fear. Few, however, who are lost feel such fear. Even many who have heard the gospel and recognize its truth do not have this fear. So the writer urges them, pleads with them, to be afraid of what they are doing and of what they are facing.

As long as **a promise remains,** there is opportunity to be saved and to enter God's rest. Otherwise appeal for belief would be a mockery. There is still time. God still holds the door open. When Israel was in the wilderness, those who refused to believe were not allowed to enter the Promised Land. But God did not forsake Israel as His chosen people. The Jews who refused His Son, who mocked Him and crucified Him, were not allowed to enter God's heavenly rest. But God did not forsake Israel even then. Many Christians, unfortunately, believe that God no longer has a plan for Israel as a nation or even as a people—that His chosen people now is the church. There is no promise left for Israel, and she will have no restoration or future kingdom. This is the view of amillennialism, common today even among evangelicals. Some argue that, because of what the Jews did in the Old Testament in unbelief, and even more importantly because of what they did to Jesus Christ, as a nation and as a distinct people they forfeited every promise of God.

But God's promise to Israel still stands. One of the clearest passages that shows Israel is still in God's economy and that God is still working with her is in Acts 3. Shortly after Pentecost Peter said to a group of Jews just outside the Temple: "But you disowned the Holy and Righteous One, and asked for a murderer to be granted to you, but put to death the Prince of life" (vv. 14-15). But after this strong and seemingly final indictment, he concludes by saying, "It is you who are the sons of the prophets, and of the covenant which God made with your fathers, saying to Abraham, 'And in your seed all the families of the earth shall be blessed.' For you first, God raised up His Servant, and sent Him to bless you by turning every one of you from your wicked ways" (vv. 25-26). Even though they had killed the Prince of life, the very Son of God, they were still children of the unconditional covenant God had made with Abraham. So the writer of Hebrews could say to them, "a promise remains of entering His rest." Rest is still available. What marvelous grace!

A more accurate translation of the last part of Hebrews 4:1 is, "lest you think you have come too late to enter into the rest of God." In other words, some Jews were in danger of talking themselves out of trusting in Christ because they thought it was too late. Perhaps they believed their people had forfeited the opportunity to receive the Messiah and be saved. They had no reason for such despair, because a promise still remained. But they did have reason to be afraid—not because they had lost the opportunity for salvation, but because they *could* lose it if they continued to put off accepting Christ as their personal Savior.

In his younger manhood Jerry McCauley was as debauched as can be imagined. His children were starving because he spent his money on alcohol. His little girl died of malnutrition when she was about four. The neighbors gave enough money to buy her some new clothes and a casket to be buried in. In the middle of the night McCauley broke into the mortuary, took the clothes off his dead child, and exchanged them for a drink. Not long afterward, however, Jesus Christ reached down and changed his life, and he became one of the great preachers America has known.

As long as a person has opportunity to decide, he *can* decide. A person is never too far gone for God to deal with him. As long as his heart is sensitive to what the Spirit is saying, as long as he can hear God's call, he has time to be saved. God's rest is still available. Only God knows how long that is for each person.

THE ELEMENTS OF REST

God's rest, His salvation, is based on three things: personal faith, sovereign decree, and immediate action.

PERSONAL FAITH

For indeed we have had good news preached to us, just as they also; but the word they heard did not profit them, because it was not united by faith in those who heard. For we who have believed enter that rest, just as He has said, "As I swore in My wrath, they shall not enter My rest," although His works were finished from the foundation of the world. (4:2-3)

From the human side, the first requirement for salvation is **faith.** Hearing the gospel is essential, but it is not enough. The ancient Israelites heard God's good news of **rest,** but it did them no good since they did not accept it. They did not trust in the God who gave them the good news. It does no good to hear if we do not believe. That is the point here.

Hearing the good news of the rest of God is of no benefit, no profit, to any person at any time unless the hearing is **united by faith.**

It is tragic that hell is going to be populated with people who will say, "Lord, Lord, did we not prophesy in Your name, and in Your name cast out demons, and in Your name perform many miracles?" To which Jesus will reply, "I never knew you; depart from Me, you who practice lawlessness" (Matt. 7:22-23; cf. Luke 13:26-27). Their knowledge and their work was not united with faith. Jews prided themselves on the fact that they had God's law and God's ordinances and God's rituals. They were especially proud to be descendants of Abraham. But Jesus warned that true children of Abraham believe and act as Abraham did (John 8:39). Paul reminded his fellow Jews that "He is a Jew who is one inwardly; and circumcision is that which is of the heart, by the Spirit, not by the letter; and his praise is not from men, but from God" (Rom. 2:29). Spiritually, an unbelieving Jew is a contradiction in terms.

If you run a red light and a policeman pulls you over and starts to give you a ticket, you do not show him your copy of the state driving laws as your defense. You do not try to establish your innocence by telling him you have read the booklet many times and know most of the regulations by heart. Far from making you innocent, this would make you all the more responsible for living up to the laws and all the more guilty for breaking them. Knowing the law is an advantage only if we obey it. "For indeed circumcision is of value, if you practice the Law," Paul says, "but if you are a transgressor of the Law, your circumcision has become uncircumcision" (Rom. 2:25).

Being a true Jew under the Old Covenant was not a matter of having the law but of obeying it. Being a true Christian under the New Covenant is not a matter of knowing the gospel but of trusting in it. Having a Bible, reading it, knowing it, taking it to church every Sunday, and even teaching from it do not make us Christians. Only trusting in the One to whom it testifies makes us Christians. "You search the Scriptures, because you think that in them you have eternal life," Jesus warned, "and it is these that bear witness of Me" (John 5:39). The issue is not knowledge or work, but faith. Paul was happy and thankful for the Thessalonian Christians not simply because they accepted the gospel as the Word of God, but because they believed it (1 Thess. 2:13; cf. 2 Thess. 2:13). This signifies whole life commitment to the Lordship of Christ.

Both the positive and negative sides of this truth are categorical, absolute. Those **who have believed enter that rest** and those who do not believe **shall not enter My rest.** Belief and unbelief are very serious things. From the human side, belief with nothing else will save us; unbelief with everything else will condemn us. These are the two equally true sides of the gospel, which is *good* news only for those who accept it with all their hearts.

OUR REST IS GOD'S REST

One other point should be made here. The rest promised to those who believe is **My rest,** that is, God's rest. God's own rest from His work of creation, and the rest that He gives us in Christ, are not the rest brought on by weariness or the rest of inactivity, but are the rest of finished work. **His works were finished from the foundation of the world.** God has finished His work. God has done it all, and for anyone who wants to enter into His finished work and to share in His rest, it is available by faith.

When God had finished the creation, He said (briefly paraphrasing Gen. 2), "It's done. I've made a wonderful world for man and woman. I've given them everything earthly they need, including each other, for a complete and beautiful and satisfying life. Even more importantly, they have perfect, unbroken, unmarred fellowship with Me. I can now rest; and they can rest in Me."

For He has thus said somewhere concerning the seventh day, "And God rested on the seventh day from all His works." (4:4)

Sabbath rest was instituted as a symbol of the true rest to come in Christ. That is why the Sabbath could be violated by Jesus, and completely set aside in the New Testament. When the true Rest Land came, the symbol was useless. "Therefore let no one act as your judge in regard to food or drink or in respect to a festival or a new moon or a Sabbath day—things which are a mere shadow of what is to come; but the substance belongs to Christ" (Col. 2:16-17).

Adam and Eve were completely righteous when they were created. They walked and talked with God as regularly and as naturally as they walked and talked with each other. They were at rest, in its original and its fullest sense. They relied on God for everything. They had no anxieties, no worries, no pain, no frustrations, no heartaches. They did not need God's forgiveness, because they had no sin to be forgiven of. They did not need His consolation, because they were never grieved. They did not need His encouragement, because they never failed. They only needed His fellowship, because they were made for Him. This was their "rest" in God. God completed His perfect work and He rested. They were His perfect work and they rested in Him.

But something terrible happened. When Satan began to impugn God's word and integrity and love, Adam and Eve chose to believe Satan. They trusted him rather than God. And when they lost their trust in God, they lost His rest. And from that time until now, man apart from God not only has been sinful but restless. The entire purpose of the Bible and the entire working of God in human history have one theme: bringing man back into His rest.

To accomplish that, God had to remove the barrier to their rest, the barrier which separated them from Him. He sent His Son to do just that, to provide again for man's rest in His Creator. Through Christ's death men are again offered life. Rest is another name for life, life as God meant it to be. Even the people who lived before Jesus were saved on the basis of what God was going to do through His Son. Christ bore sins past and future, and through Him God's rest has been available to anyone who believes.

Those who sinned while wandering in the wilderness not only forfeited Canaan. Unless they exercised personal faith in God sometime during the forty years, they also forfeited eternal life—of which Canaan was only a symbol.

DIVINE DECREE

And again in this passage, "They shall not enter My rest." Since therefore it remains for some to enter it, and those who formerly had good news preached to them failed to enter because of disobedience. (4:5-6)

Rest still **remains.** Why? Because God could not cut it off. That would mean He started something that was not worth completing. But He does not do such things. God did not establish rest for mankind for nothing. The rest He has provided, someone will enter: **It remains for some to enter it.** When man lost God's rest, God immediately began a recovery process. Through His Son, Jesus Christ, some would be brought back in. He created man for fellowship with Himself, and His plan would not be thwarted, either by a rebellious archangel or by disbelieving mankind. By divine decree, therefore, there has always been a remnant of believers, even among mostly disbelieving Israel. "In the same way then, there has also come to be at the present time a remnant according to God's gracious choice" (Rom. 11:5). The way of God's rest has always been narrow, and only a few, relative to all of mankind, have ever found it. But some must enter into it, because God's purpose must be fulfilled. By sovereign decree He designed a rest for mankind and some, therefore, are going **to enter it.**

The second element of rest mentioned here is God's sovereign decree. It is mentioned second, but it came first. Without God's decree, man's faith would be futile and worthless. We are saved by two things: God's will, expressed in His sending His Son to save men; and our will, expressed in our trust in His Son to save us. We can be saved because He planned to save us before the world was created. That is predestination, or election. Jesus said, "No one can come to Me, unless the Father who sent Me draws him," and, "No one can come to Me, unless it has been granted him from the Father" (John 6:44, 65). Personal faith is necessary before God can apply His redemption to us. Yet our personal faith is effective because the Father has first drawn us to the Son. Because *God wants* us to be saved, we *can* be saved. Only **disobedience** keeps us out.

IMMEDIATE ACTION

He again fixes a certain day, "Today," saying through David after so long a time just as has been said before, "Today if you hear His voice, do not harden your hearts." (4:7)

The third element of rest is immediate action. God fixes **a certain day, "Today."** Opportunity for God's rest remains, but it will not remain indefinitely. For each individual it will end before or with death; and for all mankind it will end in the Last Day. The age of grace is not forever. This is why immediate action is a basis of entering God's rest, of being saved. This is why Paul said, "Now is 'the acceptable time,' behold, now is 'the day of salvation' " (2 Cor. 6:2). When God looked down on the civilization He was ready to drown, He said, "My Spirit shall not strive with man forever, because he also is flesh; nevertheless his days shall be one hundred and twenty years" (Gen. 6:3). In other words, a person has no more than his lifetime to believe God. The average life expectancy today is much less than 120 years; and, of course, none of us has a guarantee of living even until the average. God limits the time for salvation. This is God's today, right now—the only day, the only opportunity, we can be sure of.

THE NATURE OF REST

For if Joshua had given them rest, He would not have spoken of another day after that. There remains therefore a Sabbath rest for the people of God. For the one who has entered His rest has himself also rested from his works, as God did from His. (4:8-10)

IT IS SPIRITUAL

The rest spoken of here is not the physical rest of Canaan. That was only a picture. "For if Joshua had given them rest, He would not have spoken of another day after that." God's true rest comes not through a Moses or a Joshua or a David. It comes through Jesus Christ.

God's rest is not essentially physical at all. Certainly, resting in God and trusting in His promises can relieve us of nervousness, tenseness, and other physical problems. But these are by-products of His rest. Many cults promise their followers happiness, wealth, and health in this life. The Bible does not. The rest God promises is spiritual, not physical. Whatever physical or earthly benefits the Lord may give us, His basic promise is to give us spiritual rest, spiritual blessing. Some of God's most faithful believers are the busiest, the hardest working, and sometimes even the most afflicted people imaginable. Yet they are in God's salvation rest.

IT IS FOR ISRAEL

The term **people of God** may refer generally to anyone who knows God; but here it specifically refers to Israel. Salvation is first of all for Israel. The gospel "is the power of God for salvation to everyone who believes, to the Jew first and also to the Greek" (Rom. 1:16). There is a rest remaining for the people of God, and in the Old Testament Israel is designated the people of God. His spiritual rest is promised first to Israel, and He will not be through with her until she comes into His rest.

IT IS FUTURE

For the one who has entered His rest has himself also rested from his works, as God did from His. (4:10)

God's **rest** is also future. In his vision on Patmos the apostle John heard these beautiful words from heaven: " 'Write, "Blessed are the dead who die in the Lord from now on!" ' 'Yes,' says the Spirit, 'that they may rest from their labors, for their deeds follow with them' " (Rev. 14:13). I believe Hebrews 4:10 anticipates that final day when we cease from all effort and all work and enter into the presence of Jesus Christ. It includes the promised rest to Israel, the ultimate rest when she and all of God's other people will cease from work and rest as God did when He finished His creation. That is the reality of Sabbath rest.

The Urgency of Rest

Let us therefore be diligent to enter that rest, lest anyone fall through following the same example of disobedience. For the word of God is living and active and sharper than any two-edged sword, and piercing

as far as the division of soul and spirit, of both joints and marrow, and able to judge the thoughts and intentions of the heart. And there is no creature hidden from His sight, but all things are open and laid bare to the eyes of Him with whom we have to do. (4:11-13)

The need for God's **rest** is urgent. A person should diligently, with intense purpose and concern, secure it. It is not that he can work his way to salvation, but that he should diligently seek to enter God's rest by faith—lest he, like the Israelites in the wilderness, lose the opportunity.

God cannot be trifled with. **For the word of God is living and active and sharper than any two-edged sword, . . . and able to judge the thoughts and intentions of the heart.** In the immediate context this verse means that the readers who are hesitating in trusting Christ, who are even considering falling back into Judaism, had better be urgent and **diligent** in seeking to enter God's rest, because the Word of God is alive. It is not static, but active—constantly active. It can pierce right down into the innermost part **of the heart** to see if belief is real or not.

So the Word of God is not only saving and comforting and nourishing and healing, it is also a tool of judgment and execution. In the day of the great judgment His Word is going to penetrate and lay **bare** all hearts who have not trusted in Him. The sham and hypocrisy will be revealed and no profession of faith, no matter how orthodox, and no list of good works, no matter how sacrificial, will count for anything before Him. Only **the thoughts and intentions of the heart** will count. God's Word is the perfect discerner, the perfect *kritikos* (from which we get "critic"). It not only analyzes all the facts perfectly, but all motives, and intentions, and beliefs as well, which even the wisest of human judges or critics cannot do. The sword of His Word will make no mistakes in judgment or execution. All disguises will be ripped off and only the real person will be seen.

The word translated **open** had two distinct uses in ancient times. It was used of a wrestler taking his opponent by the throat. In this position the two men were unavoidably face to face. The other use was in regard to a criminal trial. A sharp dagger would be bound to the neck of the accused, with the point just below his chin, so that he could not bow his head, but had to face the court. Both uses had to do with grave face-to-face situations. When an unbeliever comes under the scrutiny of God's Word, he will be unavoidably face-to-face with the perfect truth about God and about himself.

In light of such certain and perfect judgment and of such beautiful and wonderful rest, why will any person harden his heart to God?

Our Great
High Priest (4:14-16)

Since then we have a great high priest who has passed through the heavens, Jesus the Son of God, let us hold fast our confession. For we do not have a high priest who cannot sympathize with our weaknesses, but one who has been tempted in all things as we are, yet without sin. Let us therefore draw near with confidence to the throne of grace, that we may receive mercy and may find grace to help in time of need. (4:14-16)

The Holy Spirit continues to appeal to Jews who have heard the gospel and turned from Judaism but have not yet trusted Christ. He has been saying, in effect, "You know your dissatisfaction with Judaism and with your own lives. You know the superiority of Jesus to prophets, angels, and Moses, and the dangers of not trusting Christ and of your need for Him. What is keeping you from making the final decision?" Hebrews 4:1-13 was an urgent appeal not to delay in accepting God's salvation, His perfect rest, in Jesus Christ.

Until now the appeal has largely been negative: if you do not believe, you will be doomed—forever apart from God and His rest. God's

Word has been shown in its all-seeing and judgmental role, as a two-edged sword (4:12).

The danger of hell is certainly real, and any preacher—especially when trying to reach the unsaved—is not true to the gospel if he avoids this truth. Because it is true, and because it is so terribly important, it *must* be preached and taught. Avoiding it is not only being unfaithful to God's Word but also being unfaithful to the needs of the unsaved. To cry "Fire!" in a crowded building where there is no fire is not only against the law but extremely cruel and dangerous. But *not* to cry "Fire!" when a building *is* in flames is even more cruel and dangerous. Done in the right spirit and way, warning unbelievers of the dangers of hell is one of the greatest kindnesses we can show them.

THE POSITIVE MESSAGE

The message now turns to the positive side of the gospel. Salvation does more than keep us out of hell, immeasurably more. Many people have a caricature of fundamentalism, or evangelicalism, as having no message but "fire and brimstone, hell and damnation."

Salvation not only saves from spiritual death, it brings spiritual life. It should be sought not only because of what will happen to us if we do not accept it, but because of what will happen to us if we do. What happens to us when we accept it is based on who Jesus is. If there were no other reason in the universe to be saved, who Jesus is would be reason enough. Coming into a living relationship with Him is the greatest experience a person can have. To walk in the fellowship of the living Christ would be a glorious thing even if there were no hell to escape. So we have reason to receive Jesus Christ and enter into God's rest not only because of fear of His judgment but because of His beauty, not only because of His wrath but also because of His grace, not only because He is a judge but because He is also a merciful and faithful High Priest.

Three things make Jesus our great High Priest—His perfect priesthood, His perfect Person, and His perfect provision. Because He is perfect in these aspects, He is God's only true High Priest. All others, no matter how faithful, were but symbols of His priesthood.

HIS PERFECT PRIESTHOOD

Since then we have a great high priest who has passed through the heavens, Jesus the Son of God, let us hold fast our confession. (4:14)

Throughout the book of Hebrews the high priesthood of Jesus Christ is exalted. In chapter 1 He is seen as the One who has made "purification of sins" (v. 3). In chapter 2 He is "a merciful and faithful high priest" (v. 17) and in chapter 3 He is "the Apostle and High Priest of our confession" (v. 1). Chapters 7-9 focus almost exclusively on Jesus' high priesthood. Here (4:14) he is called **a great high priest.**

The priests of ancient Israel were appointed by God to be mediators between Himself and His people. Only the high priest could offer the highest sacrifice under the Old Covenant, and that he did only once a year on the Day of Atonement (Yom Kippur). All the sins of the people were brought symbolically to the Holy of Holies, where blood was sprinkled on the mercy seat as a sacrifice to atone for them. As no other human instrument could, he represented God before the people and the people before God.

As we learn from Leviticus 16, before the high priest could even enter the Holy of Holies, much less offer a sacrifice there, he had to make an offering for himself, since he, just as all those whom he represented, was a sinner. Not only that, but his time in the Holy of Holies was limited. He was allowed to stay in the presence of the Shekinah glory of God only while he was making the sacrifice.

To enter the Holy of Holies, the priest had to pass through three areas in the Tabernacle or the Temple. He took the blood and went through the door into the outer court, through another door into the Holy Place, and then through the veil into the Holy of Holies. He did not sit down or delay. As soon as the sacrifice was made, he left and did not return for another year.

Every year, year after year, another Yom Kippur was necessary. Between these yearly sacrifices—every day, day after day—thousands of other sacrifices were made, of produce and of animals. The process was never ended, never completed, because the priesthood was not perfect and the sacrifices were not perfect.

Jesus, our great High Priest, after He had made the one-time, perfect sacrifice on the cross, also passed through three areas. When He **passed through the heavens,** he went through the first heaven (the atmosphere), the second heaven (outer space), and into the third heaven (God's abode; 2 Cor. 12:2-4). Jesus went to where God Himself, not simply His glory, dwells. This is the holiest of all holies. But Jesus did not have to leave. His sacrifice was made once for all time. The sacrifice was perfect and the High Priest was perfect, and He sat down for all eternity at the Father's right hand (Heb. 1:3). "I glorified Thee on the earth, having accomplished the work which Thou hast given Me to do. And now, glorify Thou Me together with Thyself, Father, with the glory which I had with Thee before the world was" (John 17:4-5). He had made the perfect atonement for sin, the purpose for which He had come to earth. And the work was completed when He entered heaven and presented Himself in the Holy Place (Heb. 9:12).

Our great High Priest did not pass through the Tabernacle or the Temple. He **passed through the heavens**. When He got there He sat down, and God said, "I'm satisfied. My Son, Jesus Christ, accomplished the atonement for all sins for all time for all those who come to Him by faith and accept what He did for them." The appeal of 4:14, therefore, is for yet uncommitted Jews to accept Jesus Christ as their true High Priest. They should demonstrate that their confession is true possession by holding fast to Him as their Savior. This emphasizes the human side of the believer's security. True believers **hold fast,** as God holds them fast.

THE END OF JEWISH PRIESTHOOD AND SACRIFICES

Jesus was crucified less than forty years before Jerusalem was destroyed in A.D. 70. With it was destroyed the Temple, the only place where sacrifices could be made. From shortly after the time of Christ, therefore, no Jewish sacrifices have been made—even until the present time. Consequently, there has been no need for a Jewish priesthood since that time. Yom Kippur is still celebrated as a holy day, the highest holy day, but no priests are involved and no sacrifices are offered—because there are no priests to make the sacrifices and no temple in which to offer them.

THE END OF ALL RITUALISTIC PRIESTHOODS AND SACRIFICES

No Christian priesthood was established by Christ or the apostles. Peter refers to the church, that is to all believers, as a "holy priesthood" and "a royal priesthood" (1 Pet. 2:5, 9). Christians, as God's redeemed, are types of priests, in the general sense that we are responsible for bringing God to other men through preaching and teaching His Word and for bringing men to God through our witnessing. But no special order of priesthood or system of sacrifices is either taught or recognized in the New Testament. All claims of special priestly mediation between God and men—in offering forgiveness for sins, making atonement for sins by supposedly repeating Christ's sacrifice through a ritual, or any other such claim or practice—is entirely unbiblical and sinful. It is open defiance of the finished work of Jesus Christ.

Any formal religious priesthood on earth now implies that the final and perfect atonement for sin has not yet been made. It is equal to the rebellion of Korah, Dathan, and Abiram, whom the earth swallowed because God was so angry at their wicked presumption (Num. 16). There is absolutely no place in the economy of Christianity for a priesthood. Any that is established is illegitimate and a direct affront to the full and final priesthood of Jesus Christ Himself.

We have our perfect and great High Priest and He has already made, once and for all, the only sacrifice that will ever need to be made for sin—the only effective sacrifice that *could* be made for sin. Any other priest who attempts to reconcile men and God is a barrier rather than a mediator. By faith in Jesus Christ any person can enter directly into God's presence. When Jesus died, the veil of the Temple was torn from top to bottom. Access to God was thrown wide open to anyone who would come on His terms.

HIS PERFECT PERSON

For we do not have a high priest who cannot sympathize with our weaknesses, but one who has been tempted in all things as we are, yet without sin. (4:15)

At the end of verse 14 our great High Priest is again identified as **Jesus, the Son of God.** Here together are His human name, Jesus, and His divine title, Son of God. These two parts of His nature are also reflected in verse 15.

JESUS' HUMANITY

Most people seem to think of God as being far removed from human life and concerns. Jesus was the very Son of God, yet His divinity did not prevent Him from experiencing our feelings, our emotions, our temptations, our pain. God became man, He became Jesus, to share triumphantly the temptation and the testing and the suffering of men, in order that He might be a sympathetic and understanding High Priest.

When we are troubled or hurt or despondent or strongly tempted, we want to share our feelings and needs with someone who understands. Jesus can **sympathize with our weaknesses.** The phrase "No one understands like Jesus" in the well-known hymn is not only beautiful and encouraging but absolutely true. Our great High Priest not only is perfectly merciful and faithful but also perfectly understanding. He has an unequaled capacity for sympathizing with us in every danger, in every trial, in every situation that comes our way, because He has been through it all Himself. At the tomb of Lazarus Jesus' body shook in grief. In the Garden of Gethsemane, just before His arrest, He sweat drops of blood. He experienced every kind of temptation and testing, every kind of vicissitude, every kind of circumstance that any person will ever face. And He is at the right hand of the Father right now interceding for us.

Jesus not only had all the feelings of love, concern, disappointment, grief, and frustration that we have, but He had much greater love, infinitely more sensitive concerns, infinitely higher standards of righteousness, and perfect awareness of the evil and dangers of sin. Contrary, therefore, to what we are inclined to think, His divinity made His temptations and trials immeasurably harder for Him to endure than ours are for us.

Let me give an illustration to help explain how this can be true. We experience pain when we are injured, sometimes extreme pain. But if it becomes too severe, we will develop a temporary numbness, or we may even faint or go into shock. I remember that when I was thrown out of the car and skidded on my back on the highway, I felt pain for awhile and then felt nothing. Our bodies have ways of turning off pain when it becomes too much to endure. People vary a great deal in their pain thresholds, but we all have a breaking point. In other words, the amount of pain we can endure is not limitless. We can conclude, therefore, that there is a degree of pain we will never experience, because our bodies will turn off our sensitivity in one way or another—perhaps even by death—before we reach that point.

A similar principle operates in temptation. There is a degree of temptation that we may never experience simply because, no matter what our spirituality, we will succumb before we reach it. But Jesus Christ had no such limitation. Since He was sinless, He took the full extent of all that Satan could throw at Him. He had no shock system, no weakness limit, to turn off temptation at a certain point. Since He never succumbed, He experienced every temptation to the maximum. And He experienced it as a man, as a human being. In every way He was tempted as we are, and more. The only difference was that He never sinned. Therefore, when we come to Jesus Christ we can remember that He knows everything we know, and a great deal that we do not know, about temptation, and testing, and pain. **We do not have a high priest who cannot sympathize with our weaknesses.**

This truth was especially amazing and unbelievable to Jews. They knew that God was holy, righteous, sinless, perfect, omnipotent. They knew His divine attributes and nature and could not comprehend His experiencing pain, much less temptation. Not only this, but under the Old Covenant God's dealings with His people were more indirect, more distant. Except for special and rare instances, even faithful believers did not experience His closeness and intimacy in the way that all believers now can. Jews believed that God was incapable of sharing the feelings of men. He was too distant, too far removed in nature from man, to be able to identify with our feelings and temptations and problems.

If comprehending God's sympathy was hard for Jews, it was even harder for most Gentiles of that day. The Stoics, whose philosophy dominated much Greek and Roman culture in New Testament times, believed that God's primary attribute was apathy. Some believed that He was without feeling or emotions of any sort. The Epicureans claimed that the gods live *intermundia*, between the physical and spiritual worlds. They did not participate in either world, and so could hardly be expected to understand the feelings, problems, and needs of mortals. They were completely detached from mankind.

The idea that God could and would identify with men in their trials and temptations was revolutionary to Jew and Gentile alike. But the writer of Hebrews is saying that we have a God not only "who is there" but one "who has been here."

Weaknesses does not refer directly to sin, but to feebleness or infirmity. It refers to all the natural limitations of humanity, which, however, include liability to sin. Jesus knew firsthand the drive of human nature toward sin. His humanity was His battleground. It is here that Jesus faced and fought sin. He was victorious, but not without the most intense temptation, grief, and anguish.

In all of this struggle, however, Jesus was **without sin** (*chōris hamartia*). He was completely apart from, separated from, sin. These two Greek words express the absolute absence of sin. Though He was mercilessly tempted to sin, not the slightest taint of it ever entered His mind or was expressed in His words or actions.

Some may wonder how Jesus can completely identify with us if He did not actually sin as we do. It was Jesus' facing sin with His perfect righteousness and truth, however, that qualifies Him. Merely experiencing something does not give us understanding of it. A person can have many successful operations without understanding the least bit about surgery. On the other hand, a doctor may perform thousands of complicated and successful operations without ever having had the surgery himself. It is his knowledge of the disease or disorder and his surgical skill in treating it that qualifies him, not his having had the disease. He has great experience with the disease—much greater experience with it than any of his patients—having confronted it in all of its manifestations. Jesus never sinned, but He understands sin better than any man. He has seen it more clearly and fought it more diligently than any of us could ever be able to do.

Sinlessness alone can properly estimate sin. Jesus Christ did not sin, could not sin, had no capacity to sin. Yet His temptations were all the more terrible because He would not fall and endured them to the extreme. His sinlessness increased His sensitivity to sin. "For consider Him who has endured such hostility by sinners against Himself, so that you may not grow weary and lose heart. You have not yet resisted to the point of shedding blood in your striving against sin" (Heb. 12:3-4). If you want to talk to someone who knows what sin is about, talk to Jesus Christ. Jesus Christ knows sin, and He knows and understands our weakness. Whatever Satan brings our way, there is victory in Jesus Christ. He understands; He has been here.

Dr. John Wilson often told the following story. Booth Tucker was conducting evangelistic meetings in the great Salvation Army Citadel in Chicago. One night, after he had preached on the sympathy of Jesus, a man came forward and asked Mr. Tucker how he could talk about a loving, understanding, sympathetic God. "If your wife had just died, like mine has," the man said, "and your babies were crying for their mother who would never come back, you wouldn't be saying what you're saying."

A few days later Mr. Tucker's wife was killed in a train wreck. Her body was brought to Chicago and carried to the Citadel for the funeral. After the service the bereaved preacher looked down into the silent face of his wife and then turned to those who were attending. "The other day when I was here," he said, "a man told me that, if my wife had just died and my children were crying for their mother, I would not be able to say that Christ was understanding and sympathetic, or that He was sufficient for every need. If that man is here, I want to tell him that Christ *is* sufficient. My heart is broken, it is crushed, but it has a song, and Christ put it there. I want to tell that man that Jesus Christ speaks comfort to me today." The man was there, and he came and knelt beside the casket while Booth Tucker introduced him to Jesus Christ.

We have a sympathetic High Priest, whose priesthood is perfect and whose Person is perfect.

HIS PERFECT PROVISION

Let us therefore draw near with confidence to the throne of grace, that we may receive mercy and may find grace to help in time of need. (4:16)

The One who understands us perfectly will also provide for us perfectly. "No temptation has overtaken you but such as is common to man; and God is faithful, who will not allow you to be tempted beyond what you are able, but with the temptation will provide the way of escape also, that you may be able to endure it" (1 Cor. 10:13). Jesus Christ knows our temptations and will lead us out of them.

COME TO GOD'S THRONE OF GRACE

Again, the Holy Spirit appeals to those who are yet undecided about accepting Christ as their Savior. They should not only keep from going back into Judaism, but they should hold on to their confession of Christ and, finally—and necessarily—go on to **draw near with confidence to the throne of grace.**

Most ancient rulers were unapproachable by the common people. Some would not even allow their highest-ranking officials to come before them without permission. Queen Esther risked her life in approaching King Ahasuerus without invitation, even though she was his wife (Esther 5:1-2). Yet any penitent person, no matter how sinful and undeserving, may approach God's throne at any time for forgiveness and salvation—confident that he will be received with **mercy** and **grace.**

By Christ's sacrifice of Himself, God's throne of judgment is turned into **a throne of grace** for those who trust in Him. As the Jewish high priests once a year for centuries had sprinkled blood on the mercy seat for the people's sins, Jesus shed His blood once and for all time for the sins of everyone who believes in Him. That is His perfect provision.

The Bible speaks much of God's justice. But how terrible for us if He were only just, and not also gracious. Sinful man deserves death, the sentence of justice; but he needs salvation, the gift of grace. It is to the very throne of this grace that any person can now come with confidence and assurance. It is the **throne of grace** because grace is dispensed there.

How can anyone reject such a High Priest, such a Savior—who not only permits us to come before His throne for grace and help, but pleads with us to come in confidence? His Spirit says, "Come boldly all the way to God's throne that has been turned into a throne of grace because of Jesus. Come all the way up, receive grace and mercy when you need it—before it is too late and your heart is hard and God's 'today' is over." The **time of need** is now.

What a High Priest we have. He sympathizes and He saves. What more could He do?

Christ the Perfect Priest (5:1-10)

For every high priest taken from among men is appointed on behalf of men in things pertaining to God, in order to offer both gifts and sacrifices for sins; he can deal gently with the ignorant and misguided, since he himself also is beset with weakness; and because of it he is obligated to offer sacrifices for sins, as for the people, so also for himself. And no one takes the honor to himself, but he receives it when he is called by God, even as Aaron was. So also Christ did not glorify Himself so as to become a high priest, but He who said to Him, "Thou art My Son, today I have begotten Thee"; just as He says also in another passage, "Thou art a priest forever according to the order of Melchizedek." In the days of His flesh, He offered up both prayers and supplications with loud crying and tears to the One able to save Him from death, and He was heard because of His piety. Although He was a Son, He learned obedience from the things which He suffered. And having been made perfect, He became to all those who obey Him the source of eternal salvation, being designated by God as a high priest according to the order of Melchizekek. (5:1-10)

Among the first things a Jew might have asked another person about his religion were, "Who is your high priest? Who mediates be-

tween you and God? Who offers the sacrifices to atone for your sins?" A
Jew during the time of the early church may well have asked a Christian,
"How are your sins going to be pardoned when you have no one offering
sacrifices and no one interceding for you? How can you claim that this
new covenant supersedes and is superior to the Old Covenant made
through Moses when it leaves you without a high priest?"

The Christian would have replied, "But we *do* have a high priest, a
perfect High Priest. He *has* offered sacrifice for our sins. He does not
confine Himself to an earthly temple, nor does He have to sacrifice yearly,
much less daily. He made one sacrifice that atones for all sins ever committed, from the beginning to the end of time. That is how great a high
priest He is and how great His sacrifice was. Not only that, but our High
Priest is seated at the right hand of God and continually intercedes for
those of us who belong to Him."

The heart of the book of Hebrews (chaps. 5-9) focuses on Jesus'
high priesthood. His superior priesthood, more than anything else, makes
the New Covenant better than the Old. He has done what all the priests
together of the old economy did not do and could never have done.

The priests under the Old Covenant were bridge builders to God.
Men could not come directly into God's presence, and God therefore appointed certain men to be ushers, as it were, to bring men into His presence. The way to God was opened only as the priests offered sacrifices—
day in and day out, year after year—presenting the blood of animals to
God. The priests were God's mediators.

THE ONE, PERFECT GREAT HIGH PRIEST

But with the sacrifice of Jesus Christ on the cross, need for the
Temple and for the Levitical priesthood was ended. There was no longer
a requirement for a high priest such as those who succeeded Aaron, or for
any human priest at all. Jesus was both High Priest and sacrifice, and
provided eternally for man an opening into God's presence. At His crucifixion, the curtain of the Temple was torn in two, exposing the Holy of
Holies to anyone who would come to God through the Son. In one perfect act of sacrifice, Jesus Christ accomplished what thousands upon
thousands of sacrifices by a multitude of priests never accomplished. He
opened the way to God permanently, so that any man at any time by faith
in Christ might enter into God's presence.

THE QUALIFICATIONS FOR PRIEST

**For every high priest taken from among men is appointed on behalf
of men in things pertaining to God, in order to offer both gifts and**

sacrifices for sins; he can deal gently with the ignorant and mis-guided, since he himself also is beset with weakness; and because of it he is obligated to offer sacrifices for sins, as for the people, so also for himself. And no one takes the honor to himself, but he receives it when he is called by God, even as Aaron was. (5:1-4)

These four verses state the three basic qualifications for a Jewish **high priest.** He was appointed by God, was sympathetic with those to whom he ministered, and offered sacrifices on their behalf. The following six verses show how Jesus Christ fulfills those qualifications.

APPOINTED BY GOD FROM AMONG MEN

HE HAD TO BE A MAN

A priest has to partake of the nature of the persons for whom he officiates. A true **high priest,** therefore, had to be **taken from among men;** that is, he had to be a man. God did not choose angels to be priests. Angels do not have the nature of men. They cannot truly understand men and they do not have open communication with men. Only a man could be subject to the temptations of men, could experience suffering like men, and thereby be able to minister to men in an understanding and merciful way. Only a man could rightly minister on behalf of men.

Remembering to whom this epistle was written, we can more easi-ly see the importance of the point being made here about Jesus Christ. To be the perfect High Priest, in fact to be a high priest at all, He had to be a man. This much, of course, was completely clear and acceptable to Jews. Their problem was with the incarnation—*God's* becoming a man. The Ho-ly Spirit very simply answers the problem of the incarnation with the one basic point: the Messiah, who is God, could not be a true high priest unless He were a man. Unless God could feel what men feel and go through what men go through, He would have no experiential under-standing of those whom He represented.

Under the old economy, even after the covenants with Abraham and with Moses, God was unapproachable. At the Fall, God drove Ad-am and Eve out of the garden and man no longer had access to the Lord's presence. In the wilderness, the people were warned not to come too near Sinai, where God chose to manifest Himself to Moses when giving the covenant of the law. In the Tabernacle and in the Temple God was behind a veil and could be approached only throuqh the high priest.

But in sending His Son, Jesus Christ, God no longer kept Him-self aloof, transcendent, and separate from men. He entered into the human world and felt everything that men will ever feel in order that He might be a sympathetic, merciful, and faithful High Priest. If God had never become man, He never could have been a high priest, a mediator, or an intercessor. He never could have offered the perfect and absolute sacrifice for the sins of His people, which divine justice required. The incarnation was not an option; it was an absolute necessity. It was an imperative if men were to be saved.

John Calvin said, "It was necessary for Christ to become a real man. For as we are very far from God, we stand in a manner before him in the person of our priest, which could not be were he not one of us. Hence, that the Son of God has a nature in common with us, does not diminish his dignity, but commends it the more to us for he is fitted to reconcile us to God because he is man." God had to come down to where we are in order to pick us up and bring us back to Himself.

HE HAD TO BE GOD'S MAN

But a true priest could not be just any man. He had to be **appointed** by God. It was not an office that a man could fill simply because of his own plans or ambition. He had to be God's man—not simply in the sense of being faithful and obedient to God but in the sense of being selected by God. He was **appointed on behalf of men** but *by* God. "No one takes the honor to himself, but receives it when he is called by God, even as Aaron was" (v. 4; cf. 8:3).

When the priesthood was first established, Moses was instructed, "Then bring near to yourself Aaron your brother, and his sons with him, from among the sons of Israel, to minister as priest to Me—Aaron, Nadab and Abihu, Eleazar and Ithamar, Aaron's sons" (Ex. 28:1). From the beginning of the priesthood, the priests not only were to minister for God but by His appointment. When Korah, Dathan, and Abiram insisted on trying to democratize the priesthood and claimed that any Israelite could be a priest, the Lord caused the earth to swallow them up (Num. 16).

SYMPATHETIC WITH MEN

He can deal gently with the ignorant and misguided, since he himself also is beset with weakness. (5:2)

Omniscience knows everything; perfect sympathy feels everything. Christ did not need to learn any information when He came to earth. He was omniscient, all-knowing. But He chose to participate in men's feelings personally so that he could also be sympathetic, all-feeling. A true high priest had to be sympathetic with those to whom he ministered. A true high priest would be completely involved in the human situation, completely bound up in the bundle of life. He needed to live among men as a man, to feel with them in their highs and in their lows, so He could **deal gently** with them.

Metriopatheō, besides meaning "to deal gently," also means to treat with mildness or moderation. In the context of Hebrews 5:2, it can carry the idea of being in the middle of things—in two ways. First is the meaning of being in the midst of, being fully involved. The other is that of taking a middle ground—of knowing and understanding, but of avoiding extremes. A person with this characteristic would, for example, show a certain balance between irritation and apathy in the face of wrongdoing. He would be patient with the wrongdoer but not condone the wrong, be understanding but not indulgent.

A better example would be in relation to grief or danger. A person who is either too sympathetic or too apathetic cannot help someone in trouble. The one who is too sympathetic will himself be engulfed by the problem, becoming too grief stricken or too scared to be of help. On the other hand, the one who is apathetic possibly will not even recognize a problem someone else is having and, in any case, will not be concerned about helping. In the middle is the person metriopatheō describes. He can fully indentify with the person having a problem without losing his perspective and judgment. A true high priest needed this characteristic. He had to experience the extremes of human emotions and temptations while being stronger than them. Thereby He would be able to deal gently with those to whom he ministered, without becoming victim of their misery.

The ones with whom the priest is to **deal gently** are those who are **ignorant and misguided,** that is, those who sin through ignorance. The Old Covenant provision was: "The priest shall make atonement before the Lord for the person who goes astray when he sins unintentionally, making atonement for him that he may be forgiven" (Num. 15:28). The priest ministered only in behalf of those who sinned in ignorance and thus went astray. In all of the Old Testament economy, there is absolutely no provision made for the unrepentant, deliberate, and defiant lawbreaker. There is none. "But the person who does anything defiantly, whether he is native or an alien, that one is blaspheming the Lord; and that person shall be cut off from among his people" (Num. 15:30).

So the emphasis here is on sympathy. The high priest was meant to have sympathy toward those who ignorantly went astray. Since the Jewish priest himself was a sinner, he had the natural capacity, and he ought to have had the sensitivity, to feel a little bit of what others were feeling.

SACRIFICING FOR MEN

In his mediatorial work, the high priest made two basic kinds of offerings: gifts and sacrifices (v. 1; cf. 8:3; 9:9).

OFFERING GIFTS

In the broadest sense, gifts included all the money, jewelry, or other such valuables people gave to the Lord through the priests. But I believe that the references in Hebrews to gifts refer specifically to the grain, or meal, offering—the only bloodless offering prescribed under the Old Covenant. It was a thanksgiving and dedication offering (see Lev. 2).

The grain offering consisted of fine flour and oil, mixed with frankincense to give a pleasant aroma, and sometimes baked or fried into a cake. Part of the offering was burned on the altar, and the remainder belonged to the priests to eat. No lemon or honey could be used, because these fermented. A small measure of salt was required, because it preserved. Restricting that which would spoil and requiring that which would preserve symbolized a dedication that was lasting. The offering represented the dedication of a person and all his possessions to God in complete thanks for what God had done.

OFFERING SACRIFICES

And because of it he is obligated to offer sacrifices for sins, as for the people, so also for himself. (5:3)

The **sacrifices,** however, were for the expiation of sins. They could not take away the sin tendency or the sin capacity, but were made for the forgiveness of particular sins. Consequently, they had to be continually repeated—day after day, year after year. Offering sacrifices was the main work of the priest. And since he himself sinned, he had to make sacrifices **for himself** as well as **for the people.**

THE PERFECTLY QUALIFIED PRIEST

So also Christ did not glorify Himself so as to become a high priest, but He who said to Him, "Thou art My Son, today I have begotten Thee"; just as He says also in another passage, "Thou art a priest forever according to the order of Melchizedek." (5:5-6)

Verses 5-10 show how Jesus met all the qualifications for high priest mentioned in verses 1-4, and more.

APPOINTED BY GOD

First of all, Jesus was chosen, sent, and honored by God the Father. Again the writer chooses quotations from the Old Testament—**Thou art My Son, today I have begotten Thee** (Ps. 2:7) and **Thou art a priest forever according to the order of Melchizedek** (Ps. 110:4)—to support his point. The Jewish readers of Hebrews knew that both passages referred to the Messiah. They knew that the Messiah was to be a great king and priest, appointed by God. Those Old Testament passages confirmed that.

Yet even though He was the divine Son, Jesus did not take the position for Himself or give honor to Himself. He told the Jewish leaders who questioned Him, "If I glorify Myself, My glory is nothing; it is My Father who glorifies Me, of whom you say, 'He is our God' " (John 8:54). God invested Jesus with the authority and honor of high priest **according to the order of Melchizedek.**

Melchizedek will be discussed in some detail under Hebrews 7, but a brief word here is necessary. He was a king-priest who lived in the time of Abraham, and whose ancestry is completely unknown. He was king of Salem (the ancient name for Jerusalem) and was a priest of the true God (Gen. 14:18). He lived many centuries before the Aaronic priesthood was established and his priesthood was unending (Heb. 7:3), unlike that of Aaron, which began in the time of Moses and ended in A.D. 70, when the Temple was destroyed. His priesthood, therefore, was superior to Aaron's in two ways. Melchizedek was a king, whereas Aaron was not, and his priesthood was perpetual, whereas Aaron's was temporary. Melchizedek's priesthood, therefore, is a better picture of Christ's than even that of Aaron.

SYMPATHETIC WITH MEN

In the days of His flesh, He offered up both prayers and supplications with loud crying and tears to the One able to save Him from death, and He was heard because of His piety. Although He was a Son, He learned obedience from the things which He suffered. (5:7-8)

Second, Jesus Christ was sympathetic with men—He was identified with them, understood them, felt with them. He *was* Himself a man, just as surely as any high priest that served in the Tabernacle or Temple.

"The days of His flesh" were an interlude in the life of Jesus Christ, who existed before and after His earthly life. But they were an extremely important and necessary interlude. Among other things, "He offered up both prayers and supplications," because of the anguish He faced in becoming sin for those who believed in Him. In the Garden of Gethsemane on the night before He went to the cross, Jesus prayed and agonized so intensely that He sweat great drops of blood. His heart was broken at the prospect of bearing sin. He felt the power of sin and He felt temptation. He cried. He shed tears. He hurt. He grieved. What He had always known in His omniscience, He learned in a new way on earth by experience. He could not have been a fully sympathetic high priest had He not experienced what we experience and felt what we feel.

When Jesus prayed to "the One able to save Him from death," He was not hoping to escape either the cross or the grave. It was for this very purpose that He came to earth (John 12:27). A more accurate translation of Hebrews 5:7 is, ". . . save Him *out* of death." Jesus was not asking to be saved from dying but to be saved out of death—that is, to be saved from remaining in death. He was not asking to avoid the cross but to be assured of the resurrection (cf. Ps. 16:8-11).

Jesus was heard by His Father **because of His piety.** The Greek word *eulabeia,* translated "piety," can mean reverential fear or awe, as reflected in the King James. It carries the idea of being devoutly submissive. Jesus recognized God as sovereign and committed Himself to the Father.

Although He was a Son, He learned obedience from the things which He suffered. (5:8)

Often the best, and sometimes the only, way to learn sympathy is by suffering ourselves what another is suffering. Suffering is a very skilled teacher. We can read about and hear about the pain of being burned. We can even see people being burned. But until we have been burned ourselves, we cannot completely sympathize with a burn victim. I had read about, and even seen, many automobile accidents; but only after I was involved in one that almost took my life did I realize how horrible they can be.

Jesus had to learn certain things by suffering. He was given no exemption from hardship and pain. Even though He was God's Son, God in human flesh, He was called to suffer. He learned the full meaning of the cost of **obedience,** all the way to death, **from the things which He suffered,** and God therefore affirmed Him as a perfect High Priest.

That is the kind of high priest we need—one who knows and understands what we are going through. When we go to the Lord in prayer and fall on our knees before Him and say, "God, this problem, this loss, this pain is breaking my heart," how wonderful to feel His arms around us and to sense in our hearts that He is saying, "I know. I know."

SACRIFICING FOR MEN

And having been made perfect, He became to all those who obey Him the source of eternal salvation." (5:9)

In His suffering and death, Jesus fulfilled the third requirement for high priest. He offered the sacrifice of Himself and thereby became the **perfect** High Priest and the source of eternal salvation. Jesus went through everything He had to go through, and accomplished all He needed to, so He could be such a perfect High Priest. He was not, of course, **made perfect** in the sense of having His nature improved. He was eternally perfect in righteousness, holiness, wisdom, knowledge, truth, power, and in every other virtue and capability. Neither His nature nor His person changed. He became perfect in the sense that He completed His qualification course for becoming the eternal High Priest.

In offering His sacrifice, however, Jesus differed in two very important ways from other high priests. First, He did not have to make a sacrifice for Himself before He could offer it for others. Second, His sacrifice was once-and-for-all. It did not have to be repeated every day, or even every year or every century.

By His death, Jesus opened the way of **eternal salvation.** All the priests of all time could not provide eternal salvation. They could only provide momentary forgiveness. But by one act, one offering, one sacrifice, Jesus Christ perfected forever those who are His. The perfect High Priest makes perfect those who accept His perfect sacrifice, those **who obey Him.**

The **obedience** mentioned here of **those who obey Him** is not that regarding commandments, rules, and regulations. It is not obedience to the law. It is "the obedience of faith" (Rom. 1:5). God wants us to obey Him by believing in Christ. True obedience, just as true works, is first of all true believing. "This is the work of God," Jesus said, "that you believe in Him whom He has sent" (John 6:29). Trust in Jesus Christ is the *work* of faith and the *obedience* of faith.

Sadly and tragically, all people do not believe. And whoever does not believe does not truly obey, no matter how moral, well-meaning, religious, and sincere. In First and Second Thessalonians, Paul speaks of the two responses to the gospel—the only two possible responses. In the second letter he tells of God's retribution on those who "do not know God" and who "do not obey the gospel of our Lord Jesus" (1:8). In the first letter, by contrast, he praises the missionary work of the faithful Thessalonian Christians in Macedonia and Achaia (1:8). Their obedience *in* the faith brought others to obedience *to* the faith—and to the gift of **eternal salvation.**

The Tragedy of Rejecting Full Revelation—part 1
(5:11-14)

Concerning him we have much to say, and it is hard to explain, since you have become dull of hearing. For though by this time you ought to be teachers, you have need again for someone to teach you the elementary principles of the oracles of God, and you have come to need milk and not solid food. For everyone who partakes only of milk is not accustomed to the word of righteousness, for he is a babe. But solid food is for the mature, who because of practice have their senses trained to discern good and evil. (5:11-14)

We have come to a section of Hebrews of which there are numerous and often conflicting interpretations, even among evangelicals. The overall passage is 5:11—6:12, and deals with spiritual maturity. The first two parts (5:11-14 and 6:1-8) are, I believe, addressed to unbelievers, whereas the third (6:9-12) is to believers.

THE CONTRAST BETWEEN CHRISTIANITY AND JUDAISM

Throughout the book of Hebrews, the many comparisons and

contrasts are basically between Christianity and Judaism. This truth is essential to proper interpretation of the epistle.

Most books of the Bible have a major theme, or a group of closely related themes. One of the first rules of sound biblical hermeneutics (interpretation) is to discover this central theme and to render all other interpretations in light of it. The gospel of John, for example, contains many profound and wonderful truths about God and His plan for man. But the central, overriding message of that gospel is the deity of Jesus Christ. A person who misses this truth cannot fully and properly understand the other truths that John presents in the book.

The central theme and message of the book of Hebrews is the superiority of the New Covenant to the Old, that is, of Christianity to Judaism. Within this theme are the subthemes of the superiority of the new priesthood to the old, the new sacrifice to the old ones, the new Mediator to the old ones, and so on. This is the key that unlocks every section of Hebrews, and to use any other key is, I believe, to make forced entry.

In the book of Hebrews the Holy Spirit is not contrasting two kinds of Christianity. He is not contrasting immature Christians and mature ones. He is contrasting Judaism and Christianity, the unsaved Jew in Judaism and the redeemed Jew in Christianity. He is contrasting the substance and the shadow, the pattern and the reality, the visible and the invisible, the facsimile and the real thing, the type and the anti-type, the picture and the actual.

The Old Testament essentially is God's revelation of pictures and types, which are fulfilled in Christ in the New Testament. The book of Hebrews, therefore, compares and contrasts the two parts of God's revelation that our division of the Bible reflects.

A THIRD WARNING

Concerning him we have much to say, and it is hard to explain, since you have become dull of hearing. (5:11)

Him, of course, refers to Melchizedek, who has just been mentioned (vv. 6, 10). Before he explains the order of Melchizedek (in chap. 7), however, the writer gives his third parenthetical warning. As we have already noted, interspersed throughout Hebrews are several warnings to the intellectually convinced Jews who were on the edge of decision but had not yet come to faith in Christ. These warnings could also function in the context of encouragement and counsel to those Jews who *had* trusted Christ but were being tempted to turn back into Judaism because of doubts, criticism, and, for some, even persecution. But the main thrust was to unbelievers. The first warning (2:1-4) was about their neglecting the gospel, and the second (3:7-19) was about hardening their hearts to it.

The third warning concerns spiritual maturity—the danger of staying with the elemental truths and promises of the Old Covenant, now that it has been superseded by the New. This warning is also, I believe, to the same group as are the other two—to unbelieving Jews who knew a great deal about the gospel but who had not gone all the way to accepting it for themselves. Some may have made a shallow profession of faith but not actually believed. They are told of the danger of not claiming the blessing of the New Covenant, apart from which they cannot have eternal life. They are close, yet so far away.

UNBELIEVING BABES

There are, of course, many exhortations in the New Testament for immature Christians to grow up. Throughout the history of the church there has been need for such counsel, but I do not think that is what is given here. He is saying to hesitant Jews still hanging on to Judaism, "Come on to completeness, to maturity, in the New Covenant." This interpretation is not the most traditional, but I think it is consistent with the context of the whole book and is defensible. The warning and the appeal, as before, are evangelistic. The maturity being called for is not that of a Christian's growing in the faith, but of an unbeliever's coming into the faith—into the full-grown, mature truths and blessings of the New Covenant. It is the same maturity or perfection (from *teleioō*) as in 10:1 and 14, which can only refer to salvation, not Christian growth.

The Old Covenant was the spiritual alphabet. The Old Covenant was the baby talk, the letters and the sounds of a child's first vocabulary. You do not use an encyclopedia to start teaching a child to read. You use pictures and other visual objects. You point to the picture or the object and say, "This is a ball. That is a horse. This is a fish." Later on you begin explaining these things. You tell him that balls are round, horses eat hay, and that fish "breathe" water. God's revelation to man progressed in a similar way. The Old Testament was His elementary, foundational teaching. It began with "pictures." God was saying, in effect, "This is a feast you are to celebrate. This is a sacrifice you must make. These are the clothes a high priest should wear, and this is a ceremonial washing that is required for certain occasions." Each had purposes and benefits for the times for which it was given. But primarily they were pictures of things to come, which the people were not then ready to understand. They were symbols and shadows of realities in Christ and the New Covenant (Col. 2:17).

Now that the New Covenant had come in Jesus Christ, the writer of Hebrews is saying to his fellow Jews, "Leave the pictures, the milk and baby food, of the Old Testament. Come to the fulfilled realities and the solid food of the New Testament. Leave Judaism and come to Christ."

DULLNESS PREVENTS UNDERSTANDING

So before they could possibly understand the significance of Jesus' priesthood being like Melchizedek's, the readers needed to get beyond their limited, immature understanding of God. A key mark of that immaturity was simply dullness of hearing, spiritual lethargy. The relation of Melchizedek and his priesthood to Christ is rich and meaningful, and important to the flow of the book, but it cannot be understood by unbelievers, even ones who intellectually accept the gospel. "A natural man does not accept the things of the Spirit of God . . . because they are spiritually appraised" (1 Cor. 2:14). These borderline believers were being told that there was no use going into the deeper things of the New Covenant at that time, because they had become **dull of hearing.**

Dull comes from the Greek *nōthros,* which is made up of the words for "no" and "push." Literally, therefore, it means "no push"—slow, sluggish. When used of a person it generally meant intellectually numb or thick. In the context of this passage, however, it primarily indicates spiritual dullness.

When a person is spiritually dull, he is difficult to teach. These Jews had been lulled into sleep because of neglect and hardness of heart, and they would have to awaken and become alert if they were to appreciate the truth, significance, and necessity of the New Covenant. They could not truly understand the gospel, of course, until they put their trust in the Bearer of the gospel. To be able to see its importance, they had to spiritually "wake up and pay attention."

These lethargic unbelievers have many counterparts today. People hear the gospel and are stirred and excited. Spiritual understanding appears to begin, but the more they hear it without accepting it, the more spiritually sluggish they become. They neglect to act on the truth they know and become more and more hardened to it, often while claiming to admire and respect it. They become more and more insulated from spiritual truth and understanding, and from spiritual life itself.

Though, as we have noted, this passage is not addressed to believers, the same principle applies. When we do not trust and act on any part of God's truth that we know, we become hardened to it and less and less likely to benefit from it. Or when we avoid delving into the deeper parts of God's Word, being satisfied with the "basics," we insulate ourselves from the Holy Spirit to that extent. From a somewhat different perspective, a teacher or preacher can suffer spiritually when he does not bother to teach and preach the deeper, and sometimes harder, truths of Scripture—or is afraid to do so. The more he resists or neglects to teach them, the less they will mean to him. Paul was able to say that he did not fail to declare the whole counsel, or purpose, of God (Acts 20:27). He would not skip over or neglect any part of God's Word. No faithful servant of God will accommodate his teaching to the dull, lazy Christian.

DULLNESS IS GRADUAL

The implication of 5:11 is that those who were dull of hearing had once been alert and interested, perhaps even eager, to learn more of the gospel. They did not start out dull; they became that way gradually. These were doubtlessly among the ones who had "once been enlightened" and had "tasted of the heavenly gift" (6:4). At one time they had been stirred and moved and open. They were once on the brink of salvation. By now, however, they had sunk into a rather settled state of spiritual stupor.

DULLNESS IS UNPRODUCTIVE

For though by this time you ought to be teachers, you have need again for someone to teach you the elementary principles of the oracles of God, and you have come to need milk and not solid food. (5:12)

Because of the length of time they had been under instruction of New Testament truth, they should have known enough to be teaching it themselves. But because they had never truly accepted it, they had not grown in it—and *could not* grow in it. They had been exposed to a great deal of God's truth, on most of which they could probably have passed an examination. They had the truth in a certain factual and superficial way, but the truth did not have them.

Paul charged in Romans, "But if you bear the name 'Jew,' and rely upon the Law, and boast in God, and know His will, and approve the things that are essential, being instructed out of the Law, and are confident that you yourself are a guide to the blind, a light to those who are in darkness, a corrector of the foolish, a teacher of the immature, having in the Law the embodiment of knowledge and of the truth, you, therefore, who teach another, do you not teach yourself?" (2:17-21). In other words, they prided themselves in the idea that they were great religious teachers. But in Hebrews the Holy Spirit says explicitly what is implicit in the passage from Romans: these Jews not only were unqualified to teach, but needed to go back to kindergarten. They did not understand the ABCs of their own faith. That was evident by their unwillingness to recognize its clear fulfillment.

I have known many professing Christians like that, some of them well-known theologians. They know Scripture and the biblical languages well. They know what the Bible says. But they do not know, or accept, what it means. For the time and study they have put in, they ought to be teachers of the Word of God. But they do not even comprehend its fundamentals. They have been "advanced" students of Scripture for decades, and yet they do not even know Jesus Christ. They may teach, but it is not the pure Word of Christ that they teach.

Some years ago at a Christian youth conference I spoke on choosing the right life partner. After one session a young girl came up to me and asked to talk. As we sat on the chapel steps, she began telling me that her boyfriend said that whatever a person does, in sex or in anything else, is all right as long as no one else is hurt. After a little questioning I discovered that her boyfriend was 21 and she was only 14. When I briefly reminded her of what God says about sex outside of marriage, she hung her head and said, "I know that. You know what I need? I need to be saved." She explained that she not only had been raised in a church but that her father was a pastor. I replied, "Then you know how to be saved." "No," she said, "I don't. I have heard my father preach on it but I don't understand it."

Here was a perfect illustration of spiritual sluggishness. This girl had heard the gospel all her life, but she had rejected Jesus Christ for so long that the gospel now was foggy to her. She could not understand it anymore. She thought her father's sermons were boring and made no sense. She had become totally indifferent to God's Word. After I carefully delineated the gospel to her, we prayed together and she confessed Christ as her Lord and Savior.

Dullness Requires Being Taught Again

Because they had become spiritually listless, the informed but unbelieving Jews had **need again for someone to teach** them. Like the young girl mentioned above, they needed to start all over in the **elementary principles of the oracles of God.**

THE FIRST PRINCIPLES OF GOD'S ORACLES

What are the **elementary principles of the oracles of God?** *Stoicheia* ("elementary principles") means that which comes first. In reference to language, it meant the letters of the alphabet as the basic parts of words—the ABCs. In science it was used of the basic physical elements, and in math of the basics of proof.

Oracles of God does not refer to the gospel. Those being addressed were Jews, and to them the oracles of God meant the Old Testament. The oracles of God were the laws of God, the mind of God revealed in the Old Testament. Having been entrusted with God's oracles was a great advantage for the Jews (Rom. 3:1-2). It was the rudiments of the Old Testament revelation, the law, that they needed to be taught again. They had had considerable exposure to the New Covenant, but they did not even comprehend the Old, as evidenced by their lack of ability to handle deeper truth about Melchizedek.

These Jews did not even understand the meaning of their own law. They needed someone to go back and show them the pictures again. They were not ready to read a book; they had to go back to the ABCs— the elementary picture-truths of ordinances, ceremonies, sacrifices, holy days, washings. These foreshadowed Christ, and they could not recognize Him unless they understood the pictures.

THE NEED TO BECOME MATURE

The Old Testament is the alphabet; the New Testament is the complete, mature message. "Before faith came, we were kept in custody under the law, being shut up to the faith which was later to be revealed. Therefore the Law has become our tutor to lead us to Christ, that we may be justified by faith" (Gal. 3:23-24). The law was a tutor, a child trainer, that taught the first and basic truths about God. In the New Covenant we are not under the tutor anymore. We have grown up. That is the point being made here. Christ has arrived, the shadows are replaced with substance, the picturebook is replaced with great writings that we can read. The alphabet is replaced with the full composition. The types have given way to the truth.

PROGRESS OR REGRESS

Again they are told, **you have come** (cf. v. 11, "you have become"). A baby does not **come** to need milk. He is born with that need. The only person who *comes* to need milk, to need baby food, is one who has gone back to childhood. Instead of becoming more mature, these Jews were becoming less. They were slipping back into spiritual infancy.

If you do not progress you regress. By neglect and hardness they had come to the place where they could only handle **milk** again. It is easy for people to hear the gospel, and then hear it and hear it and hear it until it becomes commonplace and meaningless to them. Instead of pursuing the truth of Christ and giving their lives to Him, they become spiritually sluggish and stagnant. They become dull of hearing and slow of understanding, spiritually retarded. They must be fed again like babies.

These Jews who had so long spurned Christ, some of them while professing His name, were not able to take the heavy food of Melchizedek priesthood truth. They would have to start again from the bottom up, gradually increasing their spiritual perception and understanding.

For everyone who partakes only of milk is not accustomed to the word of righteousness, for he is a babe. (5:13)

A spiritual infant is **not accustomed** (*apeiros*) to deeper truths. He cannot digest them, any more than a physical infant can digest a steak. The idea is that of being inexperienced, unskillful, and therefore unprepared and incapable. The spiritual system, like the physical, has to grow in order to handle that which is more difficult. A child can get something out of looking at a picturebook but nothing out of looking at a textbook. A spiritual child could get some meaning out of the pictures and types of the Old Testament but not out of the **word of righteousness** of the gospel.

But solid food is for the mature, who because of practice have their senses trained to discern good and evil. (5:14)

The contrast here is simple. The one who continues to feed only on God's elementary revelations is not going to grow, not going to have any discernment. A small child will stick almost anything into his mouth, touch anything he can reach, go anywhere he can manage to crawl—with no concept of what is **good** for him and what is bad, what is helpful and what is dangerous. The mature adult, on the other hand, has developed considerable discernment. He is careful about what he eats, what he does, where he goes.

The same principle operates in the spiritual realm. The **mature** believer has discernment about what is right and wrong, true and false, helpful and harmful, righteous and unrighteous.

But because the writer *does,* in chapter 7, go on to explain the significance of the order of Melchizedek, it seems he expects his readers to mature spiritually before they read this part of his message. That is, he seems to believe they will soon be saved, for it is only salvation, the new birth, that could immediately put them on the level of spiritual maturity necessary to understand **the word of righteousness.** He seems to say, "Leave Judaism and, in the instant of salvation, grow up." Judaism is the infancy they are to leave in order to go on to the maturity of manhood by faith in the New Covenant Messiah.

The Tragedy of Rejecting Full Revelation—part 2
(6:1-8)

13

Therefore leaving the elementary teaching about the Christ, let us press on to maturity, not laying again a foundation of repentance from dead works and of faith toward God, of instruction about washings, and laying on of hands, and the resurrection of the dead, and eternal judgment. And this we shall do, if God permits. For in the case of those who have once been enlightened and have tasted of the heavenly gift and have been made partakers of the Holy Spirit, and have tasted the good word of God and the powers of the age to come, and then have fallen away, it is impossible to renew them again to repentance, since they again crucify to themselves the Son of God, and put Him to open shame. For ground that drinks the rain which often falls upon it and brings forth vegetation useful to those for whose sake it is also tilled, receives a blessing from God; but if it yields thorns and thistles, it is worthless and close to being cursed, and it ends up being burned. (6:1-8)

People can go to church for years and hear the gospel over and over again, even be faithful church members, and never really make a commitment to Jesus Christ. That kind of person is addressed here. The writer is specifically talking to Jews who had heard the gospel and not accepted Christ as Savior and Lord, but the warning applies to anyone,

Jew or Gentile. All who know the truth of God's saving grace in Jesus Christ, who perhaps have seen it change the lives of many of their friends and family members, who may even have made some profession of faith in Him, yet turn around and walk away from full acceptance, are given the severest possible warning. Persistent rejection of Christ may result in such persons' passing the point of no return spiritually, of losing forever the opportunity of salvation. That is what always happens to one who is indecisive. He eventually follows his evil heart of unbelief and turns his back forever on the living God.

Such people often have adopted a form of Christianity, but they do not have the reality of it. Jesus says of them, "Not everyone who says to Me, 'Lord, Lord,' will enter the kingdom of heaven; but he who does the will of My Father who is in heaven. Many will say to Me on that day, 'Lord, Lord, did we not prophesy in Your name, and in Your name cast out demons, and in Your name perform many miracles?' And then I will declare to them, 'I never knew you; depart from Me, you who practice lawlessness' " (Matt. 7:21-23). This is the issue here in the parenthetical statement to unbelievers from the writer of Hebrews.

Unlike a knife, truth becomes sharper with use, which for truth comes by acceptance and obedience. A truth that is heard but not accepted and followed becomes dull and meaningless. The more we neglect it, the more immune to it we become. By not accepting the gospel when it was still "news," these first century Jews had begun to grow indifferent to it and had become spiritually sluggish, neglectful, and hard. Because of the disuse of their knowledge of the gospel, they now could not bring themselves to make the right decision about it. They were, in fact, in danger of making a desperately wrong decision, of turning around because of pressure and persecution and completely going back to Judaism.

That was the situation the unbelieving Jews faced, and it is the theme of 5:11-14. Spiritually they were growing dull, hard, and stupid. The solution is given to them in chapter 6.

Therefore leaving the elementary teaching about the Christ, let us press on to maturity, not laying again a foundation of repentance from dead works and of faith toward God, of instruction about washings, and laying on of hands, and the resurrection of the dead, and eternal judgment. (6:1-2)

The key ideas are **leaving** and **press on to maturity,** and are really two parts of the same idea. Together they are the first step in these Jews' becoming spiritually mature. They had to leave once and for all their ties with the Old Covenant, with Judaism, and accept Jesus Christ as Savior. They should do it immediately, without further hesitation. The maturity that salvation brings is not a process. It is an instantaneous miracle. The maturity about which this passage is talking is that of leaving the ABCs of the Old Covenant to come to the full revelation and blessing of the New.

Leaving in the Greek is *aphiēmi*, which means to forsake, to put away, let alone, disregard, put off. It refers to total detachment, total separation, from a previous location or condition. *The Expositor's Greek Testament* translates Hebrews 6:1, "Therefore let us abandon [give up] the elementary teaching about Christ." Alford comments, "Therefore leaving (as behind, and done with; in order to go on to another thing)."

In 1 Corinthians 7, Paul uses *aphiēmi* in speaking of a Christian husband's not sending away (that is, divorcing) his unbelieving wife. Divorce is total marital separation, complete abandonment of the relationship. It is wrong in relation to marriage but mandatory in relation to leaving Judaism for Christ. The unbelieving Jew must completely divorce himself from his former religion before he can be saved.

The same Greek word is often used of forgiveness of sins (as in Matt. 9:2, 5, 6; Rom. 4:7; and James 5:15). When we are forgiven, our sins are put away from us, separated from us, divorced from us. In Matthew 15:14 the same term is used to speak of separating ourselves from false teachers, and in Mark 1:20 it is used of James's and John's leaving their father, Zebedee, in order to follow Jesus. As far as their life's work was concerned, they abandoned, completely separated themselves from, their father and his fishing business.

The **elementary teaching about the Christ** (Messiah) that the unbelieving Jews were to leave was the Old Testament teaching about Him—another indication that it is not immature Christians ("babes") that are being addressed. We are never to leave the basics, the elementary teachings, of the gospel, no matter how mature we grow in the faith. Remember, the issue here is not that of growing in spiritual maturity as a Christian, but of coming into the first stage of spiritual maturity by *becoming* a Christian. It is a matter of dropping, leaving, putting away, that which we have been holding onto and taking up something entirely new. Therefore it can only be a reference to unbelievers, because at no time does the Word of God suggest that a Christian drop the basics of Christianity and go on to something else.

It is the provisions and principles of the Old Covenant, of Judaism, that are to be dropped. It is not a question of adding to what one has. It is a question of abandoning what you have for something else. This is precisely what the Holy Spirit asked the Hebrews to do—to abandon the shadows, the types, the pictures, and the sacrifices of the old economy and come to the reality of the New Covenant in Jesus Christ. A paraphrase could be, "Leave the pictures of the Messiah and go on to the Messiah Himself," or "Drop the Old Covenant and accept the New."

INCOMPLETE OLD TESTAMENT FEATURES

The **foundation,** the Old Covenant, had six features that are pointed out in verses 1-2. These are: **repentance from dead works, faith toward God, instruction about washings, laying on of hands, the resurrection of the dead,** and **eternal judgment.** These are not, as is often interpreted, elementary Christian truths that are to be abandoned in order to go on to maturity. They are Old Testament concepts. To be sure, they pointed to the gospel, but they are not themselves part of the gospel.

REPENTANCE FROM DEAD WORKS

Repentance from dead works is turning away from evil deeds, deeds that bring death. "For if the blood of goats and bulls and the ashes of a heifer sprinkling those who have been defiled, sanctify for the cleansing of the flesh, how much more will the blood of Christ, who through the eternal Spirit offered Himself without blemish to God, cleanse your conscience from dead works to serve the living God?" (Heb. 9:13-14). "The soul who sins will die," said Ezekiel (18:4). In the New Testament the truth is expressed as, "The wages of sin is death" (Rom. 6:23). The Old Testament taught that a man should repent and turn from his evil works that brought about death. But this Old Testament pattern is only the first half of repentance. Men only knew that they were to turn away from evil works and turn toward God. That was the whole doctrine they knew.

In John the Baptist's preaching, and even in Jesus' own early ministry, the basic message was, "Repent, for the kingdom of heaven is at hand" (Matt. 3:2; 4:17). Only repentance was preached. Turn from evil toward God. But the doctrine of repentance becomes mature, complete, in Jesus Christ. Paul reminded the elders of the Ephesian church of his "solemnly testifying to both Jews and Greeks of repentance toward God and faith in our Lord Jesus Christ" (Acts 20:21). In his defense before King Agrippa, Paul mentioned that he had "kept declaring both to those of Damascus first, and also at Jerusalem and then throughout all the region of Judea, and even to the Gentiles, that they should repent and turn to God, performing deeds appropriate to repentance" (Acts 26:20). But he went on to explain that the focus of this message was Jesus Christ and His work of salvation (v. 23). It no longer did any good simply to turn from evil works toward God. A person could come to God only through Jesus Christ.

Now that the New Covenant is in effect, repentance is meaningless without faith in Jesus Christ. "No one comes to the Father, but through Me," said Jesus (John 14:6). A person who, no matter how sincerely, seeks to repent of his sins and turn to God apart from Christ will never reach God. Jesus Christ is the only way to Himself that God has provided.

Repentance from dead works is simply turning from evil, and is an important and wonderful truth of the Old Testament. But it is not complete. It is fulfilled, made effective, only by a person's also coming to Jesus Christ in faith. An incomplete dealing with sin must be abandoned for a complete one.

FAITH TOWARD GOD

The meaning of **faith toward God** has already been touched on. It does no good at all today to have faith in God unless there is also faith in His Son, Jesus Christ, who is the only way to God. Peter said, "Repent, and let each of you be baptized in the name of Jesus Christ for the forgiveness of your sins" (Acts 2:38). There is no acceptable repentance apart from faith in Christ. The only repentance that "leads to life" is that which is related to belief in Jesus Christ (Acts 11:17-18). The only faith toward God that is now acceptable is faith in God the Son. There is no way to the Father except through the Son.

The Old Testament taught repentance from dead works and faith toward God. The New Testament teaches repentance in faith toward the Lord Jesus Christ, the only Way to God. The distinction is clear. The Jews addressed in this letter believed in God; but they were not saved. Their repentance from works and faith toward God, no matter how sincere it may have been, could not *bring* them to God without Christ. "There is salvation in no one else; for there is no other name under heaven that has been given among men, by which we must be saved" (Acts 4:12).

INSTRUCTION ABOUT WASHINGS

The King James translation ("doctrine of baptisms") is misleading, especially since everywhere else, including Hebrews 9:10, the same Greek word (*baptismos*) is translated **washings.** It is not *baptizō*, which is always used for the ordinance of baptism. It may have been that the King James translators assumed this passage was addressed to Christians, in which case "baptisms" might be appropriate. But the use here of *baptismos* rather than *baptizō* is another strong indication that the passage is *not* addressed to Christians.

Every Jewish home had a basin by the entrance for family and visitors to use for ceremonial cleansings, of which there were many. It is these washings that the readers are told to abandon and forget. Even the Old Testament predicted that one day its ceremonial cleansings would be replaced by a spiritual one that God Himself would give: "Then I will sprinkle clean water on you, and you will be clean; I will cleanse you from all your filthiness and from all your idols" (Ezek. 36:25). The old washings were many, physical, symbolic, and temporary; the new washing is once, spiritual, real, and permanent. It is the wonderful, effective, and eternal "washing of regeneration and renewing by the Holy Spirit" (Titus 3:5). It is the being born (regeneration) of water and the spirit that Jesus told Nicodemus was necessary for entrance into the kingdom (John 3:5).

LAYING ON OF HANDS

This **laying on of hands** has nothing to do with the apostolic practices (Acts 5:18; 6:6; 8:17; 1 Tim. 4:14; etc.). Under the Old Covenant the person who brought a sacrifice had to put his hands on it, to symbolize his identification with it (Lev. 1:4; 3:8, 13).

Our identification with Jesus Christ does not come by putting our hands on Him; it comes by the Spirit's baptizing us into union with Him by faith. "Forget the teaching about laying hands on the Temple sacrifices," the writer is telling these immature Jews. "Lay hold of Christ by putting your trust in Him."

RESURRECTION OF THE DEAD

The Old Testament doctrine of **resurrection** is not clear or complete. We learn of life after death and of rewards for the good and punishment for the wicked—and not much more about resurrection than this. From Job, for instance, we learn that resurrection will be bodily, and not just spiritual (Job 19:26). There is little else that we can learn of it from the Old Testament.

In the New Testament, of course, resurrection is one of the major and most detailed doctrines. It is the theme of apostolic preaching. It comes to fullness in the very Person of Jesus Christ, who said, "I am the resurrection and the life" (John 11:25). The resurrection body is described in considerable detail in 1 Corinthians 15; and in 1 John 3:2 we are told, "We shall be like Him, because we shall see Him just as He is." Why should anyone be content with trying to understand the resurrection from the limited and vague teachings of the Old Testament?

ETERNAL JUDGMENT

We can learn little more from the Old Testament about final judgment than what is given in Ecclesiastes: "God will bring every act to judgment, everything which is hidden, whether it is good or evil" (12:14). Punishment would come to the wicked and blessing to the good.

Again in the New Testament, however, we are told a great deal about **eternal judgment**—much more than many people like to hear. We know what is going to happen to believers. "There is therefore now no condemnation for those who are in Christ Jesus" (Rom. 8:1). We will have to stand before the Lord and have our work judged—for reward or lack of reward—but we ourselves will not be judged (1 Cor. 3:12-15). We also know what is going to happen to unbelievers. We know about the judgment of the sheep and goats (Matt. 25:31-46), and the judgment of the great white throne (Rev. 20:11-15). We know that to Jesus Christ has been committed all judgment (John 5:21-29). We know this and much more about judgment from the New Testament.

The point of Hebrews 6:1-2 is simply that the unbelieving Jews should let go completely of the immature, elementary shadows and symbols of the Old Covenant and take hold of the mature and perfect reality of the New. The Holy Spirit is calling for them to leave the ABCs of **repentance from dead works** for the New Testament teaching of repentance toward God and new life in Christ. Leave the ABCs of **faith toward God** for faith in the Person of Jesus Christ. Leave the ABCs of ceremonial **washings** for the cleansing of the soul by the Word. Leave the ABCs of **laying hands** on the sacrifice for laying hold of the Lamb of God by faith. Leave the ABCs of the **resurrection of the dead** for the full and glorious resurrection unto life. Leave the ABCs of **eternal judgment** for the full truth of judgment and rewards as revealed in the New Covenant.

These six doctrines were the basics of Judaism that were to be laid aside in favor of the better things that come in Christ. The Old Testament is incomplete. It is true. It is of God. It was a necessary part of His revelation and of His plan of salvation for man. But it is only partial revelation, and is not sufficient. Judaism is abrogated. Judaism is nullified. It is no longer a valid expression of worship or of obedience to God. It must be abandoned.

THE POWER

And this we shall do, if God permits. (6:3)

Interpreting this verse is difficult, despite its brevity and simplicity. We will look at it from two angles.

Some interpreters believe **we** is an editorial reference of the writer to himself. He is saying, "I will go on and teach you what you need to know if God permits me." Others believe the writer is simply offering to identify himself with those to whom he writes, and is saying, "You will go on to maturity if God permits."

I believe that both interpretations could be correct. They are not mutually exclusive and are consistent with the rest of Hebrews. Both service (the writer's going on to teach) and salvation (the readers' going on to spiritual maturity in Christ) must be energized by the Holy Spirit (**if God permits**) if they are to be effective and fruitful. Everything revolves around the permission of God. Need for divine enablement is the point. "Not that we are adequate in ourselves to consider anything as coming from ourselves, but our adequacy is from God" (2 Cor. 3:5; cf. James 4:13). "No one can come to Me, unless the Father who sent Me draws him" (John 6:44). By teacher and seeker alike, God's sovereignty should be recognized.

FIVE GREAT ADVANTAGES

For in the case of those who have once been enlightened and have tasted of the heavenly gift and have been made partakers of the Holy Spirit, and have tasted the good word of God and the powers of the age to come. (6:4-5)

The Hebrews being addressed here had five great advantages, which are summarized in these two verses.

THEY HAD BEEN ENLIGHTENED

First of all, we should notice that this passage makes no reference at all to salvation. There is no mention of justification, sanctification, the new birth, or regeneration. Those **who have once been enlightened** are not spoken of as born again, made holy, or made righteous. None of the normal New Testament terminology for salvation is used. In fact, no term used here is ever used elsewhere in the New Testament for salvation, and none should be taken to refer to it in this passage.

The enlightenment spoken of here has to do with intellectual perception of spiritual, biblical truth. In the Septuagint, the Greek word (*phōtizō*) several times is translated "to give light by knowledge or teaching." It means to be mentally aware of something, to be instructed, informed. It carries no connotation of response—of acceptance or rejection, belief or disbelief.

When Jesus first came to Galilee to minister, He declared that He had come to fulfill the prophecy of Isaiah 9:1-2, which, in part, reads, "The people who were sitting in darkness saw a great light" (Matt. 4:16). All who saw and heard Jesus saw this "great light," but not all who saw and heard were saved. Seeing God's light and accepting it are not the same. Those people in Galilee, as all people who hear the gospel, were to some extent or other *enlightened;* but, judging by the biblical accounts, few of them believed in Jesus. They had natural knowledge, factual information. They saw Christ, they heard His message from His own lips, they saw His miracles with their own eyes. They had firsthand opportunity to see God's truth incarnate, an opportunity that only a few thousand people in all of history have had. The Light of the gospel had *personally* broken in on their darkness (cf. John 12:35-36). Life for them could never be the same again. Their lives were permanently affected by the indelible impression Jesus must have made on them. Yet many, if not most, of them did not believe in Him (cf. John 12:37-40).

The same thing had happened to the Jews being addressed in Hebrews 6:1-8. They were enlightened but not saved. Consequently, they were in danger of losing all opportunity of being saved, and of becoming apostate. It is of such people that Peter speaks in his second letter. "For if after they have escaped the defilements of the world by the knowledge of the Lord and Savior Jesus Christ, they are again entangled in them and are overcome, the last state has become worse for them than the first. For it would be better for them not to have known the way of righteousness, than having known it, to turn away from the holy commandment delivered to them" (2 Pet. 2:20-21). Because of their unbelief, the light that was given to save them became a judgment against them.

THEY HAD TASTED OF THE HEAVENLY GIFT

This group not only had seen the heavenly light but had **tasted of the heavenly gift.** The **heavenly gift** could be one of several things. The Holy Spirit is spoken of in Scripture as a heavenly gift, but, since He is mentioned in the next verse, I do not think He is the gift meant here. The greatest heavenly gift, of course, is Christ Himself (God's "indescribable gift," 2 Cor. 9:15) and the salvation He brought (Eph. 2:8). Christ's salvation is the supreme heavenly gift, and no doubt the one referred to here.

This great gift, however, was not received. It was not feasted on, but only **tasted,** sampled. It was not accepted or lived, only examined. That stands in contrast with Jesus' work on our behalf. Having tasted death for every man (Heb. 2:9), He went on to drink it all.

Jesus told the woman at Jacob's well, "If you knew the gift of God, and who it is who says to you, 'Give Me a drink,' you would have asked Him, and He would have given you living water" (John 4:10). Jesus was speaking of the gift of salvation, the "living water" that leads to "eternal life" (v. 14). Those who drank it—not sipped it or just tasted it, but drank it—would be saved. A short time later in Galilee, Jesus told His hearers, "I am the living bread that came down out of heaven; if anyone eats of this bread, he shall live forever" (John 6:51; cf. v. 35). Eternal life comes from eating, not simply tasting, God's gift of salvation in Christ.

One of the presalvation ministries of the Holy Spirit is that of giving the unsaved a taste of the blessings of salvation. This is part of His ministry of drawing men to Christ. But tasting is not eating. The Holy Spirit will give us a taste, but He will not make us eat. God placed the blessing of salvation to the lips of these New Testament Jews, but they had not yet eaten. The tasting came from what they saw and heard, as many today have seen the transforming power of Christ and heard the gospel.

THEY HAD PARTAKEN OF THE HOLY SPIRIT

Partakers (Greek, *metochos*) has to do with association, not possession. These Jews had never possessed the **Holy Spirit,** they simply were around when He was around. This word is used of fellow fishermen in Luke 5:7, and of Christ in relation to the angels in Hebrews 1:9. It has to do with sharing in common associations and events. In the context of Hebrews 6:4, it refers to anyone who has been where the Holy Spirit has been ministering. It is possible to have an association with the Holy Spirit, to share in what He does, and not be saved. As we have seen (2:4) these Jews had heard the word and had seen and even participated in numerous signs, wonders, miracles, and gifts of the Holy Spirit. They were actually involved in some of His work.

The Bible never speaks of Christians being associated with the Holy Spirit. It speaks of the Holy Spirit being *within* them.

Here, however, are some persons who are simply associated with the Holy Spirit. Like perhaps most of the multitudes whom Jesus miraculously healed and fed, they partook of the Holy Spirit's power and blessings, but they did not have His indwelling. They did not possess the Holy Spirit, nor did the Holy Spirit possess them.

THEY HAD TASTED THE WORD OF GOD

Again these readers are spoken of as having **tasted** something of God, this time His **word.** The Greek term used here for **word** (*rhēma*, which emphasizes the parts rather than the whole) is not the usual one (*logos*) for God's Word, but it fits the meaning in this context. As with His heavenly gifts, they had heard God's utterances and sampled them, tasted them, without actually eating them. They had been taught about God. No doubt they regularly came to the assembly of the church. They may have listened carefully and even thought carefully about what they heard. They took it all in, possibly with enthusiasm and appreciation. But they could not say with Jeremiah, "Thy words were found and I ate them, and Thy words became for me a joy and the delight of my heart" (Jer. 15:16). They tasted but they did not eat, just like the nation to whom Jeremiah spoke.

Herod was like this. In spite of the prophet's hard message, including accusations directly against the king, Herod enjoyed listening to John the Baptist preach (Mark 6:20). He was perplexed but fascinated by this dynamic preacher. He liked to sample the message of God. But when pressed into decision, he forsook God's man and God's message. He reluctantly, but willingly, agreed to have John beheaded. His taste of God's Word only brought on him greater guilt.

Tasting is the first step to eating. It is not wrong to taste God's Word. In fact David encourages that very thing. "O taste and see that the LORD is good" (Ps. 34:8). To some degree, everyone must taste the gospel before he accepts it. The problem is stopping with tasting. Like so many who hear the gospel for the first time, these Jews were attracted to its beauty and sweetness. It tasted very good to them. But they did not chew it or swallow it, much less digest it. They just kept tasting. Before long, its appealing taste was gone and they became indifferent to it. Their spiritual tastebuds became insensitive and unresponsive.

Any person who has heard the gospel and perhaps made a profession of Christ, but who is uncertain of salvation, should take Paul's advice: "Test yourselves to see if you are in the faith; examine yourselves!" (2 Cor. 13:5). Such a person needs to learn if he has only tasted the gospel without eating it.

THEY HAD TASTED THE POWERS OF THE AGE TO COME

The **age to come** is the future kingdom of God. The **powers** of the kingdom are miracle powers. These Jews had seen the same kind of miracles that are going to come when Jesus brings in His earthly kingdom. They **tasted** them. They saw the apostles do signs and wonders like those that will be reproduced in the millennial kingdom of Jesus Christ. They saw miracle upon miracle. And the more they saw and tasted without receiving, the more their guilt increased. They were like those who saw Jesus Himself perform miracles. How hard it is to explain the hatred and unbelief of those who saw a resurrected Lazarus, who saw the blind given sight and the dumb given voices, and yet who rejected the One who did these marvels in front of their eyes. How guilty they will stand before God in the great white throne judgment.

These Jews had been wondrously blessed by God's enlightenment, by association with His Holy Spirit, and by tasting of His heavenly gifts, His Word, and His power. Still they did not believe.

A FOURTH WARNING

For in the case of those who have once been enlightened and have tasted of the heavenly gift and have been made partakers of the Holy Spirit, and have tasted the good word of God and the powers of the age to come, and then have fallen away, it is impossible to renew them again to repentance, since they again crucify to themselves the Son of God, and put Him to open shame. (6:4-6)

Still speaking to the unsaved who have heard the truth and acknowledged it, but who have hesitated to embrace Christ, the Holy Spirit gives a fourth warning, the crux of 6:1-8. Summarized, the warning is: "You had better come to Christ now, for if you fall away it will be **impossible** for you to come again to the point of **repentance**." They were at the best point for repentance—full knowledge. To fall back from that would be fatal.

Because they believe the warning is addressed to Christians, many interpreters hold that the passage teaches that salvation can be lost. If this interpretation were true, however, the passage would also teach that, once lost, salvation could never be regained. If, after being saved, a person lost his salvation, he would be damned forever. There would be no going back and forth, in and out of grace. But Christians are not being addressed, and it is the opportunity for *receiving* salvation, not salvation itself, that can be lost.

The believer need never fear he will lose his salvation. He cannot. The Bible is absolutely clear about that. Jesus said, "My sheep hear My voice, and I know them, and they follow Me; and I give eternal life to them, and they shall never perish; and no one shall snatch them out of My hand. My Father, who has given them to Me, is greater than all; and no one is able to snatch them out of the Father's hand" (John 10:27-29). Paul is equally clear. "Who shall separate us from the love of Christ? Shall tribulation, or distress, or persecution, or famine, or nakedness, or peril, or sword? . . . For I am convinced that neither death, nor life, nor angels, nor principalities, nor things present, nor things to come, nor powers, nor height, nor depth, nor any other created thing, shall be able to separate us from the love of God, which is in Christ Jesus our Lord" (Rom. 8:35, 38-39). "He who began a good work in you will perfect it until the day of Christ Jesus" (Phil. 1:6). We are "to obtain an inheritance which is imperishable and undefiled and will not fade away, reserved in heaven," and we "are protected by the power of God through faith for a salvation ready to be revealed in the last time" (1 Pet. 1:4-5). If the power of God cannot keep us, nothing is dependable or trustworthy or worth believing in. A Christian has no reason at any point in his life to believe that his salvation is or can be lost. If by Christ's death we can be saved, certainly by His life of power and intercession we can be kept saved (Rom. 5:10).

It is unbelievers who are in danger of losing salvation—in the sense of losing the opportunity ever to receive it. The unbelieving Jews were in great danger, because of their spiritual immaturity and sluggishness, of turning back to Judaism and of never being able to repent and come to Christ. They would be lost forever, because they had rejected, at the most vital point in knowledge and conviction, the only gospel that could save them. There is no other salvation message they could hear, no evidence of the truth of the gospel they had not seen.

These particular Jews had even heard the apostles preach and had seen them perform signs and wonders and miracles (Heb. 2:4). They had been privileged to behold virtually all the manifestations of His saving Word and power that God could give. They had heard it all and seen it all. They even had accepted it all intellectually. Any who are so informed, so witnessed to, so blessed with every opportunity to know God's gospel, and who then turn their backs on it—for Judaism or anything else—are eternally lost. They not only reject the gospel, but **crucify to themselves the Son of God, and put Him to open shame.** They had either to go on to full knowledge of God through faith in Christ or else turn away from Him, to become apostate and be lost forever. There was no other alternative.

Some have translated *adunatos* (**impossible**) in 6:6 as "difficult." But it is clear even from other passages in Hebrews that such a translation is unjustified. The same Greek word is used in 6:18 ("It is impossible for God to lie"), in 10:4 ("It is impossible for the blood of bulls and goats to take away sins"), and in 11:6 ("Without faith it is impossible to please Him"). All three of these passages would be nonsense if "impossible" were changed to "difficult." The harsh finality of the danger cannot be escaped or minimized.

A vaccination immunizes by giving a very mild case of the disease. A person who is exposed to the gospel can get just enough of it to immunize him against the real thing. The longer he continues to resist it, whether graciously or violently, the more he becomes immune to it. His spiritual system becomes more and more unresponsive and insensitive. His only hope is to reject what he is holding onto and receive Christ without delay—lest he become so hard, often without knowing it, that his opportunity is forever gone.

To renew means to restore, to bring back to an original condition. The original condition of these Jews was that of excitement about the gospel when they first heard it. It was beautiful. They had moved from Judaism right up to the edge of Christianity, evidently even to repentance. They had turned from their old ways. They had tried to turn from their sin. They had begun to turn toward God.

They had come all the way up to the edge of salvation. All the revelation God had He had given them. There was nothing else He could say or do. If they fell away they did so with an evil heart of unbelief and they did it against full revelation. They had the advantage of having been raised under the Old Covenant and they had heard and seen all the beauty and perfection of the New. If they now fell away from that, if they now departed from the living God, there was no hope that they could ever be restored to the place where the gospel was fresh, where the gospel taste was sweet, where repentance was a proper response. They could never get back there. When one rejects Christ at the peak experience of knowledge and conviction, he will not accept at a lesser level. So salvation becomes impossible.

They could not return because they had crucified **to themselves the Son of God, and put Him to open shame. To themselves** simply means that, as far as they were concerned, the Son of God deserved to be crucified. Regardless of what they may still have been professing openly and publicly, they now took their stand with the crucifiers. In their hearts they said, "That's the same verdict we give." They had made trial of Jesus Christ and, with all the evidence possible, they decided He was not the true Messiah. They had turned around and gone back to Judaism. To them Jesus was an impostor and deceiver and got exactly what was coming to Him. They agreed with those who killed Jesus, and they put Him to an open shame again. **Shame** here connotes guilt. They declared openly that Jesus was guilty as charged.

When anyone has heard the gospel and then turns away, he has done exactly what these Jews did. Though he would never take up a hammer and spikes and physically nail Jesus to a cross, he nevertheless agrees to Jesus' crucifixion. He takes his place with the crucifiers. If this happens with full light, such a person has become an apostate, and for him salvation is forever out of reach. He has rejected Jesus Christ against the full light and power of the gospel. He is incurably anti-God, and for him is reserved the hottest hell. He takes his place with Judas, who walked and talked and ate and fellowshipped with God incarnate, yet finally rejected Him. "How much severer punishment do you think he will deserve who has trampled under foot the Son of God, and has regarded as unclean the blood of the covenant by which he was sanctified, and has insulted the Spirit of grace?" (Heb. 10:29).

It is dangerously self-deceptive for a person to think that, by staying on the sidelines, by holding off deciding, by thinking himself tolerant of the gospel simply because he does not outwardly oppose it, that he is safe. The longer one stays on the edge the more he leans toward the old life. Staying there too long inevitably results in falling away from the gospel forever. It may not be, and often is not, a conscious decision against Christ. But it *is* a decision and it *is* against Christ. When a person goes away from Him in full light, he places Him on the cross again, in his own heart, and puts himself forever out of the Lord's reach.

How terribly serious it is to reject Jesus Christ.

For ground that drinks the rain which often falls upon it and brings forth vegetation useful to those for whose sake it is also tilled, receives a blessing from God; but if it yields thorns and thistles, it is worthless and close to being cursed, and it ends up being burned. (6:7-8)

Do you see the illustration? All those who hear the gospel are like the earth. The **rain** falls, the gospel message is heard. The gospel seed is planted and there is nourishment and growth. Some of the growth is beautiful and good and productive. It is that which is planted, rooted, and nourished in God. But some of the growth is false, spurious, and unproductive. It has come from the same seed and has been nourished by the same ground and the same water, but has become thorny, destructive, and **worthless.** It has rejected the life offered it and become good only for burning.

The Tragedy of Rejecting Full Revelation—part 3

14

(6:9-12)

But, beloved, we are convinced of better things concerning you, and things that accompany salvation, though we are speaking in this way. For God is not unjust so as to forget your work and the love which you have shown toward His name, in having ministered and in still ministering to the saints. And we desire that each one of you show the same diligence so as to realize the full assurance of hope until the end, that you may not be sluggish, but imitators of those who through faith and patience inherit the promises. (6:9-12)

After the severest of warnings, comes the most loving of appeals. The writer was hoping earnestly that the unbelievers he so forcefully had been warning would not fall away, that they would not apostatize. His approach was to introduce them, so to speak, to the true Christians in their midst, to be **imitators of those who through faith and patience inherit the promises.**

First he gives a brief word to the believers who are to be imitated. **Beloved** is never used in Scripture to refer to unbelievers. Now he is speaking of **things that accompany salvation,** whereas in the previous part of the chapter he had been talking only about things concerning revelation. Both of these things—the use of "beloved" and the discussion of salvation conditions—indicate the writer's change of audience. The previous topics—intellectual enlightenment about God's word, tasting God's gifts and His Spirit, and so forth—accompany revelation, not salvation. They are meant, of course, to help lead to salvation, but they do not do so apart from faith in Jesus Christ.

The Christians who are to be examples came out of the same background as those who are to imitate them. They were all raised in Judaism. They had had the same opportunity to know God's revelation and to experience the work of His Spirit. They had had the same opportunity to hear the gospel and to see and experience Christ's church at work. The only difference, though it was a very great difference, was that some had trusted Christ as Savior and some had not. That is also the great difference between the wheat and the tares of Jesus' parable (Matt. 13:24-43). The same sun that hardens the clay melts the wax.

The term **beloved** (*agapētos*, from *agapē*) expresses the highest kind of relationship. It is used sixty times in the New Testament. The first nine times it is used, it is used by God the Father in speaking of Christ, His beloved Son. Everywhere else, whether referring to Jews or Gentiles, it is used only of believers. Agape love is the beautiful and unique bond of the fellowship of believers. Arthur Pink observes, "I cannot really love a brother with full rich love unless I have a well-grounded persuasion that he is a brother." This love is reserved for those in Christ.

The writer was convinced that his fellow believers to whom he was writing exhibited all the traits, all the true marks, of salvation—of true sainthood in the biblical sense. The implication is that, after considerable investigation, he was persuaded that these beloved brethren possessed all the **things that accompany salvation** and that they, therefore, would be superb examples for their yet unbelieving friends to observe and imitate.

ACCOMPANIMENTS OF SALVATION

Many things **accompany salvation.** The entire fifth and six chapters of Romans are devoted to these accompaniments. But the particular ones mentioned in this section of Hebrews are those that contrast with the accompaniments of unbelief mentioned in 5:11—6:5. For example, accompanying salvation is not infancy but maturity, not milk but solid food, not inexperience in righteousness but perfect righteousness, not repentance in dead works but repentance toward God unto life. The accompaniments of salvation are primarily positive, not negative. They do not reflect external ceremonial religion but internal regeneration, transformation, new life. Their significance comes not from repeated sacrifices but from the one perfect and complete sacrifice of Jesus Christ. They do not focus on the elementary truths of resurrection and judgment but on the believer's blessed hope, not just on being enlightened but on being made new, not just on tasting salvation but feasting on it, not just partaking of the Holy Spirit but having Him indwell, not just getting a taste of God's good word but of drinking and eating it, not just seeing God's miracles but being one. These are the things that accompany salvation.

TO WHOM THIS APPLIES

Though we are speaking in this way no doubt is meant to be an encouragement to fellow believers who, after reading the previous somber section, may have been wondering—as do many Christians today—if this warning applies to them. Moving the last part of verse 9 to the beginning helps clarify the meaning. A paraphrased reading would be, "Beloved fellow Christians, though we have been speaking about these awesome and fearful warnings to unbelievers, we know that far better things apply to you. You have the accompaniments of salvation, not of unbelief. These warnings to apostates, and potential apostates, are put in this letter to you because these people are in your midst."

Again the parable of the wheat and tares is helpful. Jesus made a special point that both true believers and mere professed believers would be in the church together until He returns, and that true believers can never be certain who the false ones are. The characteristics of unbelievers given in Hebrews 5:11—6:4 are not meant to be used by the church to try to separate the wheat from the tares. Only the condition of a person's heart determines his standing before God, and only God has this knowledge. Under certain circumstances—such as for teaching false doctrine or living immorally—the church not only may, but should, excommunicate a member. But the Lord has made it clear that we cannot determine who in the church is really saved and who is not, and that we should not try to be the ultimate court deciding on such matters.

We do know, however, that any congregation may have an unbeliever on its rolls, perhaps even in a place of leadership, and it is to such people that this warning is given by the Lord. The faithful preacher and teacher is to give this warning, though he may not be able to determine to which particular individuals it applies. He is to teach it as part of the whole counsel of God and to let the Spirit apply it where it is needed. "Beloved," the writer is saying, "I do not say these hard things because they apply to all of you. They do not. But there are some among you who very much need this warning."

GOD DOES NOT FORGET HIS OWN

For God is not unjust so as to forget your work and the love which

you have shown toward His name, in having ministered and in still ministering to the saints. (6:10)

God knows who are really His and who are faithful. He will not **forget** His own or their **work** for Him. Our names are securely in His book of life. Our salvation will not be lost and our rewards will not be forgotten. "Rest easy," the writer says. "Don't worry."

Many Christians today, as throughout history, experience times of doubt and even anguish at the supposed prospect of losing their salvation. When they read or hear a message of judgment, they are shaken and insecure. They do not know what it is to rest in the finished work of Christ and in their positional standing in Him before God.

After Malachi had given his severe warning of judgment, many of the faithful believers apparently were worried that it applied to them. But the Lord calmed their fear. "A book of remembrance was written before Him for those who fear the LORD and who esteem His name. 'And they will be Mine,' says the LORD of hosts, '. . . I will spare them as a man spares his own son who serves him' " (Mal. 3:16-17). In the next chapter, after still another warning to the wicked, God again reassures His own: "But for you who fear My name the sun of righteousness will rise with healing in its wings" (4:2). God always knows His faithful; He always knows His own. We should not fear the final judgment. If we are in Christ, we can never be condemned. We should not worry about missing the rapture. If we belong to Christ, He will be sure to take us with Him. The sovereignty of God and His faithfulness secure us.

WORKS ARE EVIDENCE OF LOVE

A Christian's works are not what saved him or what keep him saved, but they *are* an evidence of his salvation. As James tells us, faith without works is dead—not alive, not real, not genuine. Our faith is demonstrated by our works (James 2:18, 26). God is not so unfair and insensitive that He fails to see the works of love His beloved children perform. He clearly sees the fruit of our righteousness.

Paul told the Thessalonian believers that he knew God had chosen them to be His, to be saved, because of their "work of faith and labor of love and steadfastness of hope in our Lord Jesus Christ" (1 Thess. 1:3-4). They had the fruit of good works to go along with their statement of faith. Love is a product of faith.

LOVE HIS NAME

Love for and service to the brethren is an evidence of salvation (cf. John 13:34-35). But an even more significant evidence is love **shown**

toward His name. God knows when our service is truly for His glory by whether or not it is done out of love for His name.

As important as loving fellow Christians is, loving God is immeasurably more important. In fact, without loving God first and foremost, we are not able to love each other as we should. The Jewish Christians being commended here **ministered . . . to the saints** first of all out of their love for God's name. The very reason they could love each other so much and serve each other so well was because they loved God so much. The key to true Christian service is a burning love for the Lord. All Christians ought to be attractive and lovable; but all are not. In this we often do not differ from unbelievers. But our responsibility, our calling, is to love and serve fellow Christians—and also unbelievers—first of all because of God, not because of themselves.

In the introduction of his letter to the Romans, Paul tells them of his gratitude for their faithfulness and of his longing to visit them (Rom. 1:8-10). But he also tells them that the driving force behind his ministry to them is the sake of God's name and that it is first of all God that he serves (1:5, 9). God's name stands for all that He is. To love His name is to have a passionate desire for the glory of all that God is. Speaking of some traveling ministers, John says of them, "For they went out for the sake of the Name" (3 John 7). They ministered because of their overwhelming love for the Lord. When Jesus recommissioned Peter, He did not ask him if he loved men and, if so, then to go out and serve them. He asked Peter three times, "Do you love *Me?*" After each of Peter's affirmative replies, Jesus commanded him to feed His sheep (John 21:15-17). Our service to Jesus Christ must be based on an overriding love for Him. We can never properly love men, saved or unsaved, lovable or unlovable, until we properly love Christ.

These faithful believers to whom Hebrews was primarily addressed loved the name of the Lord. This was positive proof that their faith was the real thing. They were ministering to each other because they loved their Lord. We hear a great deal about loving and ministering to the Body of Christ, about serving each other in the life of the Body. No emphasis could be more scriptural—if it is in the right perspective. The genuineness and the effectiveness of the ministry we have to one another as saints is directly related to the love we have for Christ. The more we love God, the more we will want to do His will. Our concern should not be for trying to whip up love for people, but for loving God more and more. When our love for Him is right, our love for others will be right.

AN UNBROKEN MINISTRY

Keeping God as our focus and first love not only gives us the desire and power to love others and to serve them, but it also sustains us in our love and service. Only God's love has such staying power. The faithful, loving Hebrews *had* **ministered** and were **still ministering.** Their love issued in an unbroken ministry to the saints. They just kept loving and serving. They could always speak of their fellowship with the Lord and of their Christian service in the present tense.

HOW SHOULD WE SERVE?

First of all we serve by ministering our spiritual gifts (cf. Rom. 12:3-8; 1 Cor. 12:9-11; 1 Pet. 4:10-11). Our frontline of service is through our spiritual gifts. But our spiritual gifts are not given for us to take and use by ourselves, much less for ourselves. They are to be used for God's glory, in His power and for His name's sake. Whether our gift is counseling, showing mercy, helping, teaching, preaching, administration, or whatever, it is to be ministered because we love the One who gave it to us.

Much service to one another, of course, has nothing to do with our spiritual gifts but is simply part of every Christian's responsibility. Every believer's ministry, for example, involves praying for other believers. We are to "pray at all times in the Spirit, and with this in view, be on the alert with all perseverance and petition for all the saints" (Eph. 6:18). Our ministry to one another also involves rebuking sin in a brother, seeking to restore him in love, confessing to one another, forgiving, bearing one another's burdens, caring for the weaker brother, giving to the needs of the saints, and many other responsibilities. All these things are part of our ministry to one another, and none of them can be generated on its own. All must be generated by the right kind of love for Jesus Christ.

The Christian life boils down to one thing: the measure of our love for the Lord. How preoccupied are we with His name—not with saying it sentimentally in a "spiritual" tone or with vainly repeating it in our conversation and prayer—but with doing His will for the sake of His glory? How lofty and exalted is our view of God and how overwhelming are our concern and genuine love for Him? When we love Him with all our "heart and soul and mind and strength," we will then be able—and only then be able—to love our neighbor as ourselves.

The **saints** that are ministered to are simply fellow Christians. All true Christians are *hagios*, "holy ones," or saints (cf. 1 Cor. 1:2). It goes without saying that we often do not think or act like saints, in the popular sense. But the writer is speaking of our identity in Christ. We are holy ones in our Lord, even when we are unfaithful and act unsaintly. Being a saint has nothing at all to do with one's degree of spiritual maturity or rank. It refers to any person who is saved, who is set apart by God for

Himself in His Son Jesus Christ. Because God sees us as He sees His Son, we are all "holy in His sight."

The proof that the Hebrews addressed in 6:9-10 were true believers was their loving, faithful, and continuing ministry to fellow believers, fellow saints. The greatest gift our love can give God is that of loving, faithful service to each other, His children. If we love Him, we will serve one another. To say we love God while we have no use for our brothers in Christ is to lie. John, often called the apostle of love, goes into this truth in depth in his first letter. "The one who says he is in the light and yet hates his brother is in the darkness until now." A few chapters later, he puts the same truth even more strongly: "The one who does not love does not know God, for God is love." In the last chapter he summarizes the truth: "Whoever loves the Father loves the child born of Him" (1 John 2:9; 4:8; 5:1). Loving one another is not an option or an extra; it is bedrock Christian living.

FOLLOW THEIR EXAMPLE

And we desire that each one of you show the same diligence so as to realize the full assurance of hope until the end, that you may not be sluggish, but be imitators of those who through faith and patience inherit the promises. (6:11-12)

The writer is again speaking to the unbelievers, those who had made some sort of profession of faith but who were in imminent danger of falling back into Judaism and of losing forever their opportunity for salvation. The hope that is now extended to them is for them to become imitators of the true believers that have just been described—by becoming true believers themselves. "Take a look at these true believers," he is saying. "My sincerest desire is that everyone of you become as they are. How wonderful it would be if all of you were the same, if every single one of you could have the same full assurance of hope to the end. We don't want you to fall away and lose all hope." There is no hope apart from Jesus Christ, and it is therefore to Him that these are called to come before it is too late to come. Then they could all claim this hope "as an anchor of the soul, a hope both sure and steadfast" (Heb. 6:19).

Diligence (*spoudē*) can carry the idea of eagerness or haste. The suggestion in this passage is that the unbelieving Jews can get to belief quickly. Coming to Christ is not a long, drawn-out process that takes years, or even months or weeks, of preparation. All it takes is an act of faith. It may take some people a long time to come to Christ after first hearing the gospel—but it need not, and it should not. Salvation is an instantaneous experience, and it should not be postponed.

The idea of haste is also in verse 12. These Jewish unbelievers' sluggishness was a terrible hindrance to their being saved. **Sluggish** is a translation of the same word (*nothros*) that is rendered "dull" in 5:11. Just as they were sluggish in hearing, they were sluggish in believing. They had not consciously, outrightly rejected the gospel; but not to accept it, for whatever reason, is the same as rejecting it. There is a time for carefulness and deliberation, but not when you know the right thing to do and have no guarantee of how long you will have the opportunity to do it. The time for accepting Christ is never later; it is always now. "Now is 'the acceptable time,' behold, now is the 'the day of salvation' " (2 Cor. 6:2). It is quite possible that many more people who have heard the gospel are lost because they put off trusting in Christ than because they purposely reject Him.

Before it is eternally too late, those on the edge of salvation should imitate true believers. The imitation, of course, is not to be of their personalities or abilities or individual lifestyles or habits, but of their faith—evidenced by love and labor for the Lord. "Follow the saved," they are being told, "those who have had the same persecution that you have had but who have patiently endured it because their faith is real. Follow them and come to all the promises that salvation brings" (cf. Heb. 13:7).

The Securities of God's Promise (6:13-20)

For when God made the promise to Abraham, since He could swear by no one greater, He swore by Himself, saying, "I will surely bless you, and I will surely multiply you." And thus, having patiently waited, he obtained the promise. For men swear by one greater than themselves, and with them an oath given as confirmation is an end of every dispute. In the same way God, desiring even more to show to the heirs of the promise the unchangeableness of His purpose, interposed with an oath, in order that by two unchangeable things, in which it is impossible for God to lie, we may have strong encouragement, we who have fled for refuge in laying hold of the hope set before us. This hope we have as an anchor of the soul, a hope both sure and steadfast and one which enters within the veil, where Jesus has entered as a forerunner for us, having become a high priest forever according to the order of Melchizedek. (6:13-20)

There used to be a television program called "Who Do You Trust?" That is an important question. In our age we are well on our way to trusting no one. Many people have developed a kind of psychosis of distrust, commonly known as the credibility gap. Young people are being taught not to trust anyone but themselves and to learn everything by their own experience. Promises are often made lightly, with little intention of their being kept. A person's word today can seldom be his bond. Lying has all but become the norm in much of society. The world is full of liars. That is a basic problem. The Bible says that "the whole world lies in the power of the evil one" (1 John 5:19), and Jesus tells us the evil one, the devil, is "the father of lies," that lying is the essence of his nature (John 8:44).

In the midst of the confusion and turmoil that lying always brings, people are looking for something they can trust, something they can bank their lives on. Some turn to religion. They may spend an entire life in a particular religious system, devotedly and sacrificially meeting all its requirements and standards, yet never find peace or meaning or satisfaction. They may spend years praying to and putting complete trust in a particular saint, only to be told that the saint was not really canonized. Or they may put their trust in self-proclaimed healers. A mother took her young son to a faith healer in the hope of having his crippled legs straightened. She was told to take off his braces and never to put them on him again. A few weeks of pain later, emergency surgery had to be done to save the legs from amputation.

Elmer Gantry-style evangelists have always been around to take people's hearts, money, and trust. Not too many years ago in Los Angeles a minister conducted a television campaign ostensibly to raise money for missionary work. After collecting a considerable sum, he simply left town. People go to churches that claim to worship and honor Jesus Christ but that teach doctrines and ideas utterly contrary to what He taught. They learn nothing about the Jesus Christ of Scripture. False teachers, who are both deceived and deceiving, abound. Preachers with high academic credentials from prestigious seminaries teach philosophies and theologies that are totally unbiblical and heretical.

In whom can we trust? In whom can we really believe? Without being pessimistic or cynical, the Christian knows that the only one who can be trusted without reservation is God. Over and over, throughout its pages and in many forms, the Bible tells us to trust in the Lord with all our hearts. No statement of this counsel is more beautiful than David's: "Trust in the LORD, and do good; dwell in the land and cultivate faithfulness. Delight yourself in the LORD; and He will give you the desires of you heart" (Ps. 37:3-4). Only in Him is there no credibility gap.

ABRAHAM'S EXAMPLE

As we have seen, the writer of Hebrews has been urging the Jews to completely abandon the Old Covenant. Everything from Judaism is to be dropped away and they are to commit themselves entirely to Jesus Christ in the New Covenant. The forms and rituals and ceremonies and practices are to be left behind. But, as the writer says very clearly here—

and says even more clearly in chapter 11—the essence, the substance, even of the Old Covenant was faith, as far as man's part was concerned. At no time were the forms and ceremonies the most important thing. Faith was always paramount.

Probably the most outstanding example, certainly from the Old Testament, of trusting God is **Abraham.** He, in fact, is called "the father of all who believe" (Rom. 4:11; cf. Gal. 3:7). And it is Abraham whom the writer now sets before his readers as a model of faith. He is saying, "Not only can you look around you at the true believers as examples; even Abraham, who lived thousands of years before Christ came to earth, is a model for your trusting in Him. Look back in your own history and see a man who totally trusted God." In light of the Jewish persecution that these borderline believers would almost certainly face if they became Christians, they are pointed to Abraham. The father of the Jews is also the father of the faithful. He is the perfect illustration of a man of faith who, in the midst of adversity, uncertainty, and seeming impossibility, went all the way with God, totally trusting Him for everything. He went so far as to raise the knife to slay the very son who alone could fulfill God's promise—because God had told him to sacrifice this son. That is how far he trusted God.

Paul also used Abraham as the great example of faith. The whole thrust of Romans 4 is that Abraham was saved—justified, counted righteous by God—because of his faith. And he not only was saved by faith before the Old (Mosaic) Covenant was given, but he was saved even before he was circumcised, which was the mark of the covenant God made with Abraham. Paul's point is that salvation has never been by obedience to the law or by the performance of any rite, but has *always* been by faith. "But to the one who does not work, but believes in Him who justifies the ungodly, his faith is reckoned as righteousness" (Rom. 4:5; cf. James 2:23). Abraham, in fact, not only was the father of the Jewish faithful but of everyone, Jew or Gentile, who is faithful.

What sort of faith did Abraham have? Why was it so significant, so exemplary, that he would be called the father of the faithful?

Abraham, whose original name was Abram, was raised a pagan. He was a descendant of Shem, one of Noah's three sons; but apparently for many generations, his family had worshiped false gods. He grew up in Ur, an ancient Chaldean city of Mesopotamia. For His own reasons, God spoke to Abram and commanded him first to go to Haran and then to Canaan. "By faith, Abraham, when he was called, obeyed by going out to a place which he was to receive for an inheritance; and he went out, not knowing where he was going" (Heb. 11:8). With no guarantee but God's word that he would get there, Abraham believed Him and went.

The Lord promised Abraham that He would give the land of Canaan to him and his descendants and that through Abraham all the families of the earth would be blessed (Gen. 12:1-3). Although Abraham was childless, and his wife Sarah was barren, God also promised Abraham that his descendants would be too numerous to count. For years after coming into Canaan, however, Abraham remained childless.

After Isaac, the promised son, was finally born and had become a teenager, God commanded Abraham to sacrifice this only son. Having no idea of the Lord's reasons or of what would happen, Abraham obeyed. He obeyed because he believed God. Had not God miraculously intervened and provided a substitute sacrifice, Abraham would have slain Isaac on Mt. Moriah.

Yet Abraham's faith was not blind. He could not see the consequences of his obedience but he could see God's character. Abraham had gilt-edged security. For some very obvious and powerful reasons, he could trust God. When the Lord makes a promise, He puts His integrity on the line. Every promise of God is secured by His character.

God's integrity and faithfulness are the real theme of Hebrews 6:13-20. Abraham is simply an example of those who trust His integrity and faithfulness, which alone make our trust of any value. Can we trust our lives to God? Can we take Him at His word? Can He keep us from falling? Can He finish the work He has begun in us? Will He lose hold on us, or lose interest in us, at some point along the line? In short, is there really salvation and security with God? Abraham believed there was.

This passage in Hebrews gives us four reasons for trusting God: His Person, His purpose, His pledge, and His Priest.

HIS PERSON

For when God made the promise to Abraham, since He could swear by no one greater, He swore by Himself, saying "I will surely bless you, and I will surely multiply you." And thus, having patiently waited, he obtained the promise. (6:13-15)

No one in the universe is greater than God. And the reason He cannot lie is that He invented truth. He is truth. By definition, whatever He says is true. By the very nature of His person, He cannot lie. He has no capacity to lie. His promises, then, are first of all secured by His Person. Whatever He does has to be right and whatever He says has to be true. If God makes a **promise,** therefore, He not only *will* keep it, He *must* keep it.

The Hebrew readers who recognized the truth of the gospel, who had seen miracles performed by the apostles, were still afraid to let go of Judaism. They were afraid to cast themselves completely on the Messiah for fear that He might not be able to save them, that something would go amiss. And so the Holy Spirit encourages them, assures them that they can trust God to do just as He says.

In the opening of his letter to Titus, Paul reminds his young friend of "the hope of eternal life, which God, who cannot lie, promised long ages ago" (Titus 1:2). Long ago God had promised eternal life to those who come to Him, and He cannot lie. In the early part of his epistle, James also speaks of God's utter dependability. "Every good thing bestowed and every perfect gift is from above, coming down from the Father of lights, with whom there is no variation, or shifting shadow" (James 1:17). God never deviates from His will or from His promises. He *cannot.*

Since, therefore, God has promised that all who come to Him through His Son will be saved, it is impossible for anyone who trusts in Christ not to be saved or to lose salvation once it is attained. God promises again and again that if men come to Jesus Christ they will know salvation. "But as many as received Him, to them He gave the right to become children of God, even to those who believe in His name" (John 1:12).

Just as surely as God has kept His promise to Abraham, He will keep His promise to those who trust in His Son. His basic promise to Abraham was **I will surely bless you, and I will surely multiply you** (cf. Gen. 22:17). A legitimate question, then, is, Has God kept this promise to Abraham?

Over fourteen million of the physical descendants of Abraham are still in the world today. Not only that, but many more millions around the world are Abraham's spiritual descendants. God has indeed kept His promise to Abraham.

God has never failed, and He never will. Abraham was secure because of the Person of God, who cannot lie. He cannot possibly back out on His promises. We can trust God because He has no capacity for deception or failure in His nature. "The LORD is the one who goes ahead of you; He will be with you. He will not fail you or forsake you. Do not fear, or be dismayed" (Deut. 31:8).

HIS PURPOSE—TO REDEEM A LOST WORLD

Saying, "I will surely bless you, and I will surely multiply you." **(6:14)**

Abraham was secure not only because of God's Person, but also because of God's purpose. God did not take Abraham from his homeland and send him to a foreign land to sojourn the rest of his life in order to fulfill a divine whim. God had a purpose for Abraham and for the world through Abraham. Abraham had not asked God to send him to Canaan or to bless the world through him. It was God's idea, God's purpose,

God's plan. God's call of Abraham, His promise to Abraham, and His covenant with Abraham were all entirely of His own doing.

The Abrahamic covenant, with its promise, was unconditional. God did not tell Abraham he would be blessed if he fulfilled certain requirements, if he met certain conditions. God told Abraham to do many things, and Abraham was obedient. But it was not Abraham's obedience, as important and fine as this was, that guaranteed the fulfillment of God's promise to him. God's promise guaranteed its own fulfillment. God expected many things of Abraham, but as far as fulfilling the promise was concerned, Abraham was but a spectator—watching what God was doing for him and through him. God had a predetermined purpose for Abraham. And this purpose was that Abraham *would* be blessed and that the world *would* be blessed through him.

Not long after God created Adam and Eve and put them in His beautiful garden, where every one of their needs was met, they decided to do the one thing that He had told them not to do. They ate from the tree of knowledge and fell, and the rest of creation fell with them. The whole earth was cursed. Our first parents lost their fellowship with God and were exiled from Eden. Very soon after that, the first murder was committed, when Cain killed his brother Abel.

Corruption, violence, polygamy, incest, lying, stealing, adultery, idolatry, and every other sin became common and increasingly worse. Mankind, in fact, became so terribly debauched that God destroyed all people, except for the eight in Noah's family. Man's nature was still sinful, however, and in the generations after the Flood, he continued to ignore God and sinned in every conceivable way. God had tried to reach people—including through Noah, who preached while he was building the ark—but they would not listen or change. Sin reached a climax when, with the tower of Babel, men literally tried to take heaven by storm. God thwarted their scheme by causing them to speak different languages and by scattering them across the world.

Yet God did not give up on man. It was in His eternal plan that those whom He had created in His own image would worship and serve Him. To do so they had to be redeemed. God could recover man only by drastic means. It was as if a great river had been blocked by a landslide. God had to cut a new channel. He chose a certain people to be the channel to bring the river of life to the world again. The father of that people was Abraham. From his descendants was to come the nation of Israel, God's earthly, historical channel of revelation and redemption. The Old and New Covenants, the law, the prophecies, the priestly sacrifices—all came through Israel. The Messiah Himself was a Jew, the truest Jew of all. God's plan of redemption was to be carried out through these specially chosen people. "Salvation is from the Jews" (John 4:22). And all Jews are from Abraham.

God picked Abraham. God predetermined the life of Abraham. God set His love upon Abraham to be the one through whom the channel would be cut. It was a matter of divine choice. Abraham was honored by God because of his faith and he was saved because of his faith, but he was not chosen because of his faith. Abraham was not chosen because of any merit or quality or virtue. He was chosen purely out of the sovereign will of God. "The LORD did not set His love on you nor choose you because you were more in number than any of the peoples, for you were the fewest of all peoples, but because the LORD loved you and kept the oath which He swore to your forefathers" (Deut. 7:7-8).

When the Lord made the actual covenant with Abraham, he had Abraham cut some specified animals in half and set the halves opposite each other. After Abraham fell into a deep sleep, the Lord spoke to him about His promise and then, in the form of a smoking oven and a flaming torch, passed between the halves Himself (Gen. 15). Ordinarily, when such a covenant was made *both* parties would walk between the pieces, to symbolize their mutual obligations to fulfill the conditions agreed on. But Abraham had no part in determining the conditions of this covenant or in the ceremony that sealed it. The fact that only God walked between the pieces signified that the total responsibility for fulfilling the covenant was His. Abraham was not a party to the covenant, only a witness to it and a vehicle for its fulfillment. The covenant was with Abraham in the sense that, humanly speaking, it revolved around him. But its conditions and obligations were God's alone. The covenant was made between God and Himself.

The point of this for Hebrews 6:13-20 is that God's promise did not depend on anyone's faithfulness but His own. Abraham, his descendants, and all the world through them *would be blessed*. God owed Himself the fulfillment of His plan.

PURPOSES FOR ISRAEL

What were God's chosen people meant to be? What were they supposed to do—for Him and by Him—in helping fulfill His purpose of redeeming a lost world? They were supposed to do many things. But this nation, this channel cut through the landslide of sin that blocked off man's fellowship with God, this channel through which God was going to send His flowing blessings, was given seven basic purposes.

To Proclaim the True God. Their job, in the midst of idolatry and polytheism and polydemonism and animism and all other ungodliness, first of all was to proclaim the true God. "The people whom I formed for Myself, will declare My praise" (Isa. 43:21).

To Reveal the Messiah. They were to reveal the Messiah, the Anointed One, who would be the great Savior of the world. He was to come through them, and they were to be a testimony of His coming. Just as surely as the prophets and psalmists were to proclaim His coming, so was the whole nation (see Ps. 110; Isa. 42; 49-57; Zech. 6:12-13; etc.).

To Be God's Priest-Nation. As the Mosaic covenant was being given to her at Sinai, Israel was told by God, "You shall be to Me a kingdom of priests and a holy nation" (Ex. 19:6). A priest is a mediator between God and man. All of Israel was to serve as a mediator for God to the rest of the world. The Levitical priests were to minister to Israel. Israel was to minister to the world.

To Preserve and Transmit Scripture. Israel was the scribe and repository of Scripture, the agency of God's Word. All of the Old Testament, and practically all of the New, was written by Jews (cf. Rom. 9:4).

To Show the Faithfulness of God. The Israelites were to be an illustration of God's faithfulness. Over and over they failed God, but He never failed them. They were, of course, to testify to God by their faithfulness to Him. But, even had they been perfectly faithful, their faithfulness could never have matched His. Israel was to be a means of God's showing His *own* faithfulness. God is still not through using her for this purpose. Speaking of the last times, Paul writes, "And thus all Israel will be saved; just as it is written, . . . so these also now have been disobedient, in order that because of the mercy shown to you they also may now be shown mercy" (Rom. 11:26, 31). Those who claim that all the unfulfilled promises to Israel are fulfilled in the church impugn God's Word and His faithfulness. She has been, still is, and will yet be a living illustration of His faithfulness.

To Show the Blessedness of Serving God. "How blessed are the people whose God is the LORD" (Ps. 144:15). God's chosen people were to show how blessed, how happy, those are who belong to and serve God. They not only were to be a channel of His blessing but also an illustration of it.

To Show God's Grace in Dealing with Sin. The whole sacrificial system portrayed God's gracious dealing with sin. Those sacrifices could not in themselves remove sin, but they were a beautiful picture of how God *would* remove it—through the blood of the perfect, effective sacrifice of His own Son, Jesus Christ (Heb. 9:11-14).

Israel was strategic in God's purpose. He did not have to choose her, but, once she had been chosen, He *had* to use her to fulfill the purpose for which she was chosen. He could not stop using her without violating His unconditional promise to Abraham, which would be impossible because it was contrary to His nature. Just as sure as His promise to Abraham, therefore, is His promise to those who put their trust in His Son.

The promise to Abraham and the promise to everyone who trusts in Christ are as secure as God Himself. "Surely, just as I have intended so it has happened, and just as I have planned so it will stand" (Isa. 14:24). "The counsel of the LORD stands forever" (Ps. 33:11).

As believers we are secure in Christ because God purposed before the world began to conform us to the image of His Son, and if He failed in that promise He would fail in His eternal purpose. God's promise to those who believe in Christ is, in fact, an extension of His promise to Abraham. "They are not all Israel who are descended from Israel; . . . That is, it is not the children of the flesh who are children of God, but the children of the promise are regarded as descendants" (Rom. 9:6, 8).

"Blessed be the God and Father of our Lord Jesus Christ, who has blessed us with every spiritual blessing in the heavenly places in Christ, just as He chose us in Him before the foundation of the world, that we should be holy and blameless before Him" (Eph. 1:3-4). Nothing is said about our part—our work, our faithfulness, our anything. This is the sovereign side of God's plan and is alone the basis of our security. God has purposed to love us and purposed to conform us to Christ and nothing can violate that. "For whom He foreknew, He also predestined to become conformed to the image of His Son, that He might be the firstborn among many brethren; and whom He predestined, these He also called; and whom He called, these He also justified; and whom He justified, these He also glorified" (Rom. 8:29-30). The promise is so certain that Paul puts it in the past tense—even for future believers.

HIS PLEDGE

Since He could swear by no one greater, He swore by Himself, . . . For men swear by one greater than themselves, and with them an oath given as confirmation is an end of every dispute. In the same way God, desiring even more to show to the heirs of the promise the unchangeableness of His purpose, interposed with an oath. (6:13b, 16-17)

The third security God gives, first mentioned at the end of verse 13, is His pledge. It was common in New Testament times for a person to make an **oath** on something or someone greater than himself—such as the altar, or the high priest, or even God. Once such an oath was made, argument was over; the dispute was ended. It was assumed that no one would make such an oath unless he was fully determined to keep it.

God, of course, did not need to make an oath. His word is every bit as good without an oath—as ours ought to be (Matt. 5:33-37). But to accommodate to the weak faith of men, God swore His promise on Himself. Since His promise already was unbreakable, His pledge did not make His promise any more secure. But He nonetheless gave it, as further assurance to those who are slow to believe. The bare word of God is guarantee enough, but God gave an oath just to show that He meant what He said.

I believe the pledge of God's oath is the Holy Spirit. Three times Paul refers to the Holy Spirit as God's pledge to believers (2 Cor. 1:22; 5:5; Eph. 1:14). In modern Greek, the same basic word used by Paul (*arrabōn*, "pledge") means engagement ring, an earnest of marriage. As if His bare promise were not more than enough, God swears an oath on Himself and gives us the presence of the Holy Spirit as a pledge, an earnest, on the oath.

In order that by two unchangeable things, in which it is impossible for God to lie, we may have strong encouragement, we who have fled for refuge in laying hold of the hope set before us. (6:18)

The **two unchangeable things** are God's promise and His pledge, His promise and His oath. They are immutable, without any possibility of change or variance. The term (*ametathetos*) was used in relation to wills. Once properly made, a will was *ametathetos*, unchangeable by anyone but the maker. God has declared His promise and His pledge to be *ametathetos*, even by Himself. They cannot be turned around or altered. "You're secure," He says. "Come to Christ; there's nothing to fear. I'll hold you; I'll never let go of you." Our security is not in our never letting go of God but in His never letting go of us.

In the Septuagint, the Greek word here translated "refuge" is used for the cities of refuge God provided for those who sought protection from avengers for an accidental killing (see Num. 35; Deut. 19; Josh. 20). We will never know whether God can hold us until in desperation we run to Him for refuge.

The hope set before us is Jesus Himself, and the gospel He has brought. Paul speaks of his Savior as "Christ Jesus, who is our hope" (1 Tim. 1:1). In Colossians he speaks of the gospel as our hope (1:5).

HIS PRIEST

This hope we have as an anchor of the soul, a hope both sure and steadfast and one which enters within the veil, where Jesus has entered as a forerunner for us, having become a high priest forever according to the order of Melchizedek. (6:19-20)

God gave Abraham the security of His Person, His purpose, and His pledge. All these He also gives to us who have believed in Christ. But He gives us yet another, His Priest. As our High Priest, Jesus serves as the anchor of our souls, the One who will forever keep us from drifting away from God.

Jesus' entering **within the veil** signifies His entering the Holy of

Holies, where the sacrifice of atonement was made. Under the Old Covenant it was made yearly by the high priest. Under the New is has been made once for all time by Christ's sacrifice on the cross. Our anchored soul is, in God's mind, already secure within the veil, secure within His eternal sanctuary. When Jesus entered the heavenly Holy of Holies, he did not leave after the sacrifice as did the Aaronic high priests, but "He sat down at the right hand of the Majesty on high" (Heb. 1:3). In other words, Jesus remains there forever as Guardian of our souls. Such absolute security is almost incomprehensible. Not only are our souls anchored within the impregnable, inviolable heavenly sanctuary, but our Savior, Jesus Christ, stands guard over them as well! How can the Christian's security be described as anything but eternal? Truly we can trust God and His Savior, the Lord Jesus Christ, with our souls. That is good cause to come all the way to salvation and to enjoy its security.

Melchizedek—A Type of Christ (7:1-10)

For this Melchizedek, king of Salem, priest of the Most High God, who met Abraham as he was returning from the slaughter of the kings and blessed him, to whom also Abraham apportioned a tenth part of all the spoils, was first of all, by the translation of his name, king of righteousness, and then also king of Salem, which is king of peace. Without father, without mother, without genealogy, having neither beginning of days nor end of life, but made like the Son of God, he abides a priest perpetually. Now observe how great this man was to whom Abraham, the patriarch, gave a tenth of the choicest spoils. And those indeed of the sons of Levi who receive the priest's office have commandment in the Law to collect a tenth from the people, that is, from their brethren, although these are descended from Abraham. But the one whose genealogy is not traced from them collected a tenth from Abraham, and blessed the one who had the promises. But without any dispute the lesser is blessed by the greater. And in this case mortal men receive tithes, but in that case one receives them, of whom it is witnessed that he lives on. And, so to speak, through Abraham even Levi, who received tithes, paid tithes, for he was still in the loins of his father when Melchizedek met him. (7:1-10)

In biblical study, a type refers to an Old Testament person, practice, or ceremony that has a counterpart, an antitype, in the New Testament. In that sense types are predictive. The type pictures, or prefigures, the antitype. The type, though it is historical, real, and of God, is nonetheless imperfect and temporary. The antitype, on the other hand, is perfect and eternal. The study of types and antitypes is called, as one might expect, typology.

The bronze serpent that God commanded Moses to set on a standard (Num. 21:8), for example, was a type of Christ's being lifted up on the cross (John 3:14). The sacrificial lamb was a type of the Lamb of God, Jesus Christ, who was sacrificed for the sins of the world (John 1:29; Rev. 5:6, 8; etc.).

Melchizedek is also a type of Christ. As mentioned earlier, the Bible gives very little historical information about Melchizedek. All that we know is located in Genesis 14, Psalm 110, and Hebrews 5-7. The most detailed information is in Hebrews 7:1-3.

Types are frail illustrations at best. They are analogies, and, like all analogies, they correspond to the person or thing to which they are compared only in certain ways—perhaps only in one way. The bronze serpent typified Christ in that it was lifted up for all the people to see and in that looking upon it brought them deliverance. The sacrificial lamb typifies Christ in that it is very meek (innocent) and that it was sacrificed on behalf of the sins of another. Similarly, though Melchizedek is in no way the equal of Christ, his unique priesthood, and even his name, typify Jesus Christ and His work in a number of significant ways.

Chapter 7 is the focal point of Hebrews. It concerns the central, the most important, part of Judaism—the priesthood. No sacrifices could be made except by the priest and no forgiveness of sins could be had apart from the sacrifices. Obedience to the law was exceedingly important, but the offering of sacrifices was even more important. And the priesthood was essential for offering them. Consequently, the priesthood was exalted in Judaism.

The law God gave Israel was holy and good, but because the Israelites, as all men, were sinful by nature, they could not keep the law perfectly. When they broke the law, fellowship with God was also broken. The only way of restoring fellowship was to remove the sin that was committed, and the only way to do that was through a blood sacrifice. When a person repented and made a proper offering through the priest, his sacrifice was meant to show the genuineness of his penitence by obedience to God's requirement. God accepted that faithful act and granted forgiveness.

UNDERSTANDING MELCHIZEDEK IS FOR THE MATURE

The writer first introduced Melchizedek in chapter 5, but before he could explain the significance of this ancient priest-king, he gave the warning to the immature Jews who could not bring themselves to accept Christ as their Savior (5:11—6:20). At the end of the beautiful encouragement to believers about the security of their salvation which follows that warning, Jesus again is said to be "a high priest forever according to the order of Melchizedek" (6:20). The subject thus returns to that very unique priest.

There is much conjecture about Melchizedek. Some insist he is an angel who took human form for a while during the time of Abraham. But the priesthood was a human, not angelic, function (Heb. 5:1). Others suggest that He is actually, not just typically, Jesus Christ Himself, who took a preincarnate form during Abraham's time. But Melchizedek is described as **made** *like* the Son of God (7:3), not as *being* the Son of God. I believe that Melchizedek was a historical human being, whose priestly ministry typifies that of Christ, a man whom God designed to use as a picture of Jesus Christ. But we cannot be sure of the details of his identity. Those remain among the secret things that belong only to the Lord.

The accounts of Melchizedek in sacred history are one of the most remarkable proofs of the divine inspiration and unity of Scripture. The whole concept of Melchizedek is an amazing insight into the fact that God wrote the Bible. In Genesis we have only three verses about Melchizedek. Some thousand years later David makes a briefer mention of him in Psalm 110:4, declaring for the first time that the Messiah's priesthood would be like Melchizedek's. After another thousand years, the writer of Hebrews tells us even more of Melchizedek's significance. He reveals things about Melchizedek that even Melchizedek, or his contemporary, Abraham, did not know—and of which David had only a glimpse. So we reason that the God who wrote the book of Hebrews wrote the book of Genesis and Psalm 110—and all the rest of Scripture.

Hebrews 7:1-10 first presents, then proves, the superiorities of Melchizedek's priesthood over that of the Levitical-Aaronic.

For this Melchizedek, king of Salem, priest of the Most High God, who met Abraham as he was returning from the slaughter of the kings and blessed him, to whom also Abraham apportioned a tenth part of all the spoils, was first of all, by the translation of his name, king of righteousness, and then also king of Salem, which is king of peace. Without father, without mother, without genealogy, having neither beginning of days nor end of life, but made like the Son of God, he abides a priest perpetually. (7:1-3)

Verses 1-2 are essentially a summary of the Genesis 14 account. They remind us that **Melchizedek** was the **king of Salem** (an ancient name for Jerusalem), that he was a **priest of the Most High God,** that he blessed **Abraham** after the patriarch had defeated the oppressive King Chedorlaomer and his three allies, and that Abraham, in turn, offered Melchizedek a tithe of the **spoils.** The writer also points out that the literal meaning of Melchizedek's title is **king of peace** ('Salem" is from the same Hebrew root as *shālom*, "peace").

Before we look into Melchizedek's priesthood, we should review the Levitical, with which his is compared.

THE LEVITICAL PRIESTHOOD

First, as mentioned above, the entire tribe of Levi was dedicated by God for religious service. Although all priests were Levites, not all Levites were priests. All priests, in fact, not only had to be descended from Levi but also from Aaron, Moses' brother. The nonpriestly Levites served as helpers to the priests, and probably as singers, instrumentalists, and the like. The priesthood was strictly national, strictly Jewish. Second, the Levites were subject to the king just as much as were the other tribes. Their priestly functions were not under the control of the king, but in all other matters they were ordinary subjects. They were in no way a ruling class. A Levite, in fact, could not be king. They were set aside as a first fruit to God for special priestly service (Num. 8:14-16). Third, the priestly sacrifices, including the one by the high priest on the Day of Atonement, were not permanent. They had to be repeated and repeated and repeated—continually. They had no permanence. They provided no permanent forgiveness, no permanent righteousness, no permanent peace. Fourth, the Levitical priesthood was hereditary. A man who served as a priest did so because he was born into the right family, not because he lived a right life. Fifth, just as the effects of the sacrifices were temporary, so was the time of priestly service. A priest served from the age of 25 until the age of 50, after which his ministry was over (Num. 8:24-25).

MELCHIZEDEK'S SUPERIOR PRIESTHOOD

Melchizedek's priesthood was superior to the Levitical in every way, but five specific ones are given in Hebrews 7:1-3.

MELCHIZEDEK'S PRIESTHOOD WAS UNIVERSAL, NOT NATIONAL

In relation to Israel, God took the name of Jehovah, or Yahweh. But no Jew would utter this name of God. It was too holy to pronounce. And because ancient Hebrew had no vowels, even the oldest of manuscripts do not help us to know exactly how the name would have been pronounced (although probably it was Yahweh, rather than Jehovah). When the Scriptures were read aloud, the title *Lord* (Hebrew, *'ădōnāy*) was substituted for this name of God. In most English translations of the Bible, the name is given as LORD (capital and small capitals), and occasionally as Jehovah. This name was uniquely related to God's covenant with Israel. It was His covenant name.

The Levitical priests, therefore, were priests of Jehovah. The Israelites were Jehovah's people and the Levites were Jehovah's priests. The Levitical priests could minister only to Israel and only for Jehovah.

Melchizedek, however, was **priest of the Most High God** ('*Ēl 'Elyôn*, a more universal name for God). It represents God as possessor of heaven and earth, God above all national or dispensational distinctions. The Most High God is over both Jew and Gentile, and is first mentioned in Scripture in relation to Melchizedek (Gen. 14:18).

The significance is this: Jesus is not just the Messiah of Israel, but of the world. His priesthood is universal, just as Melchizedek's. This was an extremely important truth for Jews who had come to Christ, as well as those who were considering putting their trust in Christ. To them, there was no other priesthood established by the true God but the Levitical, which was restricted to Israel. Here they are reminded that their father Abraham, the first Jew, offered tithes to another type of priest. This priest served the one true God, but he lived hundreds of years before the Levitical priesthood came into existence. It is significant that, immediately after his encounter with Melchizedek, Abraham spoke to the king of Sodom about "the LORD God Most High" (Gen. 14:22), a combination of the covenant and universal names.

The indecisive Jews were told, in effect, "Even your own Scriptures recognize a priesthood not only that is completely apart from that of Aaron, but that existed long before Aaron's." This was a powerful argument.

MELCHIZEDEK'S PRIESTHOOD WAS ROYAL

Melchizedek was himself a **king.** Four times in two verses (7:1-2) he is referred to as a king. As already mentioned, rulership of any sort was totally foreign to the Levitical priesthood. Melchizedek's universal priesthood and his royal office beautifully typify Jesus' saviorhood and lordship, as perfect Priest and perfect King. Though never known in Israel, the dual role of priest-king was predicted by her prophets. Speaking of the Messiah, Zechariah writes, "Yes, it is He who will build the temple of the LORD, and He who will bear the honor and sit and rule on His throne. Thus, He will be a priest on His throne, and the counsel of peace will be between the two offices" (Zech. 6:13). In his psalm that mentions Melchizedek, David also looks forward to the Messiah who will be both Priest and King (110:1, 4).

Because **Salem** was an ancient name for Jerusalem, Melchizedek ruled over God's special city, His holy city that was always close to His heart. "For the LORD has chosen Zion [Jerusalem]; He has desired it for His habitation. This is My resting place forever; here I will dwell, for I have desired it" (Ps. 132:13-14). We are not told when God first considered Jerusalem to be His holy city, but He had a faithful king who was a faithful priest there even in the time of **Abraham**—many centuries before Israel's priests ministered there or Israel's kings ruled there.

No truth of Scripture is more definite than that God chose the Jews as His special people, His very unique and cherished people. But Scripture is equally clear that Israel continually misunderstood and presumed upon her unique relation to God. They, for example, recognized Him as absolute Creator of heaven and earth and as sovereign over His world. But they had a very difficult time understanding Him as Redeemer of the world. As Creator and Sustainer, He was the world's; but as Savior and Lord, He was theirs alone. (Jonah's reluctance to preach to Gentiles illustrates this.) They could hardly conceive of another divine covenant and another divine priesthood, especially one that was royal and superior to their own. Yet they are told that the covenant in Christ, though called new, not only has superseded theirs but, in type, actually *preceded* theirs.

MELCHIZEDEK'S PRIESTHOOD WAS RIGHTEOUS AND PEACEFUL

There was no permanent righteousness or peace related to Aaron's priesthood. Melchizedek, however, was king both **of righteousness** and **of peace.** His very name means "king of righteousness." Although we have no historical record of his monarchy, we are told that he ruled righteously and peacefully.

The purpose of the Aaronic priesthood was to obtain righteousness for the people. The sacrifices were made to restore the people to a right relationship to God. But they never succeeded, in any deep and lasting way. God honored the sacrifice that was properly made. He had, after all, prescribed them. But they were never meant to remove sin. They were only a prefigurement, a type, of the one perfect sacrifice that could and did remove sin. They symbolized the sacrifice that makes men righteous—and thereby brings men peace—but they themselves could not make men righteous or give men peace. As a temporary ritual they accomplished their God-ordained purpose. But they could not bring men to God. They were never meant to.

Melchizedek, though king of righteousness and of peace, could not make men righteous or give them peace. His priesthood was a better type of Christ's than was the Levitical, but it was still a type. Only the Divine Priest could *give* righteousness and peace. "Therefore having been justified [counted righteous] by faith, we have peace with God through our Lord Jesus Christ" (Rom. 5:1). That is the necessary order: righteousness and then peace. Christ gives us peace by giving us righteousness. "The work of righteousness will be peace, and the service of righteousness, quietness and confidence forever" (Isa. 32:17).

What the blood of bulls and goats could not do, the blood of Jesus Christ did. The Levitical sacrifices lasted only until a person sinned again. Jesus' sacrifice lasts through all eternity. Once reconciled to God through Christ, we will never be counted as sinful again, but always as righteous. Christ is the true King of Righteousness.

As the psalmist says so beautifully, in the Lord "righteousness and peace have kissed each other" (Ps. 85:10). The two things that men have longed for are a sense of righteousness before God and of being at peace with Him. These blessings have "kissed" each other and become a reality in the Messiah. Christ came to give us His righteousness that we might be at peace with God. Melchizedek pictured that.

MELCHIZEDEK'S PRIESTHOOD WAS PERSONAL, NOT HEREDITARY

The Levitical priesthood was entirely hereditary, through Aaron. Melchizedek's was personal. From the beginning of the Aaronic priesthood, genealogy determined everything, personal qualification nothing. If you descended from Aaron, you could serve; if you did not, you could not. Consequently, the priests often were more concerned about their pedigrees than their holiness.

That Melchizedek is said to have been **without father, without mother, without genealogy, having neither beginning of days nor end of life** does not mean that he came from nowhere. It simply means that in the Old Testament record nothing is said of his parents or origin.

It is interesting that the single Greek word (*agenealogētos*) translated **without genealogy** is found nowhere else in Scripture—in fact nowhere else in Greek literature. The reason, no doubt, is that it would have had no use because it would have made no sense. Everyone has a genealogy, whether he can trace it or not.

The point in Hebrews is that Melchizedek's parentage and origin are irrelevant to his priesthood. Whereas to the Aaronic priesthood genealogy was everything, to the Melchizedek priesthood it was nothing.

In this, Melchizedek was a type of Christ, not because Jesus had no genealogy but because Jesus's genealogy was not significant in regard to His priesthood. To be sure, Jesus' royal genealogy is important. It is given in some detail by both Matthew (1:1-17) and Luke (3:23-38). Matthew's gospel, in fact, begins as "The book of the genealogy of Jesus Christ" (1:1). But His lineage is not traced to Aaron or Levi, but to Judah. Jesus Christ, though God's own Son, was not qualified for the Levitical priesthood. Like Melchizedek, as far as his priesthood was concerned, He had no priestly genealogy and He needed none.

Jesus Christ was chosen as a priest because of His personal worth, His quality. He was chosen because of who He was, not because of where He came from genealogically. Jesus "has become such not on the basis of a law of physical requirement, but according to the power of an indestructible life" (Heb. 7:16). Like Melchizedek's, Jesus' qualifications were personal, not hereditary.

MELCHIZEDEK'S PRIESTHOOD IS ETERNAL, NOT TEMPORARY

Individually, a priest served only from the time he was 25 until he was 50. No priest, no matter how faithful, could serve more than 25 years. Collectively, the priesthood was also temporary. It began in the wilderness, when the covenant with Moses was made and the law was given. It ended when the Temple in Jerusalem was destroyed in A.D. 70. The Levitical priesthood was for the Old Covenant and *only* for the Old Covenant, the covenant of law.

Melchizedek's priesthood, however, had no such time or dispensational bounds. **He abides a priest perpetually.** It is not that he lived forever, but that the order of priesthood in which he ministered was forever. If he had lived forever, he would not be a type but a part of the reality. The picture of a landscape is not the landscape, but only a suggestion, a representation, of it. The fact that we have no biblical or other record of the beginning or end of Melchizedek's personal priesthood simply symbolizes the eternality of his priestly order. It is a type of Christ's truly eternal priesthood. Christ, "because He abides forever, holds His priesthood permanently. Hence, also, He is able to save forever those who draw near to God through Him, since He always lives to make intercession for them" (Heb. 7:24-25).

Jesus is a priest like Melchizedek. His priesthood is universal, royal, righteous and peaceful, personal, and eternal.

MELCHIZEDEK'S SUPERIORITIES PROVED

Now observe how great this man was to whom Abraham, the patriarch, gave a tenth of the choicest spoils. And those indeed of the sons of Levi who receive the priest's office have commandment in the Law to collect a tenth from the people, that is, from their brethren, although these are descended from Abraham. But the one whose genealogy is not traced from them collected a tenth from Abraham, and blessed the one who had the promises. But without any dispute the lesser is blessed by the greater. And in this case mortal men receive tithes, but in that case one receives them, of whom it is witnessed that he lives on. And, so to speak, through Abraham even

Levi, who received tithes, paid tithes, for he was still in the loins of his father when Melchizedek met him. (7:4-10)

In these verses we are given three reasons, or proofs, as to how and why Melchizedek's priesthood is superior to the Levitical.

ABRAHAM GAVE A TITHE TO MELCHIZEDEK

Abraham, father of the Jewish people, gave **tithes (a tenth)** of his war spoils—his **choicest spoils**—to Melchizedek. Though Melchizedek was a king, he had not fought with Abraham against Chedorlaomer. Nor do we have any record, or reason to believe, that Melchizedek had ever performed any priestly service for Abraham. Abraham simply recognized Melchizedek as a deserving and faithful priest of God Most High and consequently gave him a tithe from the best of the spoils. It was a voluntary act revealing thanks to God.

The Holy Spirit demonstrates that Melchizedek is greater than Levi and Aaron, progenitors of the Levitical priesthood, by showing that this priest-king is better than Abraham, the progenitor of both Levi and Aaron.

Abraham was under no obligation, no law or commandment, to give Melchizedek anything. He gave freely and generously, and he gave the best that he had, not his leftovers. He gave the **choicest spoils** to the Lord, through His servant Melchizedek.

Under grace we are free of the demands of the law. The New Testament specifies no definite amount or proportion of our money that we are to give to God. But this does not mean that our giving is optional, or that it should depend on our whim or personal feeling. It means that the basis of our giving should be our love and devotion to God, in gratitude for His inestimable gift to us. Just as Melchizedek's priesthood is a type of the priesthood of our Lord Jesus Christ, so Abraham's giving to Melchizedek is a type of what our giving to the Lord should be. It is not a type in its being a tenth, but in its being from his choicest possessions and being given freely, not because of legal requirement.

The Levites, as the priestly tribe, received no inheritance of land, as did all the other tribes. They were to be supported by a tithe from their brother Israelites. All the tribes, of course, were descendants of Abraham through Jacob. Under the Old Covenant, therefore, one group of Abraham's descendants tithed to another. The point of Hebrews 7:4-10 is that because Abraham, their common and supreme ancestor, had paid **tithes** to Melchizedek, even the Levites, "in advance," so to speak, also paid tithes to Melchizedek. Even before they existed, those to whom tithes were paid had themselves paid a tithe to another priesthood, proving that this priesthood was superior to theirs.

MELCHIZEDEK BLESSED ABRAHAM

One of the first things we learn in Scripture about Abraham, and that Abraham learned about himself from God, is that through him and his descendants all the world was to be blessed. It was a staggering, awesome, and marvelous promise, especially because it was made before Abraham had any descendants and when it seemed impossible that he ever would.

Just as we have no idea how much Abraham knew about Melchizedek, we have no idea how much Melchizedek knew about Abraham. We are told only of the brief encounter described in three verses of Genesis 14. Yet, just as Abraham knew he should tithe to Melchizedek, Melchizedek knew he should bless Abraham. In so doing, **without any dispute the lesser is blessed by the greater.** As the blesser, Melchizedek indisputably was superior to Abraham. If Melchizedek was superior to Abraham, then he must also be superior to the Levites, Abraham's descendants. Consequently, his priesthood is superior to theirs.

Directly or indirectly from Genesis 12 through Malachi, all of the Old Testament is the story of Abraham's descendants, God's chosen people. Yet this priest-king that both testaments together mention in only a handful of verses, was greater than Abraham, because he blessed Abraham. God operated in Melchizedek's life on the basis of personal qualification, and he was higher than Abraham in those qualifications. Therefore, he was chosen to bless Abraham. And if he was greater than Abraham, he was greater than anything that came from Abraham.

In the church God also works on the basis of personal qualifications. The standards for teaching shepherds, for ruling elders, for evangelists, and for all other offices are based on personal spiritual qualifications, not on heredity or class (cf. 1 Tim. 3:1-13; Titus 1:5-9). God calls certain people in this economy of grace on the basis of special personal qualifications. If a person is faithful over a little, he will be made lord over much. If we meet the qualifications, God will lift us to the ministry. He worked with Melchizedek in the same way. He was personally qualified to be what he was. His lineage had nothing to do with God's choosing him and sending him to bless Abraham. He was superior, and therefore he blessed Abraham.

MELCHIZEDEK'S PRIESTHOOD IS ETERNAL

The writer again points up the permanence of Melchizedek's priesthood.

And in this case mortal men receive tithes, but in that case one receives them, of whom it is witnessed that he lives on. (7:8)

Even if the Levitical priests had not been required to quit ministering when they reached 50 years of age, they would have ceased ministering when they died. That priesthood was temporary and those priests were temporary. The Jews paid **tithes** to priests who all died. Abraham paid tithes to a priest who, in type, **lives on.** Since no death is recorded of Melchizedek, his priesthood typically is eternal. In this his priesthood is clearly superior to that of Aaron.

Jesus Christ, of course, is the reality, the true Priest who is eternal, of whom Melchizedek is but a picture. Jesus Christ is a priest, the only Priest, who is alive forevermore. He is a greater priest because He is a living priest, not a dying one. Christ is Priest of a better priesthood than Aaron's. He is Priest of a better priesthood even than Melchizedek's. He is the only Priest of the only priesthood that can bring God to men and men to God. This was a great word of assurance to those Jews who had come to Jesus Christ.

Jesus, the Superior Priest—part 1 (7:11-19)

17

Now if perfection was through the Levitical priesthood (for on the basis of it the people received the Law), what further need was there for another priest to arise according to the order of Melchizedek, and not be designated according to the order of Aaron? For when the priesthood is changed, of necessity there takes place a change of law also. For the one concerning whom these things are spoken belongs to another tribe, from which no one has officiated at the altar. For it is evident that our Lord was descended from Judah, a tribe with refererence to which Moses spoke nothing concerning priests. And this is clearer still, if another priest arises according to the likeness of Melchizedek, who has become such not on the basis of a law of physical requirement, but according to the power of an indestructible life. For it is witnessed of Him, "Thou are a priest forever according to the order of Melchizedek." For, on the one hand, there is a setting aside of a former commandment because of its weakness and uselessness (for the Law made nothing perfect), and on the other hand there is a bringing in of a better hope, through which we draw near to God. (7:11-19)

The key phrase of this passage is **we draw near to God** (v. 19b).

God's ultimate desire for men is for them to come to Him. His ultimate desire for believers is that they continue to draw nearer to Him. God's goal in all that He does in behalf of men is that they might come into His presence. Drawing near to God is the essence of Christianity. Drawing near to God is the Christian's highest experience, and should be his highest purpose. This is the design of God for Christianity—access to His presence, coming into His presence with nothing between. Sometimes we forget this.

Some Christians seem to look at Jesus Christ only as a means to salvation and personal happiness. If they believe they are saved and are fairly happy with their circumstances, they consider their lives fulfilled. They are looking for happiness and security. They find these in Christ and are satisfied. Others see their Christian lives as a continuing, growing relationship to God through study of and obedience to His Word. This view of the Christian life is much more mature than the first. But the key to the Christian life is drawing near to God. The fullest expression of faith is to enter into the presence of God in His heavenly Holy of Holies and to fellowship with Him. That is something Judaism was limited in enabling men to do.

In his letter to the Ephesians, Paul gives the essence of the mature, spiritually fulfilled Christian life. "So that Christ may dwell in your hearts through faith; and that you, being rooted and grounded in love, may be able to comprehend with all the saints what is the breadth and length and height and depth, and to know the love of Christ which surpasses knowledge, that you may be filled up to all the fulness of God" (Eph. 3:17-19). This is Christianity—"the fulness of God."

That is the basic goal of the gospel. Judaism brought a man into the presence of God, but not in the purest and fullest sense. The veil was always there. Only in the New Covenant is complete entrance possible. Only by the blood of Jesus Christ, only by His priestly intercession at the right hand of God, based on His perfect sacrifice on Calvary, was access to God opened. These are the great recurring themes in Hebrews.

Aaron's priests could never bring a man fully to God. There was always a barrier in between. The veil could not be removed because sin had not been fully done away. But the fact that the Messiah was a priest after **the order of Melchizedek** opened the way. He could remove the veil because He atoned for sin. He actually bore our sin; the Levitical sacrifices only symbolically anticipated its cancellation. And now that sin had actually been dealt with, the Levitical priesthood was no longer necessary, and God set it aside. You do not need a symbol when you have the real thing. Now that the perfect had come, the imperfect passed away.

The design of Hebrews 7:11-19 is to show this truth. The point is to encourage the wavering Jews to break with the old system and come to Jesus Christ. This was not an easy thing for Jews to understand or accept.

Despite the many prophecies of the Messiah and of the new order He would bring, most Jews could not imagine that the Mosaic economy was temporary and inadequate and defective and unable to bring **perfection.** The very idea was incomprehensible to the pious Jew. All their lives they had assumed that the Levitical system was instituted by God, and that it was perfect, sufficient, and permanent. They were correct only in the first part. It was indeed instituted by God. But it was never intended or declared by Him to be perfect, eternally sufficient, or permanent.

It is the imperfection of the Levitical system that the Holy Spirit points out in our present passage. He uses invincible logic to show that the Aaronic priesthood was imperfect and that, because it was imperfect, it had to be superseded. First He shows the imperfection of the old priesthood, then the perfection of the new.

THE IMPERFECTION OF THE OLD PRIESTHOOD

God never intended for the **Levitical priesthood** to remain forever, and nowhere in Scripture is this idea taught. The Old Testament, in fact, anticipated (as in Ps. 110:4) that another priesthood was coming. If God predicted another priesthood was coming, it would have been reasonable to assume, even without further revelation, that the new one would be better and would replace the old. Israel was told that a greater priesthood was to come, of which the Messiah would be the Priest. If the Aaronic priesthood had been perfect, another would have been unnecessary. Or, if God had intended the Aaronic priesthood somehow to improve and one day introduce the age of perfect access to Him, why would He have planned for the Messiah to be a priest of a different **order?**

It was no accident or mistake that God set aside the Israelite priesthood. He had planned it that way from the beginning. That is obvious because soon after He called Abraham, before He actually made the covenant with him, God introduced him to Melchizedek, a priest of a higher order than the one that would come from Abraham's descendants.

THE MEANINGS OF PERFECTION

In Scripture, the word *perfect* is often used in the sense of maturity or completion, of being what something or someone is meant to be. Sometimes it means full-grown. Paul often uses it in this way. In Hebrews, however, it is used to refer to the goal and aim of Christianity. This goal, this maturity, is access to God. In this sense it does not mean spiritual maturity (being advanced in the faith) but salvation in Christ (coming to faith).

Hebrews 7:11 speaks of **perfection** not coming through the **Levitical priesthood.** The purpose of the priesthood was to reconcile men to God through sacrificing for their sins. But this priesthood could only picture, only typify, the actual reconciliation, because it could only typify cleansing of sin. It was therefore imperfect, in that it could not give men access to God. Verse 19 speaks of the law not being able to make men perfect, and goes on to say specifically that this imperfection, this failure, was in not being able to bring men near to God. The goals both of the Aaronic priesthood and of the Mosaic law were to bring men to God. They were both imperfect in achieving this goal, in the sense that they could not stand alone apart from the priesthood of Christ.

In Hebrews perfection first of all means access to God, not the spiritual maturity of Christians. "For by one offering He has perfected for all time those who are sanctified" (Heb. 10:14). In other words, a person is perfected when, by Christ's sacrifice, he is given full access to God in Christ.

The Levitical priesthood could not provide this full access. Jesus said, "No one comes to the Father, but through Me" (John 14:6). Jesus was speaking to Jews, to those under the Old Covenant, the Levitical priesthood. The Old Covenant sacrifices merely covered over sin, they could not remove it. There was a degree of forgiveness, but it was never comprehensive. Permanent forgiveness, and therefore permanent access to God, can come only through Jesus Christ—in the New Covenant and through the new priesthood.

> For the Law, since it has only a shadow of the good things to come and not the very form of things, can never by the same sacrifices year by year, which they offer continually, make perfect those who draw near. Otherwise, would they not have ceased to be offered, because the worshipers, having once been cleansed, would no longer have had consciousness of sins? (10:1-2)

Had the old sacrifices been able to bring a person into God's presence, they would have ceased. They would have fulfilled their purpose.

The Old Testament saints lacked the total sense of freedom from the consciousness of their sin. They came short of that full privilege, because the sacrifices of that covenant could not completely remove their sin and bring them to God. Because their sins were not finally cleansed, their consciences could not be wholly cleansed, could not be freed. The New Covenant gives greater understanding of full forgiveness, freedom from guilt, and a peaceful conscience.

Jeremiah clearly predicted the New Covenant and many of its superiorities to the Old.

> "Behold, the days are coming," declares the LORD, "when I will make a new covenant with the house of Israel and with the house of Judah, not like the covenant which I made with their fathers in the day I took them by the hand to

bring them out of the land of Egypt, . . . But this is the covenant which I will make with the house of Israel after those days," declares the LORD, "I will put My law within them, and on their heart I will write it; and I will be their God, and they shall be My people. And they shall not teach again, each man his neighbor and each man his brother, saying, 'Know the LORD,' for they shall all know Me, from the least of them to the greatest of them," declares the LORD, "for I will forgive their iniquity, and their sin I will remember no more." (Jer. 31:31-34)

A portion of this passage is quoted in Hebrews 10:16-17, where the point is made that where there is true forgiveness of sin, sacrifice is no longer necessary. Once the final sacrifice was offered, we were free from sin and therefore from guilt. But all through Old Testament times the Israelites were troubled because their sins were never fully and permanently covered. They were still anticipating the perfect sacrifice.

Hebrews 9:8-9 makes the same basic point: "The Holy Spirit is signifying this, that the way into the holy place has not yet been disclosed, while the outer tabernacle is still standing, which is a symbol for the present time. Accordingly both gifts and sacrifices are offered which cannot make the worshiper perfect in conscience." Those sacrifices could not give a person access to God's presence. They offered no "way into the holy place," where God dwells. They offered limited freedom from guilt, "since they relate only to food and drink and various washings, regulations for the body imposed until a time of reformation" (v. 10). The "time of reformation," of course, is the time of the New Covenant. No one through the old economy had complete access to God. There was only a temporary covering over of sin, not removal of sin or of the guilt that it brings.

The point of 7:11 is made clear. If the Levitical priesthood could have brought this perfection—which is access to God, or salvation—why would God have provided another priesthood?

This truth was extremely important for Jews to hear. It was important for believing Jews as assurance that they were now totally secure in Jesus Christ, that their break with Judaism and its rituals and repeated sacrifices was justified. They had no reason to look back longingly at the forms and ceremonies and symbols—as meaningful and significant as these once were. They no longer needed a picture of salvation, for they *had* the reality of the Savior. But in the argument of Hebrews 7, the truth is even more important for Jews who had not yet come all the way to Christ. It shows them that the Levitical priesthood could not bring men to perfection, to God. It was never intended to do so. As long as they held onto it and relied on its sacrifices, they would never be free of sin, they would never have access to God.

What the old economy could not do, Christ did. The old priesthood had its place in God's plan. But it was inferior and ineffective. It only *pictured* perfection. Similarly, the law had its place in God's plan. It represented God's truth and righteousness. It *demanded* perfection. **For on the basis of it** [that is, perfection] **the people received the Law.** But neither the sacrifice that pictured it nor the law that demanded it could provide perfection. Perfection is provided only in Jesus Christ.

For when the priesthood is changed, of necessity there takes place a change of law also. (7:12)

Changed (*metatithēmi*) means to put one thing in the place of another. Christianity, in a sense, comes from Judaism. But Christianity is not merely enhanced Judaism; it replaces Judaism. For a Jewish convert, his faith is changed from Judaism to Christianity. The new priesthood, after the order of Melchizedek, was not added to Aaron's, but replaced it. Aaron's priesthood now has no validity at all, not even as a picture of salvation or as a temporary covering of sin. It is defunct, totally abrogated.

Because the Aaronic **priesthood** and the Mosaic **law** were so closely tied to one another, a changed (replaced) priesthood also meant a changed law. Is the law of God, therefore, also done away with? It is in a certain way and sense. The word **law** has several meanings in Scripture. In its broadest sense, it refers to the whole Old Testament, the Old Covenant. It can also mean the Decalogue, the Ten Commandments. It can also signify the required rituals and ceremonies of the Old Covenant. Since they were commanded of Israel by God, they were part of His law for them. I believe that is clearly what is meant here. The Holy Spirit is saying that, if the old priesthood is defunct, so is all law that pertains to it.

God's moral law, however, reflected not only in the Ten Commandments but throughout the Old Testament, is part of His very nature, and therefore cannot possibly change. In the New Testament, God's standards of righteousness for His people are reaffirmed, not decreased—much less done away with. If adultery, stealing, lying, and coveting were wrong under the Old Testament, they are also under the New. As Jesus makes clear in the Sermon on the Mount, God holds us accountable to our intents, not just our actions (Matt. 5:21-48). Far from setting aside His moral law in the New Covenant, He has *strengthened* it as far as standards for His people are concerned. The New Testament demands a greater judgment on disobedience (Acts 17:30-31).

But the ceremonial law, the Aaronic system of sacrifices, *has* been set aside. "You don't need to trek to the Temple all the time," the Jews are told. "That's done with; it's over; it's been replaced—permanently." Some who had come to Christ, and many who were thinking of coming, were still worshiping at the Temple, still hanging on to the ritual of the old system. Setting this aside was extremely difficult for many Jews to do and the reasons for doing so were extremely hard to grasp.

Some believing Jews, in fact, not only insisted on maintaining their own Jewish practices, but on making them mandatory for everyone who wanted to become a Christian. These people were called Judaizers, and they were a plague to the early church for many years. They told prospective believers, and even non-Jewish Christians, that they needed to be circumcized and have sacrifices made in the Temple and follow all the prescribed Jewish laws and rituals. It was this Judaizing of Christianity that Paul opposed so strongly in several of his letters, especially Galatians.

> "You foolish Galatians, who has bewitched you? . . . Having begun by the Spirit, are you now being perfected by the flesh? . . . Now that you have come to know God, or rather to be known by God, how is it that you turn back again to the weak and worthless elemental things, to which you desire to be enslaved all over again? . . . For in Christ Jesus neither circumcision nor uncircumcision means anything, but faith working through love." (Gal. 3:1, 3; 4:9; 5:6)

On the Mount of Transfiguration, Peter was so awestruck when he saw Moses and Elijah appear and talk with Jesus that he blurted out, " 'Rabbi, it is good for us to be here; and let us make three tabernacles, one for You, one for Moses, and one for Elijah' " (Mark 9:5). Jesus said nothing, but "then a cloud formed, overshadowing them, and a voice came out of the cloud, 'This is My beloved Son, listen to Him!' And all at once they looked around and saw no one with them anymore, except Jesus alone" (vv. 7-8). God was saying to Peter—and to James and John and every person—"Don't listen to Moses and Elijah. This is My Son; hear Him and Him alone." Even before the New Covenant was finalized by Jesus' crucifixion and resurrection, God illustrated that the Old had passed. The covenant represented by Moses and Elijah was gone (cf. John 4:21-24).

At Sinai the people were fenced off at the foot of the mountain, so they could not approach God. In the Tabernacle and in the Temple the veil stood between them and God's presence in the Holy of Holies. The Old Covenant not only did not bring men into God's presence, it forbade them from trying to get there. Without full cleansing, complete forgiveness of sins, they were not qualified. But Jesus, so to speak, came down the mountain to the people and tore down the veil.

So the whole Judaistic system was changed—not just changed, but exchanged—for a new order, a new Priest, a new sacrifice, an entirely New Covenant.

For the one concerning whom these things are spoken belongs to an-

other tribe, from which no one has officiated at the altar. For it is
evident that our Lord was descended from Judah, a tribe with reference to which Moses spoke nothing concerning priests. (7:13-14)

Jesus did not come from Levi, which was the only priestly **tribe.**
He was from **Judah,** which, just as all the other non-Levitical tribes, had
nothing to do with priestly service at the altar. If Jesus became a high
priest, therefore, He obviously was of a different order of priesthood
from the Aaronic-Levitical. And His priestly qualifications obviously
were not hereditary. The hereditary Levitical priesthood—typical, temporary, and imperfect—was changed and replaced by Jesus' Melchizedek-like
priesthood, which was real, eternal, and perfect.

The Perfection of the New Priesthood

**And this is clearer still, if another priest arises according to the like-
ness of Melchizedek, who has become such not on the basis of a law
of physical requirement, but according to the power of an indestructible life. For it is witnessed of Him, "Thou art a priest forever after
the order of Melchizedek." (7:15-17)**

The Greek language has two words for **another.** *Allos* means another—that is, an additional one—of the same kind. The word used in
verse 15, however, is *heteros*, which means another of a different kind.
The first indicates a quantitative difference, the second a qualitative difference. If I traded in my small imported car for another small imported
car, I would be getting another automobile that was *allos*, of the same
kind. But if I traded it for a large American car, I would be getting another automobile that was *heteros*, of a different kind, a different quality.
In Christ we do not have another priest just like those who ministered in the Tabernacle and the Temple. He is *heteros*, of a completely
different kind and **order.** Under the Old Covenant there were many
priests, and they were all *allos*. Under the New there is but one Priest,
and He is *heteros*.

THE PERFECT PRIEST ARISES BY HIMSELF

Both verses 11 and 15 speak of another priest arising. But in verse
15, **arises** (*anistēmi*) is in the Greek middle voice, which is reflexive. The
phrase, then, could be translated, "another priest arises by Himself." This
meaning has special significance in several ways.
First of all, I believe it signifies the virgin birth. As God, Jesus
raised Himself up by giving birth to Himself, so to speak. No Aaronic

priest could make such a claim. All other priests besides Jesus "arose" by virtue of their mothers and fathers, not of themselves.

Second, arising by Himself implies that this other Priest had no priestly ancestry, no priestly heritage. Aaronic priests could only claim a right to priesthood because of who their parents were. Jesus claimed the right because of who He Himself is.

Third, Jesus' arising by Himself indicates His resurrection. In Acts 2:32, Luke uses *anistēmi* specifically to refer to Jesus' resurrection.

Who has become such not on the basis of a law of physical require-ment, but according to the power of an indestructible life. For it is witnessed of Him, "Thou art a priest forever according to the order of Melchizedek." (7:16-17)

The standard prescribed for priests in the old economy had to do only with the physical. A priest, of course, was supposed to be godly, just as all Israelites were supposed to be godly. A number of priests who were especially ungodly were severely punished by God. But godliness was not a qualification for their serving at the altar. First, they had to be pure descendants of Aaron. Even with this pedigree, however, any one of more than 100 physical blemishes or deficiencies could disqualify them from officiating. But there was not a single moral or spiritual qualification that they had to meet. Their serving had nothing at all to do with character, ability, personality, or holiness.

Like Melchizedek's priesthood, however, Jesus' was first and last based on who He was. It had nothing to do with the physical body, but everything to do with eternal power, **the power of an indestructible life.** In the case of the Levitical priesthood, no matter how ill-suited a man may have been, or how reluctant to take the office, the law made him a priest because of the family into which he was born and because of certain physical requirements he had to meet. It was outward compul-sion. For Jesus Christ, priesthood is an inner compulsion, because of who He is. He became, and He continues, a priest by eternal power—a power that can do what no priest could ever do: give us access to God.

The evidence and the logic are overwhelming that the Levitical priesthood is now obsolete and that the new priesthood that God had long predicted *could not be* Levitical. Beginning with Genesis 49:10, the Old Testament is clear that the Messiah would come from Judah. And in many passages, such as Psalm 110:4, it is also clear that the Messiah will be both priest and king and that His priesthood would not be hereditary and temporary but would be based on personal qualification and would be eternal.

Jesus Christ can do what Aaron could not do. He takes us into the presence of God and He anchors us there eternally. "This hope we have

as an anchor of the soul, a hope both sure and steadfast and one which
enters within the veil, where Jesus has entered as a forerunner for us"
(Heb. 6:19). That is ultimate power, and ultimate love. It is the accom-
plishment of the ultimate Priest through the ultimate priesthood.

**For, on the one hand, there is a setting aside of a former command-
ment because of its weakness and uselessness (for the Law made
nothing perfect), and on the other hand there is a bringing in of a
better hope, through which we draw near to God.** (7:18-19)

Here is the climax of the text. Aaron is replaced by Christ. God
has set aside the old and imperfect and has replaced it with the new and
perfect. **Setting aside** (*athetēsis*) pertains to doing away with something
that has been established. It is used, for example, of annulling a treaty, a
promise, a law, a regulation, or of removing a man's name from a docu-
ment. The whole paraphernalia of the sacrificial system, the whole ceremonial system, was canceled, annulled, done away with entirely. God assured its end in A.D. 70, when He allowed the Temple to be destroyed.

The old system could reveal sin. It could even cover sin, in a certain way and to a certain temporary degree. But it could never remove
sin, and so itself had to be removed. It brought nothing to conclusion. It
gave no security. It gave no peace. A man never had a clear conscience.
But the priesthood of Jesus Christ made all of what Israel looked forward
to a reality. It brought access to God.

Peter tells us, "As to this salvation, the prophets who prophesied
of the grace that would come to you made careful search and inquiry,
seeking to know what person or time the Spirit of Christ within them
was indicating as He predicted the sufferings of Christ and the glories to
follow. It was revealed to them that they were not serving themselves,
but you, in these things which now have been announced to you through
those who preached the gospel to you by the Holy Spirit sent from heav-
en—things into which angels long to look" (1 Pet. 1:10-12). In other
words, those Old Testament saints only saw salvation from a distance.
They were neither fully certain nor secure until Christ came. They trusted in hope, looking ahead for a conscience freed from sin. But now we
can go into God's presence and we can sit down before Him and, with the
apostle Paul, say, "Abba, Father." We have access to God.

> Since therefore, brethren, we have confidence to enter the holy place by the
> blood of Jesus, by a new and living way which He inaugurated for us through the
> veil, that is, His flesh, and since we have a great priest over the house of God, let
> us draw near with a sincere heart in full assurance of faith. (10:19-22)

A young woman had run up a lot of bills and charged far beyond what she was able to pay. She was in debt over her head and saw no way to get out. She was in trouble and the situation looked hopeless. Then a young man came along and fell deeply in love with her. After some months he proposed. She also loved him very much, but felt that she should tell him about her debts before she agreed to marry him. When told, he said, "Don't worry. I'll pay all your debts. Just leave them to me." Before the wedding he gave her an engagement ring and reassured her many times that he would take care of her debts. She trusted him implicitly and knew he was a person of his word. She had every reason to be confident and hopeful. But she was not yet actually free of her debts and, consequently, could not be at peace about them. Finally they were married, and he paid her debts. Not only that, but he told her that he was wealthy beyond her wildest dreams and gave her a joint checking account with himself. She would never again need to be concerned about debts. From that time on she was secure in the riches of the one she loved and who loved her.

That is how much better off a person is under the New Covenant than under the Old. In Christ we are freed from all sin's debts, and we live forever in the riches of the One we love and who loves us.

Jesus, the Superior Priest—part 2 (7:20-28)

And inasmuch as it was not without an oath (for they indeed became priests without an oath, but He with an oath through the One who said to Him, "The LORD has sworn and will not change His mind, 'Thou art a priest forever' "); so much the more also Jesus has become the guarantee of a better covenant. And the former priests, on the one hand, existed in greater numbers, because they were prevented by death from continuing, but He, on the other hand, because He abides forever, holds His priesthood permanently. Hence, also, He is able to save forever those who draw near to God through Him, since He always lives to make intercession for them. For it was fitting that we should have such a high priest, holy, innocent, undefiled, separated from sinners and exalted above the heavens; who does not need daily, like those high priests, to offer up sacrifices, first for His own sins, and then for the sins of the people, because this He did once for all when He offered up Himself. For the Law appoints men as high priests who are weak, but the word of the oath, which came after the Law, appoints a Son, made perfect forever. (7:20-28)

Here the Holy Spirit presents Jesus as a superior priest three ways. He is the guarantee of a better covenant, the eternal Savior, and holy and sinless.

GUARANTEE OF A BETTER COVENANT

And inasmuch as it was not without an oath (for they indeed became priests without an oath, but He with an oath through the One who said to Him, "The Lord has sworn and will not change His mind, 'Thou art a priest forever' "); so much the more also Jesus has become the guarantee of a better covenant. (7:20-22)

God did not swear to Aaron that his priesthood would be forever. In fact God never suggested, to Aaron or to anyone else, that that priesthood would be anything but temporary. However, many Israelites no doubt thought that it would be permanent, but their belief had no basis in Scripture. Neither when the old priesthood was first established nor when any priest or group of priests were consecrated had God made an oath—or any sort of promise, conditional or unconditional—that this priesthood would be eternal. But with Christ He swore an eternal priesthood, as David had written in Psalm 110:4, to which the writer here refers for the fourth time in the letter (see also 5:6; 6:20; 7:17). To make the point more emphatic, David added, **and will not change His mind.** God made an eternal decision about the new eternal priesthood.

Neither David nor the writer of Hebrews suggests that God's oath was any more reliable or valid than His bare word. It is rather that, when He makes eternal transactions, He has chosen to do so with an oath. The oath does not represent greater truthfulness but puts the emphasis on permanence.

As already emphasized several times, the Levitical priests ministered in the Temple on a temporary and repetitive basis. They were mortal, so when they died their sons had to replace them. They were also sinful, so always had to offer sacrifices for themselves before they were qualified to offer them for the people. The sacrifices themselves only had a certain temporary effectiveness, and so had to be repeated and repeated. God *intended* for that priesthood to operate in that way. He did not plan for it to be perfect or permanent, and so did not establish it with an oath.

When God made His covenantal promise to Abraham, however, He did so with an oath (Gen. 22:16-18; cf. Heb. 6:13). This promise was unconditional and eternal. "God, desiring even more to show to the heirs of the promise the unchangeableness of His purpose, interposed with an oath" (Heb. 6:17). God wanted Abraham, and eventually all Israel and all the world, to know that this promise was permanent. It was through Abraham that Messiah came, and therefore the blessing that every believer will experience throughout all of eternity is a perpetual fulfillment of the Abrahamic covenant.

Jesus' priesthood is also based on an oath of God, and is thereby shown to be eternal, unchangeable. Because of that fact, Jesus is made a

guarantee, a surety, **of a better covenant.** The covenant that God made through Jesus is better than the old one because the old one was temporary and the new one is eternal. A better priest guarantees a better covenant.

It is important to recognize that the Old Covenant was not *bad*. God did not make the new because the old was bad, but because it was imperfect and temporary. The Mosaic covenant was a very good covenant, a God-given, God-ordained covenant that served its purpose for the time it was meant to be in effect. In many respects the Old Covenant was good in its own right. It was good as the product of God's wisdom and righteous will. It served a very good purpose, for it helped to restrain sin and to promote godliness. It also pointed toward the Messiah and helped prepare the way for Him. Until the coming of Jesus Christ, the Mosaic covenant was exactly the covenant that Israel was supposed to have. The New Covenant is better simply because the Old was incomplete. The Old was good; the New is **better.**

A beautiful illustration of guaranteeing is found in Genesis. When Jacob's sons were preparing to go to Egypt for a second time to get grain for their starving families, Judah reminded his father that the Egyptian ruler (who, unknown to them, was Joseph) told them they could not expect to get more food unless they brought their youngest brother, Benjamin, with them to Egypt. Only after Judah nobly offered to be the security for Benjamin did his father reluctantly agree. "I myself will be surety for him; you may hold me responsible for him. If I do not bring him back to you and set him before you, then let me bear the blame before you forever" (Gen. 43:9). After receiving more food from Joseph, they were stopped on their way home because of Joseph's concealing his own silver cup in Benjamin's sack of food. Dismayed at what had happened, and grieved at what the loss of Benjamin would do to his father, Judah again offered to become a guarantee for his brother. After a lengthy explanation to Joseph of his concern, Judah said, "Now, therefore, please let your servant remain instead of the lad a slave to my lord, and let the lad go up with his brothers" (44:33). Judah made the second promise of surety so he could uphold the first. He was willing to go to any length to fulfill the pledge to his father that Benjamin would return home safely. In this noble gesture, Judah illustrated the idea of Christ's being the guarantee for the New Covenant.

Paul was willing to be surety for the runaway slave, Onesimus. Addressing the owner, Philemon, Paul writes of Onesimus, "But if he has wronged you in any way, or owes you anything, charge that to my account; I, Paul, am writing this with my own hand, I will repay it" (Philem. 18-19).

Jesus is the mediator of the New Covenant, and in this has provided us with eternal life. But He does more than mediate the covenant;

He also guarantees it. He has become surety for it. All of God's promises in the New Covenant are guaranteed to us by Jesus Himself. He guarantees to pay all the debts that our sins have incurred, or ever will incur, against us.

ETERNAL SAVIOR

And the former priests, on the one hand, existed in greater numbers, because they were prevented by death from continuing, but He, on the other hand, because He abides forever, holds His priesthood permanently. Hence, also, He is able to save forever those who draw near to God through Him, since He always lives to make intercession for them. (7:23-25)

The Levitical **priests** had what might be called the ultimate disqualification for permanent ministry: **death.** None of them could serve indefinitely. Each died and had to be succeeded in order for the priesthood to continue. Once again, the Jewish readers are reminded of the limitations of the Old Covenant.

As if to picture that the Levitical priesthood would never be able to bring them to salvation, God gave Israel a dramatic and significant demonstration, recorded in Numbers 20:23-29. When Aaron, the first high priest and progenitor of all succeeding priests, was about to die, God commanded Moses to bring Aaron and his son and successor, Eleazar, to Mount Hor, in view of all the people. God reminded Moses that Aaron, like Moses himself, would not be allowed to enter the Promised Land. The human giver of the law and the human progenitor of the priesthood would both die before Israel entered the Promised Land. Aaron's high priestly garments were taken from him and placed on Eleazar. After Aaron died, the people mourned for him for thirty days. The people's attention was specially focused on Aaron's death, as if God were impressing upon them the fact that the priesthood he represented was a dying priesthood.

In this brief demonstration, along with Moses' own death shortly afterward, two things about the Old Covenant were symbolized: it was not permanent, and it could not bring the people into the Promised Land. It was temporary and it could not save. Neither the law (represented by Moses) nor the sacrifices (represented by Aaron) could deliver from the wilderness of sin and bring into the land of salvation.

Jesus Christ, **on the other hand, because He abides forever, holds His priesthood permanently.** Jesus is the superior High Priest because He needs no successor. His priesthood is permanent, eternal.

Permanently (*aparabatos*) means more than incidental permanence, or something that simply will not be changed. It means unchange-able, unalterable, inviolable—something that *cannot* be changed. Jesus' priesthood does not just happen to be permanent. It cannot possibly be anything but permanent. It is not capable of anything but permanence. By its very divine nature it can never conclude or weaken or become ineffec-tive. Jesus Christ has a priesthood that is absolutely incapable of ever being altered in any way! He is the last high priest. No other will ever be needed.

Hence, also, He is able to save forever those who draw near to God through Him, since He always lives to make intercession for them. (7:25)

Here is one of the most beautiful verses in Scripture. Like John 3:16, it contains the whole essence of the gospel. Salvation is the main theme of the entire Bible. Salvation is what the text is all about.

Jesus' priesthood not only is eternal and unalterable, but is also unlimited in its scope. He saves **forever** (*panteles*). Although the meaning in the context of 7:25 can be that of eternal, the basic idea of the word is that of completeness or perfection. The King James translation ("to the uttermost") is therefore accurate and significant. Jesus' priesthood is no halfway measure, as were the old sacrifices that only symbolized removal of sin. The symbol was important for that covenant. It was God-given and God-required, but still was only a symbol. But Jesus Christ is able to save both eternally and completely.

We can learn some things about God from nature. Paul recognizes that God's "eternal power and divine nature," that is, His greatness and His glory, are evident for every person to see (Rom. 1:18-20). We call such evidence natural revelation. But it is limited revelation. The birds can suggest to us God's beauty, but they do not sing redemption's song. The ocean and its pounding waves can suggest God's greatness and His dependability, but they do not proclaim the gospel. The stars declare the glory of God, but not the way to get to Him. Natural revelation, like the Old Testament sacrifices, is God-given. It is the nature He Himself has made that proclaims His greatness and glory. But we can only learn about salvation from special revelation, from His written Word, the Bible. When people say they can find God on the beach or on the golf course or at the lake, it is a very superficial claim. In nature, we cannot possibly see clearly God's judgment on sin or His goodness or His grace or His re-demption or His Son. In nature we cannot see the need for salvation or the way to salvation. These are only seen with spiritual eyes, through the revelation of His Word.

Within the few words of Hebrews 7:25 we can see salvation's ba-sis, its nature, its power, its objects, and its security.

THE BASIS OF SALVATION

Hence, of course, refers to what has just been said—namely, that Jesus' priesthood is permanent, eternal. He can save forever because He exists and ministers forever. The basis of salvation is Jesus Christ's divine eternality.

THE POWER OF SALVATION

The power of salvation is Christ's ability—**He is able.** Other priests were never able to save, not even partially or temporarily. The old sacrifices partially and temporarily covered sin, but they did not even partially or temporarily *remove* sin. They did not to any degree or for any length of time bring deliverance from sin. But Jesus Christ is able, perfectly able.

A friend of mine had a little boy who, at the age of four, was found to have leukemia. One of our own sons was the same age. When I visited the stricken boy in the hospital, I felt particularly heartbroken and helpless. I had the strongest desire to make him well. I would have done anything in my power to bring that little fellow back to perfect health. I was completely willing, but I was not able to. I did not have the power.

Many, perhaps most, of the priests of the Old Covenant were willing to cleanse the people of sin; but they could not, no matter how strongly they desired it. But our great High Priest is not only willing, He is also able—absolutely able. Praise God for Christ, who is able!

Evangelicals are often criticized for claiming that Jesus Christ is the only way to God. The reason we make this claim is that this is what the Bible teaches. Jesus Himself said "No one comes to the Father except through Me" (John 14:6). Jesus not only is able to save, but He is the *only* One able to save. He is the only One who has the power of salvation (Acts 4:12).

THE NATURE OF SALVATION

The nature of salvation is bringing men **near to God.** By delivering from sin, it qualifies believers to come to God. Deliverance from sin has all three of the major tenses—past, present, and future. In the past tense, we *have been* freed from sin's guilt. In the present tense, we *are* freed from sin's power. In the future tense, we *shall be* freed from sin's presence. So we can say, "I have been saved," "I am saved" (or "I am being saved'), and "I shall be saved." All these statements are true; all are scriptural. Together they represent the full, complete nature of our salvation.

THE OBJECTS OF SALVATION

The objects of Christ's eternal salvation, of course, are those who come to Him to be saved, **those who draw near to God through Him.** There are no restrictions but this, no other qualification but faith in God's Son. "The one who comes to Me I will certainly not cast out" (John 6:37). There is no other way but Jesus, but this way is open to every person who puts his trust in Him. The other side of this truth is that Jesus can save *only* those who come to Him in faith. He is able to save all, but not all will be saved, because not all will believe.

We are tempted to think that when we have presented the gospel, presented the truth of salvation, that our obligation is over. But there must be a response to the gospel for it to be able to save. Parents need continually to remember this fact when teaching their children the things of God. We cannot make them believe or make them obey, but our responsibility is not over until we have urged them as strongly as we know how to trust in the Savior of whom they have heard.

THE SECURITY OF SALVATION

He **always lives to make intercession** for us. The security of our salvation is Jesus' perpetual intercession for us. We can no more keep ourselves saved than we can save ourselves in the first place. But just as Jesus has power to save us, He has power to keep us. Constantly, eternally, perpetually Jesus Christ intercedes for us before His Father. Whenever we sin He says to the Father, "Put that on My account. My sacrifice has already paid for it." Through Jesus Christ, we are able to "stand in the presence of His glory blameless with great joy" (Jude 24). In His Son we are now blameless in the Father's sight. When we are glorified we will be blameless in His presence.

Holy and Sinless

For it was fitting that we should have such a high priest, holy, innocent, undefiled, separated from sinners and exalted above the heavens; who does not need daily, like those high priests, to offer sacrifices, first for His own sins, and then for the sins of the people, because this He did once for all when He offered up Himself. For the Law appoints men as high priests who are weak, but the word of the oath, which came after the Law, appoints a Son, made perfect forever. (7:26-28)

All the Levitical priests were sinful, and they had to offer sacrifices for themselves before they could offer them for the people. Not so our present High Priest. He is **holy, innocent, undefiled, separated from sinners, and exalted above the heavens.** It was **fitting,** necessary, that He be such a person. Otherwise He, too, would have had to offer sacrifices for Himself first, and He, too, would have had to repeat the sacrifices over and over and over. He could only be the eternal and perfect High Priest if He were completely righteous and sinless. And He is.

As believers, we are all holy in the sense that we are set apart in Christ for righteousness. We are counted righteous in Him. But Christ's righteousness is in Himself. He was **holy** from the very beginning, eternally holy. He was born into this world holy. He was not capable of sin. He said of Himself, "The ruler of the world is coming, and he has nothing in Me" (John 14:30). There was no sin in Jesus to which Satan could appeal.

Jesus is also **innocent,** or harmless. Holiness points toward God, harmlessness toward men. Jesus injured no man. He lived for others. He went about always doing good to others, including those who had done, or who He knew would do, Him harm. He healed but He never harmed.

Jesus was **undefiled,** free from any moral or spiritual blemish. Think about it. For 33 years Jesus Christ was in the world, mingling continually with sinners and being tempted continually by Satan. Yet He never contracted the least taint of sin, or defilement. Just as the rays of the sun can shine into the foulest stagnant pond and not lose their radiance and purity, so Jesus lived his life in the sinful, defiled world without losing the least of His beauty and purity. He moved through the world and remained untouched by any of its blemishes. He came into the most direct and personal contact with Satan, yet left as spotless as before they met. There never was a priest who was undefiled—until Jesus.

Jesus was **separated from sinners.** He was of an utterly different class. Obviously, He was not separated from sinners in the sense of never coming in contact with them or mingling with them. His parents, his brothers and sisters, his friends, his disciples—all the people He encountered—were sinful. Yet He ate with them, traveled with them, worked with them, worshiped with them. But His nature was totally separate, totally different, from theirs—and from ours. For this, of course, we give the highest thanks, for otherwise He could not have been our Savior.

Finally, He is **exalted above the heavens.** He is exalted because of all the other things just mentioned. Because He is holy, innocent, undefiled, and separated from sinners, He is therefore exalted.

And because of all five of these things, He does not need to offer sacrifices for Himself, **like those high priests.** Sinlessness needs no sacrifice. Jesus offered only one sacrifice, and that one not for Himself but for others. He did it once. A perfect sacrifice by a perfect Priest and it was done—for all time.

All the priests of the Old Covenant, even the most dedicated and spiritual of them, were **weak** (v. 28). But God established Jesus' priesthood as eternally strong—just as it is eternally holy and eternally effective.

When he officiated, the Old Testament high priest wore an ephod, an elaborate vestment on which were two onyx stones, each inscribed with the names of six of the tribes of Israel. Attached to the ephod by gold chains was a breastplate, on which were twelve more precious stones representing the twelve tribes. Therefore whenever he went into the presence of God, he carried with him all the tribes of Israel. The high priest symbolically bore the children of Israel to God on his heart (his affections) and on his shoulders (his strength). This represented what the priesthood was to be: first, a heart for the people, and secondly, the strength to bring them to God. Many of these priests no doubt had a heart for the people. But none of them was able to bring the people to God. They could not even bring themselves to Him.

Our High Priest has no such weakness. He carries our names on His heart and on His shoulders. But He needs no ephod or breastplate as symbols, for He has true affection and true salvation. He perfectly loves us and He can perfectly save us. **He is able.**

The New Covenant— part 1 (8:1-13)

Now the main point in what has been said is this: we have such a high priest, who has taken His seat at the right hand of the throne of the Majesty in the heavens, a minister in the sanctuary, and in the true tabernacle, which the Lord pitched, not man. For every high priest is appointed to offer both gifts and sacrifices; hence it is necessary that this high priest also have something to offer. Now if He were on earth, He would not be a priest at all, since there are those who offer the gifts according to the Law; who serve a copy and shadow of the heavenly things, just as Moses was warned by God when he was about to erect the tabernacle; for, "See," He says, "that you make all things according to the pattern which was shown you on the mountain." But now He has obtained a more excellent ministry, by as much as He is also the mediator of a better covenant, which has been enacted on better promises. For if that first covenant had been faultless, there would have been no occasion sought for a second. For finding fault with them, He says, "Behold, days are coming, says the LORD, when I will effect a new covenant with the house of Israel and with the house of Judah; not like the covenant which I made with their fathers on the day when I took them by the hand to lead them out of the land of Egypt; for they did not continue in My covenant, and I did not care for them, says the LORD. For this is the covenant that I will make with the house of Israel after those days, says the LORD: I will put My laws into their minds, and I will write them upon their hearts. And I will be their God, and they shall be My people. And they shall not teach everyone his fellow citizen, and everyone his brother, saying, 'Know the LORD,' for all shall know Me, from the least to the greatest of them. For I will be merciful to their iniquities, and I will remember their sins no more." When He said, "A new covenant," He has made the first obsolete. But whatever is becoming obsolete and growing old is ready to disappear. (8:1-13)

The main point (*kephalaion*) means just that—the main, or chief, point—not a summary, as the King James Version suggests. What is given here is the primary thrust of what has been said so far in the letter. "This is what we have been emphasizing from the beginning: the high priesthood of Jesus Christ," the writer is saying. A great many things have been presented and explained, but they all relate, directly or indirectly, to Christ's high priesthood.

The primary focus of Hebrews 8 is on the New Covenant. But as an introduction to his discussion of the covenant proper, the writer first mentions two more indications of Jesus' superiority as the High Priest of this covenant: (1) His seat at God's right hand and (2) His heavenly sanctuary.

HIS SEAT

Now the main point in what has been said is this: we have such a high priest, who has taken His seat at the right hand of the throne of the Majesty in the heavens. (8:1)

As mentioned before, the Levitical priests never sat down. "And every priest stands daily ministering and offering time after time the same sacrifices, which can never take away sins" (Heb. 10:11). The priest's job was never done, because the sacrifices he offered were never permanently effective. They had to be repeated over and over again. In his ministering at the altar, therefore, the priest never rested, because he was never through. No place was provided in the Tabernacle or the Temple for the priests to sit down. The mercy seat in the Holy of Holies was not really a seat at all. In any case, it would have been utterly blasphemous for the high priest (the only person allowed in the Holy of Holies, and then only briefly once a year) to have presumed to sit on the mercy seat, which represented God's throne and His special presence.

When Jesus Christ offered His sacrifice, however, He sat down (cf. 1:3). He was qualified to sit down because His work was done. Among His last words on the cross were, "It is finished." He accomplished in one glorious act what all the priests of the Old Covenant had not accomplished and could never have accomplished—forgiveness of men's sins and thereby their reconciliation with God. What a marvelous and wonderful thing it is. He did it all in one sacrifice, the sacrifice of Himself. As far as our salvation is concerned, He **has taken His seat.** He has accomplished all that can be accomplished, all that needs to be done. Yet, people are still trying to add to the simple, pure grace of God and salvation by faith, though it is absurd to think that the work of Christ needs anything added to it. The saving effort of our Lord cannot have anything added to it, because it is absolutely perfect.

This truth should have been the most joyous news possible to Jews. Imagine, a final sacrifice, a finished work, so that the high priest could sit down—and at God's right hand!

The right hand of a monarch symbolized honor, exaltation, and power. To stand at his right hand was honor, but to sit there, supreme honor. Christ sat down at the **right hand of the throne** of thrones, God's heavenly, eternal throne.

The idea of sitting at the right hand may have reminded some Jews of the Sanhedrin, the Jewish ruling council of seventy elders. This group had both civil and religious authority and acted administratively as well as judicially. Even under Roman rule, the Sanhedrin was allowed considerable power, as evidenced by its role in Jesus' final arrest and crucifixion. It was a kind of supreme court, and more. When the members sat in judgment, a scribe, or secretary, sat on either side of the presiding judge. The scribe on the left side was responsible for writing condemnations, while the one on the right was responsible for writing acquittals. Jesus said that He came into the world not to condemn but to save (John 3:17). As High Priest, He now sits in the place not only of honor and power but of mercy. He sits there making intercession (Heb. 7:25)—writing acquittals, as it were—for His own.

Jesus Christ has been given the place of honor. He has been ushered into the heavenly Holy of Holies. He has been seated with God on His throne. Even more amazing is that, as believers, we will one day be invited to sit on that same throne. "He who overcomes, I will grant to him to sit down with Me on My throne, as I also overcame and sat down with My Father on His throne" (Rev. 3:21).

The book of Hebrews repeatedly reminds us that Christ is at the right hand of God. I think the purpose of these reminders is to assure those who were deprived of the Temple services in Jerusalem that they did not need to fear losing out on what was going on in the symbolic, temporary Holy of Holies. They had the true, perfect, eternal Priest in the real, heavenly Holy of Holies, of which the earthly one was only a poor and soon-passing picture. In the real one, Jesus Christ was ministering and interceding for them. Thus, the crowning argument for the superior priesthood of Jesus Christ is His exaltation into heaven to sit at the Father's right hand—the place of honor, mercy, and intercession.

A tragic but beautiful story from the book of Acts comes to mind in regard to Jesus' sitting at God's right hand. Just before Stephen was taken out of Jerusalem to be stoned to death for preaching so powerfully before the Sanhedrin, "he gazed intently into heaven and saw the glory of God, and Jesus standing at the right hand of God" (Acts 7:55). As far as redemption is concerned, Jesus is seated, because He rests from the finished work of redemption. But when one of His own falls into trouble, He stands up, because He takes the position of action. His power and His energy are immediately activated in behalf of His beloved. He is seated as our Redeemer, but is standing as our Helper in time of need.

The fact that Jesus Christ, in all His glory, in all His magnitude, in all His exaltation in heaven, is still preoccupied with ministering to us is awesome, and wonderful, and humbling. He is always serving. He condescends even in His glory now on the throne of God to stand up and minister in our behalf whenever we need Him. He did not receive His majesty as something to be selfishly enjoyed. It is in Jesus Christ that majesty and service are perfectly joined.

His Sanctuary

A minister in the sanctuary, and in the true tabernacle, which the Lord pitched, not man. For every high priest is appointed to offer both gifts and sacrifices; hence it is necessary that this high priest also have something to offer. Now if He were on earth, He would not be a priest at all, since there are those who offer the gifts according to the Law; who serve a copy and shadow of the heavenly things, just as Moses was warned by God when he was about to erect the tabernacle; for, "See," He says, "that you make all things according to the pattern which was shown you on the mountain." (8:2-5)

The **sanctuary** in which Jesus is **a minister** is infinitely superior to the one in which the Jewish priests ministered. As would be expected, the superior Priest ministers in a superior sanctuary. He does not minister in a temple of cedar and gold, or in a temple of white marble, beautiful and impressive as they were, much less in a tabernacle made of animal skins. When the book of Hebrews was written, the Tabernacle had not been used for a thousand years, and the Herodian Temple would be standing for less than five more years. But Jesus' sanctuary is **in the true**

tabernacle, which the Lord pitched, not man and which can never rot or crumble or be destroyed.

The word **true** is not used here as the opposite of false. The true Israelite tabernacle is not being contrasted with the false tabernacles, or temples, of her pagan neighbors. Nor is the idea that the Israelite tabernacle itself was in any sense false. It was temporary and inadequate, but it was not false. "True" is used here as opposed to the shadowy or unreal. The comparison is between the typical and temporary and the real and permanent. "The Holy Spirit is signifying this, that the way into the holy place has not yet been disclosed, while the outer tabernacle is still standing, which is a symbol for the present time" (Heb. 9:8-9).

Certain Greek mystical philosophers held that everything we see and hear and touch is but a shadow or reflection of a "real" counterpart in another world. The world we experience is not the real, true world; it is only a representation, an ephemeral copy. Somewhere there is the universal, true horse, for example, of which the ones we ride are shadows. Somewhere there is the true chair, of which those we sit in are only reflections.

The writer of Hebrews is saying very much the same thing. He was not a Greek philosopher. He was writing the revelation of God. But in some regards those philosophers were not too far afield. As far as completeness and perfection and permanence are concerned, our physical world is less real than the eternal. The Old Covenant and all its rituals and ceremonies and altars and sacrifices and tabernacle and temples, were but shadows and types, pictures and reflections, of the realities of the New. These all had heavenly patterns. Earthly worship, even the most sincere and godly, is only a remote reflection of what worship is like in heaven. The earthly priesthood is only an inadequate shadow of the real priesthood.

For every high priest is appointed to offer both gifts and sacrifices; hence it is necessary that this high priest also have something to offer. (8:3)

Verse 3 begins to take the argument from the general to the particular. The question would likely come up at this point, "If Christ has finished His work and He is seated in heaven, does He have nothing to do now? Is all of His priestly work finished?" As was just touched on above, the answer is, No. His sacrifice is finished; His atoning work is finished. But all of His priestly ministry is not finished. If **every high priest is appointed to offer both gifts and sacrifices,** then Jesus Christ, as perfect High Priest, can do no less. He is truly a ministering priest.

Under our discussion of Hebrews 5, we looked briefly at the distinction between gifts and sacrifices. Gifts referred to meal offerings and sacrifices to blood offerings. The gift offerings were given to represent personal dedication, commitment, and thanksgiving to the Lord. The blood offerings, on the other hand, were for cleansing from sin. The priests were responsible for offering both. Not even the simplest meal offering could be made by a lay person himself. He brought the offering, but it could be presented to God only by a priest.

Jesus has already ministered the one final blood sacrifice that is sufficient for all people for all time. This work of His is completely finished, because there is no need, and there will forever be no need, for any additional sacrifice for the cleansing of sin. But the need for His redeemed people to come to dedication and commitment and thanksgiving is not over. These gifts of praise and thanksgiving Jesus continues to minister for us before His Father.

None of us can praise God, or thank Him, or commit or dedicate himself in worship, obedience, and service to Him, apart from Jesus Christ. Just as no Israelite could offer either a gift or sacrifice to God except through a priest, so Christians cannot do so except through their High Priest. We cannot confess sin or seek forgiveness apart from Christ any more than we could have come to God apart from Christ. Anything of any value or consequence we do as believers must be done through our Lord. "Whatever you do in word or deed, do all in the name of the Lord Jesus, giving thanks through Him to God the Father" (Col. 3:17; cf. Eph. 5:20).

It is obviously necessary, then, for Jesus to continue to minister in our behalf. He continually brings the gifts—the worship, the praise, the repentance, the dedication, the thanks—of the hearts of His people before the Father.

Now if He were on earth, He would not be a priest at all, since there are those who offer the gifts according to the Law; who serve a copy and shadow of the heavenly things, just as Moses was warned by God when he was about to erect the tabernacle; for, "See," He says, "that you make all things according to the pattern which was shown you on the mountain." (8:4-5)

If the Temple were still standing, "He would not be a priest at all," thus Jesus could not minister for us on earth under the terms of the Old Covenant. During His earthly ministry, Jesus healed the sick, raised the dead, preached on the hillside and in the synagogue, forgave sins, and called Himself God's true Son. But He never claimed the right to minister in the Temple. He did not venture one step closer to the inner sanctuaries than any other Jew of His day who was not a priest. He was not of the priestly tribe, and therefore was not qualified for the old, earthly ministry. God never mixes the **shadow** with the substance, the type with the antitype. Jesus could not minister the old offerings in the old, earthly sanctuary. He ministers the new offerings in the new, heavenly sanctuary—built by God, not men (v. 2).

The Tabernacle built under Moses' direction **according to the pattern** was not the original model, the type, that set the pattern for the more elaborate Temple and then the immeasurably still more elaborate heavenly sanctuary. The heavenly sanctuary is not an enhanced, improved version of the earthly. Just the opposite. The earthly was but a shadowy, a barely suggestive copy of the heavenly—which preceded the earthly by all eternity. The gifts, the sacrifices, the sanctuary, and even the priests themselves served as copies and shadows of their heavenly counterparts.

A **shadow** has no substance in itself, no independent existence or meaning apart from what it is a shadow of. It exists only as evidence of the real thing. A copy, of course, can be a helpful thing. A copy of a contract, for example, can be helpful in many ways—for checking out the names, the dates, the terms, and such that were agreed on. But in a court of law, only the real contract is valid. A copy is good for checking the terms, but only the real contract can enforce them.

Why, then, should anyone be satisfied with a copy when he can have the real thing? Why should a Jew be satisfied with the old priesthood and the old sacrifices—which are only copies and shadows of forgiveness and reconciliation—when he can have real forgiveness and real reconciliation in Jesus Christ? And what Old Covenant priest could compare with the High Priest of the New Covenant?

The Superior Covenant

But now He has obtained a more excellent ministry, by as much as He is also the mediator of a better covenant, which has been enacted on better promises. (8:6)

Jesus' superior seat and His superior sanctuary are evidences of His superior ministry. His superior ministry is evidence of the superior covenant, which He mediates and which has superior promises.

Mediator (*mesitēs*) means someone who stands between two people and brings them together, a go-between in a dispute or conflict. He must represent both parties. In religion a priest is the mediator between God and men. Many false religions have priests, whose ministry is claimed to do just that—reconcile men with God, or with the gods. These, of course, are all pseudo-mediators because, though they may represent men to some degree, they do not represent God at all. The Old Covenant with Israel had its mediators. In ceremonial matters those were the priests, and only the priests. Moses, however, also acted as a mediator—of the Old Covenant (Gal. 3:19; Ex. 20:19; Deut. 5:5). In a sense, the prophets were mediators—of God's Word to Israel.

The Israelite mediators, assuming they were legitimately doing God's work, were not false mediators, as are those of other religions. Yet they were not true mediators either, in the same way that the earthly tabernacle, though not false, was not true (Heb. 8:2). The Israelite mediators were true only in the sense of being proper, of being and doing what God wanted them to be and do. They were not true, however, in the sense of being effective. They could not bring men and God together. They were not real mediators, only reflections of the true Mediator who was to come. They, too, were but copies and shadows.

The New Covenant not only has a better Mediator but **better promises.** All covenants are based on promises. Sometimes the promises are by only one party, sometimes by both. Sometimes the promises are conditional, sometimes they are not. But promises are always involved. As far as God's covenants are concerned, it is always *His* promises that are significant. Men break their promises, God does not. The benefits and the power are always from God's side, and therefore the significant promises are always from His side. Consequently, it is *God's* promises in the New Covenant that here are called "better."

For if that first covenant had been faultless, there would have been no occasion sought for a second. For finding fault with them, He says, "Behold, days are coming, says the Lord, when I will effect a new covenant with the house of Israel and with the house of Judah. (8:7-8)

The Old Covenant was not false, but it had faults. **For if that first covenant had been faultless, there would have been no occasion sought for a second.** Its faults, its limitations, had been pointed out by Jeremiah, one of the Jews' own prophets. Hebrews 8:8-12, with the exception of the first few words of verse 8, is a direct quotation from Jeremiah 31. The writer is saying, "Look what your own Scriptures have to say about the advantages of the New Covenant. You should have been expecting a New Covenant to come, and you should already have known that it would be superior to the Old. One of your own greatest prophets told you this hundreds of years ago." Yet millions of Jews even today are hanging on tenaciously to the Old Covenant, even though their own Scriptures, through their own beloved prophet, have been telling them for well over 2,000 years that a new one was to come.

In the quotation from Jeremiah, we note at least eight factors that show that the New Covenant is superior to the Old.

212

WRITTEN BY GOD

A will is a type of covenant and illustrates beautifully God's covenants with His people. Though many people may be involved in its provisions, a will is written by one person—the one whose will it is. A beneficiary has no part in determining the benefits. He can only accept or reject—he cannot change—what the will provides for him.

The New Covenant in Christ, the Messiah, is based solely on God's sovereign terms. **I will effect a new covenant,** the Lord told Jeremiah.

DIFFERENT FROM THE OLD

Just that the covenant in Christ is **new** and is better makes it obvious that it is different to some extent. But it is not just an enhancement or modification. It is not slightly different, but radically different, from the old one. As mentioned in the next point, it is like the old in that it is sovereignly made with the same people. But its basic nature and provisions are completely different. God effected a **new covenant,** which was "not like the covenant which I made with their fathers" (v. 9).

MADE WITH ISRAEL

In this regard, the New Covenant is exactly like the Old; it is made with Israel, with the Jews. **I will effect a new covenant with the house of Israel and with the house of Judah** (v. 8; cf. v. 10). God has never made a covenant with Gentiles, and, as far as I can see from Scripture, He never will. The New Covenant is not made with the church, as some seem to think. It is made with the same people the Old Covenant was made with: Israel. Gentiles can be beneficiaries of the New Covenant, just like they could be beneficiaries of the Old (cf. Gen 12:3). But both covenants were made with Israel alone. Israel as a nation rejected God by rejecting His Son. But God has never rejected Israel, nor has He transferred His covenant with her to anyone else.

The original and basic name of the Jewish nation is Israel. After the tragic division of the kingdom, the two parts were called Israel (the northern) and Judah (the southern). But the twelve tribes together are always called Israel, or Israel and Judah. We sometimes hear of the "lost tribes of Israel," referring to the fact that the northern tribes never returned from their captivity. But those who were not carried away by Assyria in 722 B.C. did become absorbed into Judah, so that the twelve tribes were still in tact. Even though they lost their tribal records, God knows who they are, and their being lost to human history does not abrogate God's covenant with them (cf. Rev. 7:4-8).

As already mentioned—and as is abundantly clear from all the New Testament—Gentiles, by faith, may share in the benefits of the gospel on an equal basis with Jews. Gentiles could share in the Mosaic covenant and even shared in the Abrahamic covenant, because all the nations of the world were to be blessed in Abraham. But none of these covenants was made with Gentiles. "Salvation is from the Jews," Jesus said (John 4:22).

God attached no conditions or demands to the covenant with Abraham. This covenant was simply a declaration of God's intention to bless Abraham and his descendants, and the whole world through them. In the Mosaic covenant, God attached many demands, many laws. It is often called the covenant of law. Israel was to obey, and at Sinai she agreed to obey, all of the requirements of the covenant. Many of God's promised blessings to Israel were conditioned on that promised obedience. But before the commandments were given, He told her, "*You shall be* to Me a kingdom of priests and a holy nation" (Ex. 19:6). Her calling was not ultimately conditional on her obedience or her faithfulness. Her blessedness was. She lost many blessings because of disobedience, but she never lost the calling (Rom. 11:29). She broke all the covenant laws, but she could not break the covenant. Jews today are still breaking the covenant laws and losing the covenant blessings. And Jews today are still rejecting the New Covenant grace and losing its blessings. But with all their disobedience and with all their unbelief and rejection, they have not broken, and they cannot break, either covenant that God has made with their race.

When Gentiles are saved they become descendants of Abraham—spiritual descendants. "Therefore, be sure that it is those who are of faith who are sons of Abraham. And the Scripture, foreseeing that God would justify the Gentiles by faith, preached the gospel beforehand to Abraham, saying, 'All the nations shall be blessed in you'" (Gal. 3:7-8). The Abrahamic covenant is fulfilled in each of us when we accept the single requirement of the New Covenant—faith in Jesus Christ. "And if you belong to Christ, then you are Abraham's offspring, heirs according to promise" (Gal. 3:29).

For the time being, in fact, Gentiles are sharing more in the New Covenant than are Jews. But one day this will change. After Gentiles have had sufficient time to respond to the gospel, all Israel will be saved (Rom. 11:26). Her day is coming. She will be grafted back into the trunk of covenant salvation (cf. Rom 11:17-24).

NOT LEGALISTIC

Not like the covenant which I made with their fathers on the day

when I took them by the hand to lead them out of the land of Egypt; for they did not continue in My covenant, and I did not care for them, says the LORD. (8:9)

The blessings of the Old Covenant were conditioned on Israel's obedience to the law that God gave with the covenant. Because Israel did not continue, God **did not care for them.** Under the law, His care depended on her continuance. Her disobedience did not abrogate the covenant, but it forfeited all the blessings of it. It was a covenant of law.

Not so the New Covenant.

INTERNAL, NOT EXTERNAL

"For this is the covenant that I will make with the house of Israel after those days, says the LORD: I will put My laws into their minds, and I will write them upon their hearts. And I will be their God, and they shall be My people." (8:10)

The New Covenant will have a different sort of law—an internal not an external law. Everything under the old economy was primarily external. Under the Old Covenant obedience was primarily out of fear of punishment. Under the New it is to be out of adoring love and worshiping thanksgiving. Formerly God's law was given on stone tablets and was to be written on wrists and foreheads and doorposts as reminders (Deut. 6:8-9). Even when the old law was given, of course, it was intended to be in His people's **hearts** (Deut. 6:6). But the people could not write on their hearts like they could write on their doorposts. And at this time the Holy Spirit, the only changer of hearts, was not yet given to believers. Now, however, the Spirit writes God's law in the **minds** and **hearts** of those who belong to Him. in the New Covenant true worship is internal, not external, real, not ritual (cf. Ezek. 11:19-20, 36:26-27; John 14:17).

PERSONAL

And they shall not teach everyone his fellow citizen, and everyone his brother, saying, 'Know the LORD,' for all shall know Me, from the least to the greatest of them. (8:11)

Being internal, the New Covenant has to be personal. It is personal not only in God's law (His Word) being within us, but in His very Spirit (who *is* a person) being within us. Every believer has a resident Helper, a resident Teacher, a resident Friend. "But the Helper, the Holy Spirit, whom the Father will send in My name, He will teach you all things, and bring to your remembrance all that I said to you" (John 14:26).

BRINGS TOTAL FORGIVENESS

For I will be merciful to their iniquities, and I will remember their sins no more. (8:12)

Here is the capstone of the New Covenant. Here is what men need more than anything else—and what the Old Covenant pictured but could not give. The promise of the Old Testament is finally fulfilled! Under the Old Covenant, sins could never really be forgotten, because they were never really forgiven. They were only covered, foreshadowing and anticipating true forgiveness in Jesus Christ. But for those who belong to His dear Son—whether they believed under the Old Covenant or under the New—God forgets every sin.

IS FOR NOW

When He said, "A new covenant," He has made the first obsolete. But whatever is becoming obsolete and growing old is ready to disappear. (8:13)

In sharing the gospel with Jews—whether in New Testament times or today—one of the biggest stumbling blocks for them is the idea that the Old Covenant is passed away, that it is no longer valid for them or for anyone else. God does not honor that covenant anymore. He has made another one, infinitely better than the old one, through His Son, Jesus Christ, the Jews' own Messiah. It is hard for a Jew to realize that the Old Covenant, with its laws and ceremonies, was only a symbol, a picture of God's plan for them and for the world.

Their refusing to recognize Jesus as the Messiah is like a person who has a picture of a long-lost dear friend. He looks at the picture often, with love and hope and expectancy. The picture is a beautiful representation and reminder of the friend, and consequently the picture itself becomes dear. One day the friend shows up and says, "Hello. Here I am in the flesh, in person." But the one he has come to see continues to look only at the picture, never recognizing his friend's presence. He has focused so long on the picture that he does not, or will not, recognize the one in the picture when he comes in person. The symbol has been substituted for the reality. The symbol is treated as the real thing, and the real thing is regarded as unreal. Whatever the friend could do for him is not done, and the picture can do nothing.

The Old Covenant symbol is not bad, and was never bad. It had a beautiful, God-given purpose. It pointed to the Son, represented the Son, foreshadowed the Son before He came to earth. But now that the Son has come, the symbol has no more purpose, and God means for it to be discarded.

By His merely saying that a new covenant was coming, God rendered the old one **obsolete,** no longer valid. In fact it would disappear. The human writer of Hebrews could not have known how literally this truth would be fulfilled within a few years of his writing. When Titus destroyed Jerusalem, he destroyed the Temple—which had been completed only for a short time. Without the Temple, there was no altar, no Holy of Holies. There could therefore be no sacrifices and no ministering priesthood. And without a priesthood and its sacrifices, there could be no Old Covenant. It was finished. When verse 13 was written, the **obsolete** covenant was **ready to disappear.** In less than five years, it had completely disappeared.

The old sacrificial system actually was over when the veil was split in two and Christ's sacrifice was complete (Matt. 27:50-51; Mark 15:37-39; Luke 23:44-46). At that time, Christ's unique, never-to-be-repeated sacrifice was finished with the result that all men in Christ had direct access to God (1 Tim. 2:5-6). The destruction of the Temple completed the closing of the Old Covenant—by removing the place of sacrifice that no longer served a purpose.

The age of the Mosaic law and the Levitical priests was over. The age of the Son was come forever.

The New Covenant – part 2
(9:1-14)

Now even the first covenant had regulations of divine worship and the earthly sanctuary. For there was a tabernacle prepared, the outer one, in which were the lampstand and the table and the sacred bread; this is called the holy place. And behind the second veil, there was a tabernacle which is called the Holy of Holies, having a golden altar of incense and the ark of the covenant covered on all sides with gold, in which was a golden jar holding the manna, and Aaron's rod which budded, and the tables of the covenant. And above it were the cherubim of glory overshadowing the mercy seat; but of these things we cannot now speak in detail. Now when these things have been thus prepared, the priests are continually entering the outer tabernacle, performing the divine worship, but into the second only the high priest enters, once a year, not without taking blood, which he offers for himself and for the sins of the people committed in ignorance. The Holy Spirit is signifying this, that the way into the holy place has not yet been disclosed, while the outer tabernacle is still standing, which is a symbol for the present time. Accordingly both gifts and sacrifices are offered which cannot make the worshiper perfect in conscience, since they relate only to food and drink and various washings, regulations for the body imposed until a time of reformation.

But when Christ appeared as a high priest of the good things to come, He entered through the greater and more perfect tabernacle, not made with hands, that is to say, not of this creation; and not through the blood of goats and calves, but through His own blood, He entered the holy place once for all, having obtained eternal redemption. For if the blood of goats and bulls and the ashes of a heifer sprinkling those who have been defiled, sanctify for the cleansing of the flesh, how much more will the blood of Christ, who through the eternal Spirit offered Himself without blemish to God, cleanse your conscience from dead works to serve the living God? (9:1-14)

God never asks anyone to give up anything without His offering something far better in return. The chief obstacle in the way of the Hebrews' faith was their failure to see that everything connected with the ceremonial law (covenant, sacrifices, priesthood, and ritual) was preparatory and transient. So the writer painstakingly and definitively pursues a clear revelation of the better character of the New.

Consequently, in Hebrews 9:1-14 the Old and New Covenants are further contrasted. The first part of the passage (vv. 1-10) outlines, or summarizes, the characteristics of the Old, whereas the second part (vv. 11-14) outlines the characteristics of the New.

CHARACTERISTICS OF THE OLD COVENANT

Now even the first covenant had regulations of divine worship and the earthly sanctuary. (9:1)

The **first covenant** was not worthless or pointless. God gave it, and He does nothing that is worthless or pointless. Through it He prescribed certain kinds of **worship** and a special place in which to worship. But it was temporary, signified by the **earthly** character of the **sanctuary.** The sanctuary and its worship were divinely instituted, but they, like the earth, were temporary. They were ordained of God and give a beautiful, meaningful, detailed picture of the eternal Messiah.

The writer of Hebrews makes many comparisons. He has compared the prophets, the angels, Joshua, and Aaron to Christ—always pointing out and proving Christ's superiority. But he never depreciates the persons or the things he compares with Christ or with Christ's work. In fact he exalts the prophets and the angels and Aaron and Moses and the Old Covenant. He does not compare Christ to persons or things that were insignificant or meaningless or worthless, but to ones that were God-ordained and faithful and purposeful. He does not try to build Christ up by running these down. Quite to the contrary, he magnifies them and praises them. In doing so, he exalts Christ all the more. The more the other persons and things are legitimately magnified, the more Jesus is magnified, the more superior He is shown to be.

The **regulations of divine worship,** the rites and ceremonies, were instituted by God to help show His Son, the Messiah, the true Savior. They were divine services, but they were also temporary services, performed in a temporary sanctuary. Verses 2-10 mention three things about the old worship: its sanctuary, its services, and its significance.

THE OLD SANCTUARY

For there was a tabernacle prepared, the outer one, in which were the lampstand and the table and the sacred bread; this is called the holy place. And behind the second veil, there was a tabernacle which is called the Holy of Holies, having a golden altar of incense and the ark of the covenant covered on all sides with gold, in which was a golden jar holding the manna, and Aaron's rod which budded, and the tables of the covenant. And above it were the cherubim of glory overshadowing the mercy seat; but of these things we cannot now speak in detail. (9:2-5)

Here is a brief description of the old sanctuary—first the Tabernacle and then the Temple. The emphasis here, however, is on the **tabernacle.** It was the first sanctuary and also the most temporary and the most earthy. Thus it serves to illustrate best the writer's point. It was made largely of skins and was designed to be portable. Even from the human view, it was the essence of impermanence. It gave every impression of being transitory.

Only two chapters in the Bible are devoted to the creation story, whereas some fifty chapters focus on the Tabernacle (see especially Ex. 25-40). The Tabernacle is important and demands attention in our study, because it is a giant portrait of Jesus Christ. Everywhere you look in the Tabernacle you can see Him.

The courtyard of the Tabernacle was one hundred fifty feet long and seventy-five feet wide. Its single gate, on the east side, was thirty feet wide and seven and a half feet high, allowing a large number of people to enter at the same time. It is a graphic picture of Jesus Christ, who said, "I am the way" and "I am the door." Just as there was only one entrance to the Tabernacle, there is only one way to God—the only Way and the only Door, Jesus Christ. Christianity is exclusive, not because Christians make it so but because God has made it so. Throughout the centuries, of course, Christians have made the earthly church exclusive in many wrong ways. But God has intentionally made His spiritual, eternal church exclusive. It can be entered only through Jesus Christ.

The first article of furniture in the outer court was the bronze altar. It was made of acacia wood sheathed with bronze. It was seven and a half feet square, stood four and a half feet off the ground, and was topped with a bronze grate. The coals were placed underneath the grate and the sacrifice was placed on top. On the four corners of the altar were horns, to which the animal was bound when it was being sacrificed. The bronze altar is again a perfect picture of Jesus Christ, who Himself was a sacrifice for sin.

The next piece of furniture in the court was the laver or basin, also made of bronze. In it the priests would wash their hands, and even sometimes their feet, as they went about the bloody services of sacrifice. Here is a picture of Jesus Christ as the cleanser of His people. Once we have received forgiveness for our sins through Christ's sacrifice of Himself, we still need His daily cleansing that restores fellowship and joy.

Still moving west across the courtyard, we come to the Tabernacle proper—forty-five feet long, fifteen feet wide, and fifteen feet high. The **holy place** took up two-thirds of this area, which means that the **holy of holies** was a perfect fifteen-foot cube. Only priests could go into the Holy Place, in which were three pieces of furniture. The writer of Hebrews mentions only two, because, as he says, he cannot **speak in detail** (9:5).

The Holy Place. On the left, as the priest entered, was a solid gold **lampstand** having seven branches, each filled with the purest olive oil. On the right was the **table** on which was the **sacred bread,** or showbread. This table, like the base of the altar, was of acacia wood overlaid with gold. It was three feet long, one and a half feet wide, and two and a quarter feet high. Every Sabbath twelve loaves of fresh bread were set on it, one for each of the twelve tribes. At the end of the week, the priests, and only the priests, were allowed to eat the loaves.

Farther in and to the center of the Holy Place was the **altar of incense.** It, too, was of gold-overlaid acacia wood, one and one-half feet square and about three feet high. On this altar were placed the burning coals from the bronze altar in the courtyard, where sacrifice was made.

These three pieces of furniture also picture Christ. Everything in the outer courtyard was connected with salvation and the cleansing of sins. Jesus accomplished His sacrificial work on earth, outside God's heavenly presence. The outer court was accessible to all the people, just as Christ is accessible to all who will come to Him. But in His heavenly sanctuary He is shut off from the world, temporarily even from His own people. From His heavenly place now, Jesus lights our path (pictured by the golden **lampstand**), He feeds us (pictured by the table of **sacred bread**), and He intercedes for us (pictured by the **altar of incense**).

"While I am in the world, I am the light of the world," Jesus said

(John 9:5). When He left the world, the world was left in darkness, and only for believers is He the light of life. He is the light that directs our paths, the One who, through the Spirit, illumines our minds to understand spiritual truth. He is the One who, by the indwelling Spirit, guides us through the world of darkness. He is our light.

Jesus is our sustenance. He is our table of sacred bread. He is the One who feeds us every day, who sustains us with the Word. The Word is not only our food but our light. And the oil is the Spirit of God, who lights the Word for us. The altar of incense pictures Jesus interceding for us, the perfect Sacrifice becoming the perfect Intercessor.

The Holy of Holies. **Behind the second veil, there was a tabernacle which is called the Holy of Holies,** into which only the high priest could enter, and that but once a year, on the Day of Atonement. In this holiest of earthly places was only one piece of furniture, **the ark of the covenant.** In it were three very precious articles: **a golden jar holding manna, Aaron's rod which budded, and the tables of the covenant.** Made of acacia wood overlaid with **gold,** it was about three feet nine inches long, two feet three inches wide and two feet high. On the lid was **the mercy seat,** on which were **the cherubim of glory,** angelic figures made of solid gold. It was between the wings of those angels, on the mercy seat, that God met men. "And there I will meet with you; and from above the mercy seat, from between the two cherubim which are upon the ark of the testimony, I will speak to you about all that I will give you in commandment for the sons of Israel" (Ex. 25:22). If God and man were to meet it could only have been there.

Unfortunately, under the Old Testament economy only one person could ever enter the Holy of Holies, and then only on an extremely limited basis. For all practical purposes, men had no access to God at all. The regular priests could not get nearer than the outer sanctuary, and the ordinary person no closer than the outer court.

The central, in fact the only, thing in the Holy of Holies was the **ark,** which represents Jesus Christ, the true **mercy seat.** When we meet Jesus Christ as Savior, we are ushered into the presence of God, into the true Holy of Holies. God no longer communes with men between the wings of cherubim on a gold mercy seat. He communes with men in His Son, by whom the veil was torn in two. Jesus Christ is the mercy seat. Only on the basis of the blood of a goat would God have fellowship with Israel, and only on the basis of the blood of Christ will God have fellowship with men. John, in using the term "propitiation," in 1 John 2:2, relates Jesus to the mercy seat, since that very word *hilastērion* is used for mercy seat in the Septuagint translation of Exodus 25:17.

The Old Covenant had a sanctuary with divine pictures and symbols, but it was earthly and temporary and it never provided true access to God.

THE OLD SERVICES

Now when these things have been thus prepared, the priests are continually entering the outer tabernacle, performing the divine worship, but into the second only the high priest enters, once a year, not without taking blood, which he offers for himself and for the sins of the people committed in ignorance. (9:6-7)

In its sanctuary the Old Covenant had divine services. Every day the **priests** had to trim the wicks and add oil in the lampstand and put incense on the altar of incense. Every Sabbath they had to change the twelve loaves of bread. They were **continually** in and out of the Holy Place, ministering in behalf of the people. Theirs was a never-ceasing work. In this they picture Jesus Christ, who does not cease enlightening and feeding and interceding on our behalf. This work of His is perpetual, continual, unceasing. How wonderful that our Lord never stops His priestly work for us. He is an ever-living High Priest.

Nothing, however, pictures Christ so perfectly as the work of **the high priest** in the Holy of Holies on the Day of Atonement (Yom Kippur), very briefly summarized in verse 7.

Whenever an Israelite sinned, his communion with God was broken. Consequently, the sacrifices for sin were never finished and the priests' work was never done. In spite of the continual sacrificing, however, many unknown or forgotten sins would accumulate, for which no sacrifice had been made. The Day of Atonement was intended to make sacrifice for all those sins that had not yet been covered.

It was a great day for liberation of the conscience (see Lev. 16). The Israelite knew that whatever sins may have been missed in the daily sacrifices would now be taken care of. The slate would be completely clean, at least symbolically for a while. Yom Kippur was a time of release and relief. The devout Jew longed for the Day of Atonement. He could not himself go into God's presence, but the high priest would go in for him and he would be delivered.

Very early on the Day of Atonement, the high priest cleansed himself ritually and put on his elaborate robes, with the breastplate (near the heart, signifying that he carried the people in his heart) and ephod (on the shoulder, signifying that he had power on their behalf) representing the twelve tribes. Then he began his daily sacrificing. Unlike Christ, he had to sacrifice for his own sin. Very likely he would have already slaughtered twenty-two different animals by the time he reached the event known as the atonement. It was an exceptionally busy and bloody thing that he did on this day. After finishing all these sacrifices, he took off the robes of glory and beauty and went and bathed himself again completely.

He then put on a white linen garment, with no decoration or ornament at all, and performed the sacrifice of atonement.

In this ritual, the high priest symbolized Jesus Christ, who, in His true and perfect work of atonement, stripped off all His glory and beauty and became the humblest of the humble. He dressed Himself in human flesh, pure but plain and unadorned. In all of His humility He never lost His holiness.

When the high priest was done with the sacrifice of atonement, he put the robes of glory and beauty back on, picturing still further the work of our Lord. In His high priestly prayer, anticipating what would happen after the crucifixion and resurrection, Jesus said, "And now, glorify Thou Me together with Thyself, Father, with the glory which I had with Thee before the world was" (John 17:5). He was saying in effect, "Give Me back My robes. I've done the job of atonement. My work of humility is over."

In the garment of white linen, the high priest took coals off the bronze altar, where sacrifice was going to be made. He put them in a gold censer with incense and carried it into the Holy of Holies. Here again is a beautiful picture of Christ, interceding for His own before God's presence. Then the high priest went out and took a bullock purchased with his own money, because it was to be offered for his own sin. After slaughtering the bullock and offering the sacrifice, he had another priest assist him in catching the blood as it drained off. He swirled some of it in a small bowl and carried it into the Holy of Holies, where he sprinkled it on the mercy seat. The people could hear the bells on his robe as he moved about. He hurried out, and the people breathed a sigh of relief at seeing him. Had he entered the Holy of Holies ceremonially unclean, he would have been struck dead.

When he came out, two goats were waiting for him by the bronze altar. In a small urn were two lots to determine which goat would be used for which purpose. One lot was marked for the Lord and the other for Azazel, for the scapegoat. As each lot was drawn it was tied to the horn of one of the goats. The goat designated for Jehovah was then killed on the altar. Its blood was caught in the same way as that of the bullock and was swirled in the bowl as it was carried into the Holy of Holies. This blood, too, was sprinkled on the mercy seat, but this time for the sins of the people. Again he hurried back out.

He then placed his hands on the goat that remained, the scapegoat, symbolically placing the sins of the people on the goat's head. That goat was taken far out into the wilderness and turned loose, to be lost and never to return.

The first goat represented satisfaction of God's justice, in that sin had been paid for. The second represented satisfaction of man's conscience, because he knew he was freed of the penalty of sin. Still again we see Christ. In His own death he paid for man's sin, thereby satisfying God's justice, and He also carried our sins far from us, giving us peace of conscience and mind. He satisfied both God and man. The two goats actually are two parts of one offering. "And he shall take from the congregation of the sons of Israel two male goats for a sin offering" (Lev. 16:5). They represented propitiation and pardon, two aspects of the one atoning sacrifice.

THE OLD SIGNIFICANCE

The Holy Spirit is signifying this, that the way into the holy place has not yet been disclosed, while the outer tabernacle is still standing, which is a symbol for the present time. Accordingly both gifts and sacrifices are offered which cannot make the worshiper perfect in conscience, since they relate only to food and drink and various washings, regulations for the body imposed until a time of reformation. (9:8-10)

In the illustration of the old sanctuary and its services, **the Holy Spirit** is teaching at least three things. First, the worship of God was limited in the Old Covenant. There was no access to God. The people, and even the high priest, could come only so close. Second, the Spirit wants to teach the imperfect cleansing accomplished through the old **sacrifices.** The Israelites never really knew that they were forgiven. The scapegoat was sent out to be lost in the wilderness, but there was always the chance of his finding his way back to the camp. There was no freedom of **conscience,** no assurance of cleansing. Third, the Spirit is teaching that the Old Covenant was temporary. Whether the scapegoat found his way back or not, the sacrifices—the daily and the yearly—all had to be repeated. The Old Covenant was limited, imperfect, and temporary. The provision of the New Covenant had to sweep back over all the believers of the past to provide access, cleansing, and permanent salvation.

No Access (Limited Cleansing). While the Tabernacle still stood, there was no way into God's presence. There was no access. The people could not even get **into the holy place,** much less into the Holy of Holies. The whole thing was meant to prove that without a Redeemer, without a Messiah, without a Savior, there is no access to God. The Holy Spirit was teaching the impossibility of access to God without a perfect priest, a perfect sacrifice, and a perfect covenant. By allowing the people to go no farther than the outer court, He was illustrating that through Judaism there was no access to Him, only a symbol of access.

Only when Jesus died and ascended to heaven did He lead "captivity captive" and provide believers access into God's presence.

" 'When He ascended on high, He led captive a host of captives, and He gave gifts to men.' (Now this expression, 'He ascended,' what does it mean except that He also had descended into the lower parts of the earth?)" (Eph. 4:8-9). That is the source of full access to God, and it was provided because of Jesus' perfect sacrifice, perfect priesthood, and perfect covenant. Jesus alone can take us to God's presence in heaven. The way into the heavenly Holy Place could not be opened while the first Tabernacle was standing.

Imperfect Cleansing. Even with all the ceremonies and rituals, perfect cleansing from sin could not be accomplished. The specific imperfection mentioned in this passage is that of **conscience.** The Old Covenant was imperfect in every way, but the writer selected only certain elements to make his point.

Symbol (*parabolē*) refers to setting side-by-side for the purpose of comparison. The old is being set beside the new and the two are compared. From this Greek word we get *parable.* The old was only a parable, an object lesson, for Israel. The old sacrifices were never meant to cleanse from sin, but only to symbolize such cleansing. The conscience of the person sacrificing was never freed from the *feeling* of guilt because the guilt itself was never removed. The cleansing was entirely external. Consequently, he could never have a clear conscience, a deep, abiding sense of forgiveness.

Temporary Cleansing. The cleansing, like the covenant as a whole, not only was limited and imperfect but temporary. It related **only to food and drink and various washings, regulations for the body imposed until a time of reformation.** This system was never intended to last forever. It was not intended even to last through human history. It was instituted thousands of years after human history began and ended thousands of years before human history will end. As of now, it has been nearly two thousand years since the last sacrifice was made in the Temple.

Reformation is from *diorthōsis* (used only here), which means "to make straight," that is, to correct, to straighten out, to make right, to reform. Only the New Covenant in Christ set things right, and the old symbols, the old forms, were meant to serve only until this time, the **time of reformation.** The Old Covenant was never capable of setting things right between men and God. Its purpose was only to symbolize the setting of things right until the true, effective sacrifice was made—the sacrifice that "re-formed" man from the inside, not merely on the outside.

The old sanctuary and services and significance were meaningful and purposeful, very purposeful. But they were limited, imperfect, and temporary, and therefore ultimately unsatisfactory. They pictured Christ, but they could not do the work of Christ. Part of their purpose, in fact, was to show Israel that they *were* only pictures of better things to come. They not only pictured Christ but also their own built-in inadequacies.

CHARACTERISTICS OF THE NEW COVENANT

But when Christ appeared as a high priest of the good things to come, He entered through the greater and more perfect tabernacle, not made with hands, that is to say, not of this creation; and not through the blood of goats and calves, but through His own blood, He entered the holy place once for all, having obtained eternal redemption. For if the blood of goats and bulls and the ashes of a heifer sprinkling those who have been defiled, sanctify for the cleansing of the flesh, how much more will the blood of Christ, who through the eternal Spirit offered Himself without blemish to God, cleanse your conscience from dead works to serve the living God? (9:11-14)

Many characteristics of the New Covenant already have been mentioned or implied in the discussion of the Old. But the writer here focuses on several that are especially important in contrasting the two covenants.

Following the pattern used in showing the inadequacies of the Old Covenant (vv. 1-10), the new sanctuary, the new services, and the new significance are described briefly. As always, the point is not to demean the old but to show its shadowy incompleteness. To condense and paraphrase verses 13 and 14, the Holy Spirit is saying, "If these old things were so good as symbols, how much better are the real things they symbolize. If the external, physical, and temporary covenant accomplished its purpose so well, how much better will the internal, spiritual, and eternal covenant accomplish its purpose?"

THE NEW SANCTUARY

But when Christ appeared as a high priest of the good things to come, He entered through the greater and more perfect tabernacle, not made with hands, that is to say, not of this creation. (9:11)

First of all, **Christ,** as heavenly **High Priest,** has an infinitely greater sanctuary in which to minister. The old Tabernacle was designed by God, but it was made by men, out of material from the present physical creation. For that time and for that purpose, it was impressive. And on the inside, where only the priests could go, it doubtlessly was also beautiful. But it was only a tent. It is not mentioned here, but the Temple in Jerusalem, though immeasurably more magnificent than the Tabernacle, was also made by men with materials from the present creation, and was subject to the deterioration and destruction to which everything of this creation is subject.

The new sanctuary, however, is not made by men or on earth or of earthly materials. It is made by God, in heaven, and of heavenly materials. The new sanctuary, in fact, *is* heaven. Earth belongs to God, but heaven is His dwelling place, His throne, and His sanctuary (Acts 7:48-50; 17:24). As the writer of Hebrews has pointed out several times, Jesus Christ, like Melchizedek, is a priest-king. And He rules and ministers from the same place. His sanctuary and His palace are the same. In this passage, of course, the emphasis is on His sanctuary. Heaven is the **perfect tabernacle, not made with hands.** Christ ministers for us in heaven, in the throne room of God at God's right hand.

The former priests had to go into the Holy Place by themselves— *for* the people, but not *with* the people. The same was true of the high priest in regard to the Holy of Holies, where he could not even take other priests. But our heavenly Priest takes His people with Him all the way into the sanctuary. He takes us into the sanctuary of sanctuaries, into heaven itself—not into the symbolic presence of God, but into the real presence of God. Not only has He gone before us, but He takes us with Him.

If we are believers, He *already has* taken us with Him. "But God, being rich in mercy, because of His great love with which He loved us, even when we were dead in our transgressions, made us alive together with Christ, . . . and raised us up with Him, and seated us with Him in the heavenly places, in Christ Jesus" (Eph. 2:4-6). When we were saved, Christ at that time took us into the Father's presence, where, spiritually speaking, we already live with Him and will forever live with Him. We live right now in heavenly places, in the presence of God—in His throne room and in His sanctuary. "Our citizenship is in heaven" (Phil. 3:20).

THE NEW SERVICES

And not through the blood of goats and calves, but through His own blood, He entered the holy place once for all, having obtained eternal redemption. (9:12)

How does Christ minister in His heavenly sanctuary? What does He do as our eternal High Priest? He does three things, primarily. First, His service is in **His own blood,** not that of sacrificial animals. The Sacrificer was the Sacrifice. Second, He made His sacrifice only **once,** and that once was sufficient for **all** people of all time. Third, He obtained permanent, **eternal redemption.** He cleansed past, present, and future sins all in one act of redemption.

THE NEW SIGNIFICANCE

For if the blood of goats and bulls and the ashes of a heifer sprinking those who have been defiled, sanctify for the cleansing of the flesh, how much more will the blood of Christ, who through the eternal Spirit offered Himself without blemish to God, cleanse your conscience from dead works to serve the living God? (9:13-14)

If the Old Covenant, weak and imperfect as it was, served its purpose, how much better will Christ's New Covenant, powerful and perfect, serve its purpose. The new not only has a better purpose, but accomplishes its purpose in a better way, a perfect way. The purpose of the old sacrifice was to symbolize, externally, the **cleansing** of sin. It accomplished this purpose. The purpose of the new sacrifice, however, was to cleanse actually, internally (where sin really exists). It accomplished its superior purpose in a superior way.

> Not all the blood of beasts on Jewish altars slain,
> Could give the guilty conscience peace or wash away the stain.
> Christ the heavenly Lamb takes all our sins away,
> A sacrifice of nobler name and richer blood than they.
>
> Isaac Watts

Jesus did everything He did on earth in obedience to the Father through the Spirit. Even, in fact *especially,* in His supreme sacrifice He **through the eternal Spirit offered Himself without blemish to God.** In doing so, He provided the cleansing of our consciences **from dead works to serve the living God.** He frees our consciences from guilt, a joy and a blessing that no Old Testament saint ever had or could have had. In Christ we can "draw near with a sincere heart in full assurance of faith, having our hearts sprinkled clean from an evil conscience and our bodies washed with pure water" (Heb. 10:22).

The former priests cleaned up the outside, and even that only symbolically, imperfectly, and temporarily. But Christ cleanses from the inside, where the real problem is. He does more than cleanse the old man; He replaces it with a new man. He cleanses our conscience, but He recreates our person. In Christ, we are not cleaned-up old creatures but redeemed new creatures (2 Cor. 5:17).

An evangelist tells a story from the days when he held tent meetings many years ago. One day, after a series of meetings was over, he was pulling up tent stakes. A young man approached him and asked what he had to do to be saved. The evangelist answered, "Sorry, it's too late." "Oh no," was the response. "You mean it's too late because the services are over?" "No," the evangelist said, "I mean it's too late because it's already been done. Everything that could be done for your salvation has already been done." After explaining Christ's finished work to the young man, he led him to saving faith.

Our salvation is based on the covenant whose redeeming work is finished—on a sacrifice that has been offered **once** and **for all,** that is complete and perfect and eternal.

The New Covenant—
part 3 (9:15-28)

And for this reason He is the mediator of a new covenant, in order that since a death has taken place for the redemption of the transgressions that were committed under the first covenant, those who have been called may receive the promise of the eternal inheritance. For where a covenant is, there must of necessity be the death of the one who made it. For a covenant is valid only when men are dead, for it is never in force while the one who made it lives. Therefore even the first covenant was not inaugurated without blood. For when every commandment had been spoken by Moses to all the people according to the Law, he took the blood of the calves and the goats, with water and scarlet wool and hyssop, and sprinkled both the book itself and all the people, saying, "This is the blood of the covenant which God commanded you." And in the same way he sprinkled both the tabernacle and all the vessels of the ministry with the blood. And according to the Law, one may almost say, all things are cleansed with blood, and without shedding of blood there is no forgiveness.

Therefore it was necessary for the copies of the things in the heavens to be cleansed with these, but the heavenly things themselves with better sacrifices than these. For Christ did not enter a holy place made with hands, a mere copy of the true one, but into heaven itself, now to appear in the presence of God for us; nor was it that He should offer Himself often, as the high priest enters the holy place year by year with blood not his own. Otherwise, He would have needed to suffer often since the foundation of the world; but now once at the consummation of the ages He has been manifested to put away sin by the sacrifice of Himself. And inasmuch as it is appointed for men to die once and after this comes judgment, so Christ also, having been offered once to bear the sins of many, shall appear a second time for salvation without reference to sin, to those who eagerly await Him. (9:15-28)

And for this reason refers back to what has just been said—namely that Christ, because of His sacrificial death had become the mediator of a new and better covenant. By God's standard of righteousness and justice, the soul that sins must die (Ezek. 18:4). The only way a person could come to God was to have the penalty of his sin paid. This payment Jesus has provided for everyone who trusts in Him. In so doing He became the bridge, the mediator—the *only* mediator—between God and men. He accomplished in one act what the work of the old priests only symbolized in many repeated acts. Jesus' supreme act of mediation was His own death on the cross.

People often wonder how Old Testament believers were saved, since salvation is only through Jesus Christ (Acts 4:12). They were saved on the same basis as believers today are saved—by the finished work of Christ. Part of Christ's work as mediator of the New Covenant was the redemption of the transgressions that were committed under the first covenant. One of the first accomplishments of Jesus' death was to redeem all those who had believed in God under the Old Covenant. After Christ died, they saw what had only before been a promise. It was a certain promise, a guaranteed promise, but until the Messiah's atoning death, it was an unfulfilled promise. The point being made here to the writer's original readers—who were Jews, both saved and unsaved—is that Christ's atoning death was retroactive. Yom Kippur (the Day of Atonement) also pictured symbolically what Christ's atonement did actually. It, too, was retroactive. When the high priest sprinkled the blood on the mercy seat, the unintentional sins of the people were covered for the previous year.

Paul presents this same truth in Romans 3. He teaches that we are "justified as a gift by His grace through the redemption which is in Christ Jesus; whom God displayed publicly as a propitiation in His blood through faith. This was to demonstrate His righteousness, because in the forbearance of God He passed over the sins previously committed" (Rom

3:24-25). God is satisfied when a man puts his faith in the shed blood of Christ. Because His blood was not shed until hundreds or even thousands of years after many Old Testament believers died, their salvation was, so to speak, on credit. By their obedient faith in God they were credited with what Jesus Christ, their promised Messiah, would one day do on their behalf and on the behalf of all sinners who have ever lived and who will ever live. Knowing this, God was forbearing and patient, and, until the true sacrifice was made, when He saw a true heart of faith, He passed over their sins. In a deeper sense, the sacrifice had already been made in God's mind long before it was made in human history, because Christ's "works were finished from the foundation of the world" (Heb. 4:3; cf. 1 Pet. 1:19-20; Rev. 13:8). From the human perspective, however, the Old Testament saints could only *look forward* to salvation.

So the Old Testament sacrifices were not means of salvation, but marks of faithful obedience and symbols of the one perfect sacrifice that *would be* the means of salvation.

The **eternal inheritance** that the Old Testament saints could not receive without Christ's death was salvation, the total **forgiveness** that alone could bring total access to God. The New Covenant was ratified by the death of Jesus Christ and provided the full salvation that Israel had been hoping for since the very beginning.

This truth introduces the subject of the death of the Christ, the Messiah, the idea of which had always been a stumbling block to Jews (1 Cor. 1:23). Despite the predictions of His death in their own Scriptures (see Ps. 22 and Isa. 53), it was a truth that they preferred to ignore, if not actually deny. They had constructed their own ideas about the Messiah. Many of the ideas were scriptural, some were partly scriptural, and some were unscriptural altogether. They could not be faulted, of course, for having a limited understanding of the Messiah, for God had only given limited revelation. The problem was that they had ignored some messianic truth and had tried to "fill in the blanks" on their own, and a dying Messiah simply did not fit into their theology.

NECESSITY OF MESSIAH'S DEATH

Being very much aware of that theological blind spot, the writer of Hebrews proceeds to give three reasons it was necessary for the Messiah to die: a testament demands death, forgiveness demands blood, and judgment demands a substitute.

A TESTAMENT DEMANDS DEATH

For where a covenant is, there must of necessity be the death of the

one who made it. For a covenant is valid only when men are dead, for it is never in force while the one who made it lives. (9:16-17)

A testament, by its very nature, requires **the death** of the testator. **Covenant,** or testament, is from the Greek *diathēkē,* the basic meaning of which corresponds closely to that of our present-day *will.* A will does not take effect until the one who made it dies. Until that time, its benefits and provisions are only promises, and necessarily future. The point being made in verses 16-17 is simple and obvious.

Its relevance to the Old Covenant, however, was anything but obvious to the Jews being addressed here, so the writer briefly explains how it applies. Building on verse 15, he is saying that God gave a legacy, an eternal inheritance, to Israel in the form of a covenant, a will. As with any will, it was only a type of promisory note until the provider of the will died. At this point, no mention is made of who the testator is or of how Christ fills that role in life and death.

FORGIVENESS DEMANDS BLOOD

Therefore even the first covenant was not inaugurated without blood. For when every commandment had been spoken by Moses to all the people according to the Law, he took the blood of the calves and the goats, with water and scarlet wool and hyssop, and sprinkled both the book itself and all the people, saying, "This is the blood of the covenant which God commanded you." And in the same way he sprinkled both the tabernacle and all the vessels of the ministry with the blood. And according to the Law, one may almost say, all things are cleansed with blood, and without shedding of blood there is no forgiveness. (9:18-22)

The second reason for the death of Christ was that **forgiveness** demands **blood.** This truth is directly in line with the previous point, but with a different shade of meaning. Blood is a symbol of death, and therefore follows closely the idea of a testator's having to die in order for a will to become effective. But blood also suggests the animal sacrifices that were marks of the Old Covenant, even, in fact, of the Abrahamic covenant. In the Old Covenant, the death of animals was typical and prophetic, looking forward to the death of Christ that would ratify the second covenant. Even before the old priestly sacrifices were begun, the covenant itself was **inaugurated,** or ratified, with blood.

As explained in verse 19, Moses sprinkled blood on the altar and on the people (see Ex. 24:6-8). "Look at your great Moses," the writer is saying, "He himself inaugurated the Old Covenant with blood." It is hard for us today to understand how bloody and messy the old sacrificial system was. But among other things, the great amount of blood was a continual reminder of the penalty of sin, death.

When He sat with the disciples on that last night before His death, Jesus picked up the cup and said, "This is My blood of the covenant, which is poured out for many for forgiveness of sins" (Matt. 26:28). He was to ratify the New Covenant through His own blood, just as the Old Covenant was ratified by Moses with the blood of animals.

It is possible to become morbid about Christ's sacrificial death and preoccupied with His suffering and shedding of blood. It is especially possible to become unbiblically preoccupied with the physical aspects of His death. It was not Jesus' physical blood that saves us, but His dying on our behalf, which is symbolized by the shedding of His physical blood. If we could be saved by blood without death, the animals would have been bled, not killed, and it would have been the same with Jesus.

Since the Tabernacle was not yet built when Moses ratified the covenant, his sprinkling **the tabernacle and all the vessels of the ministry with the blood** is obviously meant to be anticipatory. The blood he sprinkled at the initiation of the covenant continued, in a sense, to be sprinkled by the priests in the Tabernacle and Temple as long as that covenant stood.

The purpose of the blood was to symbolize sacrifice for sin, which brought cleansing from sin. Therefore, **without shedding of blood there is no forgiveness.**

Again, however, we need to keep in mind that the blood was a symbol. If Christ's own physical blood, in itself, does not cleanse from sin, how much less did the physical blood of animals. It is not surprising, then, that the Old Covenant allowed a symbol for a symbol. A Jew who was too poor to bring even a small animal for a sacrifice was allowed to bring one-tenth of an ephah (about two quarts) of fine flour instead (Lev. 5:11). His sins were covered just as surely as those of the person who could afford to offer a lamb or goat or turtledove or pigeon (Lev. 5:6-7). This exception is clear proof that the old cleansing was symbolic. Just as the animal blood symbolized Christ's true atoning blood, so the ephah of flour symbolized and represented the animal blood. This nonblood offering for sin was acceptable because the old sacrifice was entirely symbolic anyway.

Yet this was the only exception. And even the exception *represented* a blood sacrifice. The basic symbol could not be changed because what it symbolized could not be changed. "For the life of the flesh is in the blood, and I have given it to you on the altar to make atonement for your souls; for it is the blood by reason of the life that makes atonement" (Lev. 17:11). Since the penalty for sin is death, nothing but death, symbolized by shedding of blood, can atone for sin. We cannot enter into God's presence by self-effort to be righteous. If we, on our own, could be good, we would not need atonement. Nor can we enter His presence by being model citizens or even by being religious. We cannot enter His presence by reading the Bible, by going to church, by giving generously to the Lord's work, or even by praying. We cannot enter His presence by thinking good thoughts about Him. The only way we can enter into God's presence, the only way we can participate in the New Covenant, is through the atoning death of Jesus Christ, made effective for us when we trust in Him as saving Lord.

God has set the rules. The soul that sins will die. The soul that is saved will be saved through the sacrifice of God's Son. For this sacrifice there is no exception, no substitute, for this is the real thing. Because they were symbols, God provided a limited and strictly qualified exception (flour) to the old sacrifices. But there can be no exception for the real sacrifice, because it is the only way to God.

Forgiveness is a costly, costly thing. But I often think to myself how lightly we can take the forgiveness of God. I have come to the end of a day and put my head on the pillow to say, "God, I did this and this today," listing off the things I had done that I knew were not pleasing to Him. I know He knows about them, so there is no use trying to hide them. I also know He forgives them, because He has promised to forgive them, and I thank Him. I fall off to sleep in a few minutes, accepting but not fully appreciating the marvelous grace that made such assurance and peace so easily available to me.

At other times, as I study the Word of God, and look more closely at the great cost that was paid for my salvation, I am overwhelmed. When I meditate on the infinite cost to God to forgive my sins, I realize how often I abuse my loving Father's grace.

Paul tells us that "where sin increased, grace abounded all the more" (Rom. 5:20). Then, anticipating how some might distort this truth, he goes on to say, "What shall we say then? Are we to continue in sin that grace might increase? May it never be! How shall we who died to sin still live in it?" (6:1). To realize and rejoice in God's boundless grace is one thing; to presume on it by willfully sinning is quite another. How can we, as forgiven sinners, take lightly or presumptuously, the price paid for our forgiveness? We become so used to grace that we abuse it. In fact, we are so accustomed to grace that when God brings down just punishment we may think it unjust.

God does not forgive sin by looking down and saying, "It's all right. Since I love you so much, I'll overlook your sin." God's righteousness and holiness will not allow Him to overlook sin. Sin demands payment by death. And the only death great enough to pay for all of mankind's sins is the death of His Son. God's great love for us will not lead

Him to overlook our sin, but it *has* led Him to provide the payment for our sin, as John 3:16 so beautifully reminds us. God cannot ignore our sin; but He will forgive our sin if we trust in the death of His Son for that forgiveness.

Therefore it was necessary for the copies of the things in the heavens to be cleansed with these, but the heavenly things themselves with better sacrifices than these. (9:23)

The **copies of the things in the heavens** were the things of the old economy. They were but sketches, or outlines, of the realities of heaven. It was necessary for these copies to have sacrifices. It was therefore necessary for the better covenant, the better economy, to have **better sacrifices.** All the blood of the Old Covenant was just a copy, a faint picture, of the shed blood of Jesus.

God was so satisfied with what Jesus did that He "highly exalted Him, and bestowed on Him the name which is above every name, that at the name of Jesus every knee should bow, of those who are in heaven, and on earth, and under the earth, and that every tongue should confess that Jesus Christ is Lord, to the glory of God the Father" (Phil. 2:9-11). God is immeasurably satisfied with Jesus.

God is *not* satisfied with *us*, however. That is the very reason we have to come to Him through Jesus. Jesus is the only one who satisfies the Father, and therefore no one comes to Him except through Jesus. The idea that God accepts us as we are is utterly unbiblical. We come to Jesus just as we are, since there is nothing worthwhile we can bring. But He does not present us to the Father just as we are. We are totally unpresentable as we are. Otherwise we could present ourselves. When Jesus presents us to His Father, He presents us in Himself, as *He* is. When we enter into God's presence, God sees Jesus instead of us. He sees Jesus' righteousness instead of our unrighteousness. He sees Jesus' sacrifice instead of our sin, His payment for our sin instead of the penalty we deserve for our sin. Jesus recognized the indebtedness of sinners. He recognized that God had to be satisfied, and He offered His own blood—His own self—on our behalf.

Jesus told the story of two men who went to the Temple to pray. One was a Pharisee, a member of the most religious and orthodox group of Jews. The other was a tax collector, despised almost as a traitor by fellow Jews. The Pharisee gave thanks that he was not like other people, "swindlers, unjust, adulterers, or even like this tax-gatherer." Then he mentioned his faithfulness in fasting and tithing. But Jesus said this Pharisee was praying "to himself." In other words, he was not really praying at all, only congratulating himself in God's name. The tax collector, on the other hand, felt so unworthy that he would not even lift up his eyes toward heaven, as the prayer posture often was. He beat on his breast and said, "God, be merciful to me, the sinner!" This man, Jesus said, "went down to his house justified rather than the other; for everyone who exalts himself shall be humbled, but he who humbles himself shall be exalted" (Luke 18:10-14).

When the tax collector said, "be merciful," he used the same word used of Christ in Hebrews 2:17 ("to make propitiation"). He was asking God to be propitious to him, to look favorably on him, though he did not deserve it. He was saying, "I confess my guilt. I have broken your law. I have sinned against you, and I am putting myself under the blood sprinkled on the mercy seat. God, please be satisfied. Let your attitude be toward me as it is toward those who are covered by the blood of the sacrifice. Be satisfied with me because of the sacrifice, and forgive me in your love and mercy." He did not deny his sin, as the Pharisee did in effect. He recognized his guilt and put it under the blood of the sacrifice. He offered God nothing of his own—no good works, no good habits, no good intentions, not even good excuses. He simply threw himself on God's mercy, God's propitiation. For this he was justified, counted righteous by God.

No person can be justified before God until he is placed into the death of Jesus Christ and says, "God, I am a sinner. I place myself into the death of your Son. Be satisfied with me for His sake."

For Christ did not enter a holy place made with hands, a mere copy of the true one, but into heaven itself, now to appear in the presence of God for us; nor was it that He should offer Himself often, as the high priest enters the holy place year by year with blood not his own. Otherwise, He would have needed to suffer often since the foundation of the world; but now once at the consummation of the ages He has been manifested to put away sin by the sacrifice of Himself. (9:24-26)

Christ did not go into an earthly Holy of Holies. He went into the presence of God—the heavenly, real Holy of Holies. And He did it **for us.** How beautiful to realize that when He went in, *He took us with Him!* He has ushered us into the very **presence of God.** Nor did Christ have to **offer Himself often,** as did the earthly high priests, who had to make the offering of atonement every year. Jesus' sacrifice was better because He takes His people into the heavenly Holy of Holies with Him and because He had to make an offering only once.

If Jesus' sacrifice had not been once and for all, He would have had to suffer from the **foundation of the world,** that is, from the beginning of humankind. He would have had to die continuously, as it were, since the time Adam first sinned. Like the work of the Levitical priest-hood, His atoning work would never be finished. But, praise God, His sacrifice does not have to be repeated—not even once. It is finished, com-pletely finished.

His one sacrifice of Himself was made at the **consummation of the ages.** The epistles confirm this. "Children, it is the last hour" (1 John 2:18); "For the coming of the Lord is at hand" (James 5:8); "The end of all things is at hand" (1 Pet. 4:7). The consummation of the ages was Christ at Calvary. It is no wonder the apostles expected Jesus to return at any moment and set up His kingdom—to establish the final messianic age, "the age to come" (Matt. 12:32). Until that age, His prom-ise is to be with us through the present age (Matt. 28:20). He was the consummation of the ages because of His once and for all sacrifice. He put away sin. He did not simply cover sin, as the old sacrifices had done; He removed it.

The idea of the perpetual offering of Christ is a heretical doctrine that for many centuries has contradicted this and the many other clear biblical teachings about the finished work of Christ. It maintains that, inasmuch as the priesthood of Christ is perpetual and sacrifice is an es-sential part of priesthood, therefore the sacrificial offering of Christ must also be perpetual.

Ludwig Ott, a Roman Catholic theologian, explains this perpetual sacrifice dogma, which was made official by that church at the Council of Trent in the middle of the sixteenth century. "The holy Mass," he writes, "is a true and proper sacrifice. It is physical and propitiatory, removing sins and conferring the grace of repentance. Propitiated by the offering of this sacrifice, God, by granting the grace of the gift and the gift of Pen-ance, remits trespasses and sins however grievous they may be." In other words, God's satisfaction regarding sin depends upon the weekly mass. That is why attending mass is so important to Catholics.

But the theory of the perpetual offering of Jesus Christ is in abso-lute and direct opposition to Scripture. **But now once at the consum-mation of the ages He has been manifested to put away sin by the sacrifice of Himself.** No doubt some Catholics know Christ, but in holding to the doctrine of the perpetual offering of His sacrifice, they undermine the power and significance of Christ's one-time and only true sacrifice. This false doctrine is plainly reflected in the crucifix, the ubiqui-tous symbol of Roman Catholicism. Whether in pictures, in statuary, or wherever, the cross is rarely empty in Catholic representations. To Catholics, Jesus is still being crucified.

In Communion, or the Lord's Supper, we *remember* Christ's sacrifi-cial death, as He commanded us to do. But He is not resacrificed. The Lord commanded His disciples to remember His death, not to try to redo it.

JUDGMENT DEMANDS A SUBSTITUTE

And inasmuch as it is appointed for men to die once and after this comes judgment, so Christ also, having been offered once to bear the sins of many, shall appear a second time for salvation without reference to sin, to those who eagerly await Him. (9:27-28)

All men have **to die,** and our death is by divine appointment. It is one appointment everyone will keep. After death comes **judgment,** which is also appointed by God. And since men are not able to atone for their own sins, God's judgment demands that they pay or have a substitute pay for them.

Like all men, Jesus Christ was divinely appointed to die once. But unlike all other men, He will never face judgment. Because He took our sins upon Himself, He took our judgment upon Himself. But the judgment was for *our* sins, not for His, for He had none. God "made Him who knew no sin to be sin on our behalf, that we might become the righteousness of God in Him" (2 Cor. 5:21). He died the one death that judgment demanded.

As mentioned several times, the people always waited expectantly on the Day of Atonement for the high priest to come out from the Holy of Holies. If he did anything wrong, if he failed to follow God's precise instructions, he would die. So there was always a sigh of relief, for their own sakes as well as for his, when he reappeared.

That is the situation being alluded to in Hebrews 9:28. If the people were so eager to see the former high priests reappear from the earthly Holy of Holies, how much more should Christians look eagerly for their great High Priest to reappear from the heavenly Holy of Holies? This will occur at the Second Coming (Rev. 19:11-16).

When the high priest walked out of the old sanctuary, the people knew that his sacrifice had been accepted. He had done everything right. Jesus Christ's reappearing will be one more confirmation that He did everything right, that His Father is satisfied with Him. And because the Father is satisfied with Him, He is satisfied with us, for we are in Him. When He comes back, our salvation will be full. When He appears a second time to those who expect Him, it will not be to deal with sin. Sin only needs to be dealt with once, and this He did on the cross. When He comes again, it will be be **without reference to sin.**

Three appearings of Christ are mentioned in this passage. Verse 26 speaks of His appearing, or being manifested, **at the consummation of the ages,** that is, when He came to be crucified. Verse 24 speaks of His appearing back in **heaven,** before **the presence of God.** Verse 28 speaks of His appearing on earth again. It is His third appearing, but only the **second time** on earth.

At the end of that eventful Passover week when Jesus was finishing His ministry, the Romans had prepared three crosses for three criminals. On two of the crosses, thieves were to hang. The third cross was for an insurrectionist named Barabbas, who had been found guilty of treason against the empire. But Barabbas never made it to the cross. He was guilty and condemned, but he was not executed—because someone took his place. On the middle cross that day hung not a violent, profane rebel, but the sinless Son of God. Barabbas went free not because he was innocent, but because Jesus took his place. Jesus was crucified not because He was guilty, but so that He *could* take Barabbas's place—and the place of every other sinner.

Christil, the Perfect Sacrifice (10:1-18)

For the Law, since it has only a shadow of the good things to come and not the very form of things, can never by the same sacrifices year by year, which they offer continually, make perfect those who draw near. Otherwise, would they not have ceased to be offered, because the worshipers, having once been cleansed, would no longer have had consciousness of sins? But in those sacrifices there is a reminder of sins year by year. For it is impossible for the blood of bulls and goats to take away sins. Therefore, when He comes into the world, He says, "Sacrifice and offering Thou hast not desired, but a body Thou hast prepared for Me; in whole burnt offerings and sacrifices for sin Thou hast taken no pleasure. Then I said, 'Behold, I have come (in the roll of the book it is written of Me) to do Thy will, O God.'" After saying above, "Sacrifices and offerings and whole burnt offerings and sacrifices for sin Thou hast not desired, nor hast Thou taken pleasure in them" (which are offered according to the Law), then He said, "Behold, I have come to do Thy will." He takes away the first in order to establish the second. By this will we have been sanctified through the offering of the body of Jesus Christ once for all. And every priest stands daily ministering and offering time after time the same sacrifices, which can never take away sins; but He, having offered one sacrifice for sins for all time, sat down at the right hand of God, waiting from that time onward until His enemies be made a footstool for His feet. For by one offering He has perfected for all time those who are sanctified. And the Holy Spirit also bears witness to us; for after saying, "This is the covenant that I will make with them after those days, says the LORD: I will put My laws upon their heart, and upon their mind I will write them," He then says, "And their sins and their lawless deeds I will remember no more." Now where there is forgiveness of these things, there is no longer any offering for sin. (10:1-18)

There is a story of an English village whose chapel had an arch on which was written: "We Preach Christ Crucified." For years godly men preached there and they presented a crucified Savior as the only means of salvation. But as the generation of godly preachers passed, a generation arose that considered the cross and its message antiquated and repulsive. They began to preach salvation by Christ's example rather than by His blood. They did not see the necessity of His sacrifice. After a while, ivy crept up the side of the arch and covered the word "Crucified," and only "We Preach Christ" was visible. Then the church decided that its message need not even be confined to Christ and the Bible. So the preachers began to give discourses on social issues, politics, philosophy, moral rearmament, and whatever else happened to spark interest. The ivy on the arch continued to grow until it covered the third word. Then it simply read, "We Preach."

In cultured, sophisticated Corinth, Paul was "determined to know nothing among [them] except Jesus Christ, and Him crucified" (1 Cor. 2:2). Christ crucified is the only hope of men, and that is the theme of Hebrews 10:1-18. Here is the record of Jesus' death from the theological, rather than the historical, standpoint. We are shown the meaning and the depth of His death in all of its richness. In His death, Jesus was the perfect sacrifice.

In chapter 9 we saw the necessity of His sacrifice; here we see the character of His sacrifice. The first six verses lay the foundation by showing the ineffectiveness of the old sacrifices. We tread here some familiar ground in the study of this epistle.

THE FAILURE OF THE OLD SACRIFICES

Under the Old Covenant, the priests were busy all day long, from dawn to sunset, slaughtering and sacrificing animals. It is estimated that at Passover as many as three hundred thousand lambs would be slain within a week. The slaughter would be so massive that blood would run out of the Temple ground through specially prepared channels into the Brook Kidron, which seemed to be running with blood.

But no matter how many sacrifices were made, or how often, they were ineffective. They failed in three ways: they could not bring access to God; they could not remove sin; and they were only external.

THEY COULD NOT BRING ACCESS TO GOD

The great cry in the hearts of Old Testament saints was to be in the presence of God (cf. Ex. 33:15; Ps. 16:11). But they really had no way of getting there. Even the high priest on the Day of Atonement could not take the people inside the veil, where, symbolically, God dwelt. All the old ceremonies and sacrifices, though offered continually, year after year, could *never* **make perfect those who draw near.** They could never save, never bring access to God.

They were shadows and could only *reflect* the **very form** of the good things to come, the realities of the privileges and blessings of salvation. The law only pictured these things. The old rituals and practices "are a mere shadow of what is to come; but the substance belongs to Christ" (Col. 2:17). Christ is the fulfillment of the good things to come: forgiveness, peace, a clear conscience, security, and, above all, access to God. These blessings were only pictured in the Old Covenant, they were never realized.

Shadow (*skia*) refers specifically to a pale shadow, as contrasted with a sharp, distinct one. The law and the ceremonies and rituals together were only a pale shadow of the things Christ would bring. They were form without substance. They portrayed something real, but were not themselves real.

The **very form** (*eikōn*), on the other hand, indicates an exact replica, a complete representation, or detailed reproduction. If photography had been in existence then, the writer possibly would have called it a photograph—a clear, sharp, detailed photograph in full color. The Spirit is saying that the old system was a shadow, whereas the new system is the actual substance, the very reality. Before Christ, no one could get closer to the good things of God than the shadows of them.

Judaism today is even without many of the shadows. Jews have the Scriptures, what we refer to as the Old Testament, and they continue to celebrate certain feast days. But they have no tabernacle or temple or priesthood, and therefore no sacrifices—daily or yearly. Yom Kippur is still observed, but without a high priest, without an altar, and without a sacrificial lamb. Because modern unbelieving Jews refuse to recognize the New Covenant God made with them, even the Old has lost much of its significance. What at best was pale, has faded even more. What was always indistinct has become even more indistinct. Most Jews follow neither the Scriptures nor the ceremonies. They will not accept the new sacrifice and have lost even the old. If, during the time when the previous covenant was in force, the old sacrifices could never **make perfect,** how much less effective would they be now—even if, somehow, they continued?

To **make perfect** (*teleioō*) is to bring to completion, to bring to the intended end. The end to which the Old Covenant *pointed* was access to God, full salvation, but it was never intended to *bring* men to God. It did not make perfect because God never intended for it to make perfect. Its purpose was to picture, not to perfect.

Again the writer stresses that the same sacrifices were offered **year after year, . . . continually.** The repetition of the old sacrifices is a theme that itself is repeated many times in Hebrews. You can pile shadow on shadow on shadow, and you still have no substance. Repetition of a symbol is like multiplying with zero. No matter how many times you repeat the process, the result never increases.

Why, then, did God go to all the trouble to establish the Old Covenant, with its shadow ceremonies, its shadow rituals, its shadow sacrifices? What was the point? As we have learned, the first point was simply that, even as a shadow, it had a *purpose*—to reflect the reality of which it was the shadow. It pointed to the salvation that was to come. It was to make God's people expectant. "As to this salvation, the prophets who prophesied of the grace that would come to you made careful search and inquiry" (1 Pet. 1:10). A shadow of something—certainly a God-given shadow—is immeasurably better than no evidence at all.

Second, the purpose of the shadow sacrifices was to remind God's people that the *penalty* of sin is death. The blood that sometimes flowed from the altar came from animals who were killed as sacrifices for sin. The people were constantly being reminded that the wages of sin is death, because death was going on all day long throughout their history as animals were being slaughtered.

Third, God gave His people the sacrifices as a *covering* for sin. Even a shadow is better than nothing if it can to some degree cover sin. When properly offered from a true heart of faith, the old sacrifices removed immediate, temporal judgment from God. To despise the sacrifices was to be cut off from His people and to incur His temporal punishment, because it betrayed an unbelieving, disobedient heart. Those sacrifices were temporal and they had some temporal effect and value. They could not bring a person into God's presence, but they were important in maintaining a demonstration of a person's covenantal relationship to Him.

THEY COULD NOT REMOVE SIN

Otherwise, would they not have ceased to be offered, because the worshipers, having once been cleansed, would no longer have had

consciousness of sins? But in those sacrifices there is a reminder of sins year by year. (10:2-3)

With their shadow, the animal sacrifices could cover, but never remove, sin. Yet removal of sin is what men need. Sin and guilt eat away at us. But the old system could not remove sin or guilt. If it could have, the sacrifices would have stopped. Once having removed sin, they would no longer have been necessary.

The old sacrifices not only did not remove sin, but they were a continual *reminder* that they could not. **In those sacrifices there is a reminder of sins year by year.** Even the covering of sin was temporary. It lasted only until the next sin. It was a burdensome, disappointing system.

Suppose you get sick and the doctor gives you a prescription. You get it filled and start taking the medicine. If it works, every time you look at the bottle you are happy and are reminded that you are cured, that the sickness is gone. But if it does not work, every time you look at the bottle it reminds you that the medicine is ineffective and that you are still sick. It may sometimes give relief from the symptoms, but it does nothing to cure the disease. A person who must take a medicine to stay alive cannot be said to be cured.

The old sacrifices and ceremonies had somewhat this same effect on Israel. Instead of removing her sins, they only gave temporary relief and were a constant reminder that her sins were still there. Another year, another lamb, another sacrifice—and the sins were still there. The sacrifices kept reminding the people that they were sinful, and that they were at the mercy of God and could not enter into His presence. Far from erasing sin, the Tabernacle and Temple sacrifices only served to call attention to it.

Consciousness in 10:2 translates the same Greek word (*suneidēsis*) as does "conscience" in 9:9; 10:22; and 13:18. The basic meaning is the same in all four places. The word has to do with man's innate awareness of wrong in his life and of his sense of guilt because of it. Conscience is built into man's makeup. It acts on our minds and hearts much as pain acts on our bodies. Guilt reacts to moral and spiritual injury in much the same way that pain reacts to physical injury. Both are warning systems. Neither is enjoyable, but both serve a good purpose.

Old Testament believers were never freed from the presence and awareness of guilt or, consequently, from the anxiety and tension that it brings (see Rom. 5-6). It is a wonderful blessing for Christians to know that there is no condemnation to those who are in Christ (Rom. 8:1). It is a wonderful thing to be free from guilt and to recognize that our sins are continually being forgiven by the grace of God through the death of Christ.

But there was no such freedom of conscience under the previous covenant. In fact, the more faithful and godly the person was, the guiltier he was likely to feel, because he was more aware of and sensitive to God's holiness and his own sinfulness. He was torn between his knowledge of God's law and his knowledge of his own breaking of that law. We only have to read Psalm 51 to realize how deeply David felt his guilt. He was "a man after God's own heart," and yet he was never free from his consciousness of his guilt before God. David knew, as this psalm also testifies, of God's love and mercy and grace. But the deliverance he describes so beautifully is always future. He knows that salvation, with its cleansing and renewing and joy, is coming. He does not speak as one who has experienced it, when he says, "My sin is ever before me" (Ps. 51:3).

It is not that the Christian, who really is cleansed of sin, is no longer conscious of sin in his life. No one should be more aware of his own sin than the Christian, because, just as the faithful and godly Old Testament saint, he is more aware of God's holiness and standards of righteousness. The Christian should be conscious of his sin, but his conscience should no longer be unduly burdened by it.

It is the unbeliever, and the carnal or untaught believer, who is deluded about the presence of sin in his life. "If we say that we have no sin, we are deceiving ourselves, and the truth is not in us," and "we make Him a liar" (1 John 1:8, 10). Proverbs 28:13 is true in every dispensation—"He who conceals his transgressions will not prosper, but he who confesses and forsakes them will find compassion." The forgiven sinner is not insensitive to sin, but he *knows* he is forgiven in Christ and is thereby delivered from fear of judgment.

THEY WERE ONLY EXTERNAL

The old sacrifices were also ineffective because they were only external. They never got to the heart of the problem. Sin is very often manifested outwardly, but its cause is always internal. The old sacrifices had no way of reaching inside of a person and changing him. **For it is impossible for the blood of bulls and goats to take away sins.** These sacrifices only sanctified "for the cleansing of the flesh," the external, but "the blood of Christ, who through the eternal Spirit offered Himself without blemish to God" (9:13-14), cleanses our consciences, the internal.

There was no real relationship between a person's sin and an animal sacrifice. The relationship was only symbolic, typical. It was impossible for the blood of an amoral animal to bring forgiveness for a man's moral offense against God. Only Jesus Christ, the perfect union of humanity and deity, could satisfy God and purify man. Only His death could be the ultimate sacrifice, the only effective sacrifice.

Therefore, when He comes into the world, He says, "Sacrifice and

offering Thou hast not desired, but a body Thou hast prepared for Me; in whole burnt offerings and sacrifices for sin Thou hast taken no pleasure. (10:5-6)

It is essential to know that the external ceremonies had an internal requirement to make them acceptable to God. The person who did not sacrifice out of an honest heart was not covered even externally or ceremonially (see Amos 4:4-5; 5:21-25). It is this sort of sacrifice that **Thou hast not desired.** The people had taken what was meant to be a symbol of real faith and used it as a substitute for faith. Their trust was in the outward form. It came to be seen as a form of magic, wherein the prescribed words or actions automatically produced the desired result. God Himself had instituted the sacrificial system, but as a means for expressing obedience to Him, not as a means of using Him.

As Samuel reminded Saul when the old system was relatively new, "to obey is better than sacrifice, and to heed than the fat of rams" (1 Sam. 15:22). To sacrifice without obedience, to go through a ritual without faith and devotion to God, was mockery and hypocrisy that was worse than no sacrifice at all. In Psalm 51 David describes the only kind of sacrifice acceptable to God, even under the Old Covenant: "The sacrifices of God are a broken spirit; a broken and a contrite heart, O God, Thou wilt not despise" (Ps. 51:17). Isaiah says much the same thing.

> "What are your multiplied sacrifices to Me?" says the LORD. "I have had enough of burnt offerings of rams, and the fat of fed cattle. And I take no pleasure in the blood of bulls, lambs, or goats. . . . So when you spread out your hands in prayer, I will hide My eyes from you, Yes, even though you multiply prayers, I will not listen. Your hands are covered with blood. Wash yourselves, make yourselves clean; remove the evil of your deeds from My sight. Cease to do evil, learn to do good; seek justice, reprove the ruthless; defend the orphan, plead for the widow. Come now, and let us reason together," says the LORD, "Though your sins are as scarlet, they will be as white as snow; though they are red like crimson, they will be like wool." (Isa. 1:11, 15-18)

When sacrifices were not offered in the right spirit, they could not even cover sin temporarily. They even lost their symbolic value. They were mere form without content and were absolutely worthless. Instead of pleasing God, they became an abomination that He hated (Isa. 1:13-14).

THE EFFECTIVENESS OF THE NEW SACRIFICE

The ineffectiveness of animal sacrifices is now compared to the effectiveness of Christ's sacrifice. Seven superiorities of the new are mentioned.

IT REFLECTS GOD'S ETERNAL WILL

Therefore, when He comes into the world, He says, "Sacrifice and offering Thou hast not desired, but a body Thou hast prepared for Me; . . . Then I said, 'Behold, I have come (in the roll of the book it is written of Me) to do Thy will, O God.' " (10:5, 7)

Christ's sacrifice was effective first of all because it was God's will all along. In the mind of God, before the world was ever created, He knew that the old system would be ineffective. From the beginning He had planned that Jesus would come and die. **When He comes into the world, . . . He says, "a body Thou hast prepared for Me."** When Christ was ready to be incarnated, standing on the edge of heaven, as it were, talking to His Father, He acknowledged that His own body was to be the sacrifice that would please God.

God could never have been satisfied with animal offerings and He became less satisfied with them as they became a sham and a mockery. To many offerers they had come to be meaningless religious ritual, and had nothing to do with obedience or faith.

Jesus' supreme mission on earth was to do His Father's will. Over and over in the gospels, Jesus speaks of His having come to do the Father's will and only the Father's will. His was the perfect sacrifice because it was offered in perfect obedience to God. During the wilderness temptations, Satan's purpose was to deter Jesus from His divine mission, to turn Him from His Father's will. Satan even prompted the unwitting disciples to try to dissuade Jesus from His mission—as when Peter, thinking he was showing loyalty to his Master, rebuked Jesus for suggesting that He had to die and be resurrected (Mark 8:31-33). "But that the world may know that I love the Father, and as the Father gave Me commandment, even so I do. Arise, let us go from here" (John 14:31). When He said this, Jesus was about to be arrested. His saying, "Let us go," therefore, referred to the crucifixion, Jesus' ultimate act of obedience to the Father.

From Jesus' teaching to them, the disciples should long beforehand have realized that their Lord's ministry was to lead to His suffering and death. They should, in fact, already have known this from the Scriptures. They knew He was the Messiah, and they should have known that the Messiah was to come to die. What could have been a clearer prediction of the Messiah's sacrificial death than these words of Isaiah?

Surely our griefs He Himself bore, and our sorrows He carried; yet we ourselves esteemed Him stricken, smitten of God, and afflicted. But He was pierced through for our transgressions, He was crushed for our iniquities; the chastening for our well-being fell upon Him, and by His scourging we are healed. (Isa. 53:4-5)

It was not dying in itself, of course, that was Jesus' ultimate act of obedience, but rather His taking man's total sin upon Himself in His death. His greatest test of obedience was in the garden, when He prayed, "Abba! Father! All things are possible for Thee; remove this cup from Me; yet not what I will, but what Thou wilt" (Mark 14:36). Many people, before and after Jesus, have willingly and bravely faced a martyr's death. But no one else has, or could have, taken upon himself the sins of the whole world. No one else has been, or could have been, so utterly repulsed at the prospect. And no one else has been, or could have been, so obedient.

On the cross Jesus was saying, "Father, I know You are not satisfied with the old system and the old sacrifices, but I know You are satisfied with Me and with My sacrifice. So I will gladly pay the price of obedience."

IT REPLACES THE OLD SYSTEM

After saying above, "Sacrifices and offerings and whole burnt offerings and sacrifices for sin Thou hast not desired, nor hast Thou taken pleasure in them" (which are offered according to the Law), then He said, "Behold, I have come to do Thy will." He takes away the first in order to establish the second. (10:8-9)

The writer continues his commentary on Psalm 40:6-8, which he has referred to in verses 5-7, pointing out that God took away **the first,** that is, the old sacrifices, to make way for **the second,** the new sacrifice. His point was to show the Jewish readers—again—that the Old Covenant was not then, never had been, and never could have been satisfactory. It was not meant to be permanent or truly effective, only temporary and symbolic. God's focus was always on the second covenant, the superior covenant, the perfect covenant. And that second covenant has now come in Jesus Christ. "You cannot be under two covenants at the same time," they are being told, "and now that the second has come, the first has to go." Whatever purpose and validity the first one had are now past. It no longer has any purpose or validity. God has forever set it aside. All this repeated emphasis reveals a pleading heart, calling the readers to salvation in the Lord Jesus Christ.

IT SANCTIFIES THE BELIEVER

By this will we have been sanctified through the offering of the body of Jesus Christ once for all. (10:10)

The new sacrifice is effective because it sanctifies the believer, makes him holy. The old system had no way of making a man holy. To be sanctified, or made holy (*hagiazō*), basically means to be set apart. When the word is used in Scripture of men, it always refers to being set apart *by* God *for* God. From this same Greek word group we also get *saint*. In biblical terms, a saint is a person whom God has set apart for Himself. It is God's will that we be set apart, not only positionally but practically. "For this is the will of God, your sanctification" (1 Thess. 4:3).

The Greek verb form in verse 10 (**we have been sanctified**) is a perfect participle with a finite verb, which shows in the strongest way the believer's continuing and permanent salvation. The force of the statement is, "You have been permanently made holy." This fulfills the desire of our Lord, "You shall be holy, for I am holy" (1 Pet. 1:16; cf. Lev. 11:44).

One act, in one moment, provided permanent sanctification for everyone who places his trust in Jesus Christ (cf. Col. 2:10; 2 Pet. 1:3-4). On the cross, He sanctified us, set us apart unto Himself, forever holy and dear to Himself and to the Father.

Our positional standing before God and our practical standing are, of course, quite different things. If we are in Christ, we will forever be in Christ. This position before the Father will not be modified an iota throughout all eternity. But our practical holiness, as we all know, is all too changeable. Speaking to the Christians at Colossae, Paul wrote, "Therefore consider the members of your earthly body as dead to immorality, impurity, passion, evil desire, and greed, which amounts to idolatry. . . , and in them you also once walked, when you were living in them. But now you also, put them all aside: anger, wrath, malice, slander, and abusive speech from your mouth" (Col. 3:5, 7-8). All these believers to whom Paul was speaking were positionally holy, but many of them—possibly all of them—were not practically holy. It is God's will that our practice match our position, that we really become in person who we are in Christ.

It is positional holiness that is in mind in Hebrews 10:10, for the holiness here is an accomplished fact—**we have been sanctified.** Regardless of how holy our walk may be, in our *standing* we are completely and permanently set apart unto God if we have trusted in **the offering of the body of Jesus Christ once for all.**

IT REMOVES SIN

And every priest stands daily ministering and offering time after time

the same sacrifices, which can never take away sins; but He, having offered one sacrifice for sins for all time, sat down at the right hand of God. (10:11-12)

Christ's sacrifice is effective because it removes sin, which the other covenant could never do. The New Covenant went from daily sacrifice to one sacrifice, from ineffective sacrifices to the one perfectly effective sacrifice.

These two verses are a series of contrasts—the many priests with the one Priest, the continual standing of the old priests with the sitting down of the new, the repeated offerings with the once-for-all offering, and the ineffective sacrifices that only covered sin with the effective sacrifice that completely removes sin.

The Levitical system had twenty-four orders, in each of which were hundreds of priests who took turns serving at the altar. This system did not lack for priests, but it did lack effectiveness. All the priests together could not make an effective sacrifice for sin. Christ was but one priest, yet His work was perfectly and permanently effective.

The Levitical priests always stood because their ministry was never finished. Christ, after His sacrifice **sat down at the right hand of God,** because *His* work was finished.

The Levitical sacrifices, with all their priests and all their repetition, could **never take away sins.** Christ's sacrifice took away the sins of believers **for all time.**

IT DESTROYED HIS ENEMIES

Waiting from that time onward until His enemies be made a footstool for His feet. (10:13)

Christ's sacrifice was effective because it conquered His enemies. All the sacrifices of the Old Testament did nothing to get rid of Satan. They had absolutely no effect on him at all, nor on the godless demons and people who served him. But when Jesus died on the cross, He dealt a death-blow to all His enemies. First of all, He conquered "him who had the power of death, that is, the devil" (Heb. 2:14). Second, He also triumphed over all the other fallen angels (Col. 2:14-15). Third, He disarmed and triumphed over all rulers and authorities of all ages who have rejected and opposed God (Col. 2:15). He is now only waiting until all **His enemies be made a footstool,** that is, until they acknowledge His lordship by bowing at His feet (Phil. 2:10).

Jesus Christ will stand above all those who were His enemies. He won the victory over them at the cross. There, all the enemies of God throughout the ages gathered together to inflict on Him their worst, which was death. But Jesus conquered death just as He conquered the other enemies. He went in one side of death and out the other. Not only that, but He conquered death for all who ever have and ever will believe in God. Jesus Christ turned Satan's worst into God's best.

IT PERFECTS THE SAINTS FOREVER

For by one offering He has perfected for all time those who are sanctified. (10:14)

The new sacrifice was effective because it gives believers eternal perfection. Again, it must be emphasized that perfection is eternal salvation. To make **perfected** here mean "spiritually matured" would not be consistent with the context. The death of Jesus Christ removes sin forever for those who belong to Him. We are totally secure in our Savior. We need cleansing when we fall into sin, but we need never fear God's judgment on us because of our sin. As far as Christ's sacrifice is concerned, we have *already been sanctified and perfected*—which is why He had to sacrifice Himself only once. **Now where there is forgiveness of these things, there is no longer any offering for sin** (10:18). The forgiveness is permanent because the sacrifice is permanent.

IT FULFILLS THE PROMISE OF A NEW COVENANT

And the Holy Spirit also bears witness to us; for after saying, "This is the covenant that I will make with them after those days, says the LORD: I will put My laws upon their heart, and upon their mind I will write them," He then says, "And their sins and their lawless deeds I will remember no more." (10:15-17)

Finally, the new sacrifice of Christ is effective because it fulfills the promise of a New Covenant. In other words, the new sacrifice had to be made and had to be effective because God promised that it would be. The new sacrifice was central to the New Covenant, which God said would put His **laws upon their heart, and upon their mind,** and which would cause Him to forget **their sins and their lawless deeds.** The new sacrifice was effective, therefore, because it *had* to accomplish these things (prophesied in Jeremiah 31:33-34) in order for God to fulfill His promises, which cannot be broken.

Though the New Covenant was new, it was not a new revelation, but the fulfillment of an old one. Now that it had arrived, Jews, more than any others, should have welcomed it with unbounded joy and relief.

The promise was not Jeremiah's, but was God's—the very witness of **the Holy Spirit.**

The readers were being put on the horns of a great dilemma, which they could not escape. The Holy Spirit, through the writer of Hebrews, is saying, "You cannot accept the teaching of your own beloved prophet Jeremiah and yet reject the New Covenant he prophesied. You cannot accept one without the other." To accept Jeremiah is to accept Jesus Christ. To reject Jesus Christ is to reject Jeremiah (not to mention the many other prophets who spoke of the Messiah) and to reject the Holy Spirit Himself.

Now where there is forgiveness of these things, there is no longer any offering for sin. (10:18)

The work of sacrifice is done. There will be no more. Forgiveness is already provided for those who trust in this one perfect sacrifice. Why would anyone want to go back to the old sacrifices, which were never finished and never effective? To reject is to have no other hope of forgiveness—ever.

"The Lord is not slow about His promise, as some count slowness, but is patient toward you, not wishing for any to perish but for all to come to repentance" (2 Pet. 3:9). Salvation—glorious and perfect salvation—is promised in the Old Covenant and purchased in the New.

Accepting Christ
(10:19-25)

Since therefore, brethren, we have confidence to enter the holy place by the blood of Jesus, by a new and living way which He inaugurated for us through the veil, that is, His flesh, and since we have a great priest over the house of God, let us draw near with a sincere heart in full assurance of faith, having our hearts sprinkled clean from an evil conscience and our bodies washed with pure water. Let us hold fast the confession of our hope without wavering, for He who promised is faithful; and let us consider how to stimulate one another to love and good deeds, not forsaking our own assembling together, as is the habit of some, but encouraging one another; and all the more, as you see the day drawing near. (10:19-25)

There are only two possible consequences to knowing the gospel. When a person knows the truth of the gospel, he either goes on to believe or he falls back into apostasy. Hebrews 10:19-25 is speaking to the person who does the former, the one who makes a positive response to the claims of Jesus Christ.

A positive response results in salvation. As Paul makes clear in the beautiful thirteenth chapter of his first letter to the Corinthians, salvation involves faith, hope, and love. It is these three aspects of salvation that are focused on in our present passage.

DRAW NEAR IN FAITH

The primary basis on which we can draw near to God in faith is **the blood of Jesus.** The **holy place** of the Tabernacle, or the Temple, represented God's special presence, and only the high priest could enter there once a year. But in Christ's shed blood, His perfect sacrifice, **we have confidence to enter the holy place,** into God's very presence.

I believe that **brethren** refers here, as elsewhere in Hebrews and also in Romans (9:3), to fellow Jews, not fellow Christians. These physical brothers are being urged, on the basis of the careful doctrinal groundwork that has already been given, to take hold of the perfect sacrifice, Jesus Christ—to come confidently through Him into God's very presence and to dwell there for all eternity. To a Jew who took the Old Covenant the least bit seriously, this prospect was as awesome as it was wonderful. Realizing this, the writer uses every persuasive argument to bring them to a positive decision.

If a person tries to go into God's presence based on his own character, his own works, or his own religious affiliation, he will find no access. He will certainly not have access on the basis of a mere verbal profession of Christ. "Not everyone who says to Me, 'Lord, Lord,' will enter the kingdom of heaven; but he who does the will of My Father who is in heaven. Many will say to Me on that day, 'Lord, Lord, did we not prophesy in Your name, and in Your name cast out demons, and in Your name perform many miracles?' And then I will declare to them, 'I never knew you; depart from Me, you who practice lawlessness' " (Matt. 7:21-23). All the things that Jesus mentioned were seemingly good. But they were not *really* in His name, because they were not done through faith in Him and by His power. These professors, Jesus said, did not know Him personally. Obviously they knew His name, in the sense of His title and position. They recognized Him as being "Lord." But they had not received Him as their own Lord and their own Savior, and everything else counted for nothing.

The blood of Jesus Christ, however, counts for everything, and the person who trusts in His atoning work can come with complete boldness before God, claiming all the blessings and promises in His Son. We can come expecting mercy and grace (Heb. 4:16), rather than justice. For if God gave us justice, He would have to condemn us, because this is what we deserve. But Jesus, through His shed blood, satisfied God's justice in our behalf, so that we can now claim God's mercy and grace. God cannot be just and condemn us who are in Christ.

Jesus gave no clearer or more moving illustration of God's grace than the parable of the prodigal son. Actually, the son who stayed home was also prodigal, but the story focuses on his brother, because his brother finally realized his prodigality and came home. He did not deserve to come home and he certainly did not deserve to be accepted back with such lavish celebration. But it was the father's love, not the son's merit, that prompted the welcome. The son came back out of desperation, but he came; and his coming was all the father required. Everything else the father himself provided.

The concept of simply *coming* to God was revolutionary to Jews—and to many others throughout the centuries and today. When Adam sinned, had not God put him out of the Garden and placed the angels and the flaming sword to guard the entrance? And were not all men forbidden, on pain of death, to enter into His presence in the Holy of Holies? But now, the writer says Jesus' blood, in effect, has quenched the fiery sword, and He has torn the veil of the Holy of Holies in two. If you come through Him, you not only can come into God's presence, but you can come with confidence.

Jesus' way into God's presence is **a new and living way.** The old way could not even bring man into God's symbolic, ceremonial presence, much less into His real presence. But the new way can bring us there, **through the veil, that is, His flesh.** When Jesus' flesh was torn, so was the veil that kept men from God. The blood of animals allowed only the high priest to enter the veil briefly. Jesus' blood allows everyone who believes in Him to enter the veil permanently.

New (*prosphatos*) in verse 20 is used only once in the New Testament. Its original meaning was "freshly slaughtered." Jesus is the new way, the freshly slaughtered sacrifice, who opens the way to God. It seems contradictory that the freshly slaughtered way would also be the **living way.** But Jesus' death conquered death and gives life. His death is the only way to life that is everlasting.

While Jesus was preaching and teaching and healing—that is, while He was alive—His flesh was a barrier to God's presence just as was the veil in the Tabernacle. An uncrucified Savior could not have saved. If Jesus had only come into the world and ministered in His flesh, He could not have been Savior, no matter how many years He may have preached or how many thousand more miracles He may have performed. As long as His flesh was alive it was a barrier, in the sense that only by its sacrifice could men's sins be atoned for and the way to heaven be opened. When the physical veil of the earthly Temple was torn in two during Jesus' crucifixion, the spiritual veil, so to speak, of His flesh was also torn.

Jesus not only opened the way to God but He is now our **great priest over the house of God.** He does not merely show the way to God, or even just provide the way to God; He *takes* us with Him to God and ministers for us in heaven. A paraphrase of Romans 5:10 could be:

"If His death could do so much to save me, what must His life be doing in the presence of God to keep me!"

Let us draw near with a sincere heart in full assurance of faith, having our hearts sprinkled clean from an evil conscience and our bodies washed with pure water. (10:22)

Sincere (*alēthinos*) means genuine, without superficiality, hypocrisy, or ulterior motive. Coming to God with **full assurance** requires commitment that is genuine.

The nation of Judah, like many individuals, often had come to God with anything but a sincere heart. " 'Judah did not return to Me with all her heart, but rather in deception,' declares the LORD" (Jer. 3:10). But a day was to come when His people would change. "I will give them a heart to know Me, for I am the LORD; and they will be My people, and I will be their God, for they will return to Me with their whole heart" (Jer. 24:7).

Simon the magician made a profession of faith in Christ, but his heart became corrupt. He tried to use Christ's name and power for his own glory and benefit, and was harshly rebuked by Peter. "You have no part or portion in this matter, for your heart is not right before God. Therefore repent of this wickedness of yours, and pray the Lord that if possible, the intention of your heart may be forgiven you" (Acts 8:21-22). Paul counseled slaves to be obedient to their masters, "in the sincerity of your heart, as to Christ" (Eph. 6:5). From the earliest days of the Old Covenant, God had demanded a sincere heart. "You will seek the LORD your God, and you will find Him if you search for Him with all your heart and all your soul" (Deut. 4:29). The people who find God are those who seek Him with their whole heart, with total genuineness.

A certain type of faith is built into human nature. Even on the purely human, earthly level, we could not operate without it. We eat food taken from a can or box that we buy in the store, with perfect confidence that it will not harm us. We turn on the faucet, pour a glass of water, and drink it without question. We accept payment in printed paper because we have faith that the government will back its money. Without faith, society could not operate.

But saving faith not only requires faith in a different object, it requires faith from a different source. We can trust in food, water, and money by our own will, our own decision. Faith in Jesus Christ must include our own decision, but it must proceed from God's decision. "For by grace you have been saved through faith; and that not of yourselves, it is the gift of God" (Eph. 2:8). Salvation is a gift of God, and part of that gift is saving faith itself. God plants in the heart the desire and the ability to believe, and the ability to receive the gift of salvation.

When we come to God in faith, our hearts should not only be sincere but also **sprinkled clean from an evil conscience and our bodies washed with pure water.** This figure, as we might expect, is taken from the sacrificial ceremonies of the Old Covenant. The priests were continually washing themselves and the sacred vessels in the basins of clear water, and blood was continually being sprinkled as a sign of cleansing. But all the cleansing, whether with water or blood, was external. Only Jesus can cleanse a man's heart. By His Spirit He cleanses the innermost thoughts and desires.

In Christ our sins are covered in the blood and our lives are transformed. There must be both; together they make up salvation. We might say the first is positional satisfaction and the second is practical sanctification. God is satisfied with the sprinkling of the blood of Christ, and sin is removed and our consciences are free. We are changed on the inside as we are washed by the Word and born again.

POSITIONAL SATISFACTION

Having our hearts sprinkled clean from an evil conscience is a beautiful picture of deliverance, already mentioned in 9:14. Conscience condemns us and reminds us of our guilt; and the guilt cannot be removed until the sin is removed. When Jesus died, His blood removed our sins, and when we embrace Him by faith, our conscience becomes free from guilt—we are cleansed **from an evil conscience.** We do not condemn ourselves anymore.

Cleansing of our hearts refers to satisfaction of God's justice, the expiation of our sins, which is required before we can be acceptable to Him.

PRACTICAL SANCTIFICATION

The other part of the cleansing, having **our bodies washed with pure water,** does not refer to baptism, but has to do with our living, with how the Holy Spirit changes our lives. It is the same cleansing mentioned by Paul in Titus 3:5 ("the washing of regeneration and renewing by the Holy Spirit") and in Ephesians 5:26 ("the washing of water with the word").

These two aspects of cleansing are inseparable. When a man comes to Christ, they both take place. Christ's death pays the penalty of sin for us and God is satisfied; and the cleansing act of the Holy Spirit begins to change us on the inside and He is satisfied. God's justice and righteousness are both satisfied; and because of this, a believer can come into God's presence with confidence.

The Three Requirements of Faith

The faith that God honors, the faith that is from a sincere heart, requires three things: felt need, content, and commitment.

FELT NEED

Faith cannot begin until a person realizes his need for salvation. If he is without Christ, he needs salvation whether he recognizes it or not. But he will not have reason to believe until his need is *felt*, until it is recognized. When Saul was persecuting the church, he had a great need for salvation, but he certainly felt no need of it. He was thoroughly convinced he was doing God's will. Only when the Lord confronted him dramatically on the Damascus road did his need become known and felt—in Saul's case, very deeply. The need may not, at first, be clearly understood. On the Damascus road, Saul could not have explained his spiritual need in the way that he was able to do some years later when he wrote the book of Romans. He simply knew that something was desperately wrong in his life and that the answer was in God. He knew he needed something from the Lord.

Often a person's felt need is only partial. The first feeling of need may only be for a purpose in life or for someone to love us and care for us. Or it may be a sense of need for forgiveness and removal of guilt, for inner peace. The most important thing is that a person realize that the answer to his need is in God. People came to Jesus for many reasons, some of them rather superficial. But when they came, Jesus met *all* their needs. They may have felt only a need for physical healing, but He also offered spiritual healing. Felt need does not require theological understanding of the doctrine of salvation, only a **sincere heart** that knows it *needs* salvation. On the other hand, a person who does not feel a need for salvation, no matter how good his theology, is far from faith in God. Felt need is essential, but inadequate on its own.

CONTENT

A person does not have to comprehend the full knowledge and understanding of the doctrine of salvation before he can be saved, but he does need the gospel truth (1 Cor. 15:1-5) that he is lost in sin and needs the Lord Jesus Christ as Lord and Savior. He must know the gospel. The idea of "blind faith" sounds spiritual, but it is not biblical. Even great persons of faith will not know many of the things about God until they see their Lord face to face in heaven. But God does not demand faith without giving reason for faith. The writer of Hebrews, for example, piles up truth upon truth and presents Jesus as the Jews' promised Messiah. He also shows that the New Covenant is far superior to the Old, that the old sacrifices were ineffective, and that only the new sacrifice can bring a person to God—and so on and on.

The following story is told of Channing Pollock, a well-known playwright. Mr. Pollock was collaborating with another author in writing a play. As they were working late one night in Pollock's New York apartment, something in the work they were doing caused the friend to say to Pollock, "Have you ever read the New Testament?" Pollock said he had not, and they continued working until early morning, when they parted. Pollock went to bed, but could not sleep. He was bothered by his friend's question, simple and casual though it seemed. He finally got out of bed and searched the apartment until he found a New Testament. After reading the gospel of Mark through, he got dressed and walked the streets until dawn. Later, telling the story to the friend, he said, "When I returned home, I found myself on my knees, passionately in love with Jesus Christ." Beginning with a felt need, vague as it was, he then looked at the truth and its evidence—and believed.

COMMITMENT

The climax of faith is commitment. Professing Christ, without commitment to Christ, is not saving faith.

My father often told the story of a tightrope walker who liked to walk a wire across Niagara Falls—preferably with someone on his back. Many people on the bank expressed complete confidence in his ability to do it, but he always had a difficult time getting a volunteer to climb up on him.

Many people express complete confidence in Christ but never trust themselves to Him.

As a missionary translator in the New Hebrides, John Paton was frustrated in his work for a long time because the people had no word for faith. One day a man who was working for him came into the house and flopped down into a big chair. The missionary asked him what the word would be for what he had just done. The word the man gave in reply was the one Paton used for *faith* in his translation of the New Testament. Without hesitation or reservation, the man had totally committed his body to the chair. He had felt his need for rest, he was convinced that the chair provided a place for rest, and he committed himself to the chair *for* rest. A believer must, in the same way, totally commit his life to the Lord Jesus Christ. Only then is faith, saving faith.

HOLD FAST IN HOPE

Let us hold fast the confession of our hope without wavering, for He who promised is faithful. (10:23)

The second part of a positive response to the gospel is hope. The best Greek manuscripts of this text have the word *elpis* ("hope"), rather than *pistis* ("faith"), as in the King James version. A person who genuinely trusts, cannot help being hopeful. A hopeless believer is a contradiction in terms.

Just so, a person who is genuinely hopeful will hold fast. One who lets go has lost hope; and one who still has hope will still hold on. Continuing is a mark both of faith and of hope. Holding on does not keep us saved, any more than good works will make us saved. But both are evidence that we *are* saved. Many people who have confessed Christ continue to give evidence, by their lives, that they have never known Him.

I witnessed a confession of Christ, followed by baptism, of a man who soon afterward opened a pornographic nightclub and bar. His life is an extreme example of showing correspondence to the Christ he had confessed. The "confession" of his life contradicted the confession of his lips. He did not **hold fast the confession** of his faith and hope in Jesus Christ.

Holding on is the human side of eternal security. The Reformers called it "the perseverance of the saints." It is not something we do to keep ourselves saved, but it is evidence, on the human side, that we are saved. It is a paradox, just as is the doctrine of election. God sovereignly chooses those who are saved, but He will not save anyone who does not believe. God keeps us secure in His Son, but our own wills, expressed in holding on in perseverance, are also involved. As the strongest Calvinist theologian recognizes, God's sovereignty does not exclude man's responsibility. Jesus said, "No one can come to Me, unless the Father who sent Me draws him" (John 6:44), as well as, "If you abide in My word, then you are truly disciples of Mine" (John 8:31).

How sad that many come to Christ and say they believe and yet are gone so soon. In the parable of the sower, Jesus illustrated four different kinds of response to the gospel. Some people are so far from wanting salvation that the devil simply takes away the seed of God's Word before it has time to germinate at all. Others respond joyfully at hearing the Word, but their "belief" lasts only until the first temptation. Still others believe until they run into a few problems. True believers, however, "are the ones who have heard the word in an honest and good heart, and hold it fast, and bear fruit with perseverance" (Luke 8:15).

These types of response were exemplified by those who heard and saw Jesus. During the first Passover of His ministry, "many believed in His name, beholding His signs which He was doing." But Jesus, knowing their hearts were not with Him, "was not entrusting Himself to them" (John 2:23-24). These were examples of the second or third type of response. They made a superficial start with Jesus, but soon left Him. Jesus knew right away they were not sincere; in a few days or weeks, everyone knew it.

Similarly, "many even of the rulers believed in Him, but because of the Pharisees they were not confessing Him, lest they should be put out of the synagogue; for they loved the approval of men rather than the approval of God" (John 12:42-43). What promised to be a revival among the religious leaders proved to be the making of a secret society of unbelievers.

One group was so impressed with Jesus' signs and miracles that they called Him "the Prophet who is to come into the world," and "were intending to come and take Him by force, to make Him king" (John 6:14-15). But Jesus, again reading the minds of the professed believers, knew their insincerity and withdrew to a mountain to be alone. They wanted only an outward king, not an inward one.

A true believer will be around in the end. He may become discouraged or frustrated, and occasionally fall into a sinful habit. But he will **hold fast the confession** of his **hope without wavering, for He who promised is faithful.** A true believer's faith and hope are never in vain, because they are in a God who is faithful to His promises. "Faithful is He who calls you, and He also will bring it to pass" (1 Thess. 5:24). God will do His part and the true believer will also do his.

There was once a young boy whose dad left him on a downtown corner one morning and told him to wait there until he returned in about half an hour. But the father's car broke down and he could not get to a phone. Five hours went by before the father managed to get back, and he was worried that his son would be in a state of panic. But when the father got there, the boy was standing in front of the dime store, looking in the window and rocking back and forth on his heels. When the father saw him, he ran up to him and threw his arms around him and hugged and kissed him. The father apologized and said, "Weren't you worried? Did you think I was never coming back?" The boy looked up and replied, "No, Dad. I knew you were coming. You said you would."

God's answers may seem to be a long time in coming, and our waiting may be uncomfortable or even painful. But He will always do just as He has said He will do. The reason we can hold fast to our hope without wavering is that **He who promised is faithful.**

ENCOURAGE IN LOVE

And let us consider how to stimulate one another to love and good deeds, not forsaking our own assembling together, as is the habit of some, but encouraging one another; and all the more, as you see the day drawing near. (10:24-25)

The third mark of a positive response to the gospel is love. The particular expression of love mentioned here is fellowship love. The Jewish readers were having a hard time breaking with the Old Covenant, with the Temple and the sacrifices. They were still holding on to the legalism and ritual and ceremony, the outward things of Judaism. So the writer is telling them that one of the best ways to hold fast to the things of God—the real things of God that are found only in the New Covenant of Jesus Christ—is to be in the fellowship of His people, where they could love and be loved, serve and be served. There is no better place to come all the way to faith in Christ, or to hope continually in Him, than the church, His Body.

The day drawing near could refer to the imminent destruction of the Temple, which brought all the sacrifices and rituals to a close. The Old Covenant simply could not function without the Temple, which, when the book of Hebrews was written, was about to be destroyed by Titus. But I believe the primary reference is to the coming of the Lord, which makes the passage apply to all of us. The only place where we can remain steadfast until He returns is with His people. We need each other. We need to be in fellowship with each other, as we mutually strengthen each other and encourage each other.

Some years ago, a young man sat next to me on a plane and we struck up a conversation. When he discovered I was a minister, he said, "I used to belong to a church, but it seems to me that a person's relationship to Christ ought to be personal, not institutional. What do you think?" After thanking the Lord silently for providing such an open opportunity for witness, I said, "I certainly agree with you." He then asked if I knew how he could have a personal relationship with Christ—to which I also answered in the affirmative. I thought to myself, "He certainly seems to feel his need for Christ," and so I asked if he had studied the truth of the gospel and the evidence for Christ's claims. He replied, "Yes, but I just don't know how to get to Him." "Are you ready to commit yourself to Him?" I asked. He said that he was, and as we prayed together he made the commitment. The next Sunday he was in our morning worship service, and afterward asked me if our church had anything going on during the week that he could become involved in. This young man gave every evidence of being a true believer. He felt his need, he studied the evidence, he made a commitment to Jesus Christ, and was showing every desire to hold fast to Christ and to have fellowship with His people.

The writer is saying very simply, "The door is open, the way is made available to enter into God's presence. Come in and stay and fellowship with His people, and enjoy God's company forever."

Apostasy: Rejecting Christ (10:26-39)

For if we go on sinning willfully after receiving the knowledge of the truth, there no longer remains a sacrifice for sins, but a certain terrifying expectation of judgment, and the fury of a fire which will consume the adversaries. Anyone who has set aside the Law of Moses dies without mercy on the testimony of two or three witnesses. How much severer punishment do you think he will deserve who has trampled under foot the Son of God, and has regarded as unclean the blood of the covenant by which he was sanctified, and has insulted the Spirit of grace? For we know Him who said, "Vengeance is Mine, I will repay." And again, "The LORD will judge His people." It is a terrifying thing to fall into the hands of the living God.

But remember the former days, when, after being enlightened, you endured a great conflict of sufferings, partly, by being made a public spectacle through reproaches and tribulations, and partly by becoming sharers with those who were so treated. For you showed sympathy to the prisoners, and accepted joyfully the seizure of your property, knowing that you have for yourselves a better possession and an abiding one. Therefore, do not throw away your confidence, which has a great reward. For you have need of endurance, so that when you have done the will of God, you may receive what was promised. For yet in a very little while, He who is coming will come, and will not delay. But My righteous one shall live by faith; and if he shrinks back, My soul has no pleasure in him. But we are not of those who shrink back to destruction, but of those who have faith to the preserving of the soul. (10:26-39)

This chapter could be titled, "The Tragedy of Getting over It," because it deals with those who had heard the gospel, had come face-to-face with the claims of Christ, had been associated to some extent with His church, but had gone away. These were people whose hearts had been warmed toward the gospel of Christ, who had made a superficial commitment of faith in Him, and had identified themselves visibly with the true church. But their enthusiasm was cooling and the cost of being a Christian was becoming too high. They were "getting over" the gospel, and were in danger of becoming apostate.

Of the five warnings given in Hebrews, the one in this passage is by far the most serious and sobering. It may be the most serious warning in all of Scripture. It deals with apostasy.

When the gospel of Jesus Christ is presented to an unbeliever, only two responses are possible. After he has heard the basic truths and claims of Jesus Christ, he either believes and is saved or he disbelieves and becomes apostate. Apostasy, as we will see, is the sin of rejecting the gospel for which there is no forgiveness. One helpful Scripture in defining apostasy is 1 John 2:19, which says, "They went out from us, but they were not really of us; for if they had been of us, they would have remained with us; but they went out, in order that it might be shown that they all are not of us."

There have always been apostates from God's way. Deuteronomy speaks of "some worthless men [who] have gone out from among you and have seduced the inhabitants of their city, saying, 'Let us go and serve other gods' (whom you have not known)" (Deut. 13:13). These men were types of apostates.

Saul, Israel's first king, became apostate. The Lord told Samuel, "I regret that I have made Saul king, for he has turned back from following Me, and has not carried out My commands" (1 Sam. 15:11). Amaziah, another king, also turned apostate. "Now it came about after Amaziah came from slaughtering the Edomites that he brought the gods of the sons of Seir, set them up as his gods, bowed down before them, and burned incense to them. Then the anger of the LORD burned against Amaziah, . . . And from the time that Amaziah turned away from following the LORD they conspired against him in Jerusalem, and he fled to Lachish; but they sent after him to Lachish and killed him there" (2 Chron. 25:14-15, 27).

Apostasy is not new, nor is God's attitude toward it. It is the most serious of all sins, because it is the most deliberate and willful form of unbelief. It is not a sin of ignorance, but of rejecting known truth.

Judas Iscariot is, of course, the classic apostate. No other rejecter of Christ ever had the exposure to God's truth, love, and grace as did Judas. He knew the Lord intimately. He was one of the twelve of Jesus' inner circle of disciples. Had he believed, he would have become an apostle. But he rejected the truth and became an apostate. His story is the supreme contradiction to the common excuse, "I would probably believe in Christ if I just had a little more evidence, a little more light." Judas had the perfect evidence, the perfect light, the perfect example. For some three years he lived with Truth incarnate and Life incarnate, yet turned his back on the One who is truth and life.

THE NATURE OF APOSTASY

Apostasy is an intentional falling away or withdrawal, a defection. Paul was falsely accused by some of his fellow believing Jews of using the gospel to cause other Christian Jews "to forsake" (apostatize from) the teachings of Moses (Acts 21:21). Paul speaks of a large falling away when he cautions the Thessalonians not to be misled about the coming of the Lord, "for it will not come unless the apostasy comes first" (2 Thess. 2:3). Jesus is clearly speaking of the same apostasy in Matthew 24:10—"And at that time many will fall away and will deliver up one another and hate one another."

There are people who move toward Christ, right up to the edge of saving belief. They hear of Him and they are drawn to Him. They are perhaps deeply convicted of sin and even make a profession of faith. But their interest in the things of God begins to wane, and the pressures and attractions of the world distract them further still, until they have no interest at all. They may turn to another religion or to no religion at all. Apostasy is determined by what you leave, not where you go after you leave. After a person leaves God, it makes little difference where he then goes. Our Lord was illustrating this in the parable of the soils (Matt. 13:1-9, 18-23).

Many years ago I had a friend who often went with me to Pershing Square in Los Angeles to witness. He was raised in the church and was a regular and dependable member, but I always felt that something was missing in his life. Then, suddenly, I did not see him anymore. About three years later, I met a mutual friend and asked if she knew what had happened to him. "Oh, he's an atheist now," was the reply. "He doesn't believe in God anymore. He has accepted situation ethics, and sees everything as amoral. He doesn't believe anything is good nor bad in itself." Apparently he had had enough of God, and simply turned away.

The apostle Paul said that apostasy is going to be a characteristic of the last days. "The Spirit explicitly says that in later times some will fall away from the faith, paying attention to deceitful spirits and doctrines of demons, by means of the hypocrisy of liars seared in their own conscience as with a branding iron" (1 Tim. 4:1-2). In the end times, the times in which I believe we are now living, apostasy will become worse and worse.

CHARACTERISTICS OF APOSTASY

For if we go on sinning willfully after receiving the knowledge of the truth, there no longer remains a sacrifice for sins. (10:26)

Here is possibly the clearest and most concise scriptural definition of apostasy—**receiving knowledge of the truth,** that is, the gospel, but **willfully** remaining in sin. An apostate has seen and heard the truth—he knows it well—but he willfully rejects it.

Apostasy has two major characteristics: knowledge of the truth of the gospel and willful rejection of it.

THE TRUTH IS KNOWN AND RECOGNIZED

Every apostate is an unbeliever, but not every unbeliever is an apostate. Many people have never had the opportunity to hear the gospel, even in part. They are sinful and, of course, do not believe in Christ, because they have never heard of Him or of His claims. An apostate, however, is well acquainted with the gospel. He knows more than enough to be saved.

The Greek language has two primary words that can be translated "knowledge." *Gnōsis* has to do with ordinary knowledge, and in the New Testament is often used for general spiritual knowledge. But *epignōsis,* the word used in verse 26, denotes full knowledge, understanding, and discernment. In other words, the persons described here are those who have much more than a passing acquaintance with the gospel. They know it well. An apostate has all the information. He lacks nothing intellectually. He has *epignōsis.* He is among those who have "once been enlightened, . . . tasted of the heavenly gift," and even "been made partakers of the Holy Spirit" (Heb. 6:4).

An apostate can be bred only in the brilliant light of proximity to Christ. Apostates are not made in the absence, but in the presence, of Christ. They are bred almost without exception within the church, in the very midst of God's people. It is possible for a person to read the Bible on his own, to see the gospel clearly, and then reject it—apart from direct association with Christians. But by and large, apostates come from within the church.

TRUTH IS REJECTED

Eventually, sometimes even after years of pretense and self-deception, the unbeliever who acts like a believer finally falls away. He gives up, loses interest, and goes his own way. He returns to **sinning willfully,** with no more regard for the Lord's way or the Lord's people. To know God's way, to study about it and hear about it, to identify with believers, and then turn away is to become apostate. The process of falling away may be gradual, but at some point a conscious decision is made to leave the way of God, and reject the saving grace of the Lord Jesus Christ.

Willfully (*hekousiōs*) carries the idea of deliberate intention that is habitual. The reference here is not to sins of ignorance or weakness, but to those that are planned out, determined, done with forethought. The difference between sins of ignorance and **sinning willfully** is much like the difference between involuntary manslaughter and first-degree murder. *Hekousiōs* is habitual. It not only is deliberate, but is an established way of thinking and believing. It is the permanent renunciation of the gospel, the permanent forsaking of God's grace.

A believer may sometimes lapse into sin and stray from intimacy with the Lord and with His people. But, unless the Lord disciplines him and takes him to heaven, he will come back. He will be too much under conviction to stay away permanently. In the meanwhile, he will be robbed of joy and peace and of many other blessings.

We cannot always determine who is apostate and who is backsliding, and we should not try. We are not able to distinguish between a disobedient carnal believer and an apostate unbeliever. That is the Lord's business. But there is a difference between the two, a very great difference. A person's concern should be first of all that he himself is a true believer (2 Cor. 13:5) and then that he is a faithful believer. There are many calls to self-examination in the New Testament. Every time a believer comes to the Lord's Table, he faces the reality or unreality of his salvation.

Paul distinguishes between apostates and disobedient, fleshly Christians in his second letter to Timothy. "If we deny Him, He also will deny us," because we will be apostate and willingly will have no part in Him. But, "If we are faithless, He remains faithful; for He cannot deny Himself" (2 Tim. 2:12-13). If a believer falls short in his faithfulness to the Lord, the Lord still will not fail in *His* faithfulness to the believer, for He has promised never to let us go. "He cannot deny Himself," by falling short in His own faithfulness, no matter what His people do. A Christian can become weak in faith and disobedient, which is bad enough. But this is not denying the Lord, which is apostasy. The apostate habitually continues to disbelieve and habitually continues to sin. John tells us that "No one who is born of God practices sin, because His seed abides in Him; and he cannot sin, because he is born of God" (1 John 3:9).

The two major characteristics of apostasy, then, are sufficient knowledge of the gospel to be saved and willful and habitual denial of God in spite of this knowledge.

CAUSES OF APOSTASY

But why would a person who knows the gospel, has seen the light, has even experienced many of the blessings of the Holy Spirit, ever reject so wonderful a gift? What causes people to do that? In a sense, there is always just one cause, willful unbelief. Following our own wills often has no reason except that this is what we *want* to do. But in another sense, there are a number of things that strongly influence a person to forsake God, that stimulate his will to deny his Creator.

PERSECUTION

What may drive a believer closer to the Lord will likely drive an unbeliever further from Him. Whenever the church has been persecuted, the faithful have become stronger, spiritually and morally. On the other hand, continued persecution drives unbelievers away from the church and from contact with the things of God. They do not have the strength or the desire to pay a high price for something that means little to them. Words are cheap; persecution is not. Hard times are not for the self-willed unbeliever who is simply using the church for business, or social, or other personal reasons—or who may have been raised in the church and has simply never gotten out of the habit of attending. Persecution, sometimes as mild as criticism, is usually enough to break that habit.

When persecution is severe, the apostate not only will leave the church but will often join the persecutors. "Then they will deliver you to tribulation, and will kill you, and you will be hated by all nations on account of My name. And at that time many will fall away and will deliver up one another and hate one another" (Matt. 24:9-10). Some apostates not only turn away from the church but turn against it.

FALSE TEACHERS

False teachers also cause their share of apostasy. In the same passage in Matthew, Jesus says, "And many false prophets will arise, and will mislead many" (Matt. 24:11). Persecution frightens unbelievers away from the truth, whereas false teachers entice them away. False teaching can, and does, do a lot of damage even to God's own people. It can confuse and discourage and corrupt any believer or group of believers too immature to recognize and deal with the falsehoods or too sinful to resist them. But a true believer will never be led to *deny* the Lord because of false teaching, no matter how unbiblical and persuasive it is. True believers may deny some biblical truths because of false teaching, but the only person false teaching will cause to deny the Lord is a person who never belonged to Him. When unbelievers get "fed up" with the gospel, they can usually find someone who will feed them something more palatable to their sin nature. "They will not endure sound doctrine; but wanting to have their ears tickled, they will accumulate for themselves teachers in accordance to their own desires" (2 Tim. 4:3).

TEMPTATION

Apostasy is sometimes triggered by temptation. The things of this world become more attractive and more influential than the things of God. These apostates are "rocky soil" hearers (Luke 8:13), who are attracted to the gospel for a while, but who are tempted away from full commitment. Whether the temptation is in the form of many small ones over a long period of time or of a very strong one that comes suddenly, they do not have the resources or the will to resist. Demas possibly was such a person. "Having loved this present world," he may have deserted the Lord as well as Paul (2 Tim. 4:10).

NEGLECT

Perhaps the saddest cause of apostasy is neglect. A person can put off deciding for Christ so long that he loses the opportunity. Not to decide for Christ is to decide against Him. Such a person may never persecute believers. He may not publicly, or even consciously, deny Christ. But by continually resisting the gospel of Christ, he takes his stand apart from Him and is in danger of neglecting his way into apostasy. "How shall we escape if we neglect so great a salvation?" (Heb. 2:3). To make no positive decision for Christ is to decide against Him.

CLINGING TO THE OLD

Holding on to the old religion, or simply the old life-style, can eventually bring a person to apostatize. Many of the unbelieving Jews addressed in the book of Hebrews were very much in this danger. Their religion not only would not bring them salvation but had become a barrier to salvation. False religion can become so habitual, so much a part of our way of thinking and living, that to give it up seems unthinkable. It would be like cutting off part of our body, our very life. Jesus knew how hard such a break with the old ways can be, but warned, "If your right eye makes you stumble, tear it out, and throw it from you; for it is better for you that one of the parts of your body perish, than for your whole body to be thrown into hell" (Matt. 5:29). Religious tradition has long been one of the greatest barriers to the gospel and one of the foremost contributors to apostasy.

FORSAKING CHRISTIAN FELLOWSHIP

Another cause of apostasy is forsaking Christian fellowship, which the writer has already mentioned (10:25). The best place for strong influence toward Christ is to be in the company of believers. And, especialy once he has been exposed to the truth of the gospel, the worst place he can be is away from true believers.

THE RESULTS OF APOSTASY

For if we go on sinning willfully after receiving the knowledge of the truth, there no longer remains a sacrifice for sins, but a certain terrifying expectation of judgment, and the fury of a fire which will consume the adversaries. Anyone who has set aside the Law of Moses dies without mercy on the testimony of two or three witnesses. How much severer punishment do you think he will deserve who has trampled under foot the Son of God, and has regarded as unclean the blood of the covenant by which he was sanctified, and has insulted the Spirit of grace? For we know Him who said, "Vengeance is Mine, I will repay." And again, "The LORD will judge His people." It is a terrifying thing to fall into the hands of the living God. (10:26-31)

NO SACRIFICE FOR SIN REMAINS

The first result of apostasy is that the apostate no longer has a **sacrifice** that can atone for his **sins.** He is, therefore, beyond salvation. The only sacrifice that can bring a person into God's presence is the sacrifice of Christ's blood in the New Covenant. If Christ's sacrifice is rejected, then all hope of salvation is forfeited. Opportunity is gone, hope is gone, eternal life is gone. Apart from Christ, everything worth having is gone. The old, repeated sacrifices of Judaism would soon be stopped. They were ineffective, anyway. The only effective sacrifice has already been made, and will be made only once. To turn away willfully from this sacrifice leaves no sacrifice; it leaves only sin, the penalty for which is eternal death.

BRINGS GREATER JUDGMENT

**But a certain terrifying expectation of judgment, and the fury of a
fire which will consume the adversaries.** (10:27)

The second result of apostasy is greater **judgment.** The greater
the sin the greater the judgment. Since apostasy is the worst sin, it will
have the worst judgment. God sees the one who knows the truth and
walks away as an enemy, an adversary whose judgment is **certain** and
terrifying.

Just before Jesus cast the demons out of the two Gadarene men,
the demons cried out to Him, "What do we have to do with You, Son of
God? Have You come here to torment us before the time?" (Matt. 8:29).
They were well aware that their final judgment of torment was coming,
that it was certain, and were afraid that Jesus was going to bring it early.
The demons know, better than many professed Christians seem to know,
that God's judgment on His enemies is inescapable, and **the fury of a
fire** from Him is consuming.

Just as certain as the judgment of demons is the judgment of all
who turn their backs on Jesus Christ. In explaining the parable of the
tares, Jesus said to His disciples:

> The tares are the sons of the evil one; and the enemy who sowed them is the
> devil, and the harvest is the end of the age; and the reapers are angels. Therefore
> just as the tares are gathered up and burned with fire, so shall it be at the end of
> the age. The Son of Man will send forth His angels, and they will gather out of
> His kingdom all stumbling blocks, and those who commit lawlessness, and will
> cast them into the furnace of fire; in that place there shall be weeping and gnash-
> ing of teeth. (Matt. 13:38-42)

A few moments later, Jesus told another parable with the same
point: the end of the age will see the separation of believers and unbelievers, the believers to heaven and the unbelievers to hell. "So it will be at
the end of the age; the angels shall come forth, and take out the wicked
from among the righteous, and will cast them into the furnace of fire;
there shall be weeping and gnashing of teeth" (Matt. 13:49-50).

Paul gives similar warnings of judgment, including this one in his
second letter to the Thessalonians:

> The Lord Jesus shall be revealed from heaven with His mighty angels in flaming
> fire, dealing out retribution to those who do not know God and to those who do
> not obey the gospel of our Lord Jesus. And these will pay the penalty of eternal
> destruction, away from the presence of the Lord and from the glory of His pow-
> er. (2 Thess. 1:7-9)

There is nothing in the Old Testament to compare in severity to the judgment described in the New. People often think of the Old Testament as showing a harsh, judgmental God, while the New shows one of mercy and compassion. But God's mercy and His wrath are clearly revealed in *both* testaments. It is true that we have a more complete and beautiful picture of God's grace and love in the New Testament; but we also have here a more complete and terrifying picture of His wrath.

DEGREES OF SIN AND JUDGMENT

Anyone who has set aside the Law of Moses dies without mercy on the testimony of two or three witnesses. How much severer punishment do you think he will deserve who has trampled underfoot the Son of God, and has regarded as unclean the blood of the covenant by which he was sanctified, and has insulted the Spirit of grace? (10:28-29)

Jesus told Pilate, "He who delivered Me up to you has the greater sin" (John 19:11). Judas's sin was greater than Pilate's. Both were unbelievers, but Judas was an apostate. He had light and evidence far beyond what Pilate had, and was therefore far more guilty in betraying Christ.

Jesus also made it clear that judgment, like guilt, is in proportion to sin. "That slave who knew his master's will and did not get ready or act in accord with his will, shall receive many lashes, but the one who did not know it, and committed deeds worthy of a flogging, will receive but few" (Luke 12:47-48).

The teaching of punishment is not as clear in the Old Testament, but neither is the teaching about salvation. The person who sinned under the Old Covenant was guilty and deserving of punishment. Every Jew knew the severity of breaking Mosaic law. If such disobedience was affirmed by the proper witnesses, the penalty was death. But the worst offender in that age cannot compare with the person who has heard the gospel of Jesus Christ and yet rejects Him. Such persons will find themselves in the Judas section of hell, enduring **much severer punishment.**

Far from being more tolerant of sin today, God is less tolerant, because men now have immeasurably more light. "Having overlooked the times of ignorance, God is now declaring to men that all everywhere should repent, because He has fixed a day in which He will judge the world in righteousness through a Man whom He has appointed, having furnished proof to all men by raising Him from the dead" (Acts 17:30-31).

REJECTION OF GOD

How much severer punishment do you think he will deserve who has trampled under foot the Son of God, and has regarded as unclean the blood of the covenant by which he was sanctified, and has insulted the Spirit of grace? (10:29)

APOSTATES REJECT THE FATHER

Apostasy involves total rejection of the godhead—the Father, the Son, and the Holy Spirit. Just as to accept the Son is to accept the Father, so to reject the Son is to reject the Father. "This is My beloved Son, in whom I am well-pleased," said God (Matt. 3:17). Paul tells us that "God highly exalted Him, and bestowed on Him the name which is above every name" (Phil. 2:9). The Son and the Father are one (John 10:30), and it is not possible to reject one without also rejecting the other. Therefore, to trample **under foot the Son of God** is the same as to trample under foot the Father. And to reject the Son is to spurn the Holy Spirit.

To have **trampled under foot** means to have scorned, to have counted as worthless. A person who sees a coin on the sidewalk may think it is a slug and walk by it or perhaps kicks it into the gutter. He doesn't bother to pick it up and examine it. Some people walk by Christ and think He is nothing. They see Him clearly, and have gotten close enough to examine Him carefully had they chosen to. But they count Him as worthless, and go on their way. It is a fearful and damning thing to count as worthless the One whom the Father has declared to be of infinite worth.

APOSTATES REJECT THE SON

I believe the phrase **by which he was sanctified** refers to Christ. It could not refer to the apostate who is regarding **the blood** as **unclean,** because he is hardly sanctified. The reference, therefore, must be to Christ. In His high priestly prayer, Jesus spoke of His sanctifying Himself for the sake of those who believed in Him (John 17:19). He set Himself apart unto God, even as He sanctifies us, by the **blood of the covenant,** shed on Calvary. The apostate counts this sacrifice as unclean, despised, worthless. In so doing he has rejected the second Person of the Trinity, whose very blood was shed for him.

The apostate regards Christ's blood as common blood, just like that of any other person. That which cost God His Son, and that which cost the Son the agony of becoming sin for us, is counted as worthless. That which is of infinite value, he counts as valueless.

APOSTATES REJECT THE HOLY SPIRIT

The man who has been led by the Spirit of grace in the presalvation work of redemption and has been energized by Him toward repentance (John 16:8-11), insults the Spirit by turning from Christ. He rejects
the gracious work of preparation done by the Spirit in his heart—and that
is apostasy.

By trampling under foot the Son of God, he rejects God the Fath-
er. By regarding the blood of the covenant as unclean, He rejects the Son.
By insulting the gentle, gracious leading of the Spirit, he rejects the Spirit.
No wonder he deserves much severer punishment.

**For we know Him who said, "Vengeance is Mine, I will repay." And
again, "The LORD will judge His people." It is a terrifying thing to
fall into the hands of the living God.** (10:30-31)

God is long-suffering, and patient, and loving, and infinitely gracious, not willing that anyone should perish (2 Pet. 3:9). But for the one
who turns his back on God's grace, there is nothing left that God can
offer or do for him. Only judgment remains.

THE DETERRENTS TO APOSTASY

Within this severe warning, is a loving and earnest appeal not to
fall away. The near-believing Jews are told to do two things that will
prevent their becoming apostate and lead them into full belief. They are
told to look back on what they had experienced and to look forward to
the rewards that would be theirs if they carried through on what they had
learned of Christ.

REMEMBER YOUR SUFFERING AND YOUR SERVICE

**But remember the former days, when, after being enlightened, you
endured a great conflict of sufferings, partly, by being made a public
spectacle through reproaches and tribulations, and partly by becoming sharers with those who were so treated. For you showed sympathy to the prisoners, and accepted joyfully the seizure of your property, knowing that you have for yourselves a better possession and an
abiding one.** (10:32-34)

The writer obviously knew the ones to whom he was writing, or
at least knew a great deal about them. He was aware of their deep involve-
ment in the church. They were so closely identified with Christians (**becoming sharers**) that they even experienced **suffering, reproaches,**

and **tribulations** because of it. To the world, and certainly to their fellow Jews in the synagogue, they already were Christians. They were not believers, but had already suffered for being considered believers. And at this point that much persecution had not yet driven them out.

It is possible even for an unbeliever to have a kind of "first love" for Christ. On hearing of Christ's love, of His promises and teachings, of His great works and graciousness, it is easy to be strongly drawn to Him intellectually and emotionally. If He is learned of in a fellowship of believers that is caring and loving, the attraction is even stronger.

The unbelieving Jews addressed in this passage were so attracted. They had not yet trusted in the gospel, but neither were they ashamed of it. They had been somewhat ridiculed, persecuted, and had property seized because of their association with Christians. But the association seemed worth the sacrifice, so that those problems had not yet caused them to turn away. They did not outwardly apologize for or compromise their stand for Christ, which had cost them dearly.

These Jews were intellectually **enlightened.** They knew all the basics of the gospel. But this was no substitute for faith itself. They were well on their way to believing, but they had not believed. So they are told to think of how far they had already come, and what they had already endured, and to complete the process by putting their full trust in Jesus Christ. They are told, in effect, "Remember carefully all the experiences you have had in learning of Christ and in fellowshiping with His people. How terrible it would be to fall back now, when you are so close. You mustn't give up now. How terrible if, after all you have learned of the gospel and all you have suffered and sacrificed for the gospel, you would not receive the real blessing of the gospel—eternal life. You have shown great respect for Christ and great love for His people. Now put your trust in Christ, so that you can *become* one of His people." Like the seed in stony ground, they had endured to a degree, but as the persecution increased they would be offended and fall away (cf. Matt. 13:20-21).

Remember (*anamimnēskō*) means more than simply to recall. It means to carefully think back, to reconstruct in your mind. The idea is that these fellow Jews, who were so close to salvation, should, truth-by-truth and event-by-event, look back on what they had learned and on what they had experienced because of the gospel of Jesus Christ. This would be a strong deterrent to apostasy and a strong encouragement to belief.

They had the prospect of **a better possession and an abiding one.** They had given up many worldy things—reputation, friends, possessions—for what they could see were the better things of the New Covenant. But since they had not fully trusted in the Christ of the New Covenant, they were in danger of falling back into complete unbelief, from which they could never return. They had learned too much and experienced too much to have any excuse left for not believing, and so were urged gently but forcefully to go all the way to salvation before it became too late.

LOOK FORWARD TO YOUR REWARDS

Therefore, do not throw away your confidence, which has a great reward. For you have need of endurance, so that when you have done the will of God, you may receive what was promised. (10:35-36)

The second deterrent to apostasy is the prospect of the rewards for those who believe. "You know what the promises are," they are told. "You know how wonderful and unequaled and how superior they are, and you know that Christ will be faithful in fulfilling them. Don't let your confidence waver now. *Claim* the promises. *Secure* the rewards. Look back and remember how wonderful it once seemed, and look ahead to how even more wonderful it is going to be."

They needed **endurance** and patience to prevent their present circumstances from causing them to turn back. Their enlightenment in the gospel and their suffering and persecution and loss by outward association with believers were not for nothing. Their confidence was not in vain, but it was not enough. They had not **done the will of God** fully, because they had not trusted in His Son fully. And until then, they could not **receive what was promised.** They knew the promises, rejoiced in the promises, and even had suffered for the promises. But they had not *received* the promises. The church is still filled with people like this. It is the negative side of Matthew 7:22-23: "Many will say to Me on that day, 'Lord, Lord, did we not prophesy in Your name, and in Your name cast out demons, and in Your name perform many miracles?' "And then I will declare to them, 'I never knew you; depart from Me, you who practice lawlessness.' "

For yet in a very little while, He who is coming will come, and will not delay. But My righteous one shall live by faith; and if he shrinks back, My soul has no pleasure in him. But we are not of those who shrink back to destruction, but of those who have faith to the preserving of the soul. (10:37-39)

The suffering they might endure would not last forever, but their salvation in Jesus Christ would. The Lord would be coming to set His world right, and He **will not delay.** In the meanwhile, the way to *become* righteous is by **faith** and the way the righteous should *live* is by faith. From the human side, faith is the basis of spiritual life and spiritual living. Knowledge of the gospel is essential. Suffering for the gospel is possible. Serving others, especially God's people, in the name of the gospel is fine. But only **faith** will bring salvation and the **preserving of the soul.**

The warning and appeal end on a positive and hopeful note. The writer seems confident that some of those to whom he is appealing will indeed believe—so much so, in fact, that he already identifies himself with them and the other true believers. **We are not of those who shrink back to destruction.**

What Faith Is (11:1-3)

Now faith is the assurance of things hoped for, the conviction of things not seen. For by it the men of old gained approval. By faith we understand that the worlds were prepared by the word of God, so that what is seen was not made out of things which are visible. (11:1-3)

"The Saints' Hall of Fame," "The Heroes of Faith," "The Honor Roll of the Old Testament Saints," "The Westminster Abbey of Scripture," and "The Faith Chapter" are but a few of the titles that have been given to Hebrews 11. This chapter deals with the primacy and the excellency of faith, and fits perfectly into the flow of the epistle, that the new is better than the old.

First-century Jews saw everything as a matter of works. Even after being shown the basic truths of the New Covenant, the tendency was for them to try to fit these new principles into the mold of works righteousness.

By the time of Christ, Judaism was no longer the supernatural system God had originally given. It had been twisted into a works system, with all kinds of legalistic requirements. It was a system of self-effort, self-salvation, and self-glorification. It was far from the faith system that

God had given. In many ways it was a religious cult built on ethics. (And even the divinely ordained Judaism was falsified without its fulfillment in Christ.)

As all works systems, it was despised by God—particularly because it was a corruption of the true system He had given. God has never re-deemed man by works, but always by faith (cf. Hab. 2:4). As this chapter makes clear, from the time of Adam on, God has honored faith, not works. Works have always been commanded as a by-product of faith, never as a means of salvation. God does not tolerate any self-imposed ethical system as a means of reaching Him.

This theme of faith connects with chapter 10, where the writer has already presented the principle of salvation by faith, of which the saints named in chapter 11 are examples. He quoted from Habakkuk, a Jewish prophet, reinforcing the truth that this was the principle of redemption that God had always honored. "But My righteous one shall live by faith" (Heb. 10:38; Hab. 2:4). Faith is the way to life, and faith is the way to live. There has never been any other way.

These Jews who have heard the powerful arguments for the supe-riority of the New Covenant over the Old are being told that, in regard to faith, the two covenants are the same. That is, the faith principle did not originate with the New Covenant. It was also active in the Old. In fact, it was active the moment man fell and needed a way back to God. It originated even before the earth began. Since God chose us in Christ "before the foundation of the world" (Eph. 1:4), and since the only way God accepts us in Christ is by our faith, then God obviously established salvation by faith at that time. The way back to God, as far as man's part is concerned, is by faith—it has always been by faith and only by faith.

Between the statement of the faith principle and the long list of Old Testament men and women who illustrated it, is a brief definition of this faith.

The Nature of Faith

Now faith is the assurance of things hoped for, the conviction of things not seen. (11:1)

In a form the old Hebrew poets often used, the writer expresses his definition of **faith** in two parallel and almost identical phrases. It is not a full theological definition, but an emphasizing of certain basic char-acteristics of faith that are important in understanding the message the writer is trying to get across.

THE ASSURANCE OF THINGS HOPED FOR

In Old Testament times, men and women had to rest on the promises of God. God had told them of a coming Messiah, a Deliverer who would take away sin. He told them that one day all Israel would be made clean and be ruled by this righteous Messiah. God's faithful believed God's promises, as incomplete and vague as many of those promises were. They did not have a great deal of specific light, by New Testament standards, but they knew it was God's light, and put their full trust and hope in it.

That is what faith is. Faith is living in a hope that is so real it gives absolute **assurance.** The promises given to the Old Testament saints were so real to them, because they believed God, that they based their lives on them. All the Old Testament promises related to the future—for many believers, far into the future. But the faithful among God's people acted as if they were in the present tense. They simply took God at His word and lived on that basis. They were people of faith, and faith gave present assurance and substance to what was yet future.

Faith is not a wistful longing that something may come to pass in an uncertain tomorrow. True faith is an absolute certainty, often of things that the world considers unreal and impossible. Christian hope is belief in God against the world—not belief in the improbable against chance. If we follow a God whose audible voice we have never heard and believe in a Christ whose face we have never seen, we do so because our faith has a reality, a substance, an assurance that is unshakable. In doing so, Jesus said, we are specially blessed (John 20:29).

Moses considered "the reproach of Christ [Messiah] greater riches than the treasures of Egypt; for he was looking to the reward" (Heb. 11:26). Moses took a stand on the messianic hope, and forsook all the material things he could touch and see for a Messiah who would not come to earth for more than 1400 years.

Shadrach, Meshach, and Abed-nego were confronted with the choice of obeying Nebuchadnezzar, whom they could see very well, or God, whom they had never seen. Without hesitation, they chose to obey God. Man's natural response is to trust his physical senses, to put his faith in the things he can see, hear, taste, and feel. But the man of God puts his trust in something more durable and dependable than anything he will ever experience with his senses. Senses may lie; God cannot lie (Titus 1:2).

The philosopher Epicurus, who lived several hundred years before Christ, said the chief end of life is pleasure. But he was not a hedonist, as many people think. He was talking of pleasure in the long view—ultimate pleasure, not immediate, temporary gratification. He held that we should pursue that which, in the end, will bring the most satisfaction. Understood in the right way, this should also be the Christian's objective.

Christians are not masochists. Quite to the contrary, we live for ultimate and permanent pleasure. We live in the certainty that whatever discomfort or pain we may have to endure for Christ's sake on earth, will more than be compensated for by an eternity of unending bliss, of pleasure we cannot now imagine.

The Greek word *hupostasis*, translated here as **assurance,** appears two other times in Hebrews. In 1:3 it is rendered "exact representation," speaking of Christ's likeness to God, and in 3:14 it is rendered "assurance," as in 11:1. The term refers to the essence, the real content, the reality, as opposed to mere appearance. Faith, then, provides the firm ground on which we stand, waiting for the fulfillment of God's promise. Far from being nebulous and uncertain, faith is the most solid possible conviction. Faith is the present essence of a future reality.

The Old Testament saints "died in faith, without receiving the promises, but ... welcomed them from a distance" (Heb. 11:13). They saw the fulfillment of God's promise with the eye of faith, which, when it is in God, has immeasurably better vision than the best of physical eyes. They held on to the promise as the ultimate reality of their lives, as the most certain thing of their existence.

THE CONVICTION OF THINGS NOT SEEN

Conviction of things not seen carries the same truth a bit further, because it implies a response, an outward manifestation of the inward assurance. The person of faith lives his belief. His life is committed to what his mind and his spirit are convinced is true.

Noah, for example, truly believed God. He could not possibly have embarked on the stupendous, demanding, and humanly ridiculous task God gave him without having had absolute faith. When God predicted rain, Noah had no concept of what rain was, because rain did not exist before the Flood. It is possible that Noah did not even know how to construct a boat, much less a gigantic ark. But Noah believed God and acted on His instructions. He had both assurance and conviction—true faith. His outward building of the ark bore out his inward belief that the rain was coming and that God's plan was correct for constructing a boat that would float. His faith was based on God's word, not on what he could see or on what he had experienced. For 120 years he preached in faith, hoped in faith, and built in faith.

The natural man cannot comprehend that kind of spiritual faith. We see Him who is invisible (Heb. 11:27), but the unsaved man does not, because he has no means of perception. Because he has no spiritual senses, he does not believe in God or the realities of God's realm. He is like a blind man who refuses to believe there is such a thing as light because he has never seen light.

Yet there is a sense in which all men live by faith. As illustrated in an earlier chapter, society is built on a foundation of faith. We drink water out of a faucet, with perfect confidence it is safe. We eat food in a restaurant, confident that it is not contaminated. We willingly receive our pay in the form of a check or paper money—neither of which has any instrinsic value at all. We accept them because of our faith in the person or the company or the government that issues them. We put our faith in a surgeon, and in medical science in general, though we may not have the least training, competence, or experience in medicine ourselves. We submit to the surgeon's knife entirely by faith. The capacity for faith is created in us.

Spiritual faith operates in the realm of that capacity. It willingly accepts and acts on many things it does not understand. But spiritual faith is radically different from natural faith in one important way. It is not natural, as is our trust in water, money, or the doctor. "For by grace you have been saved through faith; and that not of yourselves, it is the gift of God" (Eph. 2:8). Just as natural trust comes by natural birth, so spiritual trust comes from God.

The Testimony of Faith

For by it the men of old gained approval. (11:2)

Men of old gained approval from God because of their faith, and because of nothing else. God has always approved and recognized the person of faith. This verse implies what other parts of the chapter make clear—that God makes his approval *known* to those who trust Him. How God shows His approval varies, but every saint, just as surely as Enoch (Heb. 11:5), has God's witness that his faith is pleasing to his Lord.

Faith is not simply one way to please God; it is the only way. "Without faith it is impossible to please Him, for he who comes to God must believe that He is, and that He is a rewarder of those who seek Him" (11:6). No matter what else we may think, say, or do for or in the name of God, it is meaningless and worthless apart from faith. It cannot possibly be approved by God.

Modern man has put himself in a dilemma, as evangelical scholars such as Francis Schaeffer have frequently pointed out. Throughout virtually all of history, man had what philosophers call a unified field of knowledge. That is, man understood the supernatural, human history, science, ethics, economics—everything—within one frame of reference. These areas were all part of total reality. But then we had a great movement in philosophy known as rationalism, which denied the very existence of the supernatural, including—especially including—God. Men such as Graf, Wellhausen, Bauer, Strauss, Renan, and many others began systematically to undercut every supernatural doctrine or belief.

A prime target was the Bible. Often in the name of biblical scholarship they contradicted, by supposed disproof, every supernatural claim of Scripture. They reduced all knowledge and reality to the area of natural reason, which dealt only with what the physical senses could observe and measure and with what the human mind could interpret on its own. Man became the measure of all things. Everything outside the sphere of man's physical experience and intellectual understanding was denied or discounted.

But most men could not handle this radical explanation. Even from the human perspective, it left too much unaccounted for. It made man nothing more than part of a huge, meaningless machine. Some philosophers began to see the limitations of rationalism. Kierkegaard, for example, decided to make a place for the supernatural by putting it in a different order of reality than the everyday world. This "upper story," as Schaeffer describes it, is thought not to be knowable in the same way that the lower, earthly level is knowable. It is experienced only by a "leap of faith." Because it supposedly cannot really be known, every man is free to make of the supernatural what he wants. He can believe in a "Wholly Other" kind of god, as did Paul Tillich; or he can simply believe in believing, have faith in faith. But what is believed has no definite content, no definite reality, no definite truth. It is purely existential, without content, nonrational, and nonlogical. To use a phrase from Schaeffer again, it is an "escape from reason"—the opposite extreme from that of rationalism. Both of these philosophies, of course, are escapes from the true God.

This new, nonrational philosophy first began to influence art, which had always been basically realistic. Artists varied widely in style and technique, but they all sought to portray reality. That is, a picture of a man always looked like a man, a picture of a flower looked like a flower, and so on. Art was reasonable and realistic. It corresponded to what all men saw and experienced. But with the coming of nonrational philosophy, art began to reflect this new outlook. There were no absolutes, no certainties about anything. A man was represented as the artist felt like representing him at the moment. A flower took the form of whatever the artist had in mind when he painted. Van Gogh, Gauguin, Picasso, and many others developed what became known as abstract art, which was completely subjective, imaginative, and contentless.

The next influence was on music. It, too, began to reflect only the subjective and imaginative, apart from content or structure—as seen in Debussy, Cage, and rock music.

Then came the effect on literature, with Dylan Thomas, Arthur Miller, and such writers who used their skills to undercut absolutes and standards not only in literature but in spiritual and moral areas as well.

Love, honesty, truth, purity, the sacred, the right—all were grist for their existential mills to grind into relativism.

Relativism can lead nowhere but to meaninglessness and despair, which many proponents of this philosophy realized and acknowledged. But they insisted that this is all there is to the world, to life, to man, and that we therefore have to make the best of it. Since God was ruled out, man had no measure of himself or of his world—and could not expect to find any.

The most significant area to be affected was theology. A god that *may* be there, that *may* be good, that *may* care is hardly a god that inspires devotion and commitment. A god that man makes and imagines, man can remake and reimagine. A theology of a god that cannot be known or understood is not theology at all. It is hardly surprising that the extreme form of contentless theology declared that God is dead. Of course, even this "doctrine" had no content, no exact meaning. It simply meant whatever the person who used it may have meant when he said or wrote it.

Such nonrational philosophy is perfectly illustrated in the book *Catch-22*, which centers on a squadron of World War II American fliers stationed on the ficticious island of Pianos in the Mediterranean. Their job was to fly extremely dangerous missions over southern Europe, and they had to complete 25 missions before being eligible for transfer. One of the men, Yosarian, was especially anxious to get out. But when he had completed his twenty-fifth mission, the new commanding officer raised the number to 30, and then to 40, 45, 50, and so on. Insanity became the only justification for transfer. But if a flyer turned himself in for being insane in order to get out of flying the missions, that was evidence he was sane. It became clear to the fliers that they were playing a sadistic game, with no way out. So Yosarian decided to build a raft and float to Sweden—no matter that a whole continent was between him and Sweden or that the ocean currents would have taken him anywhere but there. Despite the impossibility of accomplishing what he intended, he could not be dissuaded. He had devised a hopeless escape from a hopeless situation, and insisted on his right to pursue it. He jumped headlong into the absurd.

People take alcohol and drugs today because they have run out of rational options. They are also trying to escape into witchcraft, astrology, reincarnationism, and countless cults. They are looking for meaning and sense and reality, often while denying that there can be any such things.

These are some of the desperate lengths to which men will go when they reject God, and even the rational and the sensible. They are left only with the absurd—no faith, no hope, no peace, no assurance, no confidence. They can only leap from one vapid and empty absurdity to another, with no prospect or expectation that the next will be better than the previous.

God is the only rational answer, the only sure answer. Only the God who made men can ever satisfy men. Only the God who made reason can make life reasonable. Only the God who made the universe can show man any purpose in it. Since the time of Adam, some men have believed in God and believed what He has said. For them life has been meaningful; it has had assurance, substance, and confidence. They did not make a blind leap of faith, but put their faith in a future reality that, because of their faith, God made certain and sure for them. And with this certainty came assurance, confidence, and hope. Believing in God gives reason for living—and for dying. Just before Stephen was stoned, "he gazed intently into heaven and saw the glory of God, and Jesus standing at the right hand of God" (Acts 7:55). This glimpse of his Lord vindicated all he had endured for the gospel's sake and all he was then about to suffer. He had something to live for and to die for.

The Illustration of Faith

By faith we understand that the worlds were prepared by the word of God, so that what is seen was not made out of things which are visible. (11:3)

The writer is saying to the Jews who had not yet trusted Christ, "You already have a certain faith in God. You believe that He created the universe and everything in it." They believed this without any doubt, even though they were not there when God created. They could not see His act of creating, but they could see His creation and they believed in the Creator. They had a start of faith. They knew and accepted this truth by faith, not by sight. Their own Scriptures taught it and they believed it.

God did not just create the world, but the **worlds** (*aiōn*), which designates the physical universe itself and also its operation, its administration. He created everything simply by His word (*rhēma*), His divine utterance. He created from nothing, at least not from anything physical, or **visible.** The writer makes an absolutely stupendous claim in this short verse. The greatest claim, and the one hardest for an unbeliever to accept, is that understanding of creation comes entirely by faith.

The origin of the universe has been a long-standing problem for philosophers and scientists. Centuries of investigation, speculation, and comparing of notes and theories have brought them no closer to a solution. Every time a consensus seems to be developing about a particular theory, someone comes up with evidence that disproves it or makes it less plausible.

Bertrand Russell spent most of his 90 years as a philosopher. His most certain conviction was that Christianity was the greatest enemy of mankind, because it taught of a tyrannical God who stifled man's rightful freedom. He admitted at the end of his life that philosophy "was a washout," that it held no answers for anything. He had written that "we must conquer the world by intelligence," and yet all of his own great intellect and all of the other intellects who looked to themselves for answers never found an answer. Russell's greatest faith was in the idea that there is no God. He rejected the only source of answers, meaning, and hope.

Most philosophy is mere doodling with words, as many people do with a pencil. Without revelation, a source of basic truth, the best it can do is make verbal squiggles. Some are more impressive than others, but none can lay claim to the truth or to ultimate meaning. Paul warned the Colossians, "See to it that no one takes you captive through philosophy and empty deception, according to the tradition of men" (Col. 2:8).

Science has done no better than philosophy in offering answers to the origin of the universe. Even though science, by definition, is limited to the observable, measurable, and repeatable, some scientists persist in speculating about the origin of the earth and of the entire universe—trying to reconstruct the process from what can be observed today. They, like the philosophers, have assumed a burden far beyond their competence and resources.

For some 100 years the nebula theory was the dominant scientific explanation of the origin of the universe. It was eventually replaced by the tidal theory, which was soon replaced by the steady-state theory, the super dense (big bang) theory, and so on. None of these theories gained universal acceptance among scientists. Today, theories are still multiplying and none yet is universally accepted, much less proved. The same is true of theories of evolution. Even some nonreligious scientists are calling for science to reconsider the very notion of evolution. Discovery of origins is far outside man's scope of knowledge and investigation. His attempts to discover where the universe came from, or where man himself came from, cannot possibly end in anything but futility. He is doomed to go from one unprovable theory to another.

Physics professor T. L. Moore of the University of Cincinnati has said, "To talk of the evolution of thought from sea slime to amoeba, from amoeba to a self-conscious thinking man, means nothing. It is the easy solution of a thoughtless brain."

Through *faith* we understand that the worlds were framed by the Word of God, a truth the world's most brilliant thinkers have not discovered and cannot discover on their own. It is beyond the realm of scientific investigation, but it is not beyond knowing—if we are willing to be taught by the Word of God. The Christian has no reason to be proud of his knowledge. It is a gift from God, like every other blessing of faith. By his own resources, he could no more discover the truth about origins than could the rankest atheist.

The Christian insists that all truth is God's truth. Some of it—the natural world—is discoverable with our eyes, ears, touch, and intellect. A great deal more of it, however, is not. It is apprehended only by faith, for which the Christian should make no apology. The very attempt to explain the universe, or our own being and nature, apart from God is a fool's effort. These things we understand only by faith in the revealed Word of Scripture. Faith comprehends that which the mind of man, no matter how brilliant, cannot fathom. "Things which eye has not seen and ear has not heard, and which have not entered the heart of man, all that God has prepared for those who love Him. For to us God revealed them through the Spirit; for the Spirit searches all things, even the depths of God" (1 Cor. 2:9-10).

An evangelist of many years ago told the beautiful story of two little boys he once visited in a London hospital.

The cots were side-by-side. One boy had a dangerous fever, the other had been struck by a truck and his body was badly mangled. The second one said to the first, "Say, Willie, I was down to the mission Sunday school and they told me about Jesus. I believe that if you ask Jesus, He will help you. They said that if we believe in Him and pray to God, then when we die He'll come and take us with Him to heaven." Willie replied, "But what if I'm asleep when He comes and I can't ask Him?" His friend said, "Just hold up your hand; that's what we did in Sunday school. I guess Jesus sees it." Since Willie was too weak to hold up his arm, the other boy propped it up for him with a pillow. During that night, Willie died, but when the nurse found him the next morning, his arm was still propped up.

We can be sure that the Lord saw his arm, because the Lord sees faith and the Lord accepts faith. By faith Willie saw the way to heaven. By faith he saw what the learned will never discover on their own. God's greatest truths are discovered by simple faith. It is not the world's way to truth, but a thousand years from now—if the Lord tarries that long—the world will still be devising and rejecting its theories. The person of faith knows the truth now. Faith is the only way to God.

Abel: Worshiping in Faith (11:4)

26

By faith Abel offered to God a better sacrifice than Cain, through which he obtained the testimony that he was righteous, God testifying about his gifts, and through faith, though he is dead, he still speaks. (11:4)

James Moffatt wrote, "Death is never the last word in the life of a righteous man. When a man leaves this world, be he righteous or unrighteous, he leaves something in the world. He may leave something that will grow and spread like a cancer or a poison, or he may leave something like the fragrance of perfume or a blossom of beauty that permeates the atmosphere with blessing." Man leaves this world either a Paul or a Nero.

Dead men do tell tales. They are not silent, but still speak to those who will listen. From many thousands of years ago, Abel speaks to twentieth-century man. This man who lived when the earth was new, who was of the second generation of mankind, has something to teach modern, sophisticated, technological man. He lived in a far distant age, in a far different culture, with far less light from God than we have. But what he has to tell us is more relevant than anything we are likely to read in our current newspapers or magazines.

The obvious theme of Hebrews 11 is faith, and it is about faith that Abel speaks to us. He is the first in a long line of faithful persons who can teach us about the life of faith. He, and the others mentioned in chapter 11, illustrate a pure kind of faith that sharply isolates it from works. It is this distinction that the Jewish readers especially needed to see. They had to be shown that, from the very beginning, faith has been the only thing that God will accept to save fallen man.

Adam and Eve could not have been persons of faith in the same way as their descendants. They had seen God face-to-face, fellowshipped with Him, talked with Him, and had lived in the garden of paradise. Until they sinned, they had no need for faith, because they lived in God's very light. Even after they sinned, they had the memory and knowledge of this unique and beautiful relationship with their Creator. Their children were the first to have need of faith in its fullest sense. Abel was the first man of faith, and it is important to understand that his faith had to do with his personal salvation.

Abel's faith led to three progressive things: true sacrifice, true righteousness, and true witness. Because he believed, he offered a better sacrifice. Because he offered a better sacrifice, he obtained righteousness. Because he obtained righteousness, he is for all the ages a living voice saying, "Righteousness is by faith."

God put Adam and Eve out of the Garden because of sin. Sin violated their fellowship with God and forfeited their right to be in His presence. But even as His judgment sent them out, His grace promised a way back. Through woman a man would be born whose heel would be bruised by Satan but who would bruise Satan on the head (Gen. 3:15). That is, this One who would be born from the seed of woman would conquer and destroy Satan, and thereby deliver mankind from sin's curse. Within the very curse itself, a Redeemer was promised. While judgment was being executed, mercy was being offered.

Only one woman, the mother of Jesus, has ever possessed a seed apart from its being implanted by a man. The Holy Spirit placed the seed in her, and in this way it was the seed of woman that gave birth to Jesus, the promised Savior. Not only the coming of the Redeemer but also His virgin birth was prophesied in the first part of the first book of God's Word.

From her comments after the birth of Cain, it is possible that Eve thought her firstborn would be the promised deliverer. His name probably means "to get" or "to get something," and her statement, "I have gotten a manchild with the help of the LORD" (Gen. 4:1), might be rendered, "I have gotten 'He is here.' " If she thought this son was the deliverer, she was greatly mistaken. This son became mankind's first murderer, not its savior. Even apart from Cain's wickedness and faithlessness, he could not have been the savior, nor could any of Adam and Eve's physical descendants. Flesh can only produce flesh. In

Adam all died, and the sons of Adam could not give a life which they themselves did not have.

We do not know their age difference, but Abel was born sometime after Cain. The basic meaning of Abel could be "breath," "weakness," or "vanity," carrying the idea of brevity. In any case, his life was indeed brief, cut off by his jealous brother.

Abel was "a keeper of flocks," while Cain was "a tiller of the ground." One was a shepherd, the other a farmer. Both were conceived after the fall and were born outside of Eden. They were therefore both born in sin. They were the second and third men ever to live on earth. They lived and functioned as all mankind since their time has lived and functioned. They had the same natures and capacities and limitations and inclinations that every person since then has had. In other words, in all the essentials of human nature, they were exactly as we are. In no way do they resemble the primitive beings of evolutionist fantasy.

Showing their preconceptions and biases, evolutionists and various interpreters of Scripture have argued that the Genesis account of man's beginnings cannot possibly be correct, because Adam, Eve, Cain, Abel, and the others mentioned in the earlier chapters are far too advanced to have been the first human beings. Besides the impossible supernatural claims of Adam and Eve talking with God, critics reason that original man could not have domesticated animals, as Abel did, or plowed and planted fields, as Cain did—much less have invented musical instruments or metal tools (4:21-22).

The Bible is clear, however, that Adam and Eve were highly intelligent when God created them. Adam named all the animals, which required devising a creative vocabulary. Their sons understood animal husbandry and farming, and within a very few generations came the tools and musical instruments already mentioned. The Genesis account, brief as it is, gives the definite picture of people who were well-developed in language and in general culture.

The first human inhabitants of earth, Adam and Eve and Cain and Abel, lived and functioned as human beings in the ways that we do today.

ABEL MADE A TRUE SACRIFICE

By faith Abel offered to God a better sacrifice than Cain. (11:4a)

This verse takes us back to Genesis, where we read of Abel's sacrifice: "So it came about in the course of time that Cain brought an offering to the LORD of the fruit of the ground. And Abel, on his part also brought of the firstlings of his flock and of their fat portions. And the

LORD had regard for Abel and for his offering; but for Cain and for his offering He had no regard" (Gen. 4:3-5).

A PLACE TO WORSHIP

Cain and Abel had a place to worship. Because they brought offerings, some sort of altar must have been used on which to make the sacrifices. There is no mention of their erecting an altar at this time, and it may be that an altar already existed near the east side of the Garden of Eden, where God had placed the cherubim with the flaming sword to prevent man from reentering.

It seems perfectly consistent with God's grace that, from the beginning, He would have provided for some means of worship. Perhaps the altar here was a forerunner of the mercy seat, a place where man could come for forgiveness and atonement. Very early in man's history God promised a future Deliverer, and very early He provided a temporary means of worship and sacrifice.

A TIME FOR WORSHIP

There seems also to have been a *time* for worship. "In the course of time," means literally, "at the end of days," that is, at the end of a certain period of time. It may be, therefore, that God had designated a special time for sacrificing. God is a God of order, and we know that in later centuries He did prescribe definite times and ways of worshiping. The fact that Cain and Abel came to sacrifice at the same time also suggests that God had specified a particular time.

A WAY TO WORSHIP

I also believe that God had designated a *way* to worship. Cain and Abel would know nothing about the need for worship or sacrifice, much less the way, had they not been told by God—perhaps through their parents. It is especially significant that the first recorded act of worship was sacrifice, a sin offering, the supreme act of worship in all of God's covenants with His people. Abraham sacrificed to God, and through Moses came the complicated and demanding rituals of sacrifice of the Old Covenant. The heart of the New Covenant is Jesus' perfect, once-for-all sacrifice on the cross. It is inconceivable that Cain and Abel accidentally stumbled onto sacrifice as a way of worshiping God. The fact that God accepted only the one sacrificial offering also seems to indicate that He had established a pattern for worship.

Abel offered his sacrifice by faith. Since "faith comes from hearing" (Rom. 10:17), Abel must have had some revelation from God on which his faith was based. He must have known the place and time and way in which God wanted the sacrifice for sin to be offered.

There was nothing intrinsically wrong with a grain or fruit or vegetable offering. The Mosaic covenant included such offerings. But the blood offerings were always first, because only the blood offerings dealt with sin.

Here is where the life of faith begins, with a sacrifice for sin. It begins with believing God that we are sinners, that we are worthy of death, that we need His forgiveness, and that we accept His revealed plan for our deliverance. That is the beginning of the life of faith. It was in such faith that Abel presented his sacrifice to God. And it was because of such faith that his sacrifice was acceptable to God.

When Abel did what God said, he revealed his obedience and acknowledged his sinfulness. Cain, on the other hand, was disobedient and did not acknowledge his sin. **Abel offered to God a better sacrifice than Cain** because God had prescribed a *blood* sacrifice. Somehow Abel, and Cain as well, knew what God wanted. The difference between the two was that Abel gave what God wanted, whereas Cain gave what he himself wanted. Abel was obedient and Cain was disobedient. Abel acknowledged his sin. Cain did not.

Abel approached God and said, in effect, "Lord, this is what You said You wanted. You promised that if I brought it, You would forgive my sin. I believe You, God. I acknowledge my sin and I acknowledge Your prescribed remedy. Here it is." Cain had the same knowledge of God's requirements, but decided to worship in his own way. In the tradition of his parents, he did his own thing. In effect, he was denying his sin.

Cain believed in God, else he would not have brought Him a sacrifice. He acknowledged a supreme being and even that he owed Him some sort of worship. He recognized God, but he did not obey God. He *believed in* God, but he did not *believe* God. He thought he could approach God in whatever way he wanted, and expected Him to be impressed and satisfied. In so doing, Cain became the father of all false religion.

False religion is trying to come to God by any other way than the way God has prescribed. It says, "I can get to God by thinking myself into Nirvana," or, "I can please God by meditation," or, "I can satisfy God by my works or by following the teachings of Mary Baker Eddy, Joseph Smith, or Charles Taze Russell." God's Word says, "There is no other name under heaven that has been given among men, by which we must be saved" (Acts 4:12). False religion says that there *is* another name, another way. False religion is any way to God that God Himself has not ordained. Proverbs 14:12 marks this truth: "There is a way which seems right to a man, but its end is the way of death."

The idea that one way is just as good as another does not seem to be accepted in any area of life except religion and morality. When a person goes to a doctor with a problem, he first of all wants to know the truth. No one likes to hear a diagnosis of a terrible disease. But the sensible person would rather know the truth than live in ignorance of something that could ruin his health or even take his life. Once knowing the diagnosis, he then wants the *right* cure, not just any cure. He wants the best treatment he can find and will usually go to any lengths to get it. He would be insulted and infuriated with a doctor who told him simply to go home and do whatever he thought best—that one person's opinion was just as good as another's. The reason we think this way about medicine is that we believe there are medical *truths.* Medical science does not have all the answers, but a great deal is known and accepted as factual, reliable, and dependable. The reason this same kind of reasoning is not applied to spiritual and moral issues is that the absolute truths and standards God has given are rejected. In fact, the very *notion* of spiritual and moral absolutes is rejected. Cain rejected God's standards and became the first apostate.

Cain failed to acknowledge his sin and refused to obey God by bringing the sacrifice God required. He did not mind worshiping God, as long as it was on his own terms, in his own way. And God rejected his sacrifice and rejected him.

Cain's disobedience of God and setting up his own standards of living were the beginning of Satan's world system. Cain "went out from the presence of the LORD" (Gen. 4:16) and into a life of continuous self-will, which is the heart of worldliness and unbelief. By his own decision, his own volition, he turned away from God and God's way to himself and his own way. We should not be sorry for him because God refused to honor his sacrifice. He knew what God required, and he was able to do it. But he chose instead to do what he himself wanted.

There are all kinds of people around under the guise of religion, even Christian religion, who are denying God. "Woe to them!" Jude says, "For they have gone the way of Cain" (v. 11). Cain is an example of the religious natural man, who believes in God and even in religion but after his own will and who rejects redemption by blood. Paul says of such people that, "they have a zeal for God, but not in accordance with knowledge. For not knowing about God's righteousness, and seeking to establish their own, they did not subject themselves to the righteousness of God" (Rom. 10:2-3).

In addition to being wicked and unbelieving, Cain was a hypocrite. He did not want to worship God but only give the appearance of worship. His purpose was to please himself, not God. His sacrifice was simply a religious activity designed to suit his own purposes and fulfill his own will. Cain was like the Pharisee in the Temple who Jesus said was praying "to himself" (Luke 18:11). He was patronizing God and worshiping himself. Also like the Pharisee, Cain went home unjustified; whereas Abel, like the penitent tax gatherer, went home justified.

God is not arbitrary or whimsical or capricious. He was not playing a game with Cain and Abel. He did not hold them accountable for
what they could not have known or could not have done. Abel's sacrifice
was accepted because he knew what God wanted and obeyed. Cain's was
rejected because he knew what God wanted, yet disobeyed. To obey is
righteous; to disobey is evil. Abel was of God; Cain was of Satan (1 John
3:12).

Abel offered a better sacrifice because it represented the obedience
of faith. He willingly brought God what He asked, and he brought the
very best that he had. In Abel's sacrifice, the way of the cross was first
prefigured. The first sacrifice was Abel's lamb—one lamb for one person.
Later came the Passover—with one lamb for one family. Then came the
Day of Atonement—with one lamb for one nation. Finally came Good
Friday—one Lamb for the whole world.

ABEL OBTAINED RIGHTEOUSNESS

Through which he obtained the testimony that he was righteous.
(11:4b)

The only thing that obtained righteousness for Abel was that, in
faith, He did what God told him to do. That is the only thing that
changes a man's relationship to God. It is not how good we are, but
whether or not we trust in Him, that counts with God. That trust is
evidenced in obedience to His Word.

Abel was sinful, just as Cain was. But it is quite possible, even
likely, that Abel was a better person than Cain. He was probably more
moral, more dependable, more honest, and even more likable than Cain.
It was not, however, these qualities of Abel that made his sacrifice acceptable, or the lack of these qualities that made Cain's sacrifice unacceptable.
The difference was the way in which the sacrifices were made. One was
made in obedient faith; the other made in disobedient unbelief.

Abel's was the kind of faith that allows God to move in on our
behalf and make us **righteous.** True faith is always obedient. Jesus said
"to those Jews who had believed Him, 'If you abide in My word, then
you are truly disciples of Mine' " (John 8:31). These people believed
Jesus, but they had not yet trusted in Him, which Jesus said would be
marked by obedience to His word. Obedience does not bring faith, but
faith will always bring obedience and the desire to live righteously.

> Beloved, while I was making every effort to write you about our common salva-
> tion, I felt the necessity to write to you appealing that you contend earnestly for
> the faith which was once for all delivered to the saints. For certain persons have

crept in unnoticed, those who were long beforehand marked out for this condemnation, ungodly persons who turn the grace of our God into licentiousness and deny our only Master and Lord, Jesus Christ. (Jude 3-4)

We cannot claim to have faith in God and then continually disregard His Word. James must have known some people who thought this way, for he wrote, "What use is it, my brethren, if a man says he has faith, but he has no works? Can that faith save him? . . . Faith, if it has no works, is dead, being by itself" (James 2:14, 17). Nonworking faith, disobedient faith, is not saving faith. It is not valid faith at all. Cain believed that God exists. Even the demons believe this, James goes on to say. "But are you willing to recognize, you foolish fellow, that faith without works is useless?" (2:19-20).

James then drives the point home by reminding his readers that Abraham's faith, for which he was counted righteous, was demonstrated by his obedience in offering his son Isaac as God commanded. "You see that faith was working with his works, and as a result of the works, faith was perfected" (2:21-22).

James does not teach salvation by works. He is saying that our faith is only real when it issues in works. We cannot work our way to God, but having come to Him, works will become evident—and prove that our faith is genuine. The Christian, in fact, is "created in Christ Jesus for good works, which God prepared beforehand, that we should walk in them" (Eph. 2:10).

It seems to me that God's **testimony** that Abel's sacrifice was acceptable and that He counted Abel as righteous could have been indicated by His causing this offering to be consumed. On at least five occasions recorded in Scripture, God showed His acceptance of a sacrifice by sending fire to consume it (Lev. 9:24; Judg. 6:21; 1 Kings 18:38; 1 Chron. 21:26; 2 Chron. 7:1). In any case, it is clear from Genesis that God made His approval and disapproval of the sacrifices known to Cain and Abel. He did not leave them in doubt as to their standing before Him.

Abel was counted righteous, not because he *was* righteous, but because he trusted God. He stood righteous before God because He had faith in God. Abel was the same sinner as he was before he made the sacrifice. He did not even receive the Holy Spirit, as do believers today. He walked away with the same problems he had before. But He had God's approval, and God's righteousness credited to his account.

ABEL SPEAKS FROM THE DEAD

God testifying about his gifts, and through faith, though he is dead, he still speaks. (11:4c)

When the Lord confronted Cain after Abel's murder, He said, "What have you done? The voice of your brother's blood is crying to Me from the ground" (Gen. 4:10). Abel's first "speaking" after **death** was to God, asking for his murder to be avenged. Like the souls underneath the altar "who had been slain because of the word of God" (Rev. 6:9-10), Abel asked the Lord to avenge his blood.

His voice also spoke to his brother. "And now you are cursed from the ground, which has opened its mouth to receive your brother's blood from your hand. When you cultivate the ground, it shall no longer yield its strength to you; you shall be a vagrant and a wanderer on the earth" (Gen. 4:11-12). Every bit of soil on which Cain placed his feet would remind him of his wicked deed. The earth, in effect, rejected Cain as he had rejected God and his brother. Abel, though dead, continued to speak to his brother.

The primary meaning of Hebrews 11:4, however, has to do with Abel's speaking to later generations of believers and potential believers. **He still speaks.** He says three things: man comes to God by faith, not works; man must accept and obey God's revelation above his own reason and self-will; and sin is severely punished. This is Abel's timeless three-point sermon to the world, which he has been preaching for thousands of years to those who will hear. It could be titled, "The Righteous Shall Live by Faith."

Enoch: Walking in Faith (11:5-6)

27

By faith Enoch was taken up so that he should not see death; and he was not found because God took him up; for he obtained the witness that before his being taken up he was pleasing to God. And without faith it is impossible to please Him, for he who comes to God must believe that He is, and that He is a rewarder of those who seek Him. (11:5-6)

The second hero of faith is Enoch. Whereas Abel exemplifies *worshiping* by faith—which must always come first—Enoch exemplifies *walking* by faith.

God never intended works as a way for men to come to Him. He intended works to be a result of salvation, not a way of salvation. At no time has man been able to approach God on the basis of works. Rather, God has always intended that works be a product of the salvation men receive when they approach Him on the basis of faith.

And Enoch lived sixty-five years, and became the father of Methuselah. Then Enoch walked with God three hundred years after he became the father of Methuselah, and he had other sons and daughters. So all the days of Enoch were three hundred and sixty-five years. And Enoch walked with God; and he was not, for God took him. (Gen. 5:21-24)

Here we see a new concept in the book of Genesis. Abel knew what it was to worship by faith, but he did not really understand the concept of walking with God. Revelation in Scripture is progressive. Abel received some revelation, and Enoch received more.

Adam and Eve had walked and talked with God in the Garden, but when they fell and were thrown out of the Garden, they ceased to walk with Him. The ultimate destiny of man is reinstituted with Enoch, who stands as an illustration for all men of what it is to be in fellowship with God. In Enoch the true destiny of man is again reached, as he experienced the fellowship with God that Adam and Eve had forfeited.

I believe Enoch's faith included everything Abel's included. Enoch had to have offered a sacrifice to God, symbolic of the ultimate sacrifice of Christ, because sacrifice is the only way into God's presence. He could not have walked with God unless he had first come to God, and a person cannot come to God apart from the shedding of blood. The principle has not changed from the days of Abel and Enoch until today.

Hebrews 11:5-6 shows us five features in Enoch's life that were pleasing to God: he believed that God is; he sought God's reward; he walked with God; he preached for God; and he entered into God's presence.

ENOCH BELIEVED THAT GOD IS

And without faith it is impossible to please Him, for he who comes to God must believe that He is. (11:6a)

Absolutely nothing from men can please God apart from *faith*. Religion does not please God, because it is essentially a system developed by Satan to counteract the truth. Nationality and heritage do not please God (cf. Gal 3:28-29). The Jews thought they pleased God just because they were descendants of Abraham. But most of the time they were displeasing to Him. Good works in themselves do not please God, "because by the works of the Law no flesh will be justified in His sight" (Rom. 3:20). **Without faith it is impossible to please Him.**

The first step of faith is simply to **believe that He is.** This Enoch did. God is pleased with those who believe in Him, even with the first step of believing that He exists. This belief alone is certainly not enough to save a person, but if it is a sincere conviction and is followed up, it will lead to full faith.

In his book, *Your God is Too Small,* J. B. Phillips describes some of the common gods that people manufacture. One is the grand old man god, the grandfatherly, white-haired, indulgent god who smiles down on men and winks at their adultery, stealing, cheating, and lying. Then there are the resident policeman god, whose primary job is to make life difficult and unenjoyable, and the god in a box, the private and exclusive sectarian god. The managing director god is the god of the deists, the god who designed and created the universe, started it spinning, and now stands by far away watching it run down. God is not pleased with belief in any of these idolatrous substitutes.

Believing that the true God exists is what is pleasing to Him. Mere recognition of a deity of some sort—the "ground of being," the "man upstairs," or any of the man-made gods just mentioned—is not the object of belief in mind here. Only belief in the existence of the true God, the God of Scripture, counts.

We cannot know God by sight. "No man has seen God at any time," Jesus said (John 1:18). Nor can we know God by reason. Two chapters of the book of Job (38-39) are devoted to God's forceful and colorful illustrations of how man cannot even fathom the operations of nature. How much less can we understand God Himself by our own observations and reasonings.

God gives much evidence of His existence, but it is not the kind of evidence that men often are looking for. He cannot be proved by science, for example. At best, scientific evidence is circumstantial. Paul Little wrote, "But it can be said with equal emphasis that you can't prove Napoleon by the scientific method, either. The reason lies in the nature of history itself, and in the limitation of the scientific method. In order for something to be proven by science, it must be repeatable. One cannot announce a new finding to the world on the basis of a single experiment. But history is, by its very nature, unrepeatable. No one can rerun the beginning of the universe. Or bring Napoleon back. Or repeat the assassination of Lincoln or the crucifixion of Jesus Christ. But the fact that these events can't be proved by repetition does not disprove their reality."

The point he is making is that you cannot apply the scientific method to everything. It does not work. You cannot put love or justice or anger in a test tube either, but no sensible person doubts their existence. By the same reasoning, God's existence should not be doubted merely because it cannot be scientifically proved.

Yet many things learned from science give *evidence* of His existence. The law of cause and effect, for example, holds that for every cause there must be an effect. If you keep pushing further and further back for causes, eventually you will end up with an uncaused cause. The only uncaused cause is God. This is the argument used previously by the writer of Hebrews: "For every house is built by someone, but the builder of all things is God" (3:4).

Philosopher J. H. Stirling said, "If each link of the chain hangs on another, the whole will hang and only hang in eternity unsupported like some stark serpent unless you find a hook for it. You add weakness to weakness in any quantity and you never get strength."

According to the law of entropy, the universe is running down. If it is running down, then it is not self-sustaining. If it is not self-sustaining, then it had to have a beginning. If it had a beginning, someone had to begin it, and we are back to the uncaused cause. There must be a first cause, for which only God qualifies.

The law of design also indicates that God is. When we look at plants and animals in all their marvelous intricacy, we see hundreds, thousands of amazingly complex designs that not only function beautifully but reproduce themselves perfectly. When we look at the stars, the planets, the asteroids, the comets, the meteors, the constellations, we see them kept precisely on their courses by centrifugal, centripetal, and gravitational forces. Such massive, marvelous, complex, and wonderfully operating design demands the existence of a designer.

We learn from science that water has a high specific heat, which is absolutely essential to stabilize chemical reactions within the human body. If water had a low specific heat, we would boil over with the least activity. Without this property of water, human and most animal life would hardly be possible.

The ocean is the world's thermostat. It takes a large loss of heat for water to go from liquid to ice, and a large intake of heat for water to become steam. The oceans are a cushion against the heat of the sun and the freezing blasts of winter. Unless the temperatures of the earth's surface were modulated by the ocean and kept within certain limits, we would either be cooked to death or frozen to death. How could such intricate, exacting, and absolutely necessary design come about by accident? It *demands* a designer.

Even the size of the earth gives evidence of design. If it were much smaller, there would be no atmosphere to sustain life. Earth would then be like our moon or Mars. On the other hand, if it were much larger, the atmosphere would contain free hydrogen, as do Jupiter and Saturn, which also prevents life. The earth's distance from the sun is absolutely right. Even a small change would make it too hot or too cold. The tilt of the earth's axis ensures the seasons. And so it goes.

Science cannot prove God, but it gives overwhelming evidence of a master designer and sustainer, which roles could only be filled by God.

Like science, reason cannot prove God. But also like science, it gives a great deal of evidence for Him. Man himself is personal, conscious, rational, creative, volitional. It is inconceivable that he could have become so by accident or that his Creator could be anything *less* than personal, conscious, rational, creative, and volitional. To think that personal, thinking, decision-making man somehow could have developed from slime to amoeba and on up the evolutionary chain does not make sense.

Studies by anthropologists show that man is universally God-conscious. This does not mean that there is no man who does not believe in some sort of god—much less in the true God—but that men in general do. The fact that some men do not believe does not disprove the rule, any more than a one-legged man proves that men are not two-legged creatures.

The very idea of God lends substance to the fact that He is. The fact that a man can conceive of God suggests that someone has given the possibility of such conception and that there is someone who corresponds to this conception.

But with all the many natural, scientific, and rational evidences of God, acknowledging Him is still a matter of faith. The proof comes after belief. "The one who believes in the Son of God has the witness in himself" (1 John 5:10). Even the scientist receives proof after faith. When he develops a hypothesis, his faith becomes greater and greater as evidence for the hypothesis mounts. It is his commitment to the hypothesis, his faith in it, that eventually leads to proof, if the hypothesis is true. The witness of the Holy Spirit in the hearts of believers is infinitely greater proof of God's existence than the conclusions of a laboratory experiment for the validity of a scientific theory ever could be.

ENOCH SOUGHT GOD'S REWARD

He who comes to God must believe that He is, and that He is a rewarder of those who seek Him. (11:6b)

It is not enough simply to believe that God exists. In order to please Him it is also necessary to believe that He is moral and just, that He will reward faith in Him. We must recognize God as a personal, loving, gracious God to those who seek Him. Enoch believed this within the revelation he had. He did not believe God was merely a great impersonal cosmic force. He believed in and knew God in a personal, loving way. You cannot "walk" with a ground of being or a first mover or an ultimate cause. For three hundred years Enoch had fellowship with the true God, a God whom he knew to be just, merciful, forgiving, caring, and very personal.

It is not enough merely to postulate a God. Einstein said, "Certainly there is a God. Any man who doesn't believe in a cosmic force is a fool, but we could never know Him." Brilliant as he was, Einstein was wrong. We *can* know God. In fact, in order to please Him, we must believe that He is personal, knowable, loving, caring, moral, and responds graciously to those who come to Him. It is not enough even to believe in the right God. Many Jews to whom the letter of Hebrews was addressed acknowledged the true God, the God of Scripture. But they did not have faith in Him; they did not trust in Him. Enoch knew the true God and trusted the true God.

Both testaments are filled with teachings that God not only *can* be found but that it is His great desire **to be** found. David said to his son Solomon, "If you seek Him, He will let you find Him; but if you forsake Him, He will reject you forever" (1 Chron. 28:9). "Surely there is a reward for the righteous; surely there is a God who judges on earth!" (Ps. 58:11). "I love those who love me; and those who diligently seek me will find me" (Prov. 8:17). "And you will seek Me and find Me, when you search for Me with all your heart" (Jer. 29:13). Jesus was very explicit: "For everyone who asks, receives; and he who seeks, finds; and to him who knocks, it shall be opened" (Luke 11:10). It is not enough just to believe that He is. We must also believe that He rewards those who seek Him.

The reward that God gives for faith is salvation. "Whoever believes in Him should not perish, but have eternal life" (John 3:16). "But seek first His kingdom and His righteousness; and all these things shall be added to you" (Matt. 6:33). In other words, every good thing that God has, including eternal life, constitutes the reward for belief. For faith we receive forgiveness, a new heart, eternal life, joy, peace, love, heaven—everything! When we trust in Jesus Christ, we become mutual heirs with Him. All that God's own Son has is ours as well.

ENOCH WALKED WITH GOD

Believing that God exists is the first step *toward* faith. Believing that he rewards those who trust in Him is the first step *of* faith. Trusting fully in Jesus Christ as Lord and Savior is only the beginning of the faithful life in God. To continue pleasing God, we must fellowship with Him, commune with, "walk" with Him—just as Enoch did. In the four verses in Genesis (5:21-24) describing Enoch, he is twice spoken of as "walking with God." In the Septuagint (Greek Old Testament) this phrase is translated "pleased God," using the same Greek word (*euaresteō*, "to be well-pleasing") that is used twice in Hebrews 11:5-6. Walking with God is pleasing God.

The term *walk* is used many times in the New Testament to represent faithful living. "Therefore we have been buried with Him through baptism into death, . . . so we too might walk in newness of life" (Rom. 6:4). "For we walk by faith, not by sight" (2 Cor. 5:7). "Walk by the Spirit, and you will not carry out the desire of the flesh" (Gal. 5:16). "Walk in love, just as Christ also loved you, and gave Himself up for us"

(Eph. 5:2). Christ even speaks of our fellowship with Him in heaven as a walk: "They will walk with Me in white; for they are worthy" (Rev. 3:4). Like Enoch, every believer *should* walk with God every day he is on earth. When we get to heaven, we *will* walk with Him forever.

RECONCILIATION

The first thing implied in Enoch's walk with God is reconciliation. "Do two walk together unless they have agreed to do so?" (Amos 3:3, NIV). The point is obvious. Two people cannot really walk together in intimate fellowship unless they are agreed. Walking together, then, presupposes harmony. If Enoch walked with God, he obviously was in agreement with God. Rebellion was over for this man of faith. Since Adam fell, every person born into the world has been in rebellion against God. We do not grow into rebellion or fall into rebellion; we are *born* into rebellion. Our very nature, from before birth, is at enmity with God. We are all "by nature children of wrath" (Eph. 2:3). The purpose of salvation is to reconcile men to God, to restore the relationship broken by sin. Because of his faith, Enoch was reconciled with God; and because he was reconciled with God, he could walk with God.

A CORRESPONDING NATURE

The second truth implied in Enoch's walk with God is that Enoch and God had corresponding natures. Some animals can become very good companions to men. They may have great loyalty and sensitivity to their owners, and a close relationship can develop over the years. But man cannot fellowship with even the smartest and most devoted animal. Our natures are far too different. Animals can offer companionship but not fellowship. We can *take* a walk with a dog, but we cannot "walk" with a dog, in the sense of having fellowship with him. It is just as impossible for an unbeliever to have fellowship with God (2 Cor. 6:14-16), and for the same reason—his nature is too different from God's. Even an unbeliever is created in God's image, but that image has been so shattered by sin, his nature so corrupted, that fellowship with his Creator is not possible—there is no common sphere in which he and God can be agreed.

When we are saved, we become citizens of a new domain. We are still on earth, but our true life, our real citizenship, is in heaven (Phil. 3:20). As Peter says, we "become partakers of the divine nature" (2 Pet. 1:4). In Christ we are given a heavenly nature, His own nature, and we can therefore have fellowship with God. Because Enoch walked with God, he must have had a nature corresponding to God's.

MORAL FITNESS AND A JUDICIAL DEALING WITH SIN

Walking with God implies moral fitness as well as a judicial dealing with sin. We could not have a new nature unless God took away sin. Because a person walks with God means that his sin has been forgiven and that he has been justified, counted righteous by God. Only when sin has been dealt with can we move into God's presence and begin walking with Him. God will not walk in any way but the way of holiness. "If we say that we have fellowship with Him and yet walk in the darkness, we lie and do not practice the truth; but if we walk in the light as He Himself is in the light, we have fellowship with one another, and the blood of Jesus His Son cleanses us from all sin" (1 John 1:6-7). The only persons God walks with are those who are cleansed of sin. Since Enoch walked with God, he had to have been forgiven of his sin and declared righteous by God.

A SURRENDERED WILL

Walking with God implies a surrendered will. God does not force His company on anyone. He only offers Himself. God must first will that a person come to Him, but that person must also will to come to God. Faith is impossible without willingness to believe. Just as walking with God presupposes faith it also presupposes willingness—a surrendered will.

A surrendered will is a surrender in love. Willing surrender is not abject submissiveness, a determined resignation to the Lord's way and will. It is what might be called a willful willingness, a glad and free surrender. "And this is love, that we walk according to His commandments" (2 John 6).

Enoch walked with God for three hundred years! Small wonder that the Lord went for a walk with him one day and just took him on up to heaven. The New Testament refers to this sort of living as walking in the Spirit. We are to live continually in the atmosphere of the Spirit's presence, power, direction, and teaching. The fruit of this walk in the Spirit are: "love, joy, peace, patience, kindness, goodness, faithfulness, gentleness, self-control" (Gal. 5:22-23).

Walking in the Spirit is allowing Him to pervade your thoughts. It is saying, when you get up in the morning, "Holy Spirit, it is Your day, not mine. Use it as You see fit." It is saying throughout the day, "Holy Spirit, continue to keep me from sin, direct my choices and my decisions, use me to glorify Jesus Christ." It is putting each decision, each opportunity, each temptation, each desire before Him, and asking for His direction and His power. Walking in the Spirit is dynamic and practical. It is not passive resignation but active obedience.

The New Testament describes walking with God in many ways. Third John 4 says it is a truth walk; Romans 8:4 calls it a spiritual walk; Ephesians 5:2 describes it as a love walk, 5:8 as a light walk, and 5:15 as a wise walk.

It would have been wonderful to have had Enoch as an example—or Noah, Abraham, or any of the other faithful heroes of Hebrews 11. But we have an even greater example—our Lord Jesus Himself, the One who supremely walked with God. He did nothing, absolutely nothing, that was not the Father's will. The beloved apostle reminds us that "the one who says he abides in Him ought himself to walk in the same manner as He walked" (1 John 2:6). If we want to know how to walk, we need simply to look at Jesus. From childhood He was continually about His Father's business, and only His Father's business. He constantly walked with God.

CONTINUING FAITH

Finally, a person cannot walk with God unless he has first come to God by faith. Just so, he cannot continue to walk without continuing to have faith. Walking with God is a walk in faith and a walk by faith. "For we walk by faith, not by sight" (2 Cor. 5:7). "As you therefore have received Christ Jesus the Lord, so walk in Him, having been firmly rooted and now being built up in Him and established in your faith" (Col. 2:6-7).

Enoch believed God, and he continued to believe God. He could not have walked with God for three hundred years without trusting in God for three hundred years. Enoch never saw God. He walked with Him, but he did not see Him. He just believed He was there. That is how He pleased God.

Enoch Preached for God

And about these also Enoch, in the seventh generation from Adam, prophesied, saying, "Behold, the Lord came with many thousands of His holy ones, to execute judgment upon all, and to convict all the ungodly of all their ungodly deeds which they have done in an ungodly way, and of all the harsh things which ungodly sinners have spoken against Him." (Jude 14-15)

That Enoch preached for God we learn only from the book of Jude. Judging from this account, his message on ungodliness was brief and perhaps repetitious, but it was inspired. We have no hint as to how effective it was, but Enoch's purpose was to be faithful, not effective. He did what God required of him and left the results to Him. One thing is certain: because of his faithful preaching and faithful living, no one who heard Enoch or lived around him had any excuse for not believing in God. Whether any of these people believed or not, the influence Enoch had on them must have been powerful.

Jude's report of Enoch's preaching contradicts any notion that Enoch lived in an easy time for believing. He was surrounded by false teachers and false teaching. We do not know if he had the fellowship of any fellow believers, but we know that he lived in the midst of a host of unbelievers. He could not possibly have preached as strongly as he did without considerable opposition. He battled against his own generation in the same way that Noah would later battle against his. He let them know they were ungodly, and he let them know God was going to judge them. I believe God was pleased with Enoch because his faith was not just something he felt in his heart. It was heard on his lips and seen in his life. His faith was active and dynamic, vocal and fearless.

Enoch Entered into God's Presence

By faith Enoch was taken up so that he should not see death; and he was not found because God took him up; for he obtained a witness that before his being taken up he was pleasing to God. (11:5)

At last, after three hundred years of believing and walking and preaching, he went to be with the Lord—in a marvelously unique way. God just **took him up** without his experiencing death. He pleased God so much that God just reached down and lifted him up to heaven. One moment he was there, and the next moment "he was not, for God took him" (Gen. 5:24). By faith Enoch was translated. He walked so closely with God for so long that he just walked into heaven, as it were.

We do not know the reason God waited three hundred years before taking Enoch to be with Himself. Perhaps it was to allow sufficient time for him to preach and witness to the hard and unbelieving generation in which he lived. Furthermore, we do not know why God took Enoch in that unusual way at all. Perhaps it was to spare him further ridicule and persecution, which he was bound to have experienced. Perhaps it was because God wanted to be even closer to the one who pleased Him so much. "Precious in the sight of the LORD is the death of His godly ones" (Ps. 116:15). God loves His saints and loves the fellowship of His saints. Enoch was so precious to the Lord that He bypassed the death stage for this remarkable saint.

Enoch is a beautiful picture of believers who will be taken up directly to heaven when our Lord returns for His bride, the church. Just as Enoch was translated to heaven without seeing death, so also will be those of God's people who are alive at the rapture. "Then we who are alive and remain shall be caught up together with them in the clouds to meet the Lord in the air, and thus we shall always be with the Lord" (1 Thess. 4:17).

Noah: Obeying in Faith (11:7)

By faith Noah, being warned by God about things not yet seen, in reverence prepared an ark for the salvation of his household, by which he condemned the world, and became an heir of the righteousness which is according to faith. (11:7)

"Faith without works is dead" (James 2:26). True faith always has actions to support its claim. Earlier in the second chapter of his letter, James condemns the man who says he has faith but who does nothing to help a fellow Christian in need. In order for faith to be valid, it must visibly radiate itself in good deeds. If you really believe in God, there will be evidence of it in the way you live, in the things you say, and in the things you do.

Abel illustrates the worship of faith, and Enoch the walk of faith. Noah, perhaps more than any other person in history, illustrates the work of faith—obedience.

Satan has continually tried to confuse and mislead people, including God's people, about faith and works. If possible, he will convince a person that he can be saved by doing certain good works. If this strategy works, the person will be lost to God. If a person trusts in God and is saved, Satan then tries to convince him of one of two extremes—that he must do good works to *keep* his salvation (legalism) or that, now that he is saved by faith, he can forget about good works (license). From Genesis to Revelation, however, the Bible is clear that a person is saved only by faith, and that when he is saved, good works should follow as a result.

Paul, who so strongly proclaimed justification by faith alone, also proclaimed a life of good works for those who are justified. "Instruct them to do good, to be rich in good works, to be generous and ready to share" (1 Tim. 6:18). Believers are, in fact, "created in Christ Jesus for good works, which God prepared beforehand, that we should walk in them" (Eph. 2:10). For all the saints listed in Hebrews 11, their genuine faith was made known in something they did. Faith cannot be seen except in the things that it does. And if it is true faith, it will do many good things.

Noah was a man of faith, and his life continually showed his faith by his utter obedience to God. "Noah was a righteous man, blameless in his time; Noah walked with God" (Gen. 6:9). He worshiped God faithfully, as Abel had, and he walked with God faithfully, as Enoch had. He also worked for God faithfully.

I once heard a sports announcer interview a professional football player shortly before he was scheduled to play in the Super Bowl. He asked the lineman what he thought his team's chances were in the upcoming game. He replied, "We believe that if we just do what the coach says, we will win." The team had absolute faith in its coach's wisdom and judgment. But the players also knew that winning depended on their *doing* what he told them to do.

Noah's faith was stupendous. It was stupendous because of his absolute trust in God and because of his unhesitating and persistent obedience for 120 years in an undertaking that, from the human perspective, looked totally absurd and absolutely impossible.

Three things in Hebrews 11:7 give proof that Noah's faith was genuine. First, he responded to God's word. That is always a characteristic of true faith. Second, he rebuked the world. He was such a man of God that his very life was a rebuke to the wicked people that surrounded him. Third, he received God's righteousness. These are the classic marks of true faith.

NOAH RESPONDED TO GOD'S WORD

By faith Noah, being warned by God about things not yet seen, in reverence prepared an ark for the salvation of his household. (11:7a)

When God told Noah that He was getting ready to destroy the world because of its wickedness and instructed him to build **an ark** (Gen. 6:13-14), Noah dropped everything and started building. Noah probably lived in Mesopotamia, between the Tigris and Euphrates rivers, a long way from any ocean or sizable lake. It is difficult to imagine how God's message must have sounded to Noah. To most of us it would have been so strange, so demanding, so embarrassing, so absolutely overwhelming, that we would have done anything to get out of it. We would have thought up a thousand excuses for not doing it. We would have done our best to talk God out of the whole idea, or at least convince Him to get someone else for the job.

But Noah, who had but a fraction of the divine light that we have, did not argue, quibble, make excuses, complain, or procrastinate. He did not question God, but simply began obeying Him. He spent over one hundred years fulfilling this single command. True faith does not question, and Noah did not question. Among the countless faithful saints who have endured and persisted in obedience to God, Noah stands supreme, if for nothing else than the shear magnitude and time span of his one incredible assignment from the Lord.

Noah doubtlessly had a lot of things of his own to do. To surrender all his time and effort to building a boat took a special kind of commitment. He probably had little idea about what an ocean-going ship was like. Certainly he had never seen, or even heard of, a giant ship such as the ark was to be. He had no experience in shipbuilding, no easy access to building supplies, and no help except that of his sons. Even they were not able to help for many years after the ark was begun, because they were not born until after Noah was 500 years old (Gen. 5:32). One of the greatest practical acts of faith in all history was Noah's cutting down the first gopher tree for wood to make the ark.

Noah was **warned by God about things not yet seen.** He had never seen rain, because it probably did not exist before the Flood. He had never seen a flood, since floods could not have occurred without rain. Noah responded to God's message by faith, "the assurance of things hoped for, the conviction of things not seen" (Heb. 11:1). **By** *faith* **Noah . . . prepared an ark.** He had nothing to go on but God's word, which for him was more than sufficient.

Noah built the ark **in reverence.** The Greek word (*eulabeia*) can be translated "pious care, or concern," with *pious* taken in the original sense of genuine spiritual devotion. He treated the message of God with great respect and awe. He "was a righteous man, blameless in his time; Noah walked with God" (Gen. 6:9). He was a man of obedient faith even before God called him to build the ark. He had been faithful over smaller things, and now the Lord gave him a great thing to do.

The ark symbolized many of God's future dealings with men. The Hebrew word for pitch, for example, has the same root (*kpr*) as that used for atonement. The pitch kept the waters of judgment from entering the ark just as Christ's atoning blood keeps judgment from the sinner.

The exact length of the cubit during Noah's time is not certain, but using the lowest, most conservative figure it would be about seventeen and a half inches. On this basis, the ark was 438 feet long, 73 feet wide, and 44 feet high. In other words it was nearly one and a half times the length of a football field and more than four stories high. Since it had three decks, the total deck area was almost 96,000 square feet, and the total volume within the decks was about 1.3 million cubic feet. Naval engineers have discovered that the dimensions and shape of the ark form the most stable ship design known. The ark was not designed for maneuverability but for stability, in order to best protect those within it.

The ark is a beautiful picture of the salvation offered in Jesus Christ. The ark was easily large enough to hold all the animals needed to assure each species' survival. It had plenty of room for every person who wanted to come to God for safety. The fact that only eight persons came into the ark means that only eight wanted to be saved on God's terms. God does not wish "for any to perish but for all to come to repentance" (2 Pet. 3:9). God's nature does not change. His will in Peter's time was the same in Noah's time. Only those perished in the Flood who rejected God's way of salvation. Had more come to Him for safety, we can be sure the ark would have accommodated them. Just so, Jesus' blood is more than sufficient to atone for all the sins ever committed since the Fall. That no more people are saved than are simply means that these are the only ones who *want* to be saved. Jesus declared absolutely that no one who comes to Him will be cast out (John 6:37).

When God first called Noah to his gargantuan task, He told him of the covenant He would make with him (Gen. 6:18). As the Lord explained later, the covenant was also with "every living creature of all flesh that is on the earth" (9:16) that survived the Flood, including, of course, all mankind. But the covenant was first of all with Noah, the man who had "found favor in the eyes of the LORD" (6:8).

Though Noah was "blameless in his time" and "walked with God" (6:9), he was still a sinner. He was a fallen son of Adam, as seen so clearly in his shameful display of drunkenness and immodesty when things began going well after the Flood (9:20-21). He was saved because of God's "favor," because of God's grace, working through his faith. Noah's righteousness, just as that of every believer before and after him, was "in the eyes of the LORD." Noah was *counted* righteous, justified by God's pure grace, applied because of faith. Not even Noah's faith in itself, amazing as it was compared to that of most of us, saved Him. God would not be obligated to save a single person even because of faith, had He not in His love and mercy declared faith to be the condition on which He would save. It is God's right to save whom He will, and He wills to save those who believe in His Son. He takes our faith and, by His grace, *counts* it as righteousness (Rom. 4:5).

That Noah's faith was genuine is proved by his obedience to God's word. In God's economy, trust and obedience are inseparable. As we love to sing, there is no other way than "to trust and obey." Just as Noah trusted and obeyed, God wants all who belong to Him to do the same. He wants us to trust Him in the trial we are going through, the temptation we are facing, the decision we are making. He wants us to worship Him rightly, as Abel did, and to walk with Him, as Enoch did. He also wants us to obey him, as Noah did. The Lord has arks for every believer to build. It is just as important for us to build the ark He gives us as it was for Noah to build the one God assigned him. Ours may not be as big or as awesome or as time-consuming as Noah's, but it is the only one *we* can build that will please God. And, like Noah's, when we build it in faith, according to God's plan and by His power, it will accomplish what God wants it to accomplish. Also like Noah's, our work for the Lord may look foolish and purposeless in the world's eyes. But if it is His work, it will please Him, the only one a believer needs to be concerned about pleasing.

My father used to tell the story of a man who walked up and down the sidewalks wearing a sandwich board with "I am a fool for Christ" painted on the front. On the back was "Whose fool are you?" In a sense, every person is a fool for something in the eyes of someone. Many political activists and cultists are perfectly willing to look like fools for the sake of their causes. How much more should a Christian be willing to look like a fool for Christ's cause.

Peter and his partners had fished all night and caught nothing. As they were washing their nets on shore, Jesus got into one of the boats, preached for a while to the crowd that was gathered there, and then told Peter to put out into the deep and drop the nets again. Peter let the Lord know he thought the effort was useless, but he obeyed anyway. They caught so many fish they had to ask for help, and two boats nearly sank under the load. Peter's faith was small, but he obeyed and was rewarded far out of proportion to his faith. Like Noah, he faithfully obeyed God, and God honored his faith and his obedience.

Noah believed God's word about the coming judgment, and about the right size and way to build the ark, and about the promise to save him and his family. He did not pick and choose what to believe and what to obey. He believed everything and obeyed everything God said.

NOAH REBUKED THE WORLD

By faith Noah . . . condemned the world. (11:7b)

Noah's obedience included his passing on to the rest of the world

God's message of coming judgment. In 2 Peter 2:5, he is called "a preacher of righteousness." God called Noah to preach while he built. The preaching was probably more difficult than the building. Hard jobs are always easier to deal with than hard people.

The times in which Noah grew up were among the most evil and corrupt in history. "The LORD saw that the wickedness of man was great on the earth, and that every intent of the thoughts of his heart was only evil continually" (Gen. 6:5). If any man had reason to regret the time in which he lived it was Noah. But he did not complain about when he was born, his lot in life, or his calling. He obeyed as he was and where he was.

Noah's job was to warn the people of his time that God would soon judge them because of their wickedness and unbelief. They had had the same opportunity to know God and His will as had Noah. The difference between Noah and everyone around him was not a difference in the amount of light but a difference in response to it.

Mankind had become largely demon possessed. I believe the "sons of God" who came down and cohabited with the "daughters of men" (Gen. 6:2) were fallen angels, demons (cf. 1 Pet. 3:19-20). Because of this cohabitation, the fallen race fell even further. The evil of man's own nature was compounded, and it became too much for the Lord to bear. Judgment had to come. Donald Barnhouse said, "Hell is as much a part of the love story as God in heaven is." Righteousness and sin cannot coexist. God cannot establish righteousness until sin is destroyed.

As always, the Lord's judgment was tempered by His mercy. He is never happy with judgment, no matter how deserved. God was "grieved in His heart" (Gen. 6:6) about man's wickedness and the fact that he would have to be judged so severely. He allowed 120 years for the people to be warned and to repent, thereby staying the judgment (6:3). Actually a type of warning was given when Noah was born, 500 years before he started the ark. As he was being named, his father, Lamech, said, "This one shall give us rest from our work and from the toil of our hands arising from the ground which the LORD has cursed" (Gen. 5:29). And then, while God had Noah build the ark—a dramatic picture of the coming Flood—He also had Noah witness to the people, warning them. "The patience of God kept waiting in the days of Noah, during the construction of the ark" (1 Pet. 3:20). In other words, at the same time He was preparing judgment He was also preparing a way of escape.

The people had ample warning of judgment, and they also had ample knowledge of the truth. For one thing, they had the witness of nature. "Since the creation of the world His invisible attributes, His eternal power and divine nature, have been clearly seen, being understood through what has been made, so that they are without excuse" (Rom. 1:20). They also had Abel's testimony about proper worship of God and Enoch's testimony about proper fellowship with God. In addition to this positive light, God's punishment of Cain should have been a constant reminder of what He thought of sin. God's very Spirit was striving with men (Gen. 6:3), seeking to turn them back to their Creator. Then they had 120 years of righteous preaching by Noah. What more could God have done?

The people had no excuse for their sin before Noah began building the ark, and they had even less excuse after he finished. One hundred and twenty years, even when men sometimes lived to be nearly a thousand, was more than ample time for anyone to repent who *wanted* to repent.

C.H. Spurgeon said, "He who does not believe God will punish sin will not believe that he will pardon it through atoning blood." Many people are glad to hear about God's gracious promises but want to hear nothing of His judgment. Spurgeon went on to say, "I charge you who profess the Lord not to be unbelieving with regard to the terrible threatenings of God to the ungodly. Believe the threat even though it should chill your blood. Believe though nature shrinks from the overwhelming doom. For if you do not believe, disbelieving God at one point will drive you to disbelieve God upon the other points of revealed truth."

Just as the people must have made excuses for not repenting or for putting it off, Noah too must have been tempted to make excuses about his qualifications for preaching and boat building. Surely Satan suggested to him more than once that he had plenty of time to build the ark "later." One hundred and twenty years gives a great deal of opportunity for procrastination. But Noah did not make excuses or procrastinate; he simply preached and built, just as he was called to do. Amidst ridicule, wickedness, long years with little evidence of success, and many unanswered questions, Noah obeyed and obeyed and continued to obey.

Not only is God's warning of judgment an act of mercy, but even the judgment itself has a merciful aspect. For the sake of the believing remnant on earth in Noah's day, the Lord had to cut out the malicious and destructive spiritual cancer or it would have overwhelmed the world.

Against that wicked, cruel, and dark world, Noah's life and testimony shined in glistening condemnation. Black never seems so black as when white is put beside it. The man of faith rebukes the world just by his living, even if he never utters a word of reproach. A young man of Athens told Socrates, "I hate you, because every time I meet you, you show me what I am."

Perhaps the saddest lesson from Noah's day is that men have not changed in their attitude toward God since then, and will not change until the Lord returns. "For the coming of the Son of Man will be just like the days of Noah. For as in those days which were before the flood they were eating and drinking, they were marrying and giving in marriage, until the day that Noah entered the ark, and they did not understand until the flood came and took them all away, so shall the coming of the Son of Man be" (Matt. 24:37-39).

The parallels of Noah's day to our own are sobering. In Noah's day God's message was rejected, as it is today. In his day, wickedness, immorality, violence, lewdness, vulgarity, profanity, lying, killing, and blasphemy were rampant, as they are today. In his day a remnant found grace, just as a remnant believes today. In Noah's day or shortly before it, Enoch was translated, picturing the rapture of believers when the Lord returns, which could be in our day. We can be as sure as they should have been that judgment is coming, because God has promised it just as clearly and men deserve it just as much. Someone has said, "If God doesn't destroy our world, He'll have to apologize to Sodom and Gomorrah." The next judgment will be different in two ways, however. First, it will not be by flood (Gen. 9:15) but by fire (2 Pet. 3:10). Second, it will be the last. And again the only security is refuge in God's ark, Jesus Christ.

NOAH RECEIVED GOD'S RIGHTEOUSNESS

Noah . . . became an heir of the righteousness which is according to faith. (11:7c)

Noah's faith was proved by his receiving God's righteousness, which is only bestowed on those who trust in Him. "A righteous man, blameless in his time; Noah walked with God" (Gen. 6:9). He was the first person in Scripture to be called righteous.

All who believe in God are righteous, not always in practice but always in position. Christ's righteousness is imputed to us by faith (Rom. 3:22). The Father sees us as He sees the Son, holy and righteous, because by faith we are *in* the Son. If we put on colored glasses, everything we look at will appear that color. God looks at believers through the lens of His Son, and He sees us as He sees the Son. Thousands of years before Jesus became incarnate, God looked at Noah and saw the Son, because Noah believed.

Abraham: The Life of Faith (11:8-19)

By faith Abraham, when he was called, obeyed by going out to a place which he was to receive for an inheritance; and he went out, not knowing where he was going. By faith he lived as an alien in the land of promise, as in a foreign land, dwelling in tents with Isaac and Jacob, fellow heirs of the same promise; for he was looking for the city which has foundations, whose architect and builder is God. By faith even Sarah herself received ability to conceive, even beyond the proper time of life, since she considered Him faithful who had promised; therefore, also, there was born of one man, and him as good as dead at that, as many descendants as the stars of heaven in number, and innumerable as the sand which is by the seashore.

All these died in faith, without receiving the promises, but having seen them and having welcomed them from a distance, and having confessed that they were strangers and exiles on the earth. For those who say such things make it clear that they are seeking a country of their own. And indeed if they had been thinking of that country from which they went out, they would have had opportunity to return. But as it is, they desire a better country, that is a heavenly one. Therefore God is not ashamed to be called their God; for He has prepared a city for them.

By faith Abraham, when he was tested, offered up Isaac; and

he who had received the promises was offering up his only begotten
son; it was he to whom it was said, "In Isaac your descendants shall
be called." He considered that God is able to raise men even from the
dead; from which he also received him back as a type. (11:8-19)

There are only two ways to live. One way, by far the most common, is to live by sight, to base everything on what you can see. This is
the empirical way. The other way, far less common, is to live by faith, to
base your life primarily and ultimately on what you cannot see. The
Christian way, of course, is the faith way. We have never seen God, or
Jesus Christ, or heaven, or hell, or the Holy Spirit. We have never seen
any of the people who wrote the Bible or an original manuscript of the
Bible. Though we see the results of them, we have never seen any of the
virtues that God commands or any of the graces that He gives. Yet we
live in the conviction of all these things by faith. We bank our earthly
lives and our eternal destiny on things which we have never seen. That is
the way the people of God have always lived.

The life of faith has some specific ingredients, which are pointed
out in this text as reflected in the life of Abraham. Abraham is a compos-
ite of God's pattern of faith. He reveals the totality of the true faith life,
all the ingredients that constitute it. Abraham was the father of the Jewish people, and he is therefore presented to the Jews to whom the book of
Hebrews was written as the most strategic example of faith. They needed
to realize that Abraham was more than the father of their race; he also
was, by example, the father of the faithful, the father of everyone who
lives by faith in God.

The rabbis had long taught that Abraham pleased God because of
his works. They believed that God looked around the earth and finally
found an outstandingly righteous man, Abraham, who because of his
goodness was selected to be the father of God's chosen people. That false
teaching needed to be corrected. It was necessary to show, from the Old
Testament itself, that Abraham was not righteous in himself but was
counted righteous by God because of his faith.

When Stephen was preaching to the Jewish leaders in Jerusalem,
he began by showing how Abraham had obediently trusted God by leaving his homeland and believing God's promises of blessing (Acts 7:2-5).
In his powerful argument in Romans for justification by faith, Paul uses
Abraham as the central illustration (Rom. 4). Abraham is the classic example of the life of faith.

For a Jew to accept the truth that salvation is by faith, he would
have to be shown that this truth applied to Abraham. The Jews were
right in looking to Abraham as a great example. The problem was that
they looked at him in the wrong way. They knew that he pleased God,

but they had to be shown that God was pleased with him not because of any good works he did, but because he trusted Him.

The New Testament makes it clear that Abraham was the first true man of faith. Since his time, everyone who trusts in God, Jew or Gentile, is spiritually a child of Abraham. "Therefore, be sure that it is those who are of faith who are sons of Abraham" (Gal. 3:7; cf. v. 29). Those who trusted God before the Flood—such as Abel, Enoch, and Noah—were only partial examples of faith. Abraham was the first established man of faith, and he is the pattern, the prototype, of faith for men of all ages.

In this passage are five features of faith that show us the complete pattern: the pilgrimage of faith, the patience of faith, the power of faith, the positiveness of faith, and the proof of faith.

THE PILGRIMAGE OF FAITH

By faith Abraham, when he was called, obeyed by going out to a place which he was to receive for an inheritance; and he went out, not knowing where he was going. (11:8)

It was not Abraham's plan to leave Ur and then Haran, and eventually settle in the land of Canaan. In fact, when he left Ur he had no idea where he was going. He was called by God, and only God knew what was in store for him.

In the Greek, **he was called** is a present participle, and the translation could be, "when he was being called." In other words, as soon as he understood what God was saying, he started packing. It was instant obedience. It may have taken several days, or even weeks or months, to make final preparation for the trip, but in his mind he was already on the way. From then on, everything he did revolved around obeying God's call.

Abraham was a sinful heathen who grew up in an unbelieving and idolatrous society. We do not know exactly how or when God first made Himself known to Abraham, but he was raised in a home that was pagan (Josh. 24:2). His native city of Ur was in Chaldea, in the general region called Mesopotamia, between the Tigris and Euphrates rivers. It was a fertile land and was culturally advanced. It was near where the Garden of Eden was located (cf. Gen. 2:14) and was some 140 miles from where the great city of Babylon would one day be built.

Isaiah refers to Abraham as "the rock from which you were hewn" and "the quarry from which your were dug" (Isa. 51:1-2), reminding his fellow Jews that God sovereignly condescended to call Abraham out of paganism and idolatry in order to bless him and the world through him. He may have had higher moral standards than his friends and neighbors, but this was not the reason God chose him. God chose him because He wanted to choose him. And when God spoke to him, he listened; when God promised, he trusted; when God commanded, he obeyed.

When any person comes to Jesus Christ, God demands of him a pilgrimage from his old pattern of living into a new kind of life, just as Abraham's faith separated him from paganism and unbelief and started him toward a new land and a new kind of life. "Therefore if any man is in Christ, he is a new creature; the old things passed away; behold, new things have come" (2 Cor. 5:17). Salvation brings separation from the world. The Lord works in the heart the total willingness to leave behind everything that is not pleasing to Him. He cannot lead us into new ways of living until He leads us out of the old. We should respond, "I don't know what You are going to do with me, Lord, but I'm going to drop all those old things. I don't know what You're going to substitute for them, but I'm going to let them go."

That is the attitude of the faith pilgrim. The life of faith begins with the willingness to leave one's Ur, one's own place of sin and unbelief—to leave the system of the world. "Do not be conformed to this world, but be transformed by the renewing of your mind, that you may prove what the will of God is, that which is good and acceptable and perfect" (Rom. 12:2; cf. 2 Cor. 6:14; Gal. 1:4).

Giving up the old life is one of the greatest obstacles to coming to Christ, and is also one of the greatest obstacles to faithful living once we are in Christ. From the perspective of the old life and the old nature the new life in Christ can appear dull and unexciting. When we think this way we fail to understand that, once we become a Christian, we are given a new set of values, interests, and desires—which we cannot experience in advance. We cannot "see" the blessings and satisfaction of life in Christ before we trust Him as Lord and Savior. We believe and then we experience. We must first be willing to "go out to Him outside the camp, bearing His reproach. For here we do not have a lasting city, but we are seeking the city which is to come" (Heb. 13:13). Often the reproach is all we are able to see at first. We look forward to the "city which is to come" by faith.

The force that makes us want to hold on to the old life is sometimes called *worldliness*. Worldliness may be an act, but primarily it is an attitude. It is wanting to do things that are sinful or selfish or worthless, whether we actually do them or not. It is wanting men's praise whether we ever receive it or not. It is outwardly holding to high standards of conduct, but inwardly longing to live like the rest of the world. The worst sort of worldliness is religious worldliness, because it pretends to be godly. It holds to God's standards outwardly (usually adding a few of its own), but it is motivated by selfish, worldly desires. It is pretentious and hypocritical. This was the Pharisees' great sin, as Jesus so often pointed out.

Worldliness is not so much what we do as what we want to do. It is not determined so much by what our actions are as by where our heart is. Some people do not commit certain sins only because they are afraid of the consequences, others because of what people will think, others from a sense of self-righteous satisfaction in resisting—all the while having a strong desire for these sins. It is the desire for sin that is the root of worldliness, and from which the believer is to be separated. "Do not love the world, nor the things in the world. If anyone loves the world, the love of the Father is not in him" (1 John 2:15; cf. James 4:4). The root meaning of holiness is separation, being set apart for God.

One of the surest marks of the demise of worldliness is a change in desires, in loves. As we grow in Christ and in love for Him, our love for the things of the world diminishes. They will simply lose their attraction. We will not *want* to do them like we used to. The pilgrimage of faith begins by separating ourselves from the world, and as we concentrate on Jesus and fellowship with Him, soon we do not care about the things we once loved so much. When we slip and engage in them, we hate what we do in the weakness of the flesh (cf. Rom. 7:14-25).

Paradoxical as it may seem at first, the highest mark of spiritual maturity is being able to do what we want to do. "By faith Moses, when he had grown up, refused to be called the son of Pharaoh's daughter; choosing rather to endure ill-treatment with the people of God, than to enjoy the passing pleasures of sin; considering the reproach of Christ greater riches than the treasures of Egypt; for he was looking to the reward" (Heb. 11:24-26). Moses did not forsake Egypt because he had to or because he felt obligated to, but because he wanted to. Egypt had lost its attraction. It could not compare with what Christ offered. In this regard the spiritually mature Christian is like the worldly person—he does what he wants to do. The great difference is that the mature Christian wants what God wants.

THE PATIENCE OF FAITH

By faith he lived as an alien in the land of promise, as in a foreign land, dwelling in tents with Isaac and Jacob, fellow heirs of the same promise; for he was looking for the city which has foundations, whose architect and builder is God. (11:9-10)

The second standard of faith mentioned here seems to be somewhat at odds with the first. As a pilgrim, Abraham was immediately willing to give up his homeland, his friends, his business, his religion—everything. He wasted no time putting all these things behind him. But faith also has a time for waiting and for being patient.

Dwelling in tents was the way of travelers and nomads. Even in Abraham's time, tents were not considered permanent residences. Not only Abraham but also his son and grandson, **Isaac and Jacob,** lived out their lives in tents. They were in the land God had promised, but they did not settle down in it. Those great patriarchs, in fact, would *never* possess the land, except by faith. The land was in sight but not in hand. Near as it was, the land was still only a promise. Abraham did not build any houses or cities. **He lived as an alien in the land of promise, as in a foreign land.**

As a transient in the land, he had to be patient. Because the land was promised to him, patience must have been all the harder. He may have needed patience in Haran, too. But he never expected to possess Haran; it was never promised. All the rest of his life, however, Abraham walked up and down the land God had promised him, yet never owned more than a small plot in which to bury Sarah (Gen. 23:9-20). It was promised but never possessed. Abraham's faith required a great deal of patience in order to live without grumbling as an alien in his own land.

Abraham waited patiently for the really valuable things. He never saw God's promise fulfilled; he just waited and waited and waited. Often the hardest times for us as believers are the in-between times, the times of waiting. We are tempted to say, even to God, "Promises! Promises!" Abraham spent a great deal of time waiting. He waited long years for the son of promise, who was finally given. He waited all his life for the land of promise, which was never given. Yet he waited and watched and worked in the patient belief that God is faithful.

If we knew that Christ would be coming in a month, we would give full attention to forsaking sin, praying, witnessing, serving, and to all the other things of our heavenly Father's business. To devote a whole month entirely to the Lord would not be so hard if we knew that it would all be over that soon. But to be about His business month after month, year after year, with His promises seemingly no nearer being fulfilled than when we were first saved, takes patience.

William Carey spent thirty-five years in India and saw only a handful of converts. Yet every Christian missionary who has gone to India since that time owes a debt to Carey. He planted so that they could harvest. He translated the Word of God into Indian dialects, so that virtually all missionary effort in India has been based to some extent on his pioneer work. Most of the fruits of his labor he saw only by faith. He had faith's patience and did not "grow weary in well-doing." "Be patient, therefore, brethren, until the coming of the Lord. Behold, the farmer waits for the precious produce of the soil, being patient about it, until it gets the early and late rains. You too be patient" (James 5:7-8).

It is discouraging to pray and trust and work and see no results. A mother may pray for 15, 20, or 30 years for the salvation of her son, and never see him come to Christ. A minister may serve in a church faithfully for ten years and see little evidence of spiritual growth. Noah worked for more than 100 years on the ark, preaching all the while. Progress on the ark was unimaginably slow and success in witnessing was nil. Yet he continued to build and to preach until both were finished. True faith is deaf to doubt, dumb to discouragement, and blind to impossibility. No matter what it experiences, it sees only the promised success.

The secret of Abraham's patience was his hope in the ultimate fulfillment of the promise of God. His ultimate Promised Land was heaven, just as ours is. Even had he possessed the land of Canaan in his lifetime, it would not have been his ultimate inheritance. He was patient because his eyes were on **the city which has foundations, whose architect and builder is God.** As important as the earthly land was to him and to God's promise, he looked up toward the heavenly land, which he knew he would inherit without fail.

In one sense it is possible "to be so heavenly minded that we are of no earthly good." But in a much deeper sense, it is impossible to be of any real earthly good unless we *are* heavenly minded. Only the heavenly minded will have the patience to continue faithful in God's work when it becomes hard, unappreciated, and seemingly unending. There is no greater cure for discouragement, fatigue, or self-pity than to think of being in the presence of the Lord one day and of spending eternity with Him. We should make no apology for being heavenly minded.

It is when we concentrate on things below that we live and die with every little thing that goes wrong or seems to last too long or is not successful or appreciated. That is why Paul tells us to set our minds "on the things above, not on the things that are on earth" (Col. 3:2). When our minds are on heaven we will be patient with what happens down here. If we look continually at the things of this world—its trials, troubles, and struggles on the one hand, or its money, fame, and pleasures on the other, then we cannot help becoming absorbed in the impatient desires of the flesh. But if we keep focusing on heaven, on God, on Jesus Christ, then we do not care about what goes on here. "Suffer hardship with me, as a good soldier of Christ Jesus," Paul tells Timothy. "No soldier in active service entangles himself in the affairs of everyday life, so that he may please the one who enlisted him as a soldier" (2 Tim. 2:3-4).

The divine city is called many things in Scripture, but perhaps its most encouraging name is the one Ezekiel gave it: "The LORD is there" (Ezek. 48:35). Of all the things about it that are beautiful and inviting, by far the most beautiful and most inviting is that the Lord is there.

Moses' forty years in the wilderness taking Israel to the Promised Land were the most demanding years of his life. But the previous forty years may have been the hardest as far as patience was concerned. He had been trained in pharaoh's court, treated as pharaoh's son, and then forced to flee for his life into the desert, where for this middle forty years he tended sheep for his father-in-law. He must often have been tempted to think that his talent, abilities, and training were going to waste. But "he endured, as seeing Him who is unseen" (Heb. 11:27). Like Abraham, Moses' eyes were on God, not his circumstances.

THE POWER OF FAITH

By faith even Sarah herself received ability to conceive, even beyond the proper time of life, since she considered Him faithful who had promised; therefore, also, there was born of one man, and him as good as dead at that, as many descendants as the stars of heaven in number, and innumerable as the sand which is by the seashore. (11:11-12)

Faith is powerful. Faith sees the invisible, hears the inaudible, touches the intangible, and accomplishes the impossible. Unfortunately, some faith is all talk and never really gets down to action. True faith is active, powerfully active.

Faith was active in the miracle of Isaac's birth. From the human standpoint, it was impossible for Abraham and Sarah to have a child. Not only had Sarah always been barren (Gen. 16:1), but by the time she was 90 years of age she was far **beyond the proper time of life** for child-bearing. Yet at that age she conceived and gave birth to the promised son (Gen. 21:2).

The Genesis account gives no indication that Sarah ever showed much faith in God. Both Abraham and Sarah, on different occasions, had laughed at God's promise of a son in their old age (Gen. 17:17; 18:12), but Sarah had even taken matters into her own hands by persuading Abraham to have a son by her maid, Hagar (16:1-4). She did not trust God's promise and was bent on doing things her own way, which, she soon found out, was not the way either of obedience or of happiness. Her idea and Abraham's acquiescence produced a son, Ishmael, whose descendants from that day to this have been a plague on the descendants of the son of promise. Ishmael became the progenitor of the Arabs and every Jew since his birth has faced the antagonism of the Arab world because of Abraham's and Sarah's disobedience. Sarah's impatience was costly.

If we study Hebrews 11:11 carefully, I believe we discover that the faith mentioned here does not apply *to* Sarah but rather *for* her. **Received ability to conceive** (*katabolēn spermatos*) means literally "to lay down seed." A woman, however, does not lay down the seed that produce conception. This phrase, therefore, must refer to Abraham, making him the understood subject of the sentence. Looking further at the Greek, we see that *autē* (**herself**) is a dative of accompaniment or association, and basically means only "self." The "her" is supplied by translators from the context. In other words, the verse could read, "he (that is, Abraham), in association with Sarah, received power to lay down seed." I believe the faith was Abraham's, not Sarah's. Through Abraham's faith God miraculously fulfilled His promise.

Therefore, also, there was born of one man, and him as good as dead at that, as many descendants as the stars of heaven in number, and innumerable as the sand which is by the seashore. (11:12)

Abraham had children upon children, the whole of the people of Israel. Every Jew that ever has been and ever will be born is a result of Abraham's faith. Such is the power of faith.

Abraham's faith was in God. God's promise of a special son and of innumerable descendants was the basis of Abraham's faith. Jesus said, "All things are possible to him who believes" (Mark 9:23), and "With God all things are possible" (Matt. 19:26). God's power and will are on one side and man's trust is on the other. Whatever we know to be God's will, faith has the power to accomplish.

If God is unable to meet any of our needs, it is simply because we do not entrust them to Him. He gives us many things for which we never ask and of which we are often unaware. But many other things, especially spiritual blessings He has promised, we cannot receive because we are not open to them. Paul claimed, "I can do all things through Him who strengthens me" (Phil. 4:13), and he reminds us of "Him who is able to do exceeding abundantly beyond all that we ask or think, according to the power that works within us" (Eph. 3:20). God's power is for us to claim according to His will. That the things claimed seem impossible has no bearing on the matter. The only hindrance to fulfillment is lack of faith.

THE POSITIVENESS OF FAITH

All these died in faith, without receiving the promises, but having seen them and having welcomed them from a distance, and having confessed that they were strangers and exiles on the earth. For those who say such things make it clear that they are seeking a country of their own. And indeed if they had been thinking of that country from which they went out, they would have had opportunity to return. But as it is, they desire a better country, that is a heavenly one.

Therefore God is not ashamed to be called their God; for He has prepared a city for them. (11:13-16)

Not Abraham, Isaac, or Jacob, ever possessed the Promised Land. In fact it was almost 500 years after Jacob died that Israel first began to possess Canaan. **All these died in faith, without receiving the promises.** Far from being a lament, however, this statement is a positive declaration that these men died in perfect hope and assurance of fulfillment. For the person of faith, God's promise is as good as the reality. His promise of the glory ahead was as encouraging and certain to the patriarchs as actually possessing it could have been.

These men of faith did not know what was happening. God had given them no inside information, no word as to when or how the promises would be fulfilled. He only gave the promises, and that was enough. They had a sampling of the Promised Land. They walked on it and pastured their flocks on it and raised their children on it, but they were not impatient to possess it. It was enough to possess it **from a distance,** because their primary concern was for a **better country, that is a heavenly one.**

In the meantime they were quite happy to be **strangers and exiles on the earth.** In the ancient world **strangers** (*zenoi*) were often regarded with hatred, suspicion, and contempt. They had few rights, even by the standards of that day. They were also **exiles** (*parepidēmoi*), pilgrims or sojourners. They were refugees in their own Promised Land. But these faithful patriarchs were passing through Canaan to a better place, and they did not mind.

The most positive thing about our faith is not what we can see or hold or measure, but the promise that one day we will forever be with the Lord. Christians whose faith does not extend to heaven will have their eyes on the things of this world and will wonder why they are not happier in the Lord. Nothing in this life, including God's most abundant earthly blessings, will give a believer the satisfaction and joy that come with absolute assurance of future glory.

David declared, "One thing I have asked from the LORD, that I shall seek: that I may dwell in the house of the LORD all the days of my life, to behold the beauty of the LORD" (Ps. 27:4). Job, after unbelievable trials, destitution, and illness, could say, "As for me, I know that my Redeemer lives, and at the last He will take His stand on the earth. Even after my skin is destroyed, yet from my flesh I shall see God" (Job 19:25-26). This is the hope and the security of the believer—the positiveness of faith.

It is people of such faith that God blesses. He **is not ashamed to be called their God, for He has prepared a city for them.** Regardless of what we are in ourselves, if we trust Him, God is not ashamed to be called our God. "Those who honor Me I will honor," God says (1 Sam. 2:30). The patriarchs honored God, and God honored them. Nothing is so honoring to Him as the life of faith. In fact, nothing honors Him *but* the life of faith.

THE PROOF OF FAITH

By faith Abraham, when he was tested, offered up Isaac; and he who had received the promises was offering up his only begotten son; it was he to whom it was said, "In Isaac your descendants shall be called." He considered that God is able to raise men even from the dead; from which he also received him back as a type. (11:17-19)

The proof of Abraham's faith was his willingness to give back to God everything he had, including the son of promise, whom he had miraculously received *because* of his faith. After all the waiting and wondering, the son had been given by God. Then, before the son was grown, God asked for him back, and Abraham obeyed. Abraham knew that the covenant, which could only be fulfilled through Isaac, was unconditional. He knew, therefore, that God would do whatever was necessary, including raising Isaac from the dead, to keep His covenant. **He considered that God is able to raise men even from the dead.** The thought of sacrificing Isaac must have grieved Abraham terribly, but he knew that he would have his son back. He knew that God would not, in fact could not, take his son away permanently, or else He would have to go back on His own word, which is impossible.

If Noah illustrates the duration of faith, Abraham shows the depth of faith. In tremendous, monumental faith Abraham brought Isaac to the top of Mt. Moriah and prepared to offer him to God. He believed in resurrection from the dead even before God revealed the doctrine. He had to believe in resurrection, because, if God allowed him to carry out the command to sacrifice Isaac, resurrection was the only way God could keep His promise.

As it turned out, because he did not actually die, Isaac became only a **type** of the resurrection. He was offered but he was not slain. God provided a substitute. It was the fact that Abraham **offered up Isaac** that proved his faith. The final standard of faith, its real proof, is willingness to sacrifice. "If anyone wishes to come after Me," Jesus commands, "let him deny himself, and take up his cross, and follow Me" (Matt. 16:24). "I urge you therefore, brethren, by the mercies of God, to present your bodies a living and holy sacrifice, acceptable to God, which is your spiritual service of worship" (Rom. 12:1).

When John Bunyan was in jail for preaching the gospel, he was deeply concerned about his family. He was particularly grieved about his little blind daughter, for whom he had a special love. He wrote, "I saw in this condition I was a man who was pulling down his house upon the head of his wife and children. Yet, thought I, I must do it; I must do it. The dearest idol I have known, what err that idol be, help me to tear it from Thy throne and worship only Thee."

The patriarchs, therefore, held to the five great standards of faith: its pilgrimage, in separation from the world; its patience, in waiting for God to work; its power, in doing the impossible; its positiveness, in focusing on God's eternal promise; and its proof, in obedient sacrifice.

Faith That Defeats Death (11:20-22)

By faith Isaac blessed Jacob and Esau, even regarding things to come. By faith Jacob, as he was dying, blessed each of the sons of Joseph, and worshiped, leaning on the top of his staff. By faith Joseph, when he was dying, made mention of the exodus of the sons of Israel, and gave orders concerning his bones. (11:20-22)

Matthew Henry said, "Though the grace of faith is of universal use throughout the Christian's life, yet it is especially so when we come to die. Faith has its great work to do at the very last, to help believers to finish well, to die to the Lord so as to honor Him, by patience, hope and joy so as to leave a witness behind them of the truth of God's Word and the excellency of His ways."

God is glorified when His people leave this world with their flags flying at full mast. If anyone should die triumphantly it should be believers. When the Holy Spirit triumphs over our flesh, when the world is consciously and gladly left behind for heaven, when there is anticipation and glory in our eyes as we enter into the presence of the Lord, our dying is pleasing to the Lord. "Precious in the sight of the LORD is the death of His godly ones" (Ps. 116:15).

The three patriarchs mentioned in Hebrews 11:20-22 illustrate the power of faith in facing death. These men had not always lived faithfully. They trusted God imperfectly, just as we do. All three men's names appear frequently and favorably in Scripture, and we are inclined to think of them as models of the life of faith. In some regards they were. Joseph especially stands out. Though he was hated by his brothers and sold into slavery, he trusted and obeyed God amid many temptations and hardships, while completely separated from his family in a pagan foreign land.

The emphasis of this passage, however, is on the faith that Isaac, Jacob, and Joseph exhibited at the ends of their lives. Each one faced death in full, confident faith. For that they are in the Hebrews heroes gallery.

Many believers find it difficult to anticipate and to face death. Yet a Christian who, for the most part, has walked with God faithfully often finds that the last hours of his life are the sweetest. Whatever the ups and downs of their lives, Isaac, Jacob, and Joseph went out basking in the sunlight of true faith.

What makes the dying faith of these three men so significant is that, like Abraham, they died without seeing the fulfillment of God's promises. They passed them on to their children by faith. They had received the promises by faith and they passed them on by faith. In His covenant with Abraham, God had promised three things—possession of the land of Canaan, the creation of a great nation of his descendants, and the blessing of the world through these descendants. But Abraham never saw any of these things come to pass. He died in faith, saying, "Isaac, you will see the beginnings of these promises." But Isaac also died in faith, saying the same thing to Jacob; and so Jacob also to Joseph. Hebrews 11:13 applies to all four men: "All these died in faith, without receiving the promises, but having seen them and having welcomed them from a distance, and having confessed that they were strangers and exiles on the earth." Yet they were so confident in God's word that they passed on the promises to their children. They believed what they had never seen, and they passed on what they had never seen to their children. That is the assurance of faith. They had no inheritance to pass on but the promises of God, and these they considered a great treasure to bequeath their children. They had not seen the land possessed, the nation established, or the world blessed, but they saw the promises, and that was enough.

These men never doubted that the promises would come true. They did not die in the despair of unfulfilled dreams, but in the perfect peace of unfulfilled promises, confident because they were God's promises. They knew by faith that God would fulfill the promises because they knew He was a covenant-keeping God and a God of truth. They died saying, "They will come. In God's time the fulfillments will come." They died defeating death, knowing that, even though they died, God's promises could not die. That is a magnificent kind of faith, the kind of faith God honors.

Just as the saints mentioned in verses 4-19, these three men are presented to show that the principles of salvation by faith and of pleasing God by faith did not originate with the New Covenant. Faith has always been the way, never works. Without a single exception, every man of God has been a man of faith. Not Abel, Enoch, Noah, Abraham, Isaac, Jacob, or Joseph was saved by works. All were saved by faith. Without faith it has *always* been impossible to please God (Heb. 11:6).

ISAAC'S FAITH

By faith Isaac blessed Jacob and Esau, even regarding things to come. (11:20)

Just as his father had done with him, Isaac passed on the blessings of God's promise to his sons **by faith.** He had absolute certainty that they would come to pass. For the time being, the promises *were* the inheritance, which the patriarchs cherished as much as most people cherish material possessions, fame, and power.

Isaac lived longer than any of the other patriarchs, yet less space in Genesis and Hebrews is devoted to him than to the others. Whereas Abraham, Jacob, and Joseph each have about twelve chapters in Genesis that center on them, Isaac has just over two—chapters 26 and 27 and about half of 25. Isaac was easily the least spectacular and the most ordinary of the four. He was less dynamic and colorful, being generally quiet and passive. And, overall, he probably had the weakest faith. We know more of his failures than of his successes.

Because of a famine, Isaac had moved his family to Gerar. While he was there, God spoke to him in a remarkable and encouraging vision. "Sojourn in this land and I will be with you and bless you, for to you and to your descendants I will give all these lands, and I will establish the oath which I swore to your father Abraham. And I will multiply your descendants as the stars of heaven, and will give your descendants all these lands; and by your descendants all the nations of the earth shall be blessed" (Gen. 26:3-4). In other words, the covenant promises to Abraham were passed on to Isaac directly by God. Those promises alone should have kept Isaac from worry and fear, for God could not have fulfilled them if Isaac were not protected. Not only that, but the Lord specifically told him, "I will be with you and bless you."

Yet at the first sign of possible danger, Isaac proved faithless. When the men of Gerar asked about Rebekah, he said she was his sister instead of his wife, for fear that one of those Philistines might kill him in order to have her (v. 7). In that, of course, he was merely following in his father's footsteps, because Abraham had twice lied in the same way about Sarah (Gen. 12:13; 20:2). Rebekah was beautiful and the Philistines were not above doing what Isaac feared. But rather than trusting the Lord for protection, he lied. Not only that, but he seems to have been more concerned for himself than for Rebekah.

God disclosed to King Abimelech Rebekah's true relationship to Isaac, and the king put them both under a protective order. Abimelech, a pagan Philistine, was more concerned about the ethics of the matter than was Isaac, a chosen man of God. He rebuked Isaac sharply, saying, "What is this you have done to us? One of the people might easily have lain with your wife, and you would have brought guilt upon us" (v. 10). God's grace prevailed, though it was through an unbeliever, with no help, or even expectation, from Isaac.

The Lord continued to bless Isaac, who became wealthy. The envy of the Philistines caused them to keep filling up his wells until he finally moved out of their land, which seems to have been what the Lord wanted all along. At that point Isaac acknowledged God's hand in the matter. "At last the LORD has made room for us, and we shall be fruitful in the land" (v. 22). Yet even this statement shows little faith, because Isaac seems to be saying, "It's about time!"

Then he moved to Beersheba, which was part of the Promised Land, and perhaps the Lord now said, "It's about time." He had to get Isaac back into the land by the back door and almost by force. Again the Lord spoke to Isaac and repeated the covenant promises, and Isaac "built an altar there, and called upon the name of the LORD, and pitched his tent there" (26:24-25). By His sovereign work, God brought the prodigal home. That is how grace operates.

Isaac often was cowardly and spiritually weak, but he had earlier believed God and was established in the scroll of the faithful. He followed his father's example in some good things as well as some bad. Like Abraham, he trusted God for a son. Rebekah was barren, just as Sarah had been, and Isaac prayed earnestly for a son. "The LORD answered him and Rebekah his wife conceived" (Gen. 25:21).

Isaac was basically materialistic. He lived mostly by sight and by taste. He was partial to Esau, possibly because this son was a hunter and provided his father with many good meals. Even when Isaac was old and about to die, he asked Esau to go out and kill "some game and prepare a savory dish" for him before he pronounced the blessing on this elder son (27:7). He was thinking more of his stomach than of God's promise. He must have known from Rebekah that God intended for Jacob to receive the inheritance rather than Esau (25:23), and he must have known from both his sons that Esau had sold his birthright to Jacob (25:33). Yet he was determined to give the blessing to Esau. This story is of no credit to

Isaac, Esau, or Jacob. Isaac insisted on giving the blessing to the son who he knew was not God's choice. Esau, who had despised and sold his birthright, thought he could just as easily buy it back. And Jacob, at his mother's instigation, tried to secure the blessing by deception rather than by faith. The entire family acted shamefully. Father and son tried to do the wrong thing in the wrong way, and mother and son tried to accomplish the right thing but in the wrong way. God produced the outcome that Rebekah and Jacob wanted, but not for their reasons or by their methods. He did not honor what they did any more than what Isaac and Esau did. God only honors faith, and none of these had acted in faith. The right outcome was the result of His faithfulness, not theirs.

Not until the irreversibility of the blessing was obvious did Isaac begin to evidence faith. If Jonah was the reluctant prophet, Isaac was the reluctant patriarch. Only when he realized that the blessing was going to be on God's man regardless, did he acquiesce. He finally said yes to God's way. God had to box him into a corner before he believed; but he did believe. As he faced death, he blessed Jacob with the blessing that neither he nor his father had possessed and that neither Jacob nor his sons would possess. Isaac blessed Jacob in faith, knowing that God would fulfill the promises in His own way and in His own time.

In some ways Isaac was a blot on the Old Testament record. But in the end he was God's man. He submitted and believed and obeyed.

JACOB'S FAITH

By faith Jacob, as he was dying, blessed each of the sons of Joseph, and worshiped, leaning on the top of his staff. (11:21)

Jacob's life was like his father's in many ways. It was up and down spiritually. Sometimes he walked by faith and sometimes he stumbled by sight. He had times of great faith and times of fear and anxiety. He bargained with God on occasion (Gen. 28:20-21) and on other occasions he readily acknowledged God's blessing (31:5). He reverently praised the Lord when he had the dream of the heavenly ladder (28:16-17), and once he was so intent on receiving God's blessing that he wrestled with Him all night (32:24-26).

Unlike his father, Jacob did not try to circumvent God's plan for his heirs. Joseph, though younger than all his brothers except Benjamin, was the chosen son to bless, just as Jacob, though younger, was chosen above Esau. In fact Joseph received a double blessing, in that his two sons, Ephraim and Manasseh, were both **blessed;** although again the younger son, Ephraim, received the greater blessing (48:19). Consequently, instead of only one tribe descending from Joseph, as with his brothers, two tribes (often referred to as half-tribes) descended from him.

As he was dying, Jacob blessed his son through his two grandsons. "Then Israel [Jacob's new name] said to Joseph, 'Behold, I am about to die, but God will be with you and bring you back to the land of your fathers. And I give you one portion more than your brothers" (48:21-22). Once again, what was never possessed was passed on in faith. Jacob died as a man of faith.

JOSEPH'S FAITH

By faith Joseph, when he was dying, made mention of the exodus of the sons of Israel, and gave orders concerning his bones. (11:22)

Joseph spent all of his adult life in Egypt. Though a fourth-generation heir of the promise, he could not claim even to have sojourned in the Promised Land, much less to have inherited it. It had been some two hundred years since God made the initial covenant with Abraham. Two hundred years of promise, and no fulfillment in sight. In fact, by the time of Joseph's death, *none* of Abraham's descendants (that is, the descendants of promise) lived in the Promised Land at all. Because of the famine in Canaan, Joseph had brought his father and his brothers to Egypt. Jacob was carried back to Canaan after he died, and Joseph would be satisfied if only **his bones** could be buried there. If he could not inherit the land, at least the land could "inherit" him. It was not until the Exodus that Joseph's bones were actually taken to Canaan (Ex. 13:19), but his heart and his hope had always been there.

He had to look ahead to see the promise, yet he saw it clearly and confidently. "I am about to die, but God will surely take care of you, and bring you up from this land to the land which He promised on oath to Abraham, to Isaac and to Jacob" (Gen. 50:24). While he was making his brothers swear to take his bones back to Canaan, he repeated the assuring words of faith, "God will surely take care of you" (v. 25).

All three of these men believed God in the face of death. Their faith had sometimes wavered in life, but it was strong and confident in death. Death is the acid test of faith. For hundreds, perhaps thousands, of years, courts of law have taken a dying man's word at face value. The need for lying and deception is over, and what is said on a deathbed is usually believed. So with our testimony of faith. Not only is the need for hypocrisy and pretense over, but it is extremely difficult to fake faith when you know you are facing eternity. A dying man's faith is believable because a sham cannot stand this test.

A Christian who fears death has a serious weakness in his faith, for to die in Christ is simply to be ushered into the Lord's presence. "For to me, to live is Christ," Paul says, "and to die is gain" (Phil. 1:21). For those who believe, "Death is swallowed up in victory" (1 Cor. 15:54).

Moses: The Decisions of Faith (11:23-29)

By faith Moses, when he was born, was hidden for three months by his parents, because they saw he was a beautiful child; and they were not afraid of the king's edict. By faith Moses, when he had grown up, refused to be called the son of Pharaoh's daughter; choosing rather to endure ill-treatment with the people of God, than to enjoy the passing pleasures of sin; considering the reproach of Christ greater riches than the treasures of Egypt; for he was looking to the reward. By faith he left Egypt, not fearing the wrath of the king; for he endured, as seeing Him who is unseen. By faith he kept the Passover and the sprinkling of the blood, so that he who destroyed the first-born might not touch them. By faith they passed through the Red Sea as though they were passing through dry land; and the Egyptians, when they attempted it, were drowned. (11:23-29)

Life is made up of decisions. Some are simple and unimportant, and some are complex and extremely important. Many are made almost unconsciously, whereas others we think about carefully for a long time. Some decisions are made by default. When we put off deciding, a decision is made for us. But it is still our decision, because we decide to put it off. The course and the quality of our lives are determined much more by our decisions than by our circumstances.

Christian living involves making right decisions. You can note the maturity of a Christian by the decisions he makes. Holiness is making right decisions, carnality is making wrong ones. Our Christian living rises or falls in maturity and holiness on the basis of the decisions we make. When Satan tempts us, we decide either to say yes or no. When we have opportunity to witness, we either take advantage of it or we do not. We decide whether or not to take time to read the Bible and to pray. It is not a matter of having time but of taking time, and taking time requires a decision. In business we often have to choose between making more money and being honest and ethical, or between getting ahead and giving enough time to our families and to the Lord's work. Virtually everything we do involves a decision.

Shakespeare said,

> There is a tide in the affairs of men,
> Which, taken at the flood, leads on to fortune;
> Omitted, all the voyage of their life
> Is bound in shallows and in miseries.

Napoleon believed there is a crisis in every battle, a period of ten to fifteen minutes on which the outcome depends. To take advantage of this period is victory, to lose it is defeat.

Everything in a believer's life is an opportunity to glorify God. The ancient Greeks had a statue called Opportunity. The front of the figure had long flowing hair, but the back of its head was bald—symbolizing the fact that we can grasp an opportunity as it comes toward us, but once it is past there is nothing to hold on to.

Since the beginning of time, God has given men choices that determine their lives. The first man to choose was Adam. He made the wrong choice, and started the tragic chain of wrong choices that has plagued his descendants ever since.

Speaking to Israel in the wilderness, God said, "I call heaven and earth to witness against you today, that I have set before you life and death, the blessing and the curse. So choose life in order that you may live, you and your descendants" (Deut. 30:19). At Shechem, Joshua charged the people, "Choose for yourselves today whom you will serve" (Josh. 24:15). And on Mt. Carmel, Elijah asked the wavering Israelites, "How long will you hesitate between two opinions? If the LORD is God, follow Him; but if Baal, follow him" (1 Kings 18:21).

Abel chose God's way by offering the proper sacrifice, and was blessed. Cain rejected God's way by offering his own kind of sacrifice, and was cursed. Enoch chose God's way by walking with Him all his life, and God took him directly to heaven. Noah and his family chose God's way by continually obeying Him, and they were saved from the Flood. Everyone else on earth rejected God's way and was drowned. Abraham chose God's way by believing Him, regardless of how things looked from his own perspective, and he was counted righteous. Others in his day rejected God's way and died in their sins. Isaac, Jacob, and Joseph chose God's way, and they exhibited faith that conquered death. The unbelieving peoples around them chose another way and death conquered them.

Right choices are made on the basis of right faith. Often we cannot see the consequences of our choices. Satan tries to make his way seem attractive and good and God's way seem hard and unenjoyable. When we know God's will in a matter, we choose it by faith. We know it is the right choice because it is God's will, even before we see the results. God's will is the only reason we need. When we choose God's way, we put up the shield of faith, and the temptations and allurements of Satan are deflected (Eph. 6:16).

The opposite of choosing God's way is always Satan's way, and not believing God is believing Satan. Whenever we sin, we believe Satan; we believe that his way is better than God's. We believe the father of lies above the Father of truth.

Moses lived most of his life before the covenant of Mt. Sinai, with its system of commandments and rituals. But both before and after Sinai he lived by faith, not by works. No person in Scripture, other than Jesus, illustrates the power of right decision better than Moses. His decisions were right because his faith was right. Because Moses received the covenant from God at Sinai, he was always associated with God's law. This law, in fact, was often referred to as the law of Moses. In the Jewish mind he was associated with commandments, rituals, and ceremonies—with all the religious requirements and works of the Old Covenant. But he was a man who lived by faith.

Because to the Jews Moses ranks as one of the most respected Old Testament figures, to show that he lived by faith, not legalism, is one of the most powerful arguments possible to convince Jews that God's way has always been the way of faith.

The life of Moses illustrates both positive and negative decisions of faith, the things it accepts and the things it rejects. Hebrews 11:23-29 mentions three things that faith accepts and four that it rejects.

FAITH ACCEPTS GOD'S PLANS

By faith Moses, when he was born, was hidden for three months by his parents, because they saw he was a beautiful child; and they were not afraid of the king's edict. (11:23)

To stem the population explosion among the Hebrew slaves in

Egypt, the pharaoh gave an edict that all male babies were to be drowned in the Nile. To protect their newborn son, Amram and Jochebed first hid him for three months, and then put him in a waterproofed basket and placed him in the Nile near the place where Pharaoh's daughter bathed. He was found by the princess and taken to be raised as her own child. Moses' sister, Miriam, was watching and persuaded the princess to get one of the Hebrew women to nurse the infant. Miriam, of course, got her mother, who was then able to raise her own son almost as if he had been at home.

Moses' parents, Amram and Jochebed, **were not afraid of the king's edict.** They ignored the pressures and threats of the world when these conflicted with God's way. That their concern was for more than just a **beautiful child,** is indicated in Stephen's sermon before the Sanhedrin. "Moses . . . was lovely in the sight of God" (Acts 7:20). Not only Moses' parents, but also God Himself, had a special affection for this child. I believe that Moses' parents were somehow aware of God's special concern, for **by faith** in God they hid him and opposed Pharaoh's order. It was for God's sake, as well as for Moses' and their own sakes, that the baby was protected.

Moses' parents were willing to risk their own lives to follow God's way. Their decision was clear: save the child, whatever the consequences. Saving Moses was more than their own will, it was also God's will. We have no way of knowing how much they knew about God's plan for the destiny of their son, but it was enough for them to know that He had a special reason for Moses' protection.

It took considerable faith to put Moses in the basket and to trust that Pharaoh's daughter, of all people, would take pity on this baby, which she immediately recognized as a Hebrew. It also took faith to believe that, if he were adopted by the princess, he would be raised in the way of the Lord rather than in the occultic paganism of Egypt. From a human perspective, his parents had no way of knowing even that his life would be spared, much less that, for all purposes, he would be given back to them. Yet they willingly let him go, entrusting him to God.

Jochebed nursed Moses and trained him and taught him Israel's promises from God—that they were to inherit the land of Canaan and be a great nation and bless the world. She instilled in him God's promise of a great deliverer, the messianic hope in which Abraham had rejoiced (John 8:56). His mother helped build in him the faith that was to become characteristic of his life. She did not fully know why God allowed her son to be raised in the court of Egypt, within the very household of the one who wanted him and all the other male Hebrew babies slain. She knew, however, that this was in God's plan and, unlike Sarah, did not try to adjust His plan to her own.

Trying to improve on God's plan is more pretentious than taking a felt-tipped pen and trying to improve the Mona Lisa. Our scribbling would do nothing but ruin the masterpiece. God needs our obedience, not our help, our trust, not our counsel. He makes the plans; we walk in them by faith.

FAITH REJECTS THE WORLD'S PRESTIGE

By faith Moses, when he had grown up, refused to be called the son of Pharaoh's daughter. (11:24)

For forty years Moses had been a prince of Egypt, the wealthiest, most cultured, and advanced society of that day. He was therefore highly educated and skilled, as well as being a part of the royal court. "And Moses was educated in all the learning of the Egyptians, and he was a man of power in words and deeds" (Acts 7:22). His formal education would have included learning to read and write hieroglyphics, hieratic, and probably some Canaanite languages. He had, of course, learned Hebrew from his mother. He could enjoy everything Egypt had to offer. But his training in Egypt never blunted his knowledge of the hope of Israel and of the promises of God.

When Moses reached the age of forty, he faced a crucial decision. He had to decide between becoming a full-fledged Egyptian, with absolute loyalty and no reservations, and joining his own people, Israel.

The deciding factor was his faith in God. **By faith Moses . . . refused to be called the son of Pharaoh's daughter.** In all those years he had never wavered in his devotion to the Lord. Somehow God also indicated to him that he had been chosen for special service and that, from then on he would be an Israelite first and only. Again we learn from Stephen that Moses knew he had a mission to perform for God and for his people. "And he supposed that his brethren understood that God was granting them deliverance through him; but they did not understand" (Acts 7:25). The people of Israel did not understand his mission, but he did. They were slaves in the land that had once highly honored them because of Joseph. Moses was now in a position similar to Joseph's, but God had a much different work for him to do. Joseph used Egypt's power for the good of God's chosen people. Moses would have to oppose Egypt's power for the same purpose.

In the world, fame always brings a certain amount of honor. If you are born into the right family or are a successful athlete or entertainer, the world will think of you as great, whether you are or not. If you have a lot of money, regardless of how you got it, the world will hold you in high esteem. If you have enough degrees behind your name, certain people will think you have arrived. The same is true in regard to political power and many other types of human success. Moses had most of these things, yet he gave them up.

From the worldly standpoint, he was sacrificing everything for nothing. But from the spiritual standpoint, he was sacrificing nothing for everything. He renounced the world's power, honor, and prestige for the sake of God, and knew that for so doing he would gain immeasurably more than he would lose, **for he was looking to the reward** (v. 26).

The things the world counts great have nothing to do with what God considers great. He honors people on a totally different basis. He is not interested in what family we came from or how much money we have or how much education we have or what positions we hold. These are not related to His primary concerns for us.

Jesus told of a man who was greater than all the pharaohs. He was even greater than Noah, Abraham, Moses, David, or Elijah. He was greater than any person in the Old Testament. His birth was announced by an angel, who told his father, "He will be great in the sight of the Lord, . . . and he will be filled with the Holy Spirit, while yet in his mother's womb. And he will turn back many of the sons of Israel to the Lord their God" (Luke 1:15-16). Jesus said that no one born of woman had ever lived who was greater than this man—John the Baptist (Matt. 11:11).

John was born into a simple family. His father, Zacharias, was a priest, but was far from being famous or influential. His mother, Elizabeth, was the cousin of Mary, Jesus' mother; but in that day the relationship was hardly a distinction. John may not have had much education. He spent his early adult years in the desert, and "was clothed with camel's hair and wore a leather belt around his waist, and his diet was locusts and wild honey" (Mark 1:6). He had absolutely nothing to qualify him for greatness in the eyes of the world. Yet in God's eyes, he was the greatest person ever born before the birth of the Son of God.

John the Baptist was great because he was obedient to God, because he was filled with the Spirit, and because he won many of God's chosen people to the Lord. John loved the Lord, not the world. "Do not love the world, nor the things in the world. If anyone loves the world, the love of the Father is not in him, . . . but the one who does the will of God abides forever" (1 John 2:15, 17). As long as we can break with God in order to protect our worldly interests, we are not living by faith. The strength of faith is proved by self-denial.

Baron Justinian von Weltz renounced his title, estates, and income, and went as a missionary to what was then Dutch Guiana. Today his body lies there in a lonely grave, and he is forgotten by the world. But we can be sure he is not forgotten by God. As he was preparing to go into missionary service he said, "What is it to me to bear the title 'well-born,' when I am born again to Christ? What is it to me to have the title 'lord,' when I desire to be the servant of Christ? What is it to be called, 'your grace,' when I have need of God's grace? All these vanities I will away with and all else I will lay at the feet of my dear Lord Jesus."

Moses cared nothing for his Egyptian heritage or advantages. They were both pagan and worldly, and he had given himself to much greater things.

The world has little to offer compared to the riches and satisfaction of Christ. Moses gladly joined with God's chosen people, though they were slaves, rather than take advantage of the prestige and privileges of Egypt and be unfaithful to God.

FAITH REJECTS THE WORLD'S PLEASURE

Choosing rather to endure ill-treatment with the people of God, than to enjoy the passing pleasures of sin. (11:25)

No one needs to be convinced that sin is often fun. It can feed our pride, satisfy physical desires and appetites, and offer many other pleasures. But it has two characteristics that the world does not notice: it is always evil and it is always **passing.** And, no matter how temporarily satisfying it may be, its satisfaction is destined to fade. It has no good in it and it can bring no good to us, to anyone else, or to God. Any seeming good is both deceptive and fleeting.

Sometimes we wonder why unbelievers, worldly people, the grossly immoral, and sometimes even criminals seem to get along so well. They are successful, famous, wealthy, healthy—well-off in practically every way. On the other hand, many of God's most faithful saints are poor, sickly, unsuccessful in business, and ridiculed. We want to ask with Job, "Why do the wicked still live, continue on, also become very powerful? Their descendants are established with them in their sight, and their offspring before their eyes, their houses are safe from fear, neither is the rod of God on them" (Job 21:7-9). He goes on to mention how successful they are in ranching, how their children are healthy and happy, and how they are carefree and always celebrating. "They spend their days in prosperity," and even "say to God, 'Depart from us! We do not even desire the knowledge of Thy ways. Who is the Almighty, that we should serve Him, and what would we gain if we entreat Him?' " (see Job 21:10-15).

We want to plead with Jeremiah, "Why has the way of the wicked prospered? Why are all those who deal in treachery at ease?" (Jer. 12:1). The psalmist had the same question. "Behold, these are the wicked; and always at ease, they have increased in wealth. Surely in vain I have kept my heart pure" (Ps. 73:12-13). He was asking, "Why is it that they are wicked and wealthy and I am pure but poor?"

Job answers the question when he says, "And suddenly they go down to Sheol" (21:13). They die and it is all over, except for judgment. They enjoy and get by with sin for a while, but only for a while. Zophar, one of Job's three counselor friends, was right in one point: "The triumphing of the wicked is short, and the joy of the godless momentary" (Job 20:5). If we take James seriously, we will not envy the wicked, of whom he writes, "You have lived luxuriously on the earth and led a life of wanton pleasure; you have fattened your hearts in a day of slaughter. You have condemned and put to death the righteous man; he does not resist you" (James 5:5-6). But he precedes these comments with, "Come now, you rich, weep and howl for your miseries which are coming upon you. Your riches have rotted and your garments have become moth-eaten. Your gold and your silver have rusted; and their rust will be a witness against you and will consume your flesh like fire. It is in the last days that you have stored up your treasure!" (5:1-3). The wicked are going to inherit a "treasure" of judgment they do not expect. As Paul says in Romans 2:5-6, they are piling up wrath that will break loose in the day of divine judgment.

David learned the hard way that sinful pleasure is both brief and disastrous. For the pleasure of having Bathsheba for himself, he first committed adultery and then had her husband killed. Later in his life he cried, "I know my transgressions, and my sin is ever before me" (Ps. 51:3). He watched his infant son, the product of his relationship with Bathsheba, die. He saw another son, Absalom, rebel against him and be hanged. David's sin was short-lived in pleasure but long-lived in consequences.

Moses knew God was calling him to give his life for his people. He had a choice. He could have obeyed or disobeyed. Disobeying had many attractions. Among other things, it would have been a lot easier and a lot more enjoyable in the short run. It is hard enough to stop seeking worldly things. It is even harder to give them up once we have them, and Moses had a great many of them by the time he was forty. We have no reason to believe that he was ever involved in any immoral practices, but he enjoyed the pleasures of an extremely comfortable life. He had the best food, the best living quarters, the best recreation, the best of everything that his age could provide. These were not sins in themselves. Joseph had enjoyed the same pleasures in the same place, while being perfectly obedient to God. But they would have been sin for Moses, had he decided to stay in the Egyptian court, and he forsook them for the sake of God's call. He made a conscious choice to **endure ill-treatment with the people of God,** rather **than to enjoy the passing pleasures of sin.** This was an act of faith. He believed that if He did what God wanted, he would be be immeasurably better off in the end.

God has called us all to holiness. He has called us to come apart from sin. Obedience is not always easy, but in the end sin is much, much harder. God's way is not only for His own honor but for our own good. Satan's way is for *his* honor and for our harm.

FAITH REJECTS THE WORLD'S PLENTY

Considering the reproach of Christ greater riches than the treasures of Egypt; for he was looking to the reward. (11:26)

Living in Pharaoh's palace, Moses had everything material he could have wanted. He had more than enough food, possessions, and money. Discoveries such as the tomb of King Tutankhamen, who lived only a hundred or so years after Moses, have shown us how vastly rich Egypt was at its peak. Moses had access to a great deal of wealth, and likely had much in his own possession. He had all the things the world holds dear. He must have been strongly tempted to hold on to them; but he did not.

Considering (*hēgeomai*) involves careful thought, not quick decision. Moses thought through his decision, weighing the pros and cons. He weighed what Egypt had to offer against what God offered. When he reached a conclusion it was well-founded and certain. God's offer was infinitely superior in every way. In the eyes of the world no **reproach** (being ridiculed and persecuted) would be worth sacrificing riches for. Yet Moses believed that the worst he could endure for Christ would be more valuable than the best of the world.

It is interesting that the writer of Hebrews speaks of Moses' **considering the reproach of Christ,** since he lived nearly 1500 years before Christ. *Christ* is the Greek form of *Messiah,* the Anointed One. Many of God's special people in the Old Testament are spoken of as being anointed. Anointing set aside a person for special service to the Lord. It is possible, therefore, that Moses was thinking of himself as a type of messiah, a deliverer. If so, verse 26 could read, "considering the reproach of his own messiahship as God's deliverer, . . ." It is also possible that the reference is to Moses as a type of Christ, just as Joseph and Joshua are types of Christ.

I believe, however, that the meaning is just as it seems to be in most translations—with "Christ" capitalized. That is, Moses suffered reproach for the sake of Jesus Christ, the true Messiah, because he identified with Messiah's people and purpose long before Christ came to earth. Every believer since Adam's fall has been saved by the blood of Jesus Christ, no matter in what age he has lived. It is also true, therefore, that any believer at any time who has suffered for God's sake has suffered for Christ's sake. In a sense, David suffered just as surely for Christ's sake as did Paul. In one of his psalms, David says, "The reproaches of those who reproach Thee have fallen on me" (Ps. 69:9). From the other side of the cross Paul made a similar statement: "I bear on my body the brand-marks of Jesus" (Gal. 6:17). The Messiah has always been identified with His people. In a very real sense, when Israel suffered, Messiah suffered, and when Moses suffered, He suffered. In their afflictions on His behalf, He was afflicted. A comparison of Matthew 2:15 with Hosea 11:1 shows that Messiah is identified intimately with His people. Hosea refers to Israel, Matthew to Jesus Christ. Both Israel and Christ are the son called out of Egypt.

All Christians should willingly bear the same reproach. "Hence, let us go out to Him outside the camp, bearing His reproach" (Heb. 13:13). Everyone who has stood with God by faith, who has lived for Him and turned his back on the world's plenty and gone the way of God's direction, has received the reproach of God and of His Anointed, His Christ. It belongs to all who suffer for God's sake. The church bears the reproach of Christ. After being flogged by the Sanhedrin, the apostles "went on their way from the presence of the Council, rejoicing that they had been considered worthy to suffer shame for His name" (Acts 5:41). Moses would have agreed with what Peter wrote: "If you are reviled for the name of Christ, you are blessed, because the Spirit of glory and of God rests upon you" (1 Pet. 4:14). Moses rejected the treasures of Egypt and took his stand with God's Anointed.

We do not know how much Moses knew about God's future great Deliverer. But he had considerably more light than Abraham, and Jesus tells us plainly that Abraham looked forward to Jesus' day and rejoiced (John 8:56). In the same way, Moses looked forward to Jesus.

God's **reward** is always greater than the world's. "God shall supply all your needs according to His riches in glory in Christ Jesus" (Phil. 4:19). He supplies *according to* His riches, not just *out of* them. A millionaire who gives ten dollars to help someone in need is giving out of his riches but not according to them. If he gave a hundred thousand dollars, however, he would be giving according to his riches. Moses surely saw the reward of a blessed life, but the emphasis is best seen as being on the eternal reward.

"Better is the little of the righteous than the abundance of many wicked" (Ps. 37:16). It is not a sin to be rich, but it is a sin to want to be rich. If we work hard and honestly and to God's glory, and become wealthy in the process, fine. But if we set our minds on getting rich, we have the wrong motivation. Paul told Timothy, "For the love of money is a root of all sorts of evil, and some by longing for it have wandered away from the faith, and pierced themselves with many a pang. But flee from these things, you man of God; and pursue righteousness, godliness, faith, love, perseverance and gentleness" (1 Tim. 6:10-11). In other words, if along the way God happens to make us rich, wonderful. If in His wisdom he keeps us poor, also wonderful. It should make us no difference, as long as we are in His will. It made Moses no difference. For forty years he enjoyed the riches of Egypt. For the rest of his life, he forsook them, because they interfered with his obedience to God and would have prevented his receiving immeasurably greater riches when it came time for eternal rewards.

Portia, a beautiful and wealthy heiress, is the heroine of Shakespeare's *Merchant of Venice*. She had many suitors of noble birth who wanted to marry her. But her father's will decreed that her husband would be chosen by a certain test. She would belong to the one who chose the right chest out of the three that were prepared. One chest was made of gold. On it was inscribed, "Who chooseth me shall gain what many men desire," and inside was a skull. The second chest was of silver, with the inscription, "Who chooseth me shall get as much as he deserves," and inside was the picture of a fool. The winning chest was made of lead and held Portia's picture. On the outside was the inscription, "Who chooseth me must give and hazard all he hath." All of her suitors but Bassanio chose one of the first two chests, because both the precious metals and the inscriptions were so attractive. Bassanio picked the one of lead and got Portia's hand in marriage, because he was willing to give everything he had for the sake of the one he loved.

That is the attitude every Christian should have about Christ. We should be willing to forsake and hazard all we have for the sake of God's will, knowing with Moses and with Paul that our "momentary, light affliction is producing for us an eternal weight of glory far beyond all comparison" (2 Cor. 4:17; cf. Rom. 8:18).

FAITH REJECTS THE WORLD'S PRESSURE

By faith he left Egypt, not fearing the wrath of the king; for he endured, as seeing Him who is unseen. (11:27)

The first time he left Egypt, Moses was fleeing from the pharaoh, who wanted to kill him for slaying the Egyptian slavemaster (Ex. 2:15). The second time he left Egypt, another pharaoh wanted to keep Moses from taking the children of Israel with him. In both cases he was in trouble.

In addition to his problems with the kings, Moses faced other pressures. For one thing, he was under pressure to preserve the prestige, pleasure, and plenty that have already been discussed. The prospects of desert living could not have been very appealing. When he fled for his life, he had no idea that he would marry a shepherdess and tend her father's sheep for the next forty years in Midian. But at best, he knew life in the desert could not begin to compare with life in Egypt's royal court.

The greatest pressure Moses faced, however, was fear, because of **the wrath of the king.** It is the same fear, though perhaps of a different sort and source, that believers may face on occasion. Fear is one of Satan's most effective, and therefore most used, weapons. We are afraid of being thought different, or of losing our job, reputation, or popularity. We are afraid of criticism, often from people that we do not even respect.

Moses was doubtlessly tempted to fear, but he did not. He **left** Egypt with full determination to follow a better way. In this context, the King James translation seems more appropriate—"By faith he forsook Egypt." He did more than simply leave; he turned his back on Egypt and all that it represented. He renounced it permanently. Like Peter, James, and John (Luke 5:11), Moses forsook everything to follow the Lord. He was not thwarted or delayed or intimidated by Satan's fear. He had put his hand to the plow and would not look back. He is joined in the Old Testament by another fearless man of God—Daniel. He, too, was uncompromising, and he inspired his three friends to be the same (Dan. 1-2).

Fear had worked on Abraham on several occasions. He was also afraid of being killed by an Egyptian king, and some years later by a Philistine king, because of his beautiful wife, Sarah. He thought they might want her for themselves and kill him in order to have her. In both cases he lied instead of trusting God (Gen. 12:12; 20:2). Aaron became afraid of the people while Moses was on Mt. Sinai and yielded to their insistence on making the golden calf (Ex. 32:1-5). Ten of the twelve spies sent into Canaan gave a negative and exaggerated report about the dangers of the inhabitants, and the Israelites became afraid (Num. 13:32-33). Gideon's army was afraid and 22,000 were discharged (Judg. 7:3). The disciples were afraid of the storm at sea and were rebuked by Jesus for their lack of faith (Mark 4:38-40). Peter was afraid of criticism and arrest, and he denied Jesus three times (John 18:17, 25, 27).

Fear is a great pressure, and all of us are tempted at times to bend when standing for the Lord requires us to say or do something that is unpopular or dangerous. But true faith does not fold under the world's pressure.

Fear did not work on Moses, at least not when God called him out of Egypt. He knew he had an invisible but powerful means of support, **as seeing Him who is unseen.** He knew that, no matter what happened, whatever he had to face, he would be held up and strengthened and rewarded. He believed with David, "The LORD is my light and my salvation; whom shall I fear? The LORD is the defense of my life; whom shall I dread?" (Ps. 27:1).

When Moses wanted to leave Egypt the second time and take all the people of Israel with him, he not only met the resistance of the king but of his own people. When he first told them of God's plan of deliverance, they were thankful (Ex. 4:31). But when Pharaoh made things worse on them every time Moses made a demand, they lost heart and turned against Moses' leadership (6:9; 14:11-12). Now he had both the king and his own people against him. But he was afraid of neither. He continued to say what God wanted him to say and do what God wanted him to do.

Moses was the kind of man he was because he chose to focus his sights on God rather than on a monarch in Egypt. Yet how many times do we fall apart or back down in face of a much lesser threat. When we are afraid of the world, when we are afraid of what people will say or do, we are exposing ourselves to God's displeasure and discipline for lack of faith. Faith rejects the world's pressure, whatever it may be.

FAITH ACCEPTS GOD'S PROVISION

By faith he kept the Passover and the sprinkling of the blood, so that he who destroyed the first-born might not touch them. (11:28)

Here is the second of three things faith accepts. This is the positive side of making right decisions. True faith accepts the Lord's provision as well as His plan. (See discussion above under 11:23.)

The tenth and last plague that God sent on the Egyptians was the death of all first-born (Ex. 11:5). To protect the Israelites from this plague the Passover was instituted, in which a lamb's blood was sprinkled on the doorposts and lintels of their houses (12:7). Obviously the blood itself had no power to stave off the death angel, but sprinkling it as God had commanded was an act of faith and obedience and the blood was symbolic of Christ's sacrifice by which He conquered death for all who believe in Him. The people of Israel, including Moses, did not understand the full significance of the ceremony, but they knew it was part of God's plan. God required it and they obeyed. Moses accepted God's provision. Faith always accepts God's provision, no matter how strange and pointless it may seem to human understanding.

When a believer accepts Jesus Christ by faith, he accepts God's provision for salvation. To the world, good works seem like a much better way to please God than faith. But the world's way is not God's way. To Him, "All our righteous deeds are like a filthy garment" (Isa. 64:6). Faith accepts Christ's righteousness applied on our behalf. This is God's way, and is therefore faith's way.

FAITH ACCEPTS GOD'S PROMISE

By faith they passed through the Red Sea as though they were pass-

ing through dry land; and the Egyptians, when they attempted it, were drowned. (11:29)

Finally, in addition to God's plan and provision, faith accepts God's promise. When Moses and his people got to the Red Sea, Pharaoh and his army were not far behind. From all they could see they were trapped; there was no escape. At first the people lost heart and complained sarcastically to Moses, "Is it because there were no graves in Egypt that you have taken us away to die in the wilderness?" (Ex. 14:11). But they took heart again when Moses told them, "Do not fear! Stand by and see the salvation of the LORD which He will accomplish for you today; . . . The LORD will fight for you while you keep silent" (vv. 13-14). For a while at least they trusted God, and **by faith they passed through the Red Sea as though they were passing through dry land.**

They believed Moses' promise from God and started walking across the seabed as soon as the waters were parted. This took considerable faith, since the waters piled up on either side must have seemed terribly threatening. Had the waters returned too soon, Israel would have drowned instead of the Egyptians. The people had no guarantee except God's word that He would not change His mind or forget them. But His word was enough. For the faithful, God's word is always enough.

Faith takes God at His word and is victorious. Presumption denies God's word and is destroyed. The Egyptians persistently hardened their hearts to the Lord and presumed to trust themselves, and they drowned. The test of faith is trusting God when all we have are His promises. When the waters are piled high all around us and problems and dangers are about to overwhelm us, this is when faith is tested, and when the Lord takes special pleasure in showing us His faithfulness, His love, and His power. When we have nothing but His promise to rely on, His help is the nearest and His presence the dearest to those who believe.

At every juncture in our lives, we either fulfill the will of God and are filled with His Spirit, or we fulfill our own will and quench the Spirit. When we truly believe God, we will know that in *everything* He has our best interest at heart, and we will always decide for Him.

The Courage of
Faith (11:30-40)

32

By faith the walls of Jericho fell down, after they had been encircled for seven days. By faith Rahab the harlot did not perish along with those who were disobedient, after she had welcomed the spies in peace.

And what more shall I say? For time will fail me if I tell of Gideon, Barak, Samson, Jephthah, of David and Samuel and the prophets, who by faith conquered kingdoms, performed acts of righteousness, obtained promises, shut the mouths of lions, quenched the power of fire, escaped the edge of the sword, from weakness were made strong, became mighty in war, put foreign armies to flight. Women received back their dead by resurrection; and others were tortured, not accepting their release, in order that they might obtain a better resurrection; and others experienced mockings and scourgings, yes, also chains and imprisonment. They were stoned, they were sawn in two, they were tempted, they were put to death with the sword; they went about in sheepskins, in goatskins, being destitute, afflicted, ill-treated (men of whom the world was not worthy), wandering in deserts and mountains and caves and holes in the ground. And all these, having gained approval through their faith, did not receive what was promised, because God had provided some-

thing better for us, so that apart from us they should not be made perfect. (11:30-40)

Faith is trusting completely in God's Word. It is unconditional confidence in what He says, strictly on the basis that He has said it. The fact is that we either trust what God says or we are left to trust our own intellect, instincts, and attitudes. These are our only two options. Our own way is the way of unbelief; God's way is the way of faith.

The faith illustrated in Hebrews 11 is that which takes the bare word of God and acts on it, risking all. It is faith that does not question or ask for signs or miraculous direction. Looking for signs and wonders and explanations that we can understand or glory in is not faith. It is doubt looking around for proofs. Anything that demands more than God's Word is doubt, not faith. God sometimes gives explanations and reasons for His Word, but He is not obligated to give them, and faith does not require them. As Jesus said to Thomas, "Blessed are they who did not see, and yet believed" (John 20:29). Faith is therefore opposite from human nature, opposite from the world system. It often requires accepting from God that for which we can see no logic or reason.

For a Jew to become a Christian in the first century was nearly always costly. It often cost him his friends, family, synagogue privileges, job, social status, and community respect. It also cost the ceremonies, rituals, and traditions which Jews held so dear—including some that had been instituted by God for a certain time. The Jews receiving this epistle were tempted to try to keep a foot in both worlds, to accept Christianity while holding onto as much of Judaism as possible. Some were trying to take the voyage of the New Covenant while keeping their boats securely tied to the dock of the Old.

Such reluctant Jews are being shown in this chapter that God's faithful followers in the Old Testament were not like them. When those Old Testament faithful decided for God, it was everything for Him, because they had the right view of who God is. Right faith is based on right theology. Faith believes and obeys God because faith knows that God cannot lie, cannot make a mistake, cannot do wrong, cannot be defeated, cannot be surpassed. A God like this can be trusted. In fact, with a God like this, it does not make sense to do anything else but trust and obey Him. Unbelief, of course, is blind to this sort of God and therefore sees trust and obedience as foolish. It walks by sight.

Faith, then, is based on a person's attitude toward God. As J.B. Phillips observes in his book, *Your God is Too Small*, if we have a tiny god, we should *not* trust him. Only the true God, the great sovereign, loving, faithful, omniscient, omnipotent, and holy God of Scripture, deserves trust. It is because the heroes of Hebrews 11 knew *this* God that they trusted Him so completely.

Perhaps the supreme mark of true faith is courage. It is not so hard to believe and follow God when things are going well, when most of the people around us are believers, and when our faith costs little. Faith is proved when it faces disaster, trial, persecution, and ridicule—and still stands unwavering. Faith is the source of courage. We do not have great faith by having great courage, we have great courage when we have great faith. Certainly Moses demonstrated this courage in facing Pharaoh. But the writer chooses other models of the courage of faith.

Hebrews 11:30-40 shows us three ways in which courage demonstrates faith: it conquers in struggle, continues in suffering, and counts on salvation.

CONQUERING IN STRUGGLE

Life is always a struggle for the believer. God's way is not the world's way, and as long as the believer is in the world he will have to struggle in that conflict. The only effective weapon he has in this struggle is faith. It is because of faith that many of our struggles come, and it is only by faith that our struggles can be faced and conquered.

JOSHUA AND THE ISRAELITES AT JERICHO

By faith the walls of Jericho fell down, after they had been encircled for seven days. (11:30)

The **walls of Jericho** were massive structures. Some city walls of this period were wide enough at the top to drive two chariots on side-by-side. Jericho was a frontier fortress city, located strategically near the mouth of the Jordan River, and its walls were designed to protect it from the strongest enemy attack. By the standards of that day, it was virtually impregnable.

Forty years had passed since Israel had crossed the Red Sea by faith (v. 29), and that was the last faithful act of any consequence that they had collectively exhibited. The trip through the wilderness of Sinai that should have required much less than forty weeks took forty years, because God judged the sin of the older generation by forcing them to die out. Their gross unbelief, manifested in their grumbling discontent and idolatry, made them unworthy of entering the Promised Land. Nothing in that forty years was worth mentioning in a chapter on faith. Only as Israel came to Jericho did she show faith again.

Jericho was the first obstacle in Canaan, and from the human perspective seemed an impossible obstacle to the ragtag multitude of ex-slaves who had been wandering in circles in the wilderness for so many years. Its location was strategic, its walls were high and thick, and its soldiers were well-trained and well-armed.

The negative report of the ten spies who had helped scout out the land was not inaccurate. It was somewhat exaggerated, but was basically correct: "The people are bigger and taller than we; the cities are large and fortified to heaven" (Deut. 1:28). Moses rebuked them not because the report was erroneous but because of the unbelieving and fearful way in which it was given and received. "Do not be shocked, nor fear them. The LORD your God who goes before you will Himself fight on your behalf, just as He did for you in Egypt before your eyes" (vv. 29-30). The real obstacle was not Canaan but unbelief. The only difficulty for God was getting His own people to go with Him.

God would later use the army of Israel to conquer the land, but His plan for Jericho was for the people to do nothing more than a few symbolic acts—to show them, as well as the Canaanites, how powerful He is. All the Israelites had to do was march around the city once a day for six days, with seven priests in front carrying rams' horns before the ark. The seventh day they were to march around seven times, with the priests blowing their horns. When the priests finally made one loud blast, all the people were to shout, and then "the wall of the city will fall down flat" (Josh. 6:3-5). The people obeyed in faith, and the walls fell as predicted.

Militarily, the seven days of marching demanded nothing. But psychologically they demanded a great amount of courage. The scheme must have been embarrassing to Israel. This is not the way cities are conquered. The entire effort appeared utterly preposterous to the inhabitants of Jericho, and probably even to many of the Israelites. It is often easier to fight than to have faith. If we fight, we will at least have a certain respect from the world, even if we lose. But faith always looks foolish in the eyes of the world.

One of the most amazing things about Joshua 6 is that not a single word of doubt or complaint is recorded. The Israelites believed Joshua's report from the Lord, and they immediately began to prepare for the marching (v. 8). For a full week they carefully and faithfully marched. It was a milestone of faith in the life of Israel.

God delights in slaying men's pride. He slew the pride of the city of Jericho by making its city walls collapse in the most foolish possible way, just as some years later He would send a little boy to kill the giant Goliath and send the Philistines running. In the defeat of Jericho, He also demolished any pride the Israelites might have had. It was obvious that their part was purely symbolic. They could take absolutely no credit for themselves. All God wanted from them was faith, and this they gave, for **by faith the walls of Jericho fell down.**

Someone has said there are four types of faith. There is faith that *receives,* as when we come empty-handed to Christ for salvation. There is faith that *reckons,* that counts on God to undertake for us. There is faith that *risks,* that moves out in God's power, daring to do the impossible. And there is faith that *rests*—the kind that, in the middle of pain and suffering and rejection, sits back in confidence that God will deliver.

In the fall of Jericho we see the faith that risks. The people of Israel were willing to do everything and to risk everything, because they believed God. In exact compliance with God's instruction, they marched, blew the horns, and shouted. They did not add anything or leave anything out. They simply obeyed.

The great missionary Robert Moffatt worked for years in Bechuanaland in South Africa without seeing a single convert. When some friends in England wrote asking what they might send him as a present, he requested a communion set. Since there were no other believers there, they were surprised, but complied with his wishes. When the set arrived several months later, more than a dozen natives had been won to Christ and were served their first Lord's Supper. Such is the beauty and courage of faith.

Whether the obstacle is direct opposition, apathy, ridicule, or whatever, every Christian runs into his Jerichos and his Bechuanalands. If we trust the Lord, and demonstrate our trust by courageously continuing to do what the Lord has called us to do, in God's time the obstacle will fall.

RAHAB

By faith Rahab the harlot did not perish along with those who were disobedient, after she had welcomed the spies in peace. (11:31)

Rahab was an unlikely candidate for the faithfuls' hall of fame. For one thing, she was a prostitute. For another, she was a Gentile, and a Canaanite at that. She was, in fact, an Amorite, a race that God had long before marked for destruction (Gen. 15:16). Yet that is how God's grace works. His mercy is open to all who will receive it, and His grace has always been wider than Israel, even in Old Testament times.

Rahab had no more light than any other inhabitant of Jericho; yet she believed, while the others disbelieved. They were more than simply unbelieving, they **were disobedient.** The implication is that they not only knew that the true God was with Israel but that He had also called them (that is, the Jerichoites) in some way. Yet they rejected God's word. They had wanted to kill the Israelite spies, but Rahab had **welcomed the spies in peace.** They were prepared to fight Israel when she attacked the city, but Rahab again welcomed God's people. For her faith, she and her family were spared. For their disbelief, all the others in the city were destroyed.

The destruction of the Canaanites was as great a social as it was a spiritual gain to the welfare of humanity. They were a debauched, idolatrous, and wicked people. They were noted for their grossly immoral and perverted sexual practices as well as for their general cruelty. Among other things, they frequently put live babies in jars and built them into their city walls as foundation sacrifices. They were begging for judgment.

In the midst of this pagan unbelief, Rahab believed, and confessed, "The LORD your God, He is God in heaven above and on earth beneath" (Josh. 2:11). And in the midst of barbaric cruelty, she was kind and **welcomed the spies in peace.** She staked her life on the fact that God had said He would save and protect His people, Israel, and she wanted to be on His side. She had faith's courage.

For her faithful courage Rahab not only was spared but was honored. She became the mother of Boaz, who married Ruth, the great-great-grandmother of David, and she thereby came to be an ancestor of Jesus (Matt. 1:5).

MANY OTHERS

And what more shall I say? For time will fail me if I tell of Gideon, Barak, Samson, Jephthah, of David and Samuel and the prophets, who by faith conquered kingdoms, performed acts of righteousness, obtained promises, shut the mouths of lions, quenched the power of fire, escaped the edge of the sword, from weakness were made strong, became mighty in war, put foreign armies to flight. (11:32-34)

The six men named, who are not listed in chronological order, were all rulers of one kind or another. Several are outstanding Bible characters, while the others are less known. Samuel was both a judge and a prophet, and David was a king and a prophet. But none of the men is praised for his office. All are praised for what they accomplished by faith.

Gideon, a judge and military leader, had assembled 32,000 men to fight the Midianites and the Amalekites. To keep Israel from thinking the coming victory was by her own power, God cut her forces down to 10,000 and then to a mere 300. These 300 were separated out solely on the basis of how they drank water from a spring. The enemy, by contrast, were "as numerous as locusts; and their camels were without number, as numerous as the sand on the seashore" (Judg. 7:12). Yet Gideon's men were outfitted only with trumpets and with pitchers with torches inside. With even fewer men and less effort than used to defeat Jericho, the entire heathen enemy army was routed (7:16-22). Only a fool would have attempted such a courageous approach to battle apart from God's direction and power. From the perspective of faith, only a fool would *not* attempt such a thing when he *has* God's direction and power.

Barak is unknown in Scripture outside the brief account in Judges 4-5 and the mention of his name in Hebrews 12:32. We are told nothing of his background or training. Through Deborah, the judge, God promised that Israel would be delivered from Jabin, the Canaanite king, whose great commander, Sisera, had a large, powerful army that boasted 900 iron chariots. According to the Lord's instruction, Deborah asked Barak to assemble an Israelite force of only 10,000 men, taken from two tribes, Naphtali and Zebulun. The rest of the tribes were not asked to participate, apparently to show Israel, and the Canaanites, that God could be victorious with only a token army from a small part of Israel. Barak assembled his men on Mt. Tabor and charged Sisera as he had been commanded by God. "And the LORD routed Sisera and all his chariots and all his army, with the edge of the sword before Barak" (Judg. 4:15). Barak and his men were involved, and probably fought valiantly, but the success of the campaign was the Lord's. Without His help, Israel would easily have been slaughtered. Barak was told in advance that the glory of victory would not be his. Not only did the Lord fight the battle for His people, but he allowed a woman to kill Sisera, so that Barak would have even less cause for claiming credit for himself (4:9).

Barak believed God's promise of victory and was not the least concerned that a woman would get credit for slaying Sisera. In fact he insisted that Deborah, a woman judge, go to battle with him (v. 8). He wanted her spiritual, not her military, help. She was the Lord's special representative in those days, and Barak wanted the Lord's person with him. The fact that he wanted her along was another indication of his trust in the Lord. As God's prophetess, she was of greater value to him than his 10,000 men. Barak was not concerned about Sisera's power, because he had God's power. By such courageous faith he **conquered kingdoms.**

Samson is not most remembered for his faith, but for his physical strength and personal gullibility. In many ways he was immature and self-centered, unable to cope with the miraculous power God had given him. Yet he was a man of faith. He never doubted that God was the source of his power, of which his hair was only a symbol.

Samson was a judge of Israel and was given the special task of opposing the Philistines, who then ruled over Israel. Samson's own motives for fighting the Philistines were often mixed, but he knew he was doing the Lord's will in the Lord's power. From his early manhood the Spirit of the Lord had been with him, and we are told specifically that it was the Spirit that strengthened him in his amazing one-man battles (Judg. 13:25; 14:19; 15:14; 16:28).

Samson knew that God had called him and that God had empowered him to "begin to deliver Israel from the hands of the Philistines," just as He had told Samson's mother before her son was even conceived (13:5). God had promised him power and Samson trusted God for that power. He faced the Philistines not in the courage of physical prowess but in the courage of faith.

We are inclined to judge Samson by his weaknesses. But God commends him for his faith.

Jephthah preceded Samson as judge of Israel, and his responsibility was to subdue the Ammonites, one of Israel's many enemies. Despite his foolish vow (Judg. 11:30-31), Jephthah's trust was in the Lord, and his power was from the Lord (vv. 29, 32). Even people of faith make mistakes, and God honored Jephthah for his faith.

David stands out as one of the obviously great men of the Old Testament. His trust in the Lord began when he was a boy, tending sheep, killing lions and bears, and taking on Goliath with a slingshot. David faced Goliath in utter confidence that the Lord would give him power to defeat this giant. While the rest of Israel, including the king and David's own brothers, were cowering in fear, David calmly walked up to Goliath and announced, "This day the LORD will deliver you up into my hands, and I will strike you down and remove your head from you" (1 Sam. 17:46). It seems never to have occurred to David not to trust the Lord.

Like the other heroes of faith, David was not perfect, but God called him "a man after My heart, who will do all My will" (Acts 13:22). He pleased God because of the courage of his faith to trust Him and do His will.

Samuel is added to this list of warriors, though he was not a warrior. But he fought a battle equal to any that soldiers face. His great foes were idolatry and immorality. He had to stand up in the middle of a polluted society and fearlessly speak God's truth. His severest opponents frequently were not the Philistines, the Amorites, or Ammonites—but his own people. It often takes more courage to stand up against our friends than against our enemies. Social pressure can be more frightening than military power. This prophet of God, who was also Israel's last judge, began "ministering before the LORD, as a boy wearing a linen ephod" (1 Sam. 2:18) and continued faithful to God throughout his life. In the courage of faith, he ruled and prophesied.

The prophets are unnamed except for Samuel. As the writer mentions in the opening of verse 32, he does not have time to go into detail about the many other faithful people of the Old Covenant, or even to mention them all by name. These prophets, just as Gideon, Barak, and the others, risked everything for the Lord. They cheerfully, courageously, and confidently accepted God's commands and faced whatever opposition came along. They did not fight on battlefields, but they had many victories in the Lord because they believed Him. They, too, conquered through the courage of faith.

The exploits of 11:33-34 are general and refer collectively to the persons in verse 32. **The mouths of lions** may refer to Daniel, and **quenched the power of fire** to Shadrach, Meshach, and Abed-nego. The point of mentioning these works is to show that, whether the need was for political victory, helping those in need, receiving promises, overcoming natural enemies, protection from war or weakness, or winning in war—the power to accomplish these things was from God and the power was received by faith in Him.

Continuing in Suffering

Women received back their dead by resurrection; and others were tortured, not accepting their release, in order that they might obtain a better resurrection; and others experienced mockings and scourgings, yes, also chains and imprisonment. They were stoned, they were sawn in two, they were tempted, they were put to death with the sword; they went about in sheepskins, in goatskins, being destitute, afflicted, ill-treated (men of whom the world was not worthy), wandering in deserts and mountains and caves and holes in the ground. (11:35-38)

Elijah brought back to life the child of the widow of Zarephath (1 Kings 17:8-23), and his successor, Elisha, did the same for a Shunammite woman's son (2 Kings 4:18-37). These mothers and these prophets believed God for resurrection, and He performed it.

The **women** suffered for a while, but the pain was alleviated when their children were restored to life. God does not always work in this way, however. Many of the afflictions mentioned in Hebrews 11:35-38 were long-term, even lifetime. God gave power through faith to see some of His people through these problems, not to escape them. Just as it is sometimes God's will for His people to conquer in a struggle, it is also sometimes His will for His people to continue in their suffering. He will give them victory, too, but it may only be spiritual—the only kind of victory He guarantees. It often takes more courage to hold on than to fight on, and where there is need for more courage there is need for more faith.

Sometimes affliction is inescapable; sometimes it is not. To the person of faith, no affliction is escapable that requires denial or compromise of God's Word. What is easily escaped for the worldly person is not for the faithful. When it is suffered because of God's Word and standing for Him, God's people will take torture, **not accepting their release, in**

order that they might obtain a better resurrection. Here is the pin-
nacle of faith, willingness to accept the worst the world has to offer—
death—because of trust in the best God has to offer—resurrection.

Tortured is from the Greek *tumpanizō*, from the same root as the
English tympani, a kettledrum. The particular torture referred to involved stretching the victim over a large drum-like instrument and beating him with clubs, often until dead. God's faithful are willing to be beat-
en to death rather than compromise their faith in Him. They would not
sacrifice the future on the altar of the immediate. They preferred being
put to death, because by faith they knew that one day they would be
resurrected.

They endured both mental and physical anguish, mockings as
well as scourgings. Jeremiah was as emotionally abused as he was physically abused, and it is not strange that he was called the weeping prophet.
He did not weep so much for himself as for the people, who rejected God
by rejecting him. He endured, and continued to endure, all sorts of pain
for the sake of God's Word.

Tradition holds that Isaiah was sawn in two. The people became
so irritated at his powerful preaching that they cut him in half. Like Abel,
however (11:4), he continues to speak even after death.

The many kinds of suffering mentioned in these verses, just as the
conquests mentioned in the preceding verses, apply generally to the faithful saints. They are a summary of the many and varied kinds of affliction
God's people face and are often called to endure for Him. Whether they
were killed or made outcasts, the point is the same—they courageously
and uncompromisingly suffered for the Lord because of their faith.
Whether for conquering in a struggle or continuing in suffering, they
trusted the Lord.

The world is not worthy of having such people in its midst, just
as these people did not deserve the sufferings they received. For its inflicting the suffering, the world will be judged and punished; for their
enduring the suffering the faithful saints will be resurrected and rewarded. They knew with Paul that "the sufferings of this present time are not
worthy to be compared with the glory that is to be revealed to us" (Rom.
8:18), and they looked forward with Peter to "an inheritance which is
imperishable and undefiled and will not fade away, reserved in heaven" (1
Pet. 1:4).

God does not promise His saints deliverance from all suffering. To
the contrary, Jesus told us to take up our crosses and to follow Him
(Mark 8:34), and that "if they persecuted Me, they will also persecute
you" (John 15:20). Both Paul (Phil. 3:10) and Peter (1 Pet. 4:13) advise us
to rejoice in our sufferings for Christ's sake. Paul told the Corinthian
believers, "I am overflowing with joy in all our affliction" (2 Cor. 7:4).

Shadrach, Meshach, and Abed-nego were perfectly confident that

God would save them from the blazing furnace. "Our God whom we serve is able to deliver us from the furnace of blazing fire; and He will deliver us out of your hand, O king" (Dan. 3:17). But their greatest faith was not shown in their certainty of deliverance. They went on to say, "But even if He does not, let it be known to you, O king, that we are not going to serve your gods or worship the golden image that you have set up" (v. 18). Their primary concern was not for the safety of their lives but for the safety of their faith. Physical deliverance or not, they would not forsake their trust in God.

COUNTING ON SALVATION

And all these, having gained approval through their faith, did not receive what was promised, because God had provided something better for us, so that apart from us they should not be made perfect. (11:39- 40)

True faith has the courage to count on salvation. These faithful saints had to live in hope. They knew very little about the nature or the time or the means of God's salvation. But they knew it was coming, and this was the basis of their trust. They had abiding confidence that one day God would do the necessary thing to redeem them and reward them. What happened to them before that time was not consequential. They **did not receive what was promised** but they had **gained approval through their faith.** Their faith was not in some immediate fulfillment, but in the ultimate fulfillment of the promises. Here is where faith is most tested and where it most matters.

The ultimate promise was of a redeemer, the Messiah, and of His covenant that would bring righteousness before God. "As to this salvation, the prophets who prophesied of the grace that would come to you made careful search and inquiry, seeking to know what person or time the Spirit of Christ within them was indicating as He predicted the sufferings of Christ and the glories to follow" (1 Pet. 1:10-11). **All these,** from Enoch through the prophets, had that courageous faith which counts, without reservation, on final salvation.

Many of them never received the land. Sometimes they had earthly victory; sometimes they did not. Sometimes their faith saved them from death; sometimes it brought them death. No matter. They knew that **God had provided something better.**

God has provided this "something better" **for us,** that is for those under the New Covenant, which is why **apart from us they should not be made perfect.** That is, not until our time, the time of Christianity, could their salvation be completed, made perfect. Until Jesus' atoning work on the cross was accomplished, no salvation was complete, no matter how great the faith a believer may have had. Their salvation was based on what Christ would do; ours is based on what Christ has done. Their faith looked forward to promise; ours looks back to historical fact.

Yet, though their salvation was not completed in their lifetimes, these were not second-rate believers. They were believers of the highest order. They courageously struggled, suffered, and counted on salvation. They believed all of God's Word that they had, which is what counts with Him. How much less faith do we often have, in spite of our much greater light. "Blessed are they who did not see, and yet believed" (John 20:29).

Run for Your Life
(12:1-3)

Therefore, since we have so great a cloud of witnesses surrounding us, let us also lay aside every encumbrance, and the sin which so easily entangles us, and let us run with endurance the race that is set before us, fixing our eyes on Jesus, the author and perfecter of faith, who for the joy set before Him endured the cross, despising the shame, and has sat down at the right hand of the throne of God. For consider Him who has endured such hostility by sinners against Himself, so that you may not grow weary and lose heart. (12:1-3)

Effective teaching makes use of figures of speech, and we find a great many of them, especially metaphors and similes, in the Bible. In the New Testament the Christian life is repeatedly compared to everyday things, events, or practices.

Several times, for example, Christian living is compared to warfare. Paul counsels us to endure hardship "as a good soldier of Jesus Christ" (2 Tim. 2:3) and to "put on the full armor of God" (Eph. 6:11). Paul also uses boxing as a comparison. "I box in such a way, as not beating the air" (1 Cor. 9:26; cf. 2 Tim. 4:7). The Christian is often spoken of as a slave of Jesus Christ. Paul frequently refers to himself as a slave, or bond-servant, of Christ, and in several of his letters he introduces himself first of all as a bond-servant (Rom. 1:1; Phil. 1:1; Titus 1:1). Jesus spoke of His followers as lights and salt in the world (Matt. 5:13-16). Peter refers to Christians as babes and as living stones (1 Pet. 2:2, 5).

Paul was particularly fond of the figure of the race. He uses such phrases as "run in a race" (1 Cor. 9:24), "running well" (Gal. 5:7), and "run in vain" (Phil. 2:16). This is also the figure used by the writer in Hebrews 12:1-3.

In these few verses we see various aspects of the race, as they are compared to the faithful life in Christ: the event itself, encouragement to run, encumbrances to running, an Example to follow, the end or goal of the race, and a final exhortation.

THE EVENT

Therefore, since we have so great a cloud of witnesses surrounding us, let us also lay aside every encumbrance, and the sin which so easily entangles us, and let us run with endurance the race that is set before us. (12:1)

The key phrase of this passage is **let us run with endurance the race that is set before us.** In the book of Hebrews, as in many places in the New Testament, "let us" may refer to believers, to unbelievers, or to both. As a matter of courtesy and concern, an author frequently identifies himself with those to whom he is writing, whether or not they are fellow Christians.

In Hebrews 4 (vv. 1, 14, 16), for example, I think unbelievers are being addressed. Similarly, 6:1 speaks of unbelievers going on to the maturity of salvation. In 10:23-24, the reference can be both to believers and unbelievers.

In 12:1, I believe "let us" may be used to refer to Jews who have made a profession of Christ, but have not gone all the way to full faith. They have not yet begun the Christian race, which starts with salvation—to which the writer is now calling them. The truths, however, apply primarily to Christians, who are already running.

The writer is saying, "If you are not a Christian, get in the race, because you have to enter before you can hope to win. If you are a Christian, run with endurance; don't give up."

Unfortunately, many people are not even in the race, and many Christians could hardly be described as running the race at all. Some are merely jogging, some are walking slowly, and some are sitting or even lying down. Yet the biblical standard for holy living is a race, not a morning constitutional. **Race** is the Greek *agōn*, from which we get agony. A race is not a thing of passive luxury, but is demanding, sometimes grueling and agonizing, and requires our utmost in self-discipline, determination, and perseverance.

God warned Israel, "Woe to those who are at ease in Zion, and to those who feel secure in the the mountain of Samaria" (Amos 6:1). God's people are not called to lie around on beds of ease. We are to run a race that is strenuous and continuous. In God's army we never hear "At ease." To stand still or to go backward is to forfeit the prize. Worse yet is to stay in the stands and never participate at all, for which we forfeit everything—even eternal heaven.

Endurance (*hupomonē*) is steady determination to keep going. It means continuing even when everything in you wants to slow down or give up. I can still remember the excruciating experience I had in high school when I first ran the half-mile. I was used to the 100-yard dash, which requires more speed but is over quickly. So I started out well; in fact I led the pack for the first 100 yards or so. But I ended dead last, and almost felt I *was* dead. My legs were wobbly, my chest was heaving, my mouth was cottony, and I collapsed at the finish line. That is the way many people live the Christian life. They start out fast, but as the race goes on they slow down, give up, or just collapse. The Christian race is a marathon, a long-distance race, not a sprint. The church has always had many short-spurt Christians, but the Lord wants those who will "make the distance." There will be obstacles and there will be weariness and exhaustion, but we must endure if we are to win. God is concerned for steadfastness.

Many of the Hebrew Christians to whom the letter was written had started well. They had seen signs and wonders and were thrilled with their new lives (Heb. 2:4). But as the new began to wear off and problems began to arise, they began to lose their enthusiasm and their confidence. They started looking back at the old ways of Judaism, and around them and ahead of them at the persecution and suffering, and they began to weaken and waver.

Paul knew some Christians in the same condition, and to them he wrote, "Prove yourselves to be blameless and innocent, children of God above reproach in the midst of a crooked and perverse generation, among whom you appear as lights in the world" (Phil. 2:15) and "Do you not know that those who run in a race all run, but only one receives the prize? Run in such a way that you may win. And everyone who competes in the games exercises self-control in all things. They then do it to receive a perishable wreath, but we an imperishable" (1 Cor. 9:24-25).

Nothing makes less sense than to be in a race that you have little desire to win. Yet I believe the lack of desire to win is a basic problem with many Christians. They are content simply to be saved and to wait to go to heaven. But in a race or in a war or in the Christian life, lack of desire to win is unacceptable.

Paul believed this principle and he had a *hupomonē* kind of determination. He did not pursue comfort, money, great learning, popularity, respect, position, lust of the flesh, or anything but God's will. "Therefore I run in such a way, as not without aim; I box in such a way, as not beating the air; but I buffet my body and make it my slave, lest possibly, after I have preached to others, I myself should be disqualified" (1 Cor. 9:26-27). That is what Christian commitment is all about.

The competition of the Christian life, of course, is different from that of an athletic race in two important ways. First, we are not to compete against other Christians, trying to outdo each other in righteousness, recognition, or accomplishments. Ours is not a race of works but a race of faith. Yet we do not compete with each other even in faith. We compete *by* faith, but not with each other. Our competition is against Satan, his world system, and our own sinfulness, often referred to in the New Testament as the flesh. Second, our strength is not in ourselves, but in the Holy Spirit; otherwise we could never endure. We are not called on to endure in ourselves, but in Him.

The Christian has only one way to endure—by faith. The only time we sin, the only time we fail, is when we do not trust. That is why our protection against Satan's temptations is "the shield of faith" (Eph. 6:16). As long as we are trusting God and doing what He wants us to do, Satan and sin have no power over us. They have no way of getting to us or of hindering us. When we run in the power of God's Spirit, we run successfully.

THE ENCOURAGEMENT TO RUN

Therefore, since we have so great a cloud of witnesses surrounding us, (12:1*a*)

We are all creatures of motivation. We need a reason for doing things and we need encouragement while we are doing them. One of the greatest motivations and encouragements to the unbelieving Jews, as well as to Christians, would be all these great believers from the past, their heroes, who lived the life of faith. The **cloud of witnesses** are all those faithful saints just mentioned in chapter 11. We are to run the race of faith like they did, always trusting, never giving up, no matter what the obstacles or hardships or cost.

They knew how to run the race of faith. They opposed Pharaoh, they forsook the pleasures and prerogatives of his court, they passed through the Red Sea, shouted down the walls of Jericho, conquered kingdoms, shut the mouths of lions, quenched the power of fire, received back their dead by resurrection, were tortured, mocked, scourged, impris-

oned, stoned, sawn in two, had to dress in animal skins, were made destitute—all for the sake of their faith.

Now the writer says, "You should run like they did. It can be
done, if you run as they did—in faith. They ran and ran and ran, and they
had less light to run by than you have. Yet they were all victorious, every
one of them."

I do not believe that the **cloud of witnesses surrounding us** is
standing in the galleries of heaven watching as we perform. The idea here
is not that we should be faithful lest they be disappointed, or that we
should try to impress them like a sports team trying to impress the fans in
the bleachers. These are witnesses *to* God, not *of* us. They are examples,
not onlookers. They have proved by their testimony, their witness, that
the life of faith is the only life to live.

To have a whole gallery of such great people looking down on us
would not motivate us but paralyze us. We are not called to please them.
They are not looking at us; we are to look at them. Nothing is more
encouraging than the successful example of someone who has "done it
before." Seeing how God was with them encourages us to trust that He
will also be with us. The same God who was their God is our God. The
God of yesterday is the God of today and tomorrow. He has not weakened, or lost interest in His people, or lessened His love and care for
them. We can run as well as they did. It has nothing to do with how we
compare with them, but in how our God compares with theirs. Because
we have the same God, He can do the same things through us if we trust
Him.

THE ENCUMBRANCES THAT HINDER US

Let us also lay aside every encumbrance. (12:1b)

One of the greatest problems runners face is weight. Several years
ago the winner of a recent Olympic gold medal for the 100 meters came
to our country for an invitational track meet. He was considered the
world's fastest human being. But when he ran the preliminary heat, he
did not even qualify. In an interview afterward he said the reason was
simple. He was overweight. He had trained too little and eaten too much.
He had not gained a great amount of weight, but it was enough to keep
him from winning—even from qualifying. Because of a few pounds, he
was no longer a winner. In that particular race, he was not even qualified
to compete.

An **encumbrance** (*onkos*) is simply a bulk or mass of something.
It is not necessarily bad in itself. Often it is something perfectly innocent
and harmless. But it weighs us down, diverts our attention, saps our ener-

gy, dampens our enthusiasm for the things of God. We cannot win when we are carrying excess weight. When we ask about a certain habit or condition, "What's wrong with that?" the answer often is, "Nothing in itself." The problem is not in what the weight is but in what it does. It keeps us from running well and therefore from winning.

In most sports, especially where speed and endurance count, weighing in is a daily routine. It is one of the simplest, but most reliable, tests of being in shape. When an athlete goes over his weight limit, he is put on a stricter exercise and diet program until he is down to where he should be—or he is put on the bench or off the team.

Too much clothing is also a hindrance. Elaborate uniforms are fine for parades, and sweatsuits are fine for warming up, but when the race comes, the least clothing that decency allows is all that is worn. When we become more concerned about appearances than about spiritual reality and vitality, our work and testimony for Jesus Christ are seriously encumbered.

We do not know exactly what sort of things the writer had in mind regarding spiritual encumbrances, and commentators venture a host of ideas. From the context of the letter as a whole, I believe the main encumbrance was Judaistic legalism, hanging on to the old religious ways. Most of those ways were not wrong in themselves. Some had been prescribed by God for the time of the Old Covenant. But none of them was of any value now, and in fact had become hindrances. They were sapping energy and attention from Christian living. The Temple and its ceremonies and pageantry were beautiful and appealing. And all the regulations, the does and don'ts of Judaism, were pleasing to the flesh. They made it easy to keep score on your religious life. But these were all weights, some of them very heavy weights. They were like a ball and chain to spiritual living by faith. These Jewish believers, or would-be believers, could not possibly run the Christian race with all their excess baggage.

Some in the Galatian church faced the same problem. Paul tells them, "I have been crucified with Christ; and it is no longer I who live, but Christ lives in me; and the life which I now live in the flesh I live by faith in the Son of God, who loved me, and delivered Himself up for me. I do not nullify the grace of God; for if righteousness comes through the Law, then Christ died needlessly" (Gal. 2:20-21). He goes on, "You foolish Galatians, who has bewitched you, before whose eyes Jesus Christ was publicly portrayed as crucified? This is the only thing I want to find out from you: did you receive the Spirit by the works of the Law, or by hearing with faith? Are you so foolish? Having begun by the Spirit, are you now being perfected by the flesh?" (3:1-3). To impress his point even more, Paul says, "But now that you have come to know God, or rather to be known by God, how is it that you turn back again to the weak and worthless elemental things, to which you desire to be enslaved all over again?" (4:9). "After you started the Christian race," he is saying, "why did you then put all those old weights back on?"

Another type of encumbrance can be fellow Christians. We need to be careful about blaming others for our shortcomings. But a lot of Christians not only are not running themselves but are keeping others from running. They are figuratively sitting on the track, and those who *are* running have to hurdle them. Often the workers in the church have to keep jumping over or running around the nonworkers. The devil does not put all the encumbrances in the way. Sometimes we do his work for him.

Let us also lay aside . . . the sin which so easily entangles us. (12:1c)

An even more significant hindrance to Christian living is sin. Obviously all sin is a hindrance to Christian living, and the reference here may be to sin in general. But use of the definite article (**the sin**) seems to indicate a particular sin. And if there is one particular sin that hinders the race of faith it is unbelief, doubting God. Doubting and living in faith contradict each other. Unbelief **entangles** the Christian's feet so that he cannot run. It wraps itself around us so that we trip and stumble every time we try to move for the Lord, if we try at all. It **easily entangles us.** When we allow sin in our lives, especially unbelief, it is quite easy for Satan to keep us from running.

THE EXAMPLE TO FOLLOW

Fixing our eyes on Jesus, the author and perfecter of faith, who for the joy set before Him endured the cross, despising the shame, and has sat down at the right hand of the throne of God. (12:2)

In running, as in most sports, where you look is extremely important. Nothing will throw off your stride or slow you down like looking at your feet or the runner coming up from behind or the crowds in the stands. The Christian race is very much like this.

Some Christians are preoccupied with themselves. They may not be selfish or egotistical, but they pay too much attention to what they are doing, to the mechanics of running. There is a place for such concern, but if we focus on ourselves, we will never run well for the Lord. Sometimes we are preoccupied with what other Christians are thinking and doing, especially in relation to us. Concern for others also has a place. We do not disregard our brothers in Christ or what they think about us. What they think about us, including their criticism, can be helpful to us. But if we focus on others, we are bound to stumble. We are not even to focus on the Holy Spirit. We are to be *filled* with the Spirit, and when we are, our focus will be on Jesus Christ, because that is where the Spirit's focus is (John 16:14).

It is not that we try hard *not* to look at this or that or the other things that may distract us. If our focus is truly on Jesus Christ, we will see everything else in its right perspective. When our eyes are on the Lord, the Holy Spirit has the perfect opportunity to use us, to get us running and winning.

We are to focus on Jesus because He is **the author and perfecter of faith.** He is the supreme example of our faith.

In 2:10 Jesus is called the author of salvation. Here He is the **author** (*archēgos*) of faith. He is the pioneer or originator, the one who begins and takes the lead. Jesus is the author, the originator, of all faith. He originated Abel's faith, and Enoch's and Noah's, as well as Abraham's, David's, Paul's, and ours. The focus of faith is also the originator of faith. As Paul explains, "Our fathers . . . all ate the same spiritual food; and all drank the same spiritual drink, for they were drinking from a spiritual rock which followed them; and the rock was Christ" (1 Cor. 10:1, 3-4). Micah had preached the same truth hundreds of years before Paul. "But as for you, Bethlehem Ephrathah, too little to be among the clans of Judah, from you One will go forth for Me to be ruler in Israel. His goings forth are from long ago, from the days of eternity" (Mic. 5:2).

But I believe the primary meaning of *archēgos* here is that of chief leader, or chief example. Jesus Christ is our preeminent example of faith. He was "tempted in all things as we are, yet without sin" (Heb. 4:15). Jesus lived the supreme life of faith. When the devil tempted Him in the wilderness, Jesus' reply each time was the expression of trust in His Father and His Word. Jesus would not bypass the Father's will just to get food, or to test His Father's protection or lordship (Matt. 4:1-10). He would wait until the Father supplied or protected or directed. When the ordeal was over, His Father did provide by sending angels to minister to Him. He trusted His Father implicitly, for everything and in everything. "I can do nothing on My own initiative. As I hear, I judge; and My judgment is just, because I do not seek My own will, but the will of Him who sent Me" (John 5:30).

In the Garden of Gethsemane, just before His arrest, trial, and crucifixion, Jesus said to His Father, "My Father, if it is possible, let this cup pass from Me; yet not as I will, but as Thou wilt" (Matt. 26:39). Whatever the prospect of hardship or suffering, He trusted His Father. His Father's will was what He lived by and died by. It was all Jesus ever considered. The faith of all the heroes of chapter 11 together could not match the faith of the Son of God. They were wonderful witnesses and examples of faith; Jesus is a more wonderful example still. Their faith was true and acceptable to God; His was perfect and even more acceptable. In fact, without Jesus' faithfulness, no believer's faith would count for anything. For if Jesus' perfect faith had not led Him to the cross, our faith would be in vain, because there would then be no sacrifice for our sins, no righteousness to count to our credit.

Jesus not only is the **author** of faith, but also its **perfecter** (*teleiōtēs*), the One who carries it through to completion. He continued to trust His Father until He could say, "It is finished!" (John 19:30). These words, along with "Father, into Thy hands I commit My spirit" (Luke 23:46), were Jesus' last before He died. His work was finished not only in that it was completed but in that it was perfected. If a composer dies while working on a masterpiece, his work on that piece is over but it is not finished. On the cross, Jesus' work was both over and finished—perfected. It accomplished exactly what it was meant to accomplish, because, from birth to death, His life was totally committed into His Father's hands. There has never been a walk of faith like Jesus'.

The world has always mocked faith, just as they mocked Jesus' faith: "He trusts in God; let Him deliver Him now, if He takes pleasure in Him; for He said, 'I am the Son of God' " (Matt. 27:43). But in faith, Jesus **endured the cross, despising the shame.** Why should we not also trust God in everything, since we have not begun to suffer what Jesus suffered? "You have not yet resisted to the point of shedding blood in your striving against sin" (Heb. 12:4). Jesus has set such a high example of faith that it is on His example that we should rivet our eyes for as long as we live. It is good to glance at the examples of the cloud of Old Testament witnesses, but it is imperative that we *fix* our eyes on Jesus (cf. 2 Cor. 3:18).

The End of the Race

Who for the joy set before Him endured the cross, despising the shame, and has sat down at the right hand of the throne of God. (12:2b)

In the ancient Isthmian games of Greece, a pedestal stood at the finish line, and on it hung a wreath—the winner's prize. No one runs a race without some expectation of reward. The reward may be nothing more than a ribbon or a trophy or a wreath of leaves. It may be a prize worth a large amount of money. Sometimes the reward is fame and recognition. Sometimes it is a healthy body. Occasionally the race is run for the sheer exhilaration.

The Isthmian races and the race spoken of in Hebrews 12, however, were not run for exhilaration. This type of race is the *agōn*, the agony race, the marathon, the race that seems never to end. It is not a race you run simply for the pleasure of running. If you do not have something important to look forward to at the end of this race, you will likely not start it and will certainly not finish it.

Jesus did not run His race of faith for the pleasure of race itself, though He must have experienced great satisfaction in seeing people healed, comforted, brought to faith, and started on the way to spiritual growth. But He did not leave His Father's presence and His heavenly glory, endure temptation and fierce opposition by Satan himself, suffer ridicule, scorn, blasphemy, torture, and crucifixion by his enemies, and experience the misunderstanding and denial of His own disciples for the sake of whatever few pleasures and satisfactions He had while on earth. He was motivated by immeasurably more than this.

Only what was at the end of the race could have motivated Jesus to leave what He did and endure what He did. Jesus ran for two things, **the joy set before Him** and sitting **down at the right hand of the throne of God.** He ran for the joy of exaltation. In His high-priestly prayer Jesus said to His Father, "I glorified Thee on the earth, having accomplished the work which Thou hast given Me to do. And now, glorify Thou Me together with Thyself, Father, with the glory which I had with Thee before the world was" (John 17:4-5). Jesus gained His reward by glorifying His Father while on earth, and He glorified God by totally exhibiting the Father's attributes and by fully doing the Father's will.

The prize Christians are to run for is not heaven. If we are truly Christians, if we belong to God by faith in Jesus Christ, heaven is already ours. We run for the same prize that Jesus ran for, and we achieve it in the same way He did. We run for the joy of exaltation God promises will be ours if we glorify Him on earth as His Son did. We glorify God by allowing His attributes to shine through us and by obeying His will in everything we do.

When we anticipate the heavenly reward of faithful service, joy will be ours now. Paul spoke of his converts as his "joy and crown" (Phil. 4:1) and his "hope or joy or crown of exultation" (1 Thess. 2:19). He had present joy because of future promise. Those he had won to the Lord were evidence that he had glorified God in his ministry. What gives us joy in this life is confidence of reward in the next.

Even if we must suffer for the Lord, we should be able to say with Paul, "I rejoice and share my joy with you all" (Phil. 2:17). And though, like Paul, we are not yet perfect, we should also forget what is behind and reach forward to what lies ahead, pressing on "toward the goal of the prize of the upward call of God in Christ Jesus" (3:13-14). We should be able to look forward to the day when our Lord says to us, "Well done, . . . enter into the joy of your master" (Matt. 25:21). "In the future," the apostle says, "there is laid up for me the crown of righteousness, which the Lord, the righteous Judge, will award to me on that day; and not only to me, but also to all who have loved His appearing" (2 Tim. 4:8). And when we get to heaven, we can join the twenty-four elders in casting our "crowns before the throne, saying, 'Worthy art Thou, our Lord and our God, to receive glory and honor and power' " (Rev. 4:10-11).

When Jesus went to the cross, He endured all that it demanded. He despised the shame and accepted it willingly, for the sake of His Father's reward and the joy that anticipation of this reward brought. As we run the race of the Christian life, we can run in the joyful anticipation of that same reward—the crown of righteousness, which one day we can cast at His feet as evidence of our eternal love for Him.

THE EXHORTATION

For consider Him who has endured such hostility by sinners against Himself, so that you may not grow weary and lose heart. (12:3)

When we get weary in the race, when our faith runs out and we think God has turned His back, when it seems we will never get out of the mess we are in and we are sure our faith cannot hold on any longer, we should read this verse. Part of the purpose for **fixing our eyes on Jesus** is the same as that for considering the **cloud of witnesses**—our encouragement. Those saints were heroes of faith; He is the epitome of faith. Nothing we will ever be called to endure will compare to that which He endured. He is the divine Son of God, but while on earth He did not live in His own power and will, but in His Father's. Otherwise, He could not be our example. And unless, by the Holy Spirit, we are truly *able* to live in the same way in which He lived, His life would not be an example but an impossible ideal to mock and to judge us.

We rejoice that one day we will "live together with Him" (1 Thess. 5:10), but we should also rejoice that we can live *like* Him right now. We do not live in our own power but in His, just as on earth He did not live in His own power but in the Father's. We can say with Paul, "It is no longer I who live, but Christ lives in me; and the life which I now live in the flesh I live by faith in the Son of God, who loved me, and delivered Himself up for me" (Gal. 2:20).

The Discipline of God (12:4-11)

You have not yet resisted to the point of shedding blood in your striving against sin; and you have forgotten the exhortation which is addressed to you as sons, "My son, do not regard lightly the discipline of the LORD, nor faint when you are reproved by Him; for those whom the LORD loves He disciplines, and He scourges every son whom He receives." It is for discipline that you endure; God deals with you as with sons; for what son is there whom his father does not discipline? But if you are without discipline, of which all have become partakers, then you are illegitimate children and not sons. Furthermore, we had earthly fathers to discipline us, and we respected them; shall we not much rather be subject to the Father of spirits, and live? For they disciplined us for a short time as seemed best to them, but He disciplines us for our good, that we may share His holiness. All discipline for the moment seems not to be joyful, but sorrowful; yet to those who have been trained by it, afterwards it yields the perfect fruit of righteousness. (12:4-11)

All the Jews to whom the book of Hebrews was written were undergoing persecution because of their break with Judaism. It was coming from their Jewish friends and relatives, who resented their

383

turning their backs on the religious customs and traditions in which they had been born and raised. The readers had been reminded about "the former days, when, after being enlightenened, you endured a great conflict of sufferings, partly, by being made a public spectacle through reproaches and tribulations, and partly by becoming sharers with those who were so treated (10:32-33). Even the unbelieving Jews who were involved with the church must have suffered because of their association with Christians.

The affliction had largely been in the form of social and economic pressure, though some of them had been imprisoned (10:34). We can imagine the arguments they heard for rejecting the new faith. "Look at what you have gotten yourselves into. You have become Christians and all you have had are problems, criticism, hardship, and suffering. You have lost your friends, your families, your synagogues, your traditions, your heritage—everything."

As we have seen, those who had made mere professions of faith were, under this pressure, in danger of reverting to Judaism, of apostatizing. The true believers were in danger of having their faith seriously weakened by adopting again the rituals and ceremonies of the Old Covenant.

Some believers perhaps were wondering why, if their God was a God of power and of peace, they were suffering so much. "Why are we not winning out over our enemies, instead of our enemies seeming always to have the upper hand? Where is the God who is supposed to supply all our needs and give us the answers to our questions, and fulfillment to our lives? Why, when we turned to a God of love, did everyone start hating us?"

The last section of chapter 11 begins to answer questions like these and also provides a foundation for the exhortations of 12:4-11. Suffering for God's sake was nothing new. The saints of the Old Covenant had known what it was to suffer for their faith. They faced warfare, weakness, torture, beatings, imprisonment, stonings, destitution, and every sort of affliction—all because of their trust in the Lord (11:34-38). And despite all this, they did not receive the fullness of blessing promised to believers under the New Covenant, such as the indwelling of the Holy Spirit, the knowledge of sins completely forgiven, and peaceful consciences. These heroes of the past "did not receive what was promised," yet they endured valiantly and "gained approval through their faith" (v. 39). They faced afflictions in the right attitude, which is what the readers of Hebrews are counseled to do—to run the race of faith as their forefathers had done (12:1).

More importantly than this, they were to fix their eyes on Jesus, who had given up more and suffered far more than any other. One of the reasons He "endured such hostility by sinners against Himself," was that

His followers might "not grow weary and lose heart" (12:3). They could look to His example for strength.

You have not yet resisted to the point of shedding blood in your striving against sin. (12:4)

None of the suffering Hebrews to whom this letter was written had endured what Jesus had endured. None had given his life for the gospel. Nor had any of them lived an absolutely sinless life as Jesus had done, living in perfect obedience to the Father, and thus deserving no punishment at all. On the contrary, some of their suffering was deserved and was intended for their spiritual discipline and growth.

The key word of 12:4-11 is **discipline,** used both as a noun and a verb. It is from the Greek *paideia,* which, in turn, comes from *pais* ("child") and denotes the training of a child. The word is a broad term, signifying whatever parents and teachers do to train, correct, cultivate, and educate children in order to help them develop and mature as they ought. It is used nine times in these eight verses.

The figure changes from that of a race to that of a family. Christian living involves running, working, fighting, and enduring. It also involves relationships, especially our relationship to God and to other believers. The emphasis of this passage is on the heavenly Father's use of discipline in the lives of His children.

PURPOSES OF DISCIPLINE

God uses hardship and affliction as a means of discipline, a means of training His children, of helping them mature in their spiritual lives. He has three specific purposes for His discipline: retribution, prevention, and education.

We must realize that there is a great difference between God's discipline and His judgmental punishment. As Christians we often have to suffer painful consequences for our sins, but we will never experience God's judgment for them. This punishment Christ took completely on Himself in the crucifixion, and God does not exact double payment for any sin. Though we *deserve* God's wrathful punishment because of our sin, we will never have to face it, because Jesus endured it for us. Neither God's love nor His justice would allow Him to require payment for what His Son has already paid in full. In discipline, God is not a judge but a Father (cf. Rom 8:1).

PUNISHMENT

We experience some of God's discipline as the direct result of our sin, but the punishment is corrective, not judgmental. It is punishment, to be sure, but not of the sort that unbelievers receive.

Because of his lust for Bathsheba and the resulting adultery and murder, God severely punished David. Most other kings of that day did this sort of thing, and worse, as a matter of course. It was considered to be a king's prerogative. But, no matter what any culture tolerates, none of God's people has a prerogative to sin, not even His own anointed king who was a "man after God's own heart." In fact, those who are especially blessed and enlightened by God have less justification for sinning. Consequently, God disciplined David, not out of wrath but out of love. David's sin did not cost him his salvation, but it cost him dearly in the loss of an infant son by Bathsheba and in countless heartaches from several of his other sons. He went through years of anguish that otherwise he never would have experienced. Through the prophet Nathan, God told David that because of this sin (really a series of sins), "Now therefore, the sword shall never depart from your house, because you have despised Me and have taken the wife of Uriah the Hittite to be your wife" (2 Sam. 12:10). It may be that even his being forbidden to build the Temple was at least an indirect result of this sin, since it was because of his warfare that God denied him the privilege (1 Chron. 22:8).

Yet David was a better man because of God's discipline. God had a purpose in the discipline—to draw His servant closer to Himself, to convince him not to sin again, and to help him grow and mature.

The church at Corinth was particularly immature and carnal. Among other things, many believers were abusing the Lord's Table. They were using it as an excuse for partying, with some even getting drunk (1 Cor. 11:20-22). Paul rebuked them strongly and told them plainly that they were suffering weakness, sickness, and even death because of this sinfulness (v. 30). They were being "disciplined by the Lord in order that [they would] not be condemned along with the world" (v. 32).

When we discipline our children, even for something serious, we do not put them out of the family. We discipline them to correct their behavior, not to disown them. Neither does God put us out of His family when He disciplines us, His children. He wants to draw us deeper into the fellowship of His family.

It is often as hard for us to see the good in God's chastening us as it is for our children to see the good in our chastening them. But we know that, because He is our loving heavenly Father, He will not do anything to harm us. His discipline may hurt, but it will not harm. It is the best thing the Lord can do for us when we sin. It restrains us from repeating the sin.

God says that when His children "forsake My law, and do not walk in My judgments, if they violate My statutes, and do not keep My commandments, then I will visit their transgression with the rod, and their iniquity with stripes" (Ps. 89:30-32). But the other side of the promise of punishment is the promise of faithfulness to His covenant. "But I will not break off My lovingkindness from him, nor deal falsely in My faithfulness. My covenant I will not violate, nor will I alter the utterance of My lips" (v. 33-34). When God chastises, He is not rejecting but correcting.

PREVENTION

Sometimes God disciplines in order to *prevent* sin. Just as we put restrictions and limits, and sometimes literal fences, around our children to protect them from harm, so God does with us. We do not allow our small children to play in busy streets, or play with matches, or splash in the swimming pool without someone to watch them. God also puts fences around His children to protect them. What seems to us a terrible inconvenience or hardship may be God's loving hand of protection.

If the apostle Paul was anything he was self-disciplined. He was also genuinely humble, always careful to give the Lord credit for anything good or miraculous that he did. Yet Paul tells us that God gave him a "thorn in the flesh" for the specific purpose of keeping him from exalting himself (2 Cor. 12:7). God allowed this "messenger of Satan" to "buffet" Paul not because His beloved and faithful apostle *was* proud but to keep him from *becoming* proud. The thorn in the flesh was sent to protect his spiritual well-being. Paul did not enjoy the thorn, and pleaded earnestly with the Lord on three occasions to remove it. But when God assured him, "My grace is sufficient for you, for power is perfected in weakness," Paul gladly accepted the thorn, in fact boasted in it (vv. 8-9). He learned that not only this thorn but also many other hardships and afflictions were being used by God to make him better. "Therefore I am well content with weaknesses, with insults, with distresses, with persecutions, with difficulties, for Christ's sake; for when I am weak, then I am strong" (v. 10). Because the Lord's discipline made him better, Paul thanked the Lord for it. It is one of God's blessings, though not as attractive as some of the others.

Our sickness, lack of business success, or other problems may be God's way of keeping us from something much worse. If God's children accepted His preventive discipline more willingly and gratefully, He would have much less need for administering His corrective discipline.

EDUCATION

Besides punishing and preventing, God's discipline also educates us for better service and better living. It will teach us, if we will listen to what He is saying through it.

First of all, discipline can help us better know God's power and sufficiency. Sometimes God can get our attention better through affliction than through blessing. Prosperity has a way of making us feel self-satisfied and independent, while problems often make us more aware of our need for the Lord. We need Him every bit as much when things are going well as when they are not, but often we do not *feel* our need for Him until we face our own helplessness.

By God's own declaration, Job was "blameless, upright, fearing God, and turning away from evil" (Job 1:1). Yet God allowed him to suffer pain, loss, grief, sickness, and ridicule that make Paul's thorn in the flesh, whatever it was, seem insignificant by comparison. Just as Paul's thorn, Job's afflictions were messengers of Satan and came upon him with God's approval (1:12; 2:6). Job went through his horrible sufferings and "did not sin with his lips" (2:10).

Job's discipline was clearly not punishment; nor was it prevention. It was sent to educate Job further in the ways and character of the Lord. It was a slow process. Job did not sin through all his suffering, but he was hard put to explain it. He kept trying to figure out on his own why he was having such a hard time. He knew it was not because of sin, and he knew that God was not wicked or capricious. But he was not willing to accept his suffering. Job endured it, but he did not accept it, until, after two long lectures directly by God, he acknowledged he did not need to know the reason behind everything that happened to him. God is sovereign and omniscient and omnipotent. What Job learned through his trials was not the reason for them but that God is supremely great and marvelous. He learned "things too wonderful for me, which I did not know," and confessed to his Lord, "I have heard of Thee by the hearing of the ear; but now my eye sees Thee; therefore I retract, and I repent in dust and ashes" (42:3, 5-6).

Through his great and seemingly unending suffering Job had been given a magnificent view of God. He experienced His holy majesty, His deliverance, His care, His power, His counsel, His defense—all through His discipline. Job also learned a great lesson about himself: that his wisdom was not God's wisdom. He learned to trust God for who He is, not for what he himself could see and comprehend. When we see God better, we see ourselves better.

Discipline can also teach sympathy for others. Again Job's experience is a perfect illustration. "And the LORD restored the fortunes of Job when he prayed for his friends" (42:10). Through his troubles, Job saw God more clearly, himself more clearly, and others more clearly. He became more sensitive and understanding. He learned a great deal in God's school of suffering.

When we have troubles, problems, heartaches, we should ask ourselves—better still, ask God to show us—if He is disciplining us as punishment, as prevention, or as education. When we ask, however, we should remember Job and realize that God may not show us the reason as quickly or as clearly as we would like Him to. We can always be sure that His discipline will correct us, protect us, or instruct us. Whatever the reason, it will be for our good, and we should be thankful.

Only faith can bring us to appreciate discipline, whatever the kind. We are able to see behind the scenes in Job's ordeal because Scripture gives a vivid picture of the workings of both Satan and God. But Job had no knowledge of this. As far as we can tell from the Bible, Job went to his grave not knowing exactly why he had to suffer as he did. When he finally acknowledged God's sovereign omnipotence and goodness in it all, it was by faith. He came to see God more clearly (42:5) but he was not shown the whys and wherefores of his problems more clearly. When we understand and trust God more deeply, we are content with whatever limited knowledge He gives.

FORGETTING GOD'S WORD

And you have forgotten the exhortation which is addressed to you as sons, "My son, do not regard lightly the discipline of the LORD, nor faint when you are reproved by Him." (12:5)

Forgetfulness causes a lot of unnecessary problems and heartaches. Our greatest need is not for new light from God, but for paying attention to light we already have. When God's Word is neglected it is forgotten. Sometimes the answer or the help we need is in a truth we learned a long time ago but have let slip away.

Jews in New Testament times had forgotten many things about the Old Testament. They had forgotten that God had never been pleased by anything apart from faith, and they had forgotten that many of His choicest saints had suffered greatly for their faith. Now they are reminded that they had also forgotten the teaching from Proverbs 3:11-12 about God's discipline.

Suffering for God's sake was nothing new. Being disciplined by Him was not new. These believers were upset about their afflictions partly because they had forgotten God's Word. In the Old Testament God not only had spoken to them about suffering and discipline, but He had spoken to them **as sons.** They had forgotten more than simply divine truths, they had **forgotten the exhortation** of their heavenly Father. Turning to Scripture is listening to God, for Scripture is His Word. For believers, it is the Word of their Father.

This forgotten exhortation tells us of two perils of discipline—regarding it lightly, and fainting because of it.

PERILS IN DISCIPLINE

My son, do not regard lightly the discipline of the LORD. (12:5*b*)

REGARDING IT LIGHTLY

The first thing that can keep God from accomplishing what He wants in our lives is to **regard lightly** His **discipline.** If we do not understand our problems as being discipline that the Lord sends for our good, we cannot profit from them as He intends. Our reactions cannot be right if our view of what is happening is not right. The spiritual weakness mentioned in this verse is not that of taking our problems lightly but of taking the Lord's discipline through them lightly. It is usually because we take our problems too seriously that we take the Lord's discipline too lightly. Our focus is on the experience rather than on our heavenly Father and on what He wants to do for us through the experience.

We can take God's discipline lightly in many ways. We can become *callous* to God and His Word, so that when He is doing something in us or for us, we do not recognize His hand in it. When we are calloused, God's discipline will harden us instead of soften us. We may also treat God's discipline lightly by *complaining.* In this case, we do not forget God; in fact our attention is on Him, but in the wrong way. Instead of showing patient endurance, like the hero saints, we gripe and grumble. We do not accuse God of anything wrong, at least not in so many words. But complaining to God amounts to just that—believing He is doing something not quite right. Fretting comes from nothing but disbelief, lack of trust in God to do everything right, especially for His children.

Arthur Pink comments, "Remind yourself of how much dross there is yet among the gold and view the corruption of your own heart and marvel that God has not smitten you more severely. Form the habit of heeding His taps, and you will be less likely to receive His raps."

We can prevent God from accomplishing His desired result through discipline by *questioning.* Like complaining, questioning shows a clear lack of faith. When a child asks his parents, "Why?" he usually is not looking for a reason but is challenging them to justify what they want him to do or not do. In exactly the same way, our questioning God implies that He is not justified in doing what He is doing to us.

Even when we recognize His discipline *as* discipline, we may question whether it is of the right kind, of the right severity, of the right length, or has come at the right time. If we spank our child, he may think that going without supper would have been a better punishment. Or if we ground him for two days, he may think that withholding his allowance for a week would have been more appropriate. A parent's discipline, of course, is never perfect, but it is much more likely to be appropriate than what the child deems right. We need to recognize that God's discipline is always the right discipline, the perfect discipline—exactly what we need.

Perhaps the greatest danger in regarding God's discipline lightly is *carelessness*. When we do not care about what purpose God has in the discipline or about how we can profit from it, His discipline cannot be effective. It becomes like a blessing that we misuse. He gives it for our benefit and His glory, but we do not use it for either. We thwart its purpose by spiritual indifference.

FAINTING

Nor faint when you are reproved by Him. (12:5c)

Some people become so overcome by their problems that they give up; they become despondent, depressed, **faint.** They become spiritually inert, unresponsive to what God is doing or why. They are not callous, complaining, questioning, or careless. They are simply immobilized. They give up and collapse. The psalmist had this experience, and cries out to himself, "Why are you in despair, O my soul? And why have you become disturbed within me?" He knew his problem, and he also knew the cure, for he continues, "Hope in God, for I shall yet praise Him, the help of my countenance, and my God" (Ps. 42:11). The cure for hopelessness is hope in God. The child of God has no need to faint because of God's discipline. God gives it to strengthen us, not to weaken us, to encourage us, not to discourage us, to build us up, not to tear us down.

When, by our taking it lightly or by our becoming despondent, God's discipline is not allowed to accomplish His purpose in us, Satan is the victor. God's purpose is lost, and our blessing is lost.

PROOFS IN DISCIPLINE

"For those whom the LORD loves He disciplines, and He scourges every son whom He receives." It is for discipline that you endure; God deals with you as with sons; for what son is there whom his father does not discipline? But if you are without discipline, of which all have become partakers, then you are illegitimate children and not sons. (12:6-8)

To the Christian who is responsive to the Lord's discipline, it proves two things: His love and our sonship.

PROVES GOD'S LOVE

The first thing we should think of when we are suffering is our Father's love, **for those whom the** LORD **loves He disciplines.** We cannot prove this to anyone, or even to ourselves, except by faith. Even less can we prove, by reason or human understanding, that we are being disciplined *because of* God's love. But faith proves it. Faith's logic is simple: "We are God's children. God loves His children and is bound by His own nature and His own covenant to do them only good. Therefore, whatever we receive from God's hand, including discipline, is from God's love." More than any earthly father, the heavenly Father wants his children to be righteous, mature, obedient, competent, responsible, capable, and trusting. We benefit in all these ways, and many more, when we accept His discipline.

Paul tells us to be "rooted and grounded in love" (Eph. 3:17), that is, to have a settled assurance that God cannot do anything apart from or contrary to His love for us. God continually loves, whether we are aware of His love or not. When we *are* aware of it, however, it can accomplish immeasurably more good in us and for us. Instead of looking at our troubles, we look at our Father's love, and thank Him that even the troubles are proof of His love.

A man who was asked why he was looking over a wall replied, "Because I can't see through it." When Christians cannot see through the wall of pain, confusion, hardship, or despair, they need only look over the wall into the face of their loving heavenly Father.

Just as God's love has predestined us (Eph. 1:4-5) and redeemed us (John 3:16), it also disciplines us.

Children have long wondered why parents insist on saying, "This spanking hurts me more than it does you." The idea is hard for a child to accept, until he himself becomes a parent. A loving parent *does* hurt when he has to discipline his child. The parent gets no joy or satisfaction out of the discipline itself, but out of the eventual benefit it will be to the child.

God is more loving than any human parent, and He suffers when He has to discipline His children. "For the Lord will not reject forever, for if He causes grief, then He will have compassion according to His abundant lovingkindness. For He does not afflict willingly, or grieve the sons of men" (Lam. 3:31-33). The Lord is tender and careful in His discipline. Nothing is more sensitive than love. Because God loves with infinite love, He is infinitely sensitive to the needs and feelings of His children. He hurts when we hurt. He takes no more pleasure in the painful discipline of His children than in the death of unbelievers (Ezek. 18:32). Nor will He discipline us beyond what we need or can bear, any more than He will allow us to be tempted beyond what we can endure (1 Cor. 10:13). He does not discipline to grieve us but to improve us.

God suffers whenever we suffer, whatever the reason for it. "In all their affliction He was afflicted" (Isa. 63:9). Everything Israel went through, the Lord went through with her. Everything she suffered, including punishment for her sins, He suffered with her. God does not understand us simply because He made us, but also because He identifies with us as our Father. We can be sure that our discipline hurts Him more than it hurts us. If He Himself is willing to endure suffering for our good, how can we not be willing to endure it gladly and thankfully?

PROVES OUR SONSHIP

And He scourges every son whom He receives. It is for discipline that you endure; God deals with you as with sons; for what son is there whom his father does not discipline? But if you are without discipline, of which all have become partakers, then you are illegitimate children and not sons. (12:6b-8)

The second thing that discipline proves is closely related to the first. It proves our sonship. All men are subject to God's punishment, but only His children receive His discipline.

At times we have all wanted to discipline someone else's children when they disturb or irritate us. When we see an unruly child throwing a tantrum in a store, we think to ourselves, "If I could have him for just about a week." But we have no continuing desire to discipline children that are not our own, because we do not love them as we love our own. The relationship is not the same and therefore the concern is not the same.

Besides the motivation of love, discipline is given because of obligation. Since our children are our special responsibility, and since discipline is for their good, we are obligated to discipline them as we are not obligated to discipline other peoples' children. God has a covenant relationship with His people, and has obligated Himself to redeem, protect, and bless them. " 'For the mountains may be removed and the hills may shake, but My lovingkindness will not be removed from you, and My covenant of peace will not be shaken,' says the LORD who has compassion on you" (Isa. 54:10).

We can know we are God's children by His leading us (Rom. 8:14) and by the witness of His Spirit to our spirits (8:15-16). We know from the fact that we have trusted in Jesus Christ that we are God's children. "But as many as received Him, to them He gave the right to become children of God, even to those who believe in His name" (John 1:12). We also know from our discipline that we are His children, because **He scourges every son whom He receives.** An undisciplined child is an unloved child and a miserable child. God's love will not allow Him not to discipline us, and His punishment is another of the many proofs of His love and of our sonship.

The other side, the tragic side, of this truth is that those who are not disciplined by God are not His children. **He scourges every son** is inclusive. Not a single one of His children will miss out on His loving discipline. **Whom He receives,** however, is exclusive. Only those He receives through their faith in His Son are His children.

Scourges (*mastigoō*) refers to flogging with a whip, and was a common Jewish practice (Matt. 10:17; 23:34). It was a severe and extremely painful beating. The point of Hebrews 12:6*b*, and of Proverbs 3:12 (from which it is quoted), is that God's discipline can sometimes be severe. When our disobedience is great or our apathy is great, His punishment will be great.

Parents often become discouraged when discipline seems to have no effect. Sometimes we just do not want to go through the trouble for ourselves, even though we know our child needs discipline for his own good. But if we love our children, we will discipline and continue to discipline them as long as they are under our care. "He who spares his rod hates his son, but he who loves him disciplines him diligently" (Prov. 13:24; cf. 23:13-14). Our juvenile courts are constant testimonies to the truth that "a child who gets his own way brings shame to his mother" (Prov. 29:15)—as well as to his whole family and community. We can be certain that because God will always love us, He will always discipline us while we are in this life.

So, discipline in the Christian life is not in spite of sonship, but because of sonship. **For what son is there whom his father does not discipline?** A truly loving father is absolutely committed to helping his child conform to the highest standards. How much more is our heavenly Father committed to our conforming to His standards, and to inflicting the pain to make such conformity a reality.

When we look at how well many unbelievers are doing and then at how much trouble we are having, we should take this as evidence that we belong to God and they do not. If they **are without discipline,** they **are illegitimate children and not sons.** We should pity, not envy, the prosperous, healthy, popular, and attractive person who does not know God. We should not wish on them our trials or suffering, but we should want to say to them, as did Paul to Agrippa, "I would to God, that whether in a short or long time, not only you, but also all who hear me this day, might become such as I am, except for these chains" (Acts 26:29).

Jerome said a paradoxical thing that fits the point of this passage of Hebrews. "The greatest anger of all is when God is no longer angry with us." The supreme affliction is to be unteachable and unreachable by

God. When the Lord disciplines us, we should say, "Thank you, Lord. You have just proved again that You love me and that I am Your child."

PRODUCTS OF DISCIPLINE

Furthermore, we had earthly fathers to discipline us, and we respected them; shall we not much rather be subject to the Father of spirits, and live? For they disciplined us for a short time as seemed best to them, but He disciplines us for our good, that we may share His holiness. All discipline for the moment seems not to be joyful, but sorrowful; yet to those who have been trained by it, afterwards it yields the peaceful fruit of righteousness. (12:9-11)

The two products of discipline mentioned in these verses are closely related to the three purposes of discipline suggested above. God's discipline produces life and produces holiness.

It is the disciplined child who respects his parents. The surest way for a parent to lose, or never gain, his child's respect is never to correct or punish him, no matter how terrible the child's behavior. Even while they are growing up, children instinctively know that a parent who disciplines fairly is a parent who loves and cares. They also realize that a parent who always lets them have their own way is a parent who does not care. **We had earthly fathers to discipline us, and we respected them,** because of what that discipline proved and produced.

LIFE

Since we respected our earthly fathers even while they were disciplining us, **shall we not much rather be subject to the Father of spirits, and live?** Our response to God's discipline should not be resentful resignation, but willing and grateful submission. We should want to benefit as much from our heavenly Father's discipline as we possibly can.

Under the Old Covenant, a son who was totally rebellious to his parents, who would not be corrected or disciplined, was to be stoned to death (Deut. 21:18-21). This punishment was severe in the extreme, but shows us how seriously God takes a child's obedience to his parents. I believe that Hebrews 12:9 suggests the same severity. A Christian's persistent rebellion against God's discipline can cost him his life. Paul speaks of believers' "sleeping," that is dying, because of partaking of the Lord's Supper unworthily (1 Cor. 11:30). John tells us of sin "leading to death" (1 John 5:16). James implies the same sort of death resulting directly from sin: "Therefore putting aside all filthiness and all that remains of wickedness, in humility receive the word implanted, which is able to save your souls" (James 1:21). A Christian who continually rejects God's discipline, who refuses to profit from divine correction, can lose his life because of his stubbornness.

More than this, however, I believe the teaching here may include the idea that when we are **subject to the Father of spirits,** we will have a richer, more abundant life. You do not know what victory is until you have fought a battle. You do not know the meaning of freedom until you have been imprisoned. You do not know the joy of relief until you have suffered, or of healing until you have been sick. You do not know what living is all about until you have experienced some problems and hardships.

I once asked a missionary to Indochina how he liked living there. The gist of his reply was, "I don't think I could ever come back to the boring existence of the United States. We have seen God work so many wonderful miracles over there. Why would we want to come back here to this humdrum routine?" He had been through war, famine, disease, political and military upheavals, and countless other experiences that most of us would do almost anything to avoid. Yet he knew he was really living in the fullness of God's presence.

"Those who love Thy law have great peace, and nothing causes them to stumble" (Ps. 119:165). No one lives so well as the believer who loves God's law and will, who receives everything from his Father's hand willingly and joyously.

HOLINESS

For they disciplined us for a short time as seemed best to them, but He disciplines us for our good, that we may share His holiness. (12:10)

To live for the Lord is to live in holiness. God's primary desire for us is that we be holy as He is holy (1 Pet. 1:16), that **we may share in His holiness.**

Because God is perfect, His discipline is always perfect. Human parents discipline as seems **best to them,** but our best is often mistaken and is always imperfect. Sometimes we punish more out of anger than love, and sometimes we punish more severely than the offense calls for. Sometimes we even mistakenly punish a child for something he did not do. I will never forget spanking one of my boys strongly for something I was sure he had done. When he kept crying longer than usual, I ask what the matter was. He said, "Dad, I didn't do it." I was crushed, and tears came to my own eyes. But the Lord never makes such mistakes with His children. His discipline is always proper, always at the right time, of the right sort, and in the right degree. It is always perfectly **for our good, that we may share His holiness.**

There is only one kind of holiness, God's holiness. He is both the source and the measure of holiness—which is separation from sin. His greatest desire for His children is to share His holiness with us, that we "may be filled up to all the fullness of God" (Eph. 3:19). The only way we can be separated from sin, and thereby partake of His holiness and be filled up with His fullness, is "to become conformed to the image of His Son" (Rom. 8:29)—which requires that we accept His discipline as a son. Positionally we already are holy, because we are justified. But practically our holiness is just beginning, which is the work of sanctification—*making us holy.*

All discipline for the moment seems not to be joyful, but sorrowful; yet to those who have been trained by it, afterwards it yields the peaceful fruit of righteousness. (12:11)

Discipline itself is not meant to be pleasant. If it were pleasant, it would have little corrective power. By its very nature, discipline is unpleasant to administer and to endure. Medicine, surgery, physical therapy, and other such treatments that we willingly endure are very often painful, uncomfortable, and inconvenient. We endure them for the sake of the end result—better health.

How much more should we be willing to endure the Lord's treatment of our spiritual needs, which **afterwards . . . yields the peaceful fruit of righteousness?** We should consider our troubles as spiritual treatment, which builds our character and our faith, our love and our righteousness. It will never look like it from the natural perspective, but from the perspective of faith, we see that discipline is one of God's richest and most rewarding blessings on His children.

Someone has written, "And so what do I say? I say let the rains of disappointment come, if they water the plants of spiritual grace. Let the winds of adversity blow, if they serve to root more securely the trees that God has planted. I say, let the sun of prosperity be eclipsed, if that brings me closer to the true light of life. Welcome, sweet discipline, discipline designed for my joy, discipline designed to make me what God wants me to be."

Falling Short of God's Grace

(12:12-17)

Therefore, strengthen the hands that are weak and the knees that are feeble, and make straight paths for your feet, so that the limb which is lame may not be put out of joint, but rather be healed. Pursue peace with all men, and the sanctification without which no one will see the Lord. See to it that no one comes short of the grace of God; that no root of bitterness springing up causes trouble, and by it many be defiled; that there be no immoral or godless person like Esau, who sold his own birthright for a single meal. For you know that even afterwards, when he desired to inherit the blessing, he was rejected, for he found no place for repentance, though he sought for it with tears. (12:12-17)

Nothing in Scripture is more important than doctrine. It is foundational to everything else. Biblical doctrine can be defined simply as "God's truth," and apart from His truth we could know nothing about Him, or anything about ourselves spiritually, or how God looks at us or what He wants us to be or to do. Apart from doctrine there could be no basis for obedience, faith in God or love of God, since we would know nothing about Him.

But Scripture contains much more than doctrine, much more than information about God and about ourselves. It also contains exhortation for living out the truths we learn. Knowing and believing are one side of the coin; living and obeying are the other. Paul joins the two in his charge to Timothy: "teach and preach" (1 Tim. 6:2). "Preach" here means to exhort or admonish. The job of a pastor is to teach right doctrine and to exhort right living, and the job of every Christian is to know right doctrine and to pursue right living.

In my earlier ministry I was asked to preach at a well-known midwestern Christian college. I spoke from 2 Corinthians 5, trying to apply practically some of Paul's rich teaching in that chapter. After the message I was handed a note by one of the students that reprimanded me for passionate exhortation and suggested that, especially with such a sophisticated audience, I should just present the facts of Scripture as I saw them and let the audience "take it from there." I was taken aback at first, but after thinking about what he said, I wrote a note back to the student that said, "Thank you for helping me examine my ministry, but be assured that I am following a pattern established in the Scriptures." Teaching without exhortation is not biblical. It is not giving the whole counsel, or purpose, of God (see 2 Tim. 4:1-2).

The basic thrust of Hebrews 12:12-17 is clearly exhortation. **Strengthen, make straight, pursue,** and **see to it** are all terms of exhortation. The purpose here is not to teach truth only but to encourage living up to the truth. With all the doctrine that the book of Hebrews contains, its primary original purpose was not to teach but to exhort. "But I urge you, brethren, bear with this word of exhortation, for I have written to you briefly" (13:22). Much of the doctrine the readers had heard before. They had a good intellectual grasp of the gospel. They were being urged now to believe it and to follow it, to trust it and obey it.

Truth that is known, but not obeyed, becomes a judgment on us rather than a help to us. Teaching and exhortation are inseparable. Teaching sound doctrine that is not applied is worthless, and exhortation that is not based on sound doctrine is misleading. God's method for instruction is simple—explain the spiritual principles and then illustrate and encourage the application of them.

Many people have an intellectual grasp of the doctrines of Scripture but know nothing of practical Christian living. As someone has said, they understand the doctrines of grace but do not experience the grace of those doctrines. It is one thing, for instance, to believe in the inspiration and inerrancy of Scripture; it is quite another to live under the authority of Scripture. It is one thing to believe that Jesus Christ is Lord; it is quite another to surrender to His lordship. It is one thing to believe God is omnipotent; it is quite another to lean on His mighty arm when we are weak or in trouble.

The "thens," "therefores," and "wherefores" of the Bible are usually transitions from teaching to exhortation, from truth to application, from knowing to doing. In the book of Romans, possibly Paul's most doctrinal letter, he focuses primarily on doctrine. But he does not let his readers "take it from there." Doctrine should lead to something. It should make a difference, a change in our lives. Chapter 12 begins with something of a climax to all he has said before. "I urge you therefore, brethren, by the mercies of God, to present your bodies a living and holy sacrifice, acceptable to God, which is your spiritual service of worship" (v. 1). After setting forth the "mercies of God" for eleven chapters, he exhorts us to respond by commitment. After the truth that "each one of us shall give account of himself to God," he says, "Therefore let us not judge one another anymore, but rather determine this—not to put an obstacle or a stumbling block in a brother's way" (Rom. 14:12-13). After teaching that all food is clean in itself, he says, "Therefore do not let what is for you a good thing be spoken of as evil" (Rom. 14:14-16).

In the book of Galatians, after spending several chapters setting forth the truth that Christians are free from the law, Paul exhorts, "Therefore keep standing firm and do not be subject again to a yoke of slavery" (Gal. 5:1). As soon as he finished explaining the doctrine of sowing and reaping, he says, "So then, while we have opportunity, let us do good to all men, and especially those who are of the household of the faith" (Gal. 6:7-10).

Hebrews 12 also begins with an exhortation. After faith has been carefully explained and defined and illustrated, the writer says, in effect, "Now that you know what the Christian race of faith is, go out and run it." It is not enough to know the New Covenant is better; we must accept it for ourselves. It is not enough to know that Christ is the superior and perfect High Priest; we must trust in His atoning sacrifice for us. It is not enough to know how we should live; we must actually live what we know. The biggest fool of all is the one who knows the truth but does not apply it to life.

Verses 12-17 give three exhortations: for continuance, for diligence, and for vigilance. They are addressed first of all to believers, although they apply to unbelievers as well. The writer is saying, "On the basis that you should be in the race of faith to win and that your suffering is part of God's loving discipline for your good, here are three things you should concentrate on doing."

CONTINUANCE

Therefore, strengthen the hands that are weak and the knees that are feeble, and make straight paths for your feet, so that the limb which is lame may not be put out of joint, but rather be healed. (12:12-13)

These verses resume the race metaphor. The first thing that happens to a runner when he starts to tire is that his arms drop. The position and motion of the arms are extremely important in running, to maintain proper body coordination and rhythm. Your arms actually help you pull through your stride, and they are the first parts of the body to show fatigue. The second to go are the knees. First the arms begin to droop and then the knees begin to wobble. But if you concentrate on the drooping or the wobbling, you are finished. The only way you can hope to continue is by focusing on the goal.

When we experience spiritual **hands that are weak** and **knees that are feeble,** our only hope is in "fixing our eyes on Jesus, the author and perfecter of faith" (12:2).

The writer of Hebrews got his metaphor from Isaiah. The faithful in Israel had been through a lot. They had many evil kings, some false prophets, generally disobedient and stubborn fellow Israelites, powerful enemies who threatened them, and seemingly no prospect of ever living in their own land in peace. They were discouraged and despondent, ready to give up. So the prophet reminds them of the coming kingdom, when "the wilderness and the desert will be glad" and "they will see the glory of the LORD, the majesty of our God" (Isa. 35:1-2). Then he counsels them to counsel each other: "Encourage the exhausted, and strengthen the feeble. Say to those with anxious heart, 'Take courage, fear not. Behold, your God will come with vengeance; the recompense of God will come, but He will save you'" (v. 3-4). In other words, "Don't give up now. A better day is coming. Look to that and you will have the encouragement and strength you need. Victory is ahead!"

The emphasis of Hebrews 12:12 is the same as that of Isaiah 35:3-4. We are not told to strengthen *our* hands or *our* weak and feeble knees, but *the* hands and *the* knees, regardless of whose they are. In other words, we are not to concentrate on our own weaknesses but to help strengthen other Christians in theirs. One of the surest ways to be encouraged ourselves is to give encouragement to someone else, "encouraging one another; and all the more, as you see the day drawing near" (Heb. 10:25). One of the best ways to keep continuing is to encourage others to continue.

And make straight paths for your feet refers to staying in your own lane in the race. When you get out of your lane, you not only disqualify yourself but often interfere with other runners. A runner never intentionally gets out of his lane; he only does so when he is distracted or careless, when he loses his concentration on the goal, or when fatigue robs him of the will to win.

"Let your eyes look directly ahead, and let your gaze be fixed straight in front of you. Watch the path of your feet, and all your ways will be established. Do not turn to the right nor to the left; turn your foot from evil," we are told in Proverbs 4:25-27. When we set out in the race of faith, nothing should distract us or cause us to waver or change course. If we do, we will not only stumble ourselves but cause others to stumble as well.

Paths (*trochia*) refers to the tracks left by the wheels of a cart or chariot, which later travelers follow. When we run, we leave a track behind us, which will either lead or mislead others. We should take great care that the tracks we leave are straight. The only way we will leave a straight track is to live right and run a straight course.

So that the limb which is lame may not be put out of joint, but rather be healed. (12:13*b*)

Lame could apply to weak, limping Christians, who are easily tripped up or misled. It is certainly true that our weaker brothers will be among the first to be hurt by our poor example (see Rom. 14).

But I believe the primary reference here is to professing Christians, those who have identified themselves with the church but who are not saved. They have made a step toward Christ but have not gone all the way. They have the appearance of being in the race of faith, but are not. They are in danger of apostatizing, and are particularly vulnerable to stumbling. They are prime candidates for Satan to trip up.

These are the borderline, fence-straddling kind of people Elijah challenged on Mt. Carmel. Elijah was clearly on the Lord's side and the prophets of Baal were against him. Some of the people no doubt were firmly with Baal and a few were firmly with Elijah. But most of the people, though they were Israelites, were undecided. They preferred not to take sides if they could avoid it. Actually, they tried to play both sides. During the week they would consort with the immoral priestesses of Baal, and on the Sabbath would go to the Temple and worship. So Elijah confronted them with, "How long will you hesitate between two opinions? If the LORD is God, follow Him; but if Baal, follow him" (1 Kings 18:21). The only response he got was silence, but the challenge had been made.

The Septuagint (Greek Old Testament) uses the same word (*chōlos*, "lame, hesitate") in 1 Kings 18:21 that the writer uses in Hebrews 12:13. Elijah was confronting lame, vacillating Israelites and trying to persuade them to take a side. The writer of Hebrews was warning believers about the danger of misleading lame, uncommitted unbelievers and of causing them to apostatize back into Judaism. Under the pressure of persecution, these professing but unbelieving Jews were beginning to doubt the gospel and to weaken in commitment. Inconsistent Christians leaving wandering paths would be no help.

Sadly, Christians sometimes are the greatest stumbling blocks to Christianity. A bad example by a true believer can tilt a person away from

full commitment to Christ, and therefore from salvation. A poor testimony can cause irreparable harm, many times without our knowing it. It can
cause an already limping unbeliever to be **put out of joint,** completely
dislocated spiritually.

God wants unbelievers **healed,** to be saved. It is not His will that
any person should perish (2 Pet. 3:9). This is a serious exhortation indeed—to be sure that our living does not cause anyone to reject the gospel. Jesus warns us,

> You are the salt of the earth; but if the salt has become tasteless, how will it be
> made salty again? It is good for nothing anymore, except to be thrown out and
> trampled under foot by men. You are the light of the world. A city set on a hill
> cannot be hidden. Nor do men light a lamp, and put it under the peckmeasure,
> but on the lampstand; and it gives light to all who are in the house. Let your light
> shine before men in such a way that they may see your good works, and glorify
> your Father who is in heaven. (Matt. 5:13-16)

Peter gives a practical illustration of the principle in a believing
wife's testimony before her unbelieving husband. "You wives, be submissive to your own husbands so that even if any of them are disobedient to
the word, they may be won without a word by the behavior of their
wives, as they observe your chaste and respectful behavior" (1 Pet. 3:1-2).
Directly and indirectly, our testimony should glorify God and therefore
be the best possible influence on those around us.

DILIGENCE

**Pursue peace with all men, and the sanctification without which no
one will see the Lord.** (12:14)

This verse is not easy to interpret, and has been a problem for
many sincere Christians. At first glance, it seems to be teaching salvation
by works—if we successfully pursue peace and sanctification, we will be
saved and will see the Lord. The truth is, however, that a person who is
not saved cannot pursue either peace or sanctification, at least not successfully. Only the Christian has the ability, through the Holy Spirit, to
live in peace and in holiness. " 'There is no peace,' says my God, 'for the
wicked' " (Isa. 57:21) and any righteousness men try to produce apart
from God is as "a filthy garment" (Isa. 64:6).

I believe the writer is speaking of practical peace and righteousness. Positionally, in Christ, Christians already are at peace and already
are righteous, but practically we have a great deal to do. Because we are at
peace with God, we should be peacemakers. Because we are counted
righteous, we should live righteously. Our practice should match our po-

sition. Otherwise the unbeliever will stand back and ask, "Why don't you practice what you preach? If you don't live like Christ says to live, why should I accept Him as my Lord and Savior?" (cf. 1 John 2:6).

Pursuing peace primarily relates to loving men, and pursuing righteousness primarily to loving God. If we love men, we will be at peace with them, and if we love God we will live righteously.

LOVING MEN

Peace is a two-way street. It is not possible for two persons, or two nations, to live at peace with each other if one of them is persistently belligerent. Jesus was peaceful toward all men, but all men were not peaceful toward Him. Paul clarifies the principle. "If possible, so far as it depends on you, be at peace with all men" (Rom. 12:18). We are only responsible for our side of the peace process, but we cannot use another's belligerence as an excuse for responding in kind. We have an obligation to live peaceably, whether or not those around us treat us peaceably. If they do not live peaceably, that is their problem; it is never our excuse.

I once witnessed an interesting drama on the street. A man driving ahead of me apparently had just picked up a brand new car. It still had the dealer's license on it. Another driver, anxious to pass him, pulled around on the right, running through a huge mud puddle as he did. The new car was a mess. A third man, probably a friend who had taken the first man to the car dealer, was in another car. The two of them forced the impatient man off onto the shoulder and blocked him in. They then proceeded to pour soda pop all over the offending vehicle. It was not a demonstration in peacemaking.

On another occasion, I inadvertently cut off another driver. He pulled up beside me at the next light and began cursing profusely. When he finished, I leaned out the window, admitted I was wrong and asked him to forgive me. That was obviously far from the response he expected, and he roared off in a huff. But an effort had been made for peace. In so far as I could, I tried to make peace (see James 3:13-18).

LOVING GOD

Sanctification has to do with our loving God. It speaks of the pure, obedient, holy life we live set apart for God's glory, because of that love. When we love Him, we will want to be like Him, and when we are like Him, others will see Him in us and be attracted to Him. Love toward men and love toward God are inseparable.

The most difficult part of the verse to interpret is **without which no one will see the Lord.** I believe the reference is to unbelievers who see and observe our pursuit of peace and holinesss, without which they would not be drawn to accept Christ themselves. The passage does not read, "without which *you* will not see the Lord," but **without which no one will see the Lord.** In other words, when unbelievers see a Christian's peacefulness and holiness, they are attracted to the Lord. Jesus said, "By this all men will know that you are My disciples, if you have love for one another" (John 13:35). And He prayed to His Father that "they may all be one; even as Thou, Father, art in Me, and I in Thee, that they also may be in Us; that the world may believe that Thou didst send Me" (John 17:21). Our love for each other is a testimony to the Father and to the Son. It is a means of drawing people to Christ, apart from whom **no one will see the Lord.** As we run the race, leaving a straight path, showing love to men by peacemaking, and showing love to God by holiness, people will see the Lord.

Paul agonized over some of the immature Christians at Galatia, to whom he wrote, "My children, with whom I am again in labor until Christ is formed in you" (Gal. 4:19). It was his heart prayer that, above all else, they grow in Christlikeness. Christlikeness is our greatest possible testimony to the world.

VIGILANCE

See to it that no one comes short of the grace of God; that no root of bitterness springing up causes trouble, and by it many be defiled. (12:15)

See to it translates a single Greek word (*episkopeō*), which is closely related to *episkopos* (an overseer, or bishop, and synonymous with elder). We are to have oversight of each other, helping each other grow in holiness and Christlikeness. We are also to look out for, oversee, those in our midst, especially within the church, who may not be believers. We are not to judge, but to be sensitive and concerned for opportunities to present them with the claims of Jesus Christ. And since this letter speaks so often to such people in the assembly, this is a critical point.

TO PREVENT THE FALLING SHORT OF GOD'S GRACE

The first purpose of our oversight should be to win the unsaved to Christ. **Comes short** means to come too late, to be left out. If an unbeliever dies before trusting in Jesus Christ, he will be lost forever, eternally short of God's grace. Tragically, countless thousands of people have spent their entire lives in church, yet have never come to salvation. Other thousands have come to church for a while, seen no evidence of anything supernatural or attractive, and turned away, apostatized. We are exhorted to **see to it,** to be on the lookout, that, in so far as we are able to influence them, no one around us lives under the illusion of being a Christian when he is not, or that no one is exposed to the gospel and turns away from it (cf. Matt. 7:21-23; 1 John 2:19).

We are tempted to hold back witnessing to those who profess to be Christians, but who we have reason to believe are not. We are afraid of offending them. Yet how much greater offense is it to their eternal souls if we fail to present Christ? We are exhorted, *commanded*, to make every effort to **see to it that no one comes short of the grace of God.**

TO PREVENT BITTERNESS

The second purpose for vigilance is to prevent bitterness. Moses warned the Israelites in the wilderness that there should not be among them "a man or woman, or family or tribe, whose heart turns away today from the LORD our God, to go and serve the gods of those nations; lest there shall be among you a root bearing poisonous fruit and wormwood. And it shall be when he hears the words of this curse, that he will boast, saying, 'I have peace though I walk in the stubbornness of my heart in order to destroy the watered land with the dry' " (Deut. 29:18-19). "Poisonous fruit" also carries the idea of bitter. The **root of bitterness** refers to a person who is superficially identified with God's people, and who falls back into paganism. But he is no ordinary apostate. He is arrogant and defiant concerning the things of God. He thumbs his nose at the Lord. God's response to such boastful unbelief is harsh and final. "The LORD shall never be willing to forgive him, but rather the anger of the LORD and His jealousy will burn against that man, and every curse which is written in this book will rest on him, and the LORD will blot out his name from under heaven" (v. 20).

An important purpose of vigilance is to be on guard against such apostates, lest they cause **trouble, and by it many be defiled.** Some apostates simply fall away from the church and are never heard from again. A person in the root of bitterness, however, is a corruptive influence, a serious contamination in the Body. He stays in or near the fellowship of the church and spreads wickedness, doubt, and general defilement. He is not content to apostatize by himself.

TO PREVENT SHALLOW SELFISHNESS

That there be no immoral or godless person like Esau, who sold his own birthright for a single meal. For you know that even afterwards, when he desired to inherit the blessing, he was rejected, for he found no place for repentance, though he sought for it with tears. (12:16-17)

Perhaps the saddest and most godless person in Scripture outside of Judas is Esau. On the surface, their acts against God do not seem as wicked as those of many brutal and heartless pagans. But the Bible strongly condemns them. They had great light. They had every possible opportunity, as much as any person in their times, of knowing and following God. They knew His word, had heard His promises, had seen His miracles, and had had fellowship with His people; yet with determined willfulness they turned their backs on God and the things of God.

Esau not only was **immoral,** but was **godless.** He had no ethics or faith, no scruples or reverence. He had no regard for the good, the truthful, the divine. He was totally worldly, totally secular, totally profane. Christians are to be vigilant that no persons such as Esau contaminate Christ's Body. **See to it . . . that there be no immoral or godless person like Esau.**

Jacob, Esau's brother, was not a model of ethics or integrity, but he genuinely valued the things of God. The birthright was precious to him, though he tried to procure it by devious means. He basically trusted God and relied on God; his brother disregarded God and trusted only in himself.

When Esau finally woke up to some extent and realized what he had forsaken, he made a half-hearted attempt to retrieve it. Just because **he sought for it with tears** does not indicate sincerity or true remorse. **He found no place for repentance.** He bitterly regretted, but he did not repent. He selfishly wanted God's blessings, but he did not want God. He had fully apostatized, and was forever outside the pale of God's grace. He went on "sinning willfully after receiving the knowledge of the truth," and there no longer remained any sacrifice to cover his sins (Heb. 10:26).

We must be vigilant so that no one turns from the truth, becomes bitter, or follows the course of selfish Esau, who wanted God's blessing desperately—but not on God's terms (cf. Mark 10:17-22).

Mount Sinai and Mount Zion (12:18-29)

36

For you have not come to a mountain that may be touched and to a blazing fire, and to darkness and gloom and whirlwind, and to the blast of a trumpet and the sound of words which sound was such that those who heard begged that no further word should be spoken to them. For they could not bear the command, "If even a beast touches the mountain, it will be stoned." And so terrible was the sight, that Moses said, "I am full of fear and trembling." But you have come to Mount Zion and to the city of the living God, the heavenly Jerusalem, and to myriads of angels, to the general assembly and church of the first-born who are enrolled in heaven, and to God, the Judge of all, and to the spirits of righteous men made perfect, and to Jesus, the mediator of a new covenant, and to the sprinkled blood, which speaks better than the blood of Abel. See to it that you do not refuse Him who is speaking. For if those did not escape when they refused him who warned them on earth, much less shall we escape who turn away from Him who warns from heaven. And His voice shook the earth then, but now He has promised, saying, "Yet once more I will shake not only the earth, but also the heaven." And this expression, "Yet once more," denotes the removing of those things which can be shaken, as of created things, in order that those things which cannot be shaken may remain. Therefore, since we receive a kingdom which cannot be shaken, let us show gratitude, by which we may offer to God an acceptable service with reverence and awe; for our God is a consuming fire. (12:18-29)

In addition to the pressures of neglect, unbelief, tradition, and impatience, which were keeping many Jews from fully trusting in Christ, was the pressure of fear. They were afraid of persecution—criticism, ridicule, economic loss, imprisonment, and perhaps even martyrdom (see Heb. 10:32-39). Some had already gotten a taste of persecution just from being associated with the church. All of them could see first-hand the suffering that many true and faithful believers were going through. It was evident that being godly in a godless society was costly.

This passage gives a warning of something far more fear-inspiring than what any human persecution can inflict—God's judgment. Every man will be judged on one of two bases. He will either be judged by the law or by grace, by his own works or by Christ's work, by the provisions of Sinai or by the provisions of Zion. God has two sets of books. In one set are recorded the names of those who have rejected God, in the other the names of those who have accepted Him through His Son, Jesus Christ (Rev. 20:12). The saved are in the book of life, sometimes called the Lamb's book of life (Rev. 13:8). Those whose names are in this book will be judged by what Christ has done on their behalf. Because they have trusted Him in faith, they will be measured and judged by His righteousness instead of their own. Those who have not trusted Him will be measured and judged by their own righteousness, which is of no more value before God than a "filthy garment" (Isa. 64:6).

The fear of those on the verge of accepting Christ should not be of persecution they might receive for believing in Him, but the judgment they will inevitably receive for rejecting Him. Their fear should not be of coming to Mount Zion but of turning back to Mount Sinai. The contrast is vivid.

MOUNT SINAI—THE FEAR OF THE LAW

For you have not come to a mountain that may be touched and to a blazing fire, and to darkness and gloom and whirlwind, and to the blast of a trumpet and the sound of words which sound was such that those who heard begged that no further word should be spoken to them. For they could not bear the command, "If even a beast touches the mountain, it will be stoned." And so terrible was the sight, that Moses said, "I am full of fear and trembling." (12:18-21)

The Old Covenant was associated with Mount Sinai because that is where God spoke to Moses when that covenant was instituted. It was a covenant of law, and it was also a covenant of judgment and of fear. It said, "Do this, or do not do that, or you will be judged." In some cases it said, "Do not do this, or you will die." That is not the place to which the New Covenant brings us. To that mountain **you have not come.**

As God was preparing to establish that covenant, the people were forbidden so much as to set foot on the mountain, under penalty of death. **May be touched** does not refer to permission but possibility. That is, Sinai was a physical mountain, and therefore was able to be touched, seen, and walked on. The earthly mountain symbolized the earthliness of that covenant, as contrasted with **the heavenly Jerusalem** (v. 22). The Old Covenant was the foundational covenant, the kindergarten covenant, which gave the rudiments, the elementary principles, of God's nature, will, and standards. It was therefore given and was to be obeyed in more physical, tangible, picturesque, and symbolic ways.

Exodus 19 describes the requirements and restrictions God gave in preparation for His giving the law. The people were to consecrate themselves by washing their clothes (v. 10) and by abstaining from sexual relations (v. 15) and were forbidden permission to touch even the edge of the mountain (v. 12). God was so concerned that none of the people break those restrictions that He sent Moses back down the mountain to give them a final warning (vv. 21-22). God was going to demonstrate His awesome holiness, and no defiled sinner could come near and witness His holiness and live. It was to be a day unique in human history. The demonstration of power was through the physical means of thunder, lightning, thick clouds, loud trumpet sounds, fire, smoke, and violent trembling of the earth (vv. 16-18). The primary purpose of all these signs was to convince the people of the absolute unapproachableness of God. Sinful man could not come near Him and live.

Understandably, the people were terrified; they were gripped with fear. "They trembled and stood at a distance," and pleaded with Moses, "let not God speak to us, lest we die" (20:18-19). At this, Moses assured them that they had no reason for being terrified unless they disobeyed. "Do not be afraid; for God has come in order to test you, and in order that the fear of Him may remain with you, so that you may not sin" (v. 20). In other words, if they had the proper fear of God by honoring His holiness and obeying His law, they had no reason to fear His wrath. God intended that His people have a reverential fear of Him "so that [they] may not sin."

The God of Sinai is truly a God to be feared, a God of judgment and of punishment. Sinai, representing the Old Covenant, was a mountain of fear and of judgment. The writer of Hebrews is saying to his readers, "If you go back to Judaism, you are going back to a covenant of law, fear, judgment, and death." Paul described it as "the ministry of death, in letters engraved on stones" (2 Cor. 3:7).

To stand at the foot of Sinai, even without touching it, is to stand under judgment and doom. It demands and it punishes. Since no man in himself can fulfill its demands, no man in himself can escape its punishment. At Sinai, sinful and unforgiven man stands before an infinitely holy and perfectly just God. Guilty, vile, and undeserving of forgiveness, he has nothing to expect from Sinai but God's condemnation. The symbols of Sinai are darkness, fire, trembling, and trumpets of judgment. For an unforgiven sinner, "It is a terrifying thing to fall into the hands of the living God" (Heb. 10:31). There is good reason to fear at the foot of Sinai.

God gave Israel the covenant of law in the middle of the wilderness, away from all distractions, all interference, and all hiding places. They had nothing to focus on but God, and in doing so became terribly aware of their own sinfulness. The first thing that leads a person to repentance and dependence on God for deliverance is the awareness of his sinfulness. Apart from seeing his sinfulness, a person has no reason to seek salvation. Only seeing our sin can make us see our need for salvation from sin and from the judgment it brings. This was the purpose of Sinai, to bring the people face to face with their own sinfulness, with no place to hide.

The law is God's great mirror. When we look into it, we see ourselves as we really are—immeasurably short of God's standard of righteousness. There is not a single commandment that we have kept perfectly or can keep perfectly, in either act or attitude. The law makes no exceptions and no allowance for less than perfect obedience. The law overwhelms us, slays us. No sinner can endure Sinai. Every sinner who stands at the foot of Sinai is paralyzed with fear. **So terrible was the sight, that Moses said, "I am full of fear and trembling."** Even Moses, to whom God had spoken through the fiery bush and through whom He had challenged Pharaoh, could not stand at Sinai fearless.

For many years the apostle Paul had been a student of the law. He knew the Old Testament as few men of his time knew it. Yet, until Jesus confronted him on the Damascus road, he had never really confronted the law of Moses. He had studied it, memorized it, and probably taught it. But he had never confronted it. He had never looked squarely into it to see himself. He had thought he was alive. In fact he had thought he was alive because of his obedience to the law. But in seeing Jesus Christ, he also saw the law—and himself reflected in the mirror of the law. Consequently, "When the commandment came, sin became alive, and I died; and this commandment, which was to result in life, proved to result in death for me; for sin, taking opportunity through the commandment, deceived me, and through it killed me" (Rom. 7:9-11). Though he had been active in Judaism all his life and was a scholar of the Old Testament, he had never before stood at the foot of Sinai. He had eyes, but had not seen, and had ears but had not heard (Jer. 5:21). He had not understood the clear and unmistakable declaration of Deuteronomy 27:26. But in Christ he came to understand it, and he quotes it to some Galatians who were beginning to fall back into Judaism: "For as many as are of the works of the Law are under a curse; for it is written, 'Cursed is everyone who does not abide by all things written in the book of the law, to perform them' " (Gal. 3:10).

MOUNT ZION—THE GRACE OF THE GOSPEL

But you have come to Mount Zion and to the city of the living God, the heavenly Jerusalem, and to myriads of angels, to the general assembly and church of the first-born who are enrolled in heaven, and to God, the Judge of all, and to the spirits of righteous men made perfect, and to Jesus, the mediator of a new covenant, and to the sprinkled blood, which speaks better than the blood of Abel. (12:22-24)

The mountain of the New Covenant is **Mount Zion,** representing the **heavenly Jerusalem.** The opposite of Sinai, it is not touchable, but it is approachable. Sinai symbolizes law and Zion symbolizes grace. No man can be saved by the law, but any man can be saved by grace. The law confronts us with commandments, judgment, and condemnation. Grace presents us with forgiveness, atonement, and salvation.

Ever since David had conquered the Jebusites and had placed the ark on Mount Zion, this mountain had been considered the special earthly dwelling place of God. "For the LORD has chosen Zion; He has desired it for His habitation. 'This is My resting place forever; here I will dwell, for I have desired it' " (Ps. 132:13-14). When Solomon moved the ark to the Temple, which was built on nearby Mt. Moriah, the name Zion was extended to include that area as well. Before long, Zion became synonymous with Jerusalem, and Jerusalem was therefore the city of God and the place of sacrifices. Isaiah, who spoke often and hopefully of Zion, says that God will "grant salvation in Zion" (46:13).

Whereas Sinai was forbidding and terrifying, Zion is inviting and gracious. Sinai is closed to all, because no one is able to please God on Sinai's terms—perfect fulfillment of the law. Zion is open to all, because Jesus Christ has met those terms and will stand in the place of anyone who will come to God through Him. Zion symbolizes the approachable God.

Sinai was covered by clouds and darkness; Zion is the city of light. "Out of Zion, the perfection of beauty, God has shone forth" (Ps. 50:2).

Sinai stands for judgment and death; Zion for forgiveness and life, "for there the LORD commanded the blessing—life forever" (Ps. 133:3).

The Jews to whom Hebrews is speaking at this point are clearly believers, for they are told, **you have come to Mount Zion.** They were already on the gracious mountain of God, already in **the city of the living God, the heavenly Jerusalem.** As Christians, we are already citizens of heaven, where we now spiritually dwell (Phil. 3:20).

In coming to Mount Zion—that is, by becoming a Christian—we come to seven other blessings: **the heavenly city; the general assembly; the church of the first-born; God, the Judge of all; the spirits of righteous men made perfect; to Jesus; and to the sprinkled blood.**

THE HEAVENLY CITY

The city of the living God, the heavenly Jerusalem, is heaven itself. Coming to Christ is coming to heaven, the only way to come to heaven. When we come to Mount Zion, we come by grace to the city Abraham looked for, "the city which has foundations, whose architect and builder is God" (Heb. 11:10). From the moment of salvation, heaven is our spiritual home—where our heavenly Father and our Savior are, and where the rest of our spiritual family is. That is where our treasure is, our inheritance is, our hope is. Everything we have of any value is there and all that we should want is there.

Until the Lord takes us there to be with Himself, however, we cannot enjoy its full citizenship. For now we are ambassadors on earth. As ambassadors we have full citizenship in our home country, but we are away from it for a while and cannot enjoy its full blessings. In the meanwhile we are to be faithful emissaries of our Savior and our heavenly Father, reflecting their nature before a world that does not know them. And Paul encourages us not to lose our perspective of the incomparable value of our heavenly inheritance (Rom. 8:17-18).

And like the writer of Hebrews, Paul uses Sinai and Jerusalem as figures of the Old and New Covenants and, consequently, of the old and new relationships to God that they represent. "Now this Hagar is Mount Sinai in Arabia, and corresponds to the present Jerusalem, for she is in slavery with her children. But the Jerusalem above is free; she is our mother. . . . So then, brethren, we are not children of a bondwoman, but of the free woman" (Gal. 4:25-26, 31). Sinai is the mountain of bondage. Zion, the heavenly Jerusalem, is the mountain of freedom.

THE GENERAL ASSEMBLY

I believe **the general assembly** (*panēguris*, "a gathering for a public festival") refers to the **myriads of angels,** rather than to **the church**

of the first-born. The translation could be, "But you have come to . . .
an innumerable company of angels in festal gathering." When we come in
Jesus Christ to Mount Zion, we come to a great gathering of celebrating
angels, whom we join in praising God. Daniel gives us an idea of just how
many angels we will be joining in heaven: "Thousands upon thousands
were attending Him, and myriads upon myriads were standing before
Him" (Dan. 7:10; cf. Rev. 5:11).

Innumerable angels were also present at Sinai, as mediators of the
Mosaic covenant (Gal. 3:19), the covenant of law and judgment. But men
could not join them there. Like the God they served, at Sinai they were
unapproachable. The angels were not celebrating at Sinai; they were
blowing the trumpets of judgment.

Contrary to what some churches teach, we are not to worship angels. We join them in worshiping God, and God alone. "Let no one keep
defrauding you of your prize," Paul warns, "by delighting in self-abasement and the worship of the angels" (Col. 2:18). During his vision on
Patmos, John once was so awestruck that he fell at the feet of an angel
and would have worshiped him. But the angel forbid him, saying, "Do
not do that; I am a fellow servant of yours and your brethren who hold
the testimony of Jesus; worship God" (Rev. 19:10). In heaven, we will
not worship angels, but will worship *with* angels. We will join them in
eternal celebration and praise of God.

THE CHURCH OF THE FIRST-BORN

The **church of the first-born who are enrolled in heaven** is
the Body of Christ. The first-born are those who receive the inheritance.
As believers, we are "heirs of God and fellow heirs with Christ," who is
"the first-born among many brethren" (Rom. 8:17, 29).

Jesus tells us that we should not rejoice in the great works that
God may do through us but that our "names are recorded in heaven"
(Luke 10:20). Our names **are enrolled in heaven** in "the Lamb's book
of life" (Rev. 21:27).

GOD, THE JUDGE OF ALL

On Mount Zion we can come into God's own presence, an incomprehensible concept to a Jew who knew only the God of Sinai. But at
Jesus' crucifixion, "the veil of the temple was torn in two" (Luke 23:45),
and the way into God's presence forever made open for those who trust
in the atoning work of that crucifixion. To come into God's presence at
Sinai was to die; to come into His presence at Zion is to live (cf. Ps. 73:25;
Rev. 21:3).

THE SPIRITS OF RIGHTEOUS MEN MADE PERFECT

The spirits of righteous men made perfect are Old Testament saints, those who could only look forward to forgiveness, peace, and deliverance. When we come to heaven we will join Abel, Abraham, Moses, David, and all the others in one great household of God (cf. Matt. 8:11).

They had to wait a long time for the perfection that we received the instant we trusted in Christ. In fact, they had to wait for us (Heb. 11:40), in the sense that they had to wait for Christ's death and resurrection before they could be glorified. In heaven we will be one with them in Jesus Christ. We will not be inferior to Abraham or Moses or Elijah, because we will all be equal in righteousness, because our only righteousness will be our Savior's righteousness.

JESUS

Supremely we come **to Jesus,** in the fullness of His beauty and glory as **the mediator of a new covenant.** Our Lord is here called by His redemptive name, Jesus, which He was given because He would "save His people from their sins" (Matt. 1:21). When we come to Mount Zion, we come to our Savior, our Redeemer, our one and only Mediator with the Father. First John 3:2 sums up the ultimate end of this truth: "we shall be like Him."

THE SPRINKLED BLOOD

To come to Christianity is to come **to the sprinkled blood,** the atoning blood, through which we have redemption, "through His blood, the forgiveness of our trespasses, according to the riches of His grace" (Eph. 1:7), and by which all who "formerly were far off have been brought near" (2:13).

The sprinkled blood of Jesus far surpasses the sacrifice of Abel (Heb. 11:4) and **speaks better than the blood of Abel.** Abel's sacrifice was acceptable to God because it was offered in faith, but it had no atoning power—not even for Abel, much less for anyone else. Jesus' blood, however, was sufficient to cleanse the sins of all men for all time, to make peace with God for whoever trusts in that blood sacrifice (Col. 1:20).

RESPONDING TO THE GOSPEL

See to it that you do not refuse Him who is speaking. For if those did not escape when they refused him who warned them on earth, much less shall we escape who turn away from Him who warns from heaven. And His voice shook the earth then, but now He has promised,

saying, "Yet once more I will shake not only the earth, but also the heaven." And this expression, "Yet once more," denotes the removing of those things which can be shaken, as of created things, in order that those things which cannot be shaken may remain. Therefore, since we receive a kingdom which cannot be shaken, let us show gratitude, by which we may offer to God an acceptable service with reverence and awe; for our God is a consuming fire. (12:25-29)

After giving the contrasts between Mount Sinai and Mount Zion, the writer says, in effect, "Here is what you must do. You must not ignore **Him who is speaking.**" "God, after He spoke long ago to the fathers in the prophets in many portions and in many ways, in these last days has spoken to us in His Son" (Heb. 1:1-2). If men were held accountable for heeding God when He **warned them on earth,** from Mount Sinai, how much more will they be held accountable now that He **warns from heaven,** from Mount Zion?

The unbelieving Israelites who ignored God at Sinai did not enter the earthly Promised Land, and unbelievers today, Jew or Gentile, who ignore God when He speaks through His Son from Mount Zion will not enter the heavenly promised land. Whether God speaks from Sinai or from Zion, no man who refuses Him will escape judgment.

The blessings of receiving the second covenant are immeasurably greater than those for receiving the first. And the consequences for refusing the second are also immeasurably greater. "Anyone who has set aside the Law of Moses dies without mercy on the testimony of two or three witnesses. How much severer punishment do you think he will deserve who has trampled under foot the Son of God, and has regarded as unclean the blood of the covenant by which he was sanctified, and has insulted the Spirit of grace?" (Heb. 10:28-29).

At Sinai, God **shook the earth.** From Zion He is also going to shake the very heavens, the entire universe. If unbelievers did not escape when the earth was shaken, how much less will they escape when both heaven and earth are shaken? The writer quotes from what the Lord had predicted through Haggai, "Once more in a little while, I am going to shake the heavens and the earth, the sea also and the dry land" (Hag. 2:6; cf. Isa. 13:13). The sun will become black, the moon will become like blood, stars will fall to earth, the sky will split apart like a scroll, and every mountain and island will be moved out of its place (Rev. 6:12-14).

Commenting on the Haggai passage, Hebrews 12:27 explains that the expression, **"Yet once more,"** denotes the **removing of those things which can be shaken, as of created things, in order that those things which cannot be shaken may remain.** Everything physical (**those things which can be shaken**) will be destroyed. Only the eternal things will remain.

Peter tells us that at that time, which "will come like a thief, . . . the heavens will pass away with a roar and the elements will be destroyed with intense heat, and the earth and its works will be burned up" and "the heavens will be destroyed by burning, and the elements will melt with intense heat!" (2 Pet. 3:10, 12). This will constitute the "shaking" **of those things which can be shaken,** the total destruction of the physical universe by the wrath of God.

But some things are unshakable, and these will **remain.** God has prepared "a new heaven and a new earth," which will include "the holy city, new Jerusalem, coming down out of heaven from God, made ready as a bride adorned for her husband" (Rev. 21:1-2). This is the kingdom **we receive.** It is **a kingdom which cannot be shaken.** It is eternal, unchangeable, immovable. We will never be taken from it, and it will never be taken from us. For this amazing blessing in Christ, we should **show gratitude, by which we may offer to God an acceptable service with reverence and awe.** The right response, then, is a worshiping life offering holy service to our worthy and awesome God.

The closing verse of chapter 12 is perhaps the severest warning in the book of Hebrews: **for our God is a consuming fire.** The writer is warning again by saying, "Some of you have come to the edge of full acceptance of Christ. Don't go back to Judaism now. Only judgment awaits you at Sinai, and even worse judgment in refusing the offer of Zion. Don't be consumed in God's fierce, unrelenting fire of judgment."

To live under Judaism is to come to Sinai and its judgment, wherein all who trust in the works of the law, even God's own law, will be condemned. To go back to Judaism, after hearing the gospel, after seeing Zion, brings even greater damnation. Those Jews who had "been enlightened" and had "tasted of the heavenly gift," and even "been made partakers of the Holy Spirit" (Heb. 6:4) could not simply revert to Judaism. They could not pick up where they had left off. If they turned back now, they would be subject not only to Sinai's judgment but to Zion's as well.

For every man the choice is the same. Whether we are Jew or Gentile, to try to approach God by our works is to come to Sinai and to discover that our works fall short and cannot save us. Whether we are Jew or Gentile, to trust in the atoning blood of Jesus Christ is to come to Zion, where our heavenly High Priest will mediate for us and bring us to the Father, and where we find reconciliation, peace, and eternal life. And if you have truly come to Zion and received all its blessings, it is inconceivable that you would want to hold on to Sinai in any way.

Christian Behavior: In Relation to Others (13:1-3)

37

Let love of the brethren continue. Do not neglect to show hospitality to strangers, for by this some have entertained angels without knowing it. Remember the prisoners, as though in prison with them, and those who are ill-treated, since you yourselves also are in the body. (13:1-3)

The first eleven chapters of Hebrews do not emphasize specific commands to Christians. There is an obvious lack of practical explanations or exhortations. The section is pure doctrine and is almost entirely directed to Jews who have received the gospel but need to be affirmed in the superiority of the New Covenant.

The exhortations in chapter 12 that apply to Christians are general, encouraging them to run the race of faith with patience and to follow peace and holiness. The specific practical exhortations for Christians are in chapter 13. This fits the pattern of New Testament teaching, which is always doctrine and then duty, position and then practice. Chapter 13 is not an afterthought, but is integral to the message of the book. True faith demands true living.

When Pliny the Younger reported on the Christians to the Roman emperor Trajan in the first century, he wrote, "They bind themselves by an oath not to any criminal end, but to avoid theft or robbery or adultery, never to break their word or repudiate a deposit when called on to refund it." Although he was looking for a charge against them, he was forced to characterize them as a people who did not commit crimes and who paid their debts.

Early Christians were a rebuke to the pagan and immoral societies in which they lived, and those societies often sought to condemn them. But the more they examined the lives of believers, the more it became obvious that Christians lived up to the high moral standards of their doctrine.

Peter may have had such criticism in mind when he wrote, "For such is the will of God that by doing right you may silence the ignorance of foolish men" (1 Pet. 2:15). Paul wrote similar words to Titus, advising him, "In all things show yourself to be an example of good deeds, with purity in doctrine, dignified, sound in speech which is beyond reproach, in order that the opponent may be put to shame, having nothing bad to say about us" (Titus 2:7-8).

Hebrews 13 gives some of the essential practical ethics of Christian living that help portray the true gospel to the world, that encourage men to trust in Christ, and that bring glory to God.

The philosopher Bertrand Russell wrote a famous essay entitled, "Why I Am Not a Christian." In this and other essays on the same general subject, he presented what he believed were irrefutable arguments for rejecting Christianity. He focused primarily on the lives of Christians he had known or heard of who lived far less than exemplary lives. He wrote, "I think there are many good points upon which I agree with Christ a great deal more than many professing Christians. I do not know that I can go all the way with Him, but I could go with him much farther than most professing Christians can. I do not profess to live up to them (that is, Christ's standards) myself, but then after all, it is not quite the same thing as for a Christian, is it?" He goes on to say, "There is the idea that we should all be wicked, if we did not hold to the Christian religion. It seems to me that the people who have held to it have been, for the most part, extremely wicked. The Spaniards, for example, in Mexico and Peru, used to baptize infants of the Indians, and immediately dash their brains out, by this means securing for them a place in heaven." With many other such examples, he argued against Christianity and the Bible.

The fact that Russell chose only examples that supported his preconceived notions and was guilty of rationalizing many of his points does not lessen the impact of some of his statements. Unfortunately, throughout the history of the church, the mean, prejudiced, and immoral lives of professed Christians have given the world an excuse not to be attracted to the claims of Christ. The fact that critics usually pick out the worst examples behooves us all the more to live by the very highest standards—to keep the bad examples to a minimum. We who are true Christians have a serious responsibility to live spotlessly to the glory of God, so that unbelievers never have a just reason for criticizing the way we live, because how we live is a reflection on our Lord.

Once when I was visiting a jail, I met a prisoner who was quite vocal about his being a Christian. When I asked if he had been converted while in prison, he answered no. Then I asked why he was in jail, thinking perhaps he had been convicted for standing up for his conscience on an important Christian principle. When he told me he was jailed for ignoring 30 or so parking tickets, I strongly suggested that he not advertise the fact he was a Christian. His life was a testimony against Christ.

"The world," said Alexander Maclaren, "takes its notion of God most of all from those who say they belong to God's family. They read us a great deal more than they read the Bible. They see us; they only hear about Jesus Christ." Our Lord commanded of His followers, "Let your light shine before men in such a way that they may see your good works, and glorify your Father who is in heaven" (Matt. 5:16).

Jesus, of course, had in mind true good works, not hypocritical pretense. At a conference where the famous evangelist D. L. Moody was present, some of the more zealous young people decided to spend a night in prayer. The next morning one of the young men said to Moody, "We have just come from a wonderful all-night prayer meeting. See how our faces shine!" The evangelist replied, "Moses knew not that his face shone." Good works that are self-conscious and hypocritical are not hard to spot. They do not impress God or unbelievers.

Ethics has to do with standards of conduct (behavior) or moral judgment. There can be no ethics without doctrine. Doctrine is the foundation on which any practical ethic must be based. So-called situation ethics is not really ethics at all, in the sense of having a pattern or standard of behavior. When what you do is based entirely on how you feel and what you desire at any given moment, the very idea of a standard or principle is nonsense. It is not possible to have *any* system of ethics without standards of right and wrong. You cannot reasonably require a certain type of living or morality from a person without underlying, undergirding, and universal moral principles that determine those standards. Otherwise you have no ethics at all, only a moral free-for-all, which is exactly what many people are advocating and exemplifying today.

The idea that doctrine is useless and divisive, that all we need to live by is love, is fantasy and foolishness. Love itself needs a standard. Without a standard, one person's idea of love often will be different from—and frequently contradictory to—someone else's. Desiring another man's wife may seem like love to the one who is desiring, but is something quite different to her husband. Trying to throw away doctrine while keeping ethics is like trying to keep your house intact while taking out the foundation.

Christian ethics not only demand right doctrine but a right relationship with Jesus Christ. Without a saving relationship to Him, a person will have neither the sustained desire nor the ability to live up to New Testament standards of morality. Every moral command in the New Testament presupposes faith in Christ. You cannot possibly live up to God's standards without God.

I was once asked to speak on the Christian view of sex at an ethics class at a state university. I introduced my talk with words to this effect: "I don't expect any of you here to believe what I say. I do not think you have the capacity either to understand or accept the Christian view of sex. It will be totally foreign to you, because you cannot comprehend or accept it without a personal relationship to Jesus Christ." Then, before presenting the basics of the New Testament teachings about sex, I spent about half an hour explaining what a personal relationship to Jesus Christ means.

The standards of Christian behavior set forth in Hebrews 13 presuppose two basic realities: that these standards are based on the doctrinal foundation of chapters 1 through 12, and that they apply to Christian believers.

SUSTAINED LOVE

Let love of the brethren continue. (13:1)

The primary moral standard of Christianity is love, and the particular love exhorted here is love of fellow Christians. **Love of the brethren** is one word (*philadelphia*) in the Greek and is often translated "brotherly love." It is composed of two root words—*phileō* (tender affection) and *adelphos* (brother, or near kinsman; literally, "from the same womb").

LOVE FOR THE BRETHREN

Brotherly love can have two significant applications. In some places in the New Testament, unbelieving Jews are spoken of as brothers. Physically, all Jews are from the same womb, descendants of Abraham by Sarah. They are God's chosen people, with whom He is not yet finished. The first idea here, then, could be that of continuing to love fellow Jews who are not Christians. Christian Jews were to be totally separated from Judaism, from the rituals, ceremonies, laws, and standards of the Old

Covenant. But they were to maintain a deep love for unbelieving fellow Jews. In turning their backs on Judaism, they were not to turn their backs on brother Jews. They were to have the same love that caused Paul to write, "For I could wish that I myself were accursed, separated from Christ for the sake of my brethren, my kinsmen according to the flesh, who are Israelites" (Rom. 9:3-4).

The primary teaching, however, is love for fellow Christians, our spiritual brothers. The admonition to let brotherly love **continue** indicates that such love already exists. Brotherly love is the natural outflow of the Christian life. It cannot be generated, but it can be stifled as well as nurtured. We are therefore not told to make it happen but to let it continue. When a person is saved he is naturally drawn to fellowship with other believers. Unfortunately, this attitude often changes, but it does so only if the love we were given at salvation (Rom. 5:5) is stifled.

Love of other Christians is vital to spiritual life. "Since you have in obedience to the truth purified your souls for a sincere love of the brethren, fervently love one another from the heart, for you have been born again not of seed which is perishable but imperishable, that is, through the living and abiding word of God" (1 Pet. 1:22-23). One of the by-products of obeying God's truth is increased love for fellow believers.

Since we were given brotherly love when we were given spiritual life, we should exercise this love. The Christian's task is not to seek God's blessings but to use them. We already possess all the blessings that are most important, "seeing that His divine power has granted to us everything pertaining to life and godliness" (2 Pet. 1:3). Our primary concern should not be to look for blessings or to ask for blessings but to use our blessings (cf. Eph. 1:3).

Paul teaches a closely related truth in Ephesians, as he appeals to brothers in Christ to be diligent "to preserve the unity of the Spirit in the bond of peace" (Eph. 4:3). They are told to preserve, not manufacture, the unity of the Spirit. In the same way, we preserve brotherly love by expressing it and nurturing it, and by not polluting it or neglecting it. "Now as to the love of the brethren, you have no need for anyone to write to you, for you yourselves are taught by God to love one another; for indeed you do practice it toward all the brethren who are in all Macedonia. But we urge you, brethren, to excel still more" (1 Thess. 4:9-10). We do not need to have more love; we need to use the love we have. We do not need more unity or more peace; we need to use the unity and peace that are already ours in Jesus Christ.

The believers to whom the book of Hebrews was written were experienced in showing love. "For God is not unjust so as to forget your work and the love which you have shown toward His name, in having ministered and in still ministering to the saints" (Heb. 6:10). They had faithfully exercised love for the brethren in the past and are encouraged to continue.

The basic principle of brotherly love is simple, and is explained by Paul. "Be devoted to one another in brotherly love; give preference to one another in honor" (Rom. 12:10). Put in its most basic form, brotherly love is caring for fellow Christians more than we care for ourselves. When we are preoccupied with ourselves, we stifle brotherly love. "Do nothing from selfishness or empty conceit, but with humility of mind let each of you regard one another as more important than himself; do not merely look out for your own personal interests, but also for the interests of others" (Phil. 2:3-4). Brotherly love is nurtured in humility, and humility grows out of right spiritual knowledge. When we measure ourselves against the Person of Jesus Christ, who is the standard for our living, we see ourselves as we really are and are humbled. Only then are we truly able to love as God wants us to love.

WHY BROTHERLY LOVE IS IMPORTANT

Brotherly love is important for three primary reasons: it reveals to the world that we belong to Christ; it reveals our true identity to ourselves; and it delights God.

Jesus said, "By this all men will know that you are My disciples, if you have love for one another" (John 13:35). In effect, God has given the world a right to evaluate us on the basis of our love for each other. As a witness to the world, and as a testimony for our Lord, it is of the greatest importance that we genuinely consider others better than ourselves, that we look out for their interests above our own. In so doing, our lives preach a powerful and eloquent sermon.

Loving fellow Christians also reveals our true identity—it gives added assurance to us of our spiritual life in Christ. "We know that we have passed out of death into life, because we love the brethren. He who does not love abides in death" (1 John 3:14). A sure proof of salvation is found in our own hearts. It is our love for each other. If we wonder about our salvation, we can ask, "Do I have a great concern for the welfare of the Christians I know? Do I enjoy their fellowship? Do I show my concern by ministering to their needs?" If the answer is yes, we have no better evidence that we are a child of God—because we love His other children, our brothers and sisters in Christ.

A third reason brotherly love is important is that it delights God. Nothing is more pleasing to parents than to see their children caring for each other. "Behold, how good and how pleasant it is for brothers to dwell together in unity!" (Ps. 133:1). When His children care for each other, help each other, and live in harmony with each other, God is both delighted and glorified. When we love each other to the degree where we are willing to give our lives for one another, we exemplify God's own Son. "We know love by this, that He laid down His life for us; and we ought to lay down our lives for the brethren" (1 John 3:16).

New Testament brotherly love is not sentimental, superficial affection. It is affection built on deep and continuing concern and is characterized by practical commitment. "Whoever has the world's goods, and beholds his brother in need and closes his heart against him, how does the love of God abide in him?" (1 John 3:17). In other words, refusing to help fellow believers when we are able to do so proves we do not really love them; and if we do not really love them, how can God's love be in our hearts? And if His love is not in our hearts, we do not belong to Him. John's logic is powerful and practical. He continues, "Little children, let us not love with word or with tongue, but in deed and truth. We shall know by this that we are of the truth, and shall assure our heart before Him" (vv. 18-19).

The obvious cause of lovelessness among Christians is sin. Jesus predicted, "And because lawlessness is increased, most people's love will grow cold" (Matt. 24:12). Nothing cools love as fast as sin, especially that of selfish pride. Contrary to the claims of much popular teaching and writing today that goes under the guise of evangelicalism, self-esteem, self-glory, and pride are the great enemies not only of God but of love. "Clothe yourselves with humility toward one another, for God is opposed to the proud, but gives grace to the humble" (1 Pet. 5:5). Apart from humility, so-called love for others is nothing more than using them for selfish ends, for our own purposes and satisfaction. Self-concern and brotherly love are as mutually exclusive and contradictory as darkness and light. Love only grows in the garden of humility.

In an unusually graphic illustration, the writer of Proverbs describes the true nature of self. "The leech has two daughters, 'Give,' 'Give' " (Prov. 30:15). The leech mentioned here, probably a large and especially repulsive creature, has two forks in its tongue, with which it sucks blood from its victims. It is said that it would often gorge itself until it exploded. Spiritually, this leech is self-love and its two daughters are self-righteousness and self-pity. It is never satisfied, and its insatiable appetite is the enemy of everything around it. It is even its own worst enemy, because self-love can never truly be satisfied.

Self-love perverts everything. Self must die if brotherly love is to continue. Pride and self-love are fatal to brotherly love. Jesus, God's own Son, came not to be ministered to but to minister, not to do His own will but His Father's. Who had more reason to be proud than Jesus, the Creator and Lord of the universe? Yet He said, "Take My yoke upon you, and learn from Me, for I am gentle and humble in heart" (Matt. 11:29). The only source of brotherly love is a gentle and humble heart, like the heart of Jesus.

LOVE FOR STRANGERS

Do not neglect to show hospitality to strangers, for by this some have entertained angels without knowing it. (13:2)

Strangers, like **brethren** (v. 1), can refer to unbelievers as well as believers. Our first responsibility is to our brothers in Christ, but our responsibility does not end there. "While we have opportunity, let us do good to all men, and especially to those who are of the household of the faith" (Gal. 6:10). Paul is just as explicit in 1 Thessalonians: "See that no one repays another with evil for evil, but always seek after that which is good for one another and for all men" (5:15). "All men" includes even our enemies. "You have heard that it was said, 'You shall love your neighbor, and hate your enemy.' But I say to you, love your enemies, and pray for those who persecute you" (Matt. 5:43-44). Even the most worldly of people love those who love them, Jesus goes on to say (v. 46).

The danger of "being taken" is no excuse for not helping someone in need. A **stranger,** by definition, is someone we do not know personally. Consequently, it is easy to be deceived when helping a stranger. A person who asks us for ten dollars to buy food for his family may spend it on alcohol or drugs. We should use our common sense in deciding how best to help him, but our primary concern should be for helping, not for avoiding being taken advantage of. If we help in good faith, God will honor our effort. Love is often taken advantage of, but this is a cost that it does not count.

In the ancient world **hospitality** often included putting a guest up overnight or longer. Inns were few, often had poor reputations, and were expensive. Among Jews and people of the Near East in general, hospitality, even to strangers and foreigners, was a great virtue. Christians are certainly to be no less hospitable.

Hospitality is a New Testament standard for overseers, or bishops (1 Tim. 3:2; Titus 1:8). Pastors and other church leaders are to have open homes, ready to serve and meet the needs of others. Showing hospitality to strangers is the work of a spiritual woman (1 Tim. 5:10). In other words, hospitality should be a mark of all Christians, a basic characteristic, not an incidental or optional practice.

For by this some have entertained angels without knowing it is not given as the basis or motivation for hospitality. We are not to be hospitable because on some occasion we might find ourselves ministering to angels. We are to minister out of brotherly love, for the sake of those we help and for God's glory. The point of the second half of verse 2 is that we can never know how important and far-reaching a simple act of helpfulness may be. We minister because of need, not because of any consequences we are able to foresee. Abraham went out of his way to

426

help the three men who were passing by his tent. He did not wait to be asked for help but volunteered. It was an opportunity more than a duty. In fact he considered the greater service was to himself, saying "My lord, if now I have found favor in your sight, please do not pass your servant by" (Gen. 18:3). At the time, he had no idea that two of the men were angels and that the third was the Lord Himself (18:1; 19:1). And if he had known they were not, it would have been no less right for him to be hospitable.

In a sense, we always minister to the Lord when we are hospitable, especially to fellow believers. "Truly I say to you, to the extent that you did it to one of these brothers of Mine, even the least of them, you did it to Me" (Matt. 25:40). To feed the hungry, take in the stranger, clothe the naked, and visit the imprisoned in Jesus' name is to serve Him. To turn our backs on those in need of such things is to turn our backs on Him (v. 45).

SYMPATHY

Remember the prisoners, as though in prison with them, and those who are ill-treated, since you yourselves also are in the body. (13:3)

Sympathy is closely related to sustained love. It is easier to help others when we ourselves have needed help. It is easier to appreciate hunger when we have been hungry, loneliness when we have been lonely, and persecution when we have been persecuted. It is not that a Christian must experience starvation or extreme loneliness or imprisonment in order to be sympathetic to those who are experiencing these things. The point is that we should do our best to identify with those in need, to try to put ourselves in their places. We know that if we were starving, we would want someone to feed us, and that if we were imprisoned, we would want to be visited. We should do for them what we would want done for us were we **in prison with them.** It is the principle of Jesus' golden rule: "Therefore, however you want people to treat you, so treat them, for this is the Law and the Prophets" (Matt. 7:12).

Among other things, Hebrews 13:3 is a warning against spiritualizing the Christian life. The Bible does not teach, as do some eastern religions, that the person in touch with God transcends physical pain, hardships, and other such realities. Our true home is heaven, but we are still **in the body.** We still get hungry, we still get lonely, and we still hurt, physically and psychologically. Our own hungers and hurts should make us more sensitive to those of others. Instead of seeing our own troubles as an excuse for not helping, we should see them as an incentive for being more helpful. Our own troubles should make us more sensitive, hospitable, and loving, not less. One of the surest cures for self-pity is loving service.

Tertullian, an early Christian apologist, wrote, "If there happen to be any in the mines, banished to the islands, or shut up in prisons, the Christians become carriers of their confession." Aristodes, the pagan orator, said of the Christians, "If they hear that any one of their number is in prison or in distress for the sake of their Christ's name, they all render aid in his necessity, and if they can, they redeem him, to set him free." In other words, if he was in jail, they would pay his fine or redemption price. The Apostolic Confession said, "If any Christian is condemned for Christ's sake to the mines by the ungodly, do not overlook him, but from the proceeds of your toil and sweat, send him something to support himself, and to reward the soldier of Christ. All money accruing from honest labor do you appoint and apportion to the redeeming of the saints, ransoming thereby slaves and captives and prisoners, people who are sore abused, and condemned by tyrants." Some early Christians sold themselves into slavery to get money to free a fellow believer.

We can show sympathy in at least three important ways. For one thing, we can simply "be there" when others are in trouble. Sometimes the mere presence of a friend is the best encouragement and strength.

Another way to show sympathy is by giving direct help. Paul thanked the Philippians for sharing with him in his affliction by giving him money to carry on his ministry in other places (Phil. 4:14-16). By supporting him financially, they also encouraged him spiritually.

A third way to show sympathy is through prayer. Again Paul's ministry gives us an example. His closing words to the Colossians, "Remember my imprisonment" (Col. 4:18), were an appeal for prayer. They could not visit him, and money would have been no help at that time. But by remembering him in prayer they could support him powerfully.

Bearing each other's burdens fulfills Christ's law (Gal. 6:2), which is love. If "we do not have a high priest who cannot sympathize with our weaknesses" (Heb. 4:15), how much more should we sympathize with others, especially fellow Christians, who are in need? Following Jesus' example, who did not come to be ministered to but to minister, we should lose ourselves in the sustained, sympathetic, and loving care of others.

Christian Behavior: In Relation to Ourselves

38

(13:4-9)

Let marriage be held in honor among all, and let the marriage bed be undefiled; for fornicators and adulterers God will judge. Let your character be free from the love of money, being content with what you have; for He Himself has said, "I will never desert you, nor will I ever forsake you," so that we confidently say, "The LORD is my helper, I will not be afraid. What shall man do to me?" Remember those who led you, who spoke the word of God to you; and considering the result of their conduct, imitate their faith. Jesus Christ is the same yesterday and today, yes and forever. Do not be carried away by varied and strange teachings; for it is good for the heart to be strengthened by grace, not by foods, through which those who were thus occupied were not benefited. (13:4-9)

The second major area of ethics dealt with in chapter 13 has to do with our responsibility to ourselves, and focuses on sexual purity, satisfaction with what we have, and steadfastness in the faith.

SEXUAL PURITY

MARRIAGE IS TO BE HONORED

In God's eyes, marriage is honorable. He established it at creation and has honored it ever since. In much of the world today, of course, marriage is anything but honored. A great many couples who marry do so as a temporary convenience, not as a social, much less a divine, requirement for their living together.

Let marriage be held in honor among all may have been a reaction to certain ascetic influences in the early church that held celibacy to be a holier state than marriage. Some men, such as the famous Origen of the third century, had themselves castrated, under the mistaken notion that they could thereby serve God more devotedly. Paul warns that in the last days apostate teachers will "forbid marriage" (1 Tim. 4:3). But God holds marriage not only to be permissible, but honorable, and we are to have the same high regard for it.

God honored marriage by establishing it. Jesus honored marriage by performing His first miracle at a wedding. The Holy Spirit honored marriage by using it to picture the church in the New Testament. The whole Trinity testifies that marriage is honorable. No person, therefore, is justified in disparaging marriage.

Scripture gives at least three reasons for marriage. One is the propagation of children. At creation, mankind was commissioned to "be fruitful and multiply, and fill the earth" (Gen. 1:28). Marriage is also provided as a means of preventing sexual sin. "Because of immoralities, let each man have his own wife, and let each woman have her own husband" (1 Cor. 7:2), Paul advises, and then goes on to counsel the unmarried and widows to marry if they do not have self-control (vv. 8-9). Marriage is also provided for companionship. "God said, 'It is not good for the man to be alone; I will make him a helper suitable for him'" (Gen. 2:18).

Marriage can be held in honor in many ways. One is by the husband's being the head. God is glorified in a family where the husband rules. "Christ is the head of every man, and the man is the head of a woman" (1 Cor. 11:3). "The husband is the head of the wife, as Christ also is the head of the church" (Eph. 5:23). Another way is a corollary of the first, namely, that wives be submissive to their husbands, as Sarah was to Abraham (1 Pet. 3:1, 6). A third way marriage is honored is by being regulated by mutual love and respect. "You husbands likewise, live with your wives in an understanding way, as with a weaker vessel, since she is a woman; and grant her honor as a fellow heir of the grace of life, so that your prayers may not be hindered" (v. 7). The concern of both husband and wife should center on the welfare and happiness of the other, on what can be given rather than on what can be obtained.

THE MARRIAGE BED IS TO BE UNDEFILED

God is serious about sexual purity. Men and women may play

around with illicit sex and be perfectly within their rights in the eyes of most people. But in the eyes of God, it is always sin and will always be judged. Paul warns, "Let no one deceive you with empty words, for because of these things the wrath of God comes upon the sons of disobedience" (Eph. 5:6). The apostle also tells us to "flee immorality. Every other sin that a man commits is outside the body, but the immoral man sins against his own body" (1 Cor. 6:18). "Immorality" (*porneia,* "fornication") is from the same basic Greek term as **fornicators** (*pornos*). In other words, the same sexual sin is involved in the two passages. Sexual sin not only is against God and other persons, it is also against ourselves. Part of our moral responsibility to ourselves is to be sexually pure.

The world today is obsessed with sex as never before. Sexual activity apart from marriage is considered acceptable and normal by more and more people. The publisher of a leading pornographic magazine maintains that "Sex is a function of the body, a drive which man shares with animals, like eating, drinking and sleeping. It's a physical demand that must be satisfied. If you don't satisfy it, you will have all sorts of neuroses and repressive psychoses. Sex is here to stay; let's forget the prudery that makes us hide from it. Throw away those inhibitions, find a girl who's like-minded and let yourself go."

Some of the more obvious results of such views are the heartbreaking increases in extramarital pregnancies, forcible rapes, illegitimate births (despite birth control measures and abortions), and in venereal diseases of all sorts. Billy Graham has commented that writings coming out of contemporary authors are "like the drippings of a broken sewer." Judgment already exists in the broken homes, the venereal disease, the psychological and physical breakdowns, and the murder and other violence that is generated when passion is uncontrolled. It is not possible to live and act against the moral grain of the universe established by God and not suffer terrible consequences.

When Christians are immoral, the immediate consequences may even be worse, because the testimony of the gospel is polluted. I will never forget a young coed who came to my office, obviously shaken. She said she was a new Christian and that soon after her conversion she started attending a church youth group. The president of the group asked her for a date, and she was flattered and thrilled to be going out with a Christian. "How different it will be from what I'm used to," she thought. But before the night was over, he had destroyed her purity, shattered her faith, and ruined his own testimony. The last I heard from the girl her life was still a shambles.

Within marriage, sex is beautiful, fulfilling, creative. Outside marriage, it is ugly, destructive, and damning. "But do not let immorality or any impurity or greed even be named among you, as is proper among saints" (Eph. 5:3).

Satisfaction with What We Have

Let your character be free from the love of money, being content with what you have; for He Himself has said, "I will never desert you, nor will I ever forsake you," so that we confidently say, "The Lord is my helper, I will not be afraid. What shall man do to me?" (13:5-6)

C. H. Spurgeon said, "I've been in a lot of testimony meetings, and I've heard a lot of people share how they've sinned, and I've had people come to me and make confession of sin. But in all my life I've never had one person confess the sin of covetousness to me." I have rarely had anyone confess covetousness to me, either.

A man once came into my office asking to confess a sin. He was obviously serious and quite broken up. He said his sin was gluttony. When I remarked that he did not look overweight, he replied, "I know. It is not that I eat too much but that I want to. I continually crave food. It's an obsession."

Covetousness is much like this man's gluttony. You do not have to acquire a lot of things to be covetous. In fact you do not have to acquire anything at all. Covetousness is an attitude; it is wanting to acquire things, longing for them, setting our thoughts and attention on them—whether we ever possess them or not.

When John D. Rockefeller was a young man, a friend reportedly asked him how much money he wanted. "A million dollars," he replied. After he had earned a million dollars, the friend asked him again how much money he wanted. The answer this time was, "Another million." Covetousness and greed follow a principle of increasing desire and decreasing satisfaction, a form of the law of diminishing returns. "He who loves money will not be satisfied with money, nor he who loves abundance with its income. This too is vanity" (Eccles. 5:10). The more you get the more you want. When we focus on material things, our having will never catch up with our wanting. It is one of God's unbreakable laws.

Love of money is one of the most common forms of covetousness, partly because money can be used to secure so many other things that we want. Loving money is lusting after material riches, whatever the form is. A Christian should be free from such love of material things. Love of money is sin against God, a form of distrust. **For He Himself has said, "I will never desert you, nor will I ever forsake you."** Among other things, loving money is trusting in uncertain riches rather than the living God (1 Tim. 6:17), looking for security in material things instead of in our heavenly Father. "Beware, and be on your guard against every form of greed," Jesus warned, "for not even when one has an abundance does his life consist of his possessions" (Luke 12:15).

Achan's love of money cost Israel a defeat at Ai, the lives of at least thirty-six of his fellow countrymen, his own life, and the lives of his family and flocks (Josh. 7:1, 5, 25). After Naaman was cleansed of leprosy, following Elisha's instruction to wash seven times in the Jordan, the prophet refused any payment. But Gehazi, Elisha's servant, later ran back to Naaman and deceived him in order to profit from the grateful captain. After lying again, he was cursed by Elisha with Naaman's leprosy (2 Kings 5:15-27). His greed led to lying, deceit, and leprosy. Judas was greedy as well as traitorous, willing to betray the Son of God for thirty pieces of silver. Ananias and Sapphira paid for their greed and attempted deceit with their lives (Acts 5:1-10). Greed is not a trifling sin before God. It has kept many unbelievers out of the kingdom, and it has caused many believers to lose the joy of the kingdom, or worse.

It is not wrong, of course, to earn or to have wealth. Abraham and Job were extremely wealthy. The New Testament mentions a number of faithful believers who had considerable wealth. It is **love of money** that "is a root of all sorts of evil, and some by longing for it have wandered away from the faith, and pierced themselves with many a pang" (1 Tim. 6:10). It is longing after it and trusting in it that is sinful. "If riches increase, do not set your heart upon them," David counsels (Ps. 62:10). Job puts the principle clearly: "If I have put my confidence in gold, and called fine gold my trust, if I have gloated because my wealth was great, and because my hand had secured so much; . . . That too would have been an iniquity calling for judgment, for I would have denied God above" (Job 31:24-25, 28). Trust in money is distrust in God.

Some persons love money but never acquire it. Other persons' love of money is in acquiring it. They live for the thrill of adding to their bank accounts, stock holdings, or conglomerates. For others, loving money is hoarding it. Misers are not so much interested in increasing their possessions as in simply holding on to them. They love money for its own sake. Still others are more interested in the things they can buy and display with their wealth. The conspicuous consumer is the big spender who flaunts his wealth. Whatever form love of money may take, the spiritual result is the same. It displeases God and separates us from Him. Nicer clothes, a bigger house, another car, a better vacation tempt all of us. But God tells us to be satisfied. **Be content with what you have.**

Many of those addressed in the book of Hebrews had lost most, or all, of their material possessions, because they knew they had "a better possession and an abiding one" (10:34). Some of them might have been longing to get back what they lost, thinking the cost was too high. They are told not to return to trust in material things. **We confidently say,**

"The LORD is my helper, I will not be afraid. What shall man do to me?" If we have the Lord, we have it all. Loss of anything else can be no worse than a bad inconvenience, an inconvenience that, surrendered to the Lord, will always be for our good. Material possessions are temporary, anyway. We are going to lose them sooner or later. If the Lord decides we should lose them sooner, we should not worry. Proverbs 23:5 says "wealth certainly makes itself wings."

Among the scriptural requirements for overseers, or bishops (also referred to as elders, Titus 1:5-7), is that of being "free from the love of money" (1 Tim. 3:3). No Christian can live effectively, much less lead effectively, who is longing after money. Love of money weakens our faith, weakens our testimony, and weakens our leadership. When we love money, our eye is on the wrong kind of gain. "Godliness actually is a means of great gain, when accompanied by contentment. For we have brought nothing into the world, so we cannot take anything out of it either. And if we have food and covering, with these we shall be content" (1 Tim. 6:6-8). Discontentment is one of man's greatest sins. Contentment is one of God's greatest blessings.

How do we enjoy contentment? How do we become satisfied with what we have? First, we must realize God's goodness. If we really believe that God is good, we know He will take care of us, His children. We know with Paul that "God causes all things to work together for good to those who love God, to those who are called according to His purpose" (Rom. 8:28).

Second, we should realize—not just acknowledge, but truly realize—that God is omniscient. He knows what we need long before we have a need or ask Him to meet it. Jesus assures us, "Your Father knows that you need these things" (Luke 12:30).

Third, we should think about what we deserve. What we want, or even need, is one thing; what we deserve is another. We should confess with Jacob, "I am unworthy of all the lovingkindness and of all the faithfulness which Thou hast shown to Thy servant" (Gen. 32:10). The smallest good thing we have is more than we deserve. The least-blessed of God's saints are rich (see Matt. 19:27-29).

Fourth, we should recognize God's supremacy, his sovereignty. God does not have the same plan for all of His children. What He lovingly gives to one, He just as lovingly may withhold from another. The Holy Spirit gives varieties of gifts, ministries, and effects, "But one and the same Spirit works all these things, distributing to each one individually just as He wills" (1 Cor. 12:4-11). In regard to material blessings, we should listen to Hannah's wisdom, "The LORD makes poor and rich" (1 Sam. 2:7). If He were to make us rich, we might be of outstanding service to Him. On the other hand, our becoming rich might be our spiritual undoing. The Lord knows what we need, and will provide us with no less.

Fifth, we should continually remind ourselves what true riches are. It is the worldly, including the wealthy worldly, who are poor, and it is believers, including poor ones, who are rich. Our treasure is in our homeland, in heaven, and we should set our minds "on the things above, not on the things that are on earth" (Col. 3:2).

Supremely, however, contentment comes from communion with God. The more we focus on Him the less we will be concerned about anything material. When you are near Jesus Christ, you are overwhelmed with the riches that you have in Him, and earthly possessions simply will not matter. Contentment is having confidence that **the LORD is my helper, I will not be afraid. What shall man do to me?**

STEADFASTNESS IN THE FAITH

Remember those who led you, who spoke the word of God to you; and considering the result of their conduct, imitate their faith. Jesus Christ is the same yesterday and today, yes and forever. Do not be carried away by varied and strange teachings; for it is good for the heart to be strengthened by grace, not by foods, through which those who were thus occupied were not benefited. (13:7-9)

I believe the primary appeal of this passage is for Jews who had heard and professed the gospel not to return to legalism. The New Covenant in Jesus Christ has standards, very high standards, but they do not involve ceremonies, rituals, holy days, and formalities. They are internal, not external.

Just as **those who led [us] who spoke the word of God,** and just as **Jesus Christ is the same yesterday and today,** so we should be in our doctrine and practices. We are not to be **carried away by varied and strange teachings.** One of Satan's most subtle approaches to the Christian is to move him away from sound doctrine, to get him wrapped up in beliefs that are unfounded, uncertain, and changing. Bad doctrine results in bad living.

PURITY OF DOCTRINE

One of the saddest things in the world is for a Christian to get drawn into false doctrine and be rendered ineffective, to lose his joy, reward, and testimony. Yet such has been happening since the earliest days of the church. Paul was amazed that some of the Galatian believers were "so quickly deserting Him who called you by the grace of Christ, for a different gospel; which is really not another; only there are some who are disturbing you, and want to distort the gospel of Christ" (Gal. 1:6-7).

Sometimes false teachers are kind, likable, and perhaps even sincere. It is often difficult to believe they would teach anything false or misleading. But we are to judge doctrine by God's Word, not by the appearance or personality of the person who holds it. "Even though we, or an angel from heaven, should preach to you a gospel contrary to that which we have preached to you, let him be accursed" (v. 8). In other words, even if Paul changed his teaching from the revealed truths he had been preaching, he should not be followed. Even an angel is not to be believed above God's Word. The point is so important that Paul repeats it in the next verse: "As we have said before, so I say again now, if any man is preaching to you a gospel contrary to that which you received, let him be accursed."

These Galatians had started out in grace but were falling back under the law. They had begun in the Spirit, but were now trying to continue in the flesh. The Jews being addressed in Hebrews 13 were in danger of doing the same thing. The **varied and strange teachings** were not necessarily new teachings. They are not named, but it is likely that many, if not most, of the teachings were traditional Jewish beliefs. But they were strange to the gospel of grace.

Paul also warned the Ephesian elders of this danger. "I know that after my departure savage wolves will come in among you, not sparing the flock; and from among your own selves men will arise, speaking perverse things, to draw away the disciples after them" (Acts 20:29-30). The apostle commended them to God's Word, the only resource they had for staying true to the faith (v. 32). The closing appeal of the book of Romans is, "Now I urge you, brethren, keep your eye on those who cause dissensions and hindrances contrary to the teaching which you learned, and turn away from them" (Rom. 16:17).

The worst false teachers are those who go under the guise of orthodoxy. An avowed liberal, cultist, or atheist is easily seen for what he is. Satan's best workers are the deceptive ones, who know they will get a better hearing from God's people if their heresy is coated with biblical ideas. "For such men are false apostles, deceitful workers, disguising themselves as apostles of Christ. And no wonder, for even Satan disguises himself as an angel of light" (2 Cor. 11:13-14). Satan's primary target is the church. He does not need to pervert the world, because it is already perverted, already in his camp. This is why the New Testament is so filled with warnings for Christians to beware of false teaching. Satan does wish to destroy the power of the truth in the church.

God knows that the greatest battle His church faces is purity of doctrine, because that is the basis of everything else. Every bad practice, every bad act, every bad standard of conduct, can be traced to bad belief. The end result of the work of apostles, prophets, evangelists, pastors, and teachers, and of believers becoming unified in the faith and maturing in Christ, is that "we are no longer to be children, tossed here and there by waves, and carried about by every wind of doctrine, by the trickery of men, by craftiness in deceitful scheming" (Eph. 4:14). A church that is not sound in doctrine is unstable and vulnerable.

One of the marks of small children is lack of discernment. They have no way of telling what is good or bad for themselves. They judge only by feeling and whim. If something looks attractive, they may try to pick it up, even if it were a poisonous snake. If something looks remotely like food, they try to eat it. A child of three left to select his own diet would never live to four. He would either sweeten or poison himself to death.

Some Christians, unfortunately, show little more discernment than this in the spiritual realm. They have been so little exposed to sound doctrine, or so long removed from it, that they judge entirely by appearance and feeling. Consequently, the church is filled with babes, who swallow almost any teaching that is put before them, as long as it is not blatant heresy and the teacher claims to be evangelical. As a body, and as individual Christians, we cannot be steadfast in Christ unless we are "constantly nourished on the words of the faith and of the sound doctrine" (1 Tim. 4:6). As long as believers are immature, false doctrine is a major danger (cf. Eph. 4:11-16).

REJECTION OF LEGALISM

Jews were used to having religious regulations for everything, and it was hard for them to adjust to freedom in Christ. It was difficult for them to accept the truth Paul expresses in 1 Corinthians 8:8, that "food will not commend us to God; we are neither the worse if we do not eat, nor the better if we do eat." All their lives they had been taught and had believed that what you ate and did not eat was extremely important to God. Even how it was prepared and eaten was important. Now they are told that **those who were thus occupied were not benefited.** Spirituality comes **not by foods.**

Being spiritually concerned about food is unnecessary under the New Testament. In fact, insisting on dietary regulations for religious reasons is *against* the gospel. Paul uses the harshest possible words to describe those who propagate such ideas.

> But the Spirit explicitly says that in later times some will fall away from the faith, paying attention to deceitful spirits and doctrines of demons, by means of the hypocrisy of liars seared in their own conscience as with a branding iron, men who forbid marriage and advocate abstaining from foods, which God has created to to be gratefully shared in by those who believe and know the truth. For everything created by God is good, and nothing is to be rejected, if it is received with gratitude; for it is sanctified by means of the word of God and prayer. (1 Tim. 4:1-5)

God had a hard time convincing Peter that the dietary and ceremonial restrictions of Judaism were no longer valid. Peter even argued
with God when He commanded him in a vision to kill and eat a variety of
unclean animals. The Lord had to tell him three times, "What God has
cleansed, no longer consider unholy" (Acts 10:15). Christ has rendered all
external observances invalid and useless. "For the kingdom of God is not
eating and drinking, but righteousness and peace and joy in the Holy
Spirit" (Rom. 14:17). The Colossians were exhorted: "let no one act as
your judge in regard to food" (2:16). As Christians, our hearts are only
strengthened by grace.

Christian Behavior: In Relation to God

(13:10-21)

We have an altar, from which those who serve the tabernacle have no right to eat. For the bodies of those animals whose blood is brought into the holy place by the high priest as an offering for sin, are burned outside the camp. Therefore Jesus also, that He might sanctify the people through His own blood, suffered outside the gate. Hence, let us go out to Him outside the camp, bearing His reproach. For here we do not have a lasting city, but we are seeking the city which is to come. Through Him then, let us continually offer up a sacrifice of praise to God, that is, the fruit of lips that give thanks to His name. And do not neglect doing good and sharing; for with such sacrifices God is pleased. Obey your leaders, and submit to them; for they keep watch over your souls, as those who will give an account. Let them do this with joy and not with grief, for this would be unprofitable for you.

Pray for us, for we are sure that we have a good conscience, desiring to conduct ourselves honorably in all things. And I urge you all the more to do this, that I may be restored to you the sooner.

Now the God of peace, who brought up from the dead the great Shepherd of the sheep through the blood of the eternal covenant, even Jesus our Lord, equip you in every good thing to do His will, working in us that which is pleasing in His sight, through Jesus Christ, to whom be the glory forever and ever. Amen. (13:10-21)

I see in this passage at least four things God wants in our behavior that are directly related to Him: separation, sacrifice, submission, and supplication.

SEPARATION

Verses 10-14 are among the most difficult in the book of Hebrews. They are subject to many interpretations and applications, and I do not want to be dogmatic in the views I present.

We have an altar, from which those who serve the tabernacle have no right to eat. For the bodies of those animals whose blood is brought into the holy place by the high priest as an offering for sin, are burned outside the camp. Therefore Jesus also, that He might sanctify the people through His own blood, suffered outside the gate. (13:10-12)

Many Christians believe the **altar** mentioned here is literal, and that it refers to the altars at which believers today are to worship. These interpreters hold that **right to eat** refers to the Lord's Supper. But who, then, would be **those who serve the tabernacle,** who **have no right to eat?** And verse 11 speaks of **the bodies of those animals whose blood is brought into the holy place by the high priest as an offering for sin.** This hardly can describe Christian worship.

Some believe the reference is to a heavenly altar, such as that spoken of in Revelation 6. But again, who would be those who had no right to eat there? And, in any case, there is no eating or sacrificing of animals at the heavenly altar.

Others believe the altar is a figure of Christ, whose body we are to eat and whose blood we are to drink (John 6:53-58). But still the questions remain about who is not allowed to eat and about the sacrificial animals.

I believe the best explanation is to consider that **We** refers to the writer's fellow Jews. That is, "We Jews have an altar. The priests serve at this altar in the Tabernacle, or the Temple. Ordinarily they are allowed to eat what remains of the sacrifices. But on the Day of Atonement, they are not allowed to eat the sin offering. The bodies of the animals used for this sacrifice are taken outside the camp and burned."

In this view, an analogy is given for Christians. As the priest of old could not have a part in the sins of the people, so the believer should be outside the camp of the world, no longer a part of its system, standards, and practices. This is what Jesus did, pictured supremely in the crucifixion, which was outside the city gates. **Therefore Jesus also, that He might sanctify the people through His own blood, suffered outside the gate.** I do not think the analogy can be pressed any further. It is simply a picture of Christians, following their Lord, separating themselves from the things of sin. As our Lord was crucified outside the walls of the city of Jerusalem, so we are to be spiritually outside the walls of sinning people.

Hence, let us go out to Him outside the camp, bearing His reproach. (13:13)

The practical point is that, as Christians, we must be willing to go out from the system, to bear the reproach and the shame that both the sin offering and Christ Himself bore, and to be rejected by men. This is the attitude Moses had toward the world. He considered "the reproach of Christ greater riches than the treasures of Egypt" (Heb. 11:26).

Paul had a great deal to say about separation. "Do not be bound together with unbelievers; for what partnership have righteousness and lawlessness, or what fellowship has light with darkness? Or what harmony has Christ with Belial, or what has a believer in common with an unbeliever?" (2 Cor. 6:14-15). Christians have nothing in common with the world system and should be separate from it (cf. 2 Tim. 2:4).

After the incident with the golden calf in the wilderness, and before the Tabernacle was built, Moses set a tent outside the camp, "a good distance from the camp, and he called it the tent of meeting. And it came about, that everyone who sought the LORD would go out to the tent of meeting which was outside the camp" (Ex. 33:7). Whenever Moses entered the tent, the "pillar of cloud would descend and stand at the entrance of the tent; and the LORD would speak with Moses" (v. 9). Those who wanted to approach God had to go outside the camp, because Israel for the most part, siding with the world system, had rejected God.

Whether the analogy is of the Old Testament sacrifice being taken outside the camp, of Christ's being crucified outside the gates of Jerusalem, or of the tent of meeting being outside the camp, the basic point seems to be that of separation.

For the Jews to whom Hebrews was written, separation from the world system meant separation from Judaism. God, so to speak, was no longer in the camp of Judaism. Whatever significance and importance the Old Covenant and traditional ceremonies, regulations, and standards of Judaism once had, they are now invalid. God now does His work completely outside the camp of Judaism. The moment Jesus died on the cross, the veil of the Temple was torn in two, and the Temple, the altar, the sacrifices, and the ritual seased to be a part of God's program. These were now a part of the world system, a part of man's religion, man's way, man's work. God cast them aside and they became as pagan as any sacrifice in the temples of Baal or Diana. A Christian Jew had no more right to hold on to Judaism than a Gentile Christian had to hold on to the worship of Jupiter.

Separation from the system does not mean separation from unbelievers in the sense of never having contact with them. If this were so, we could never witness to them or be hospitable to them. Nor does it mean we try to escape the world by becoming monastics. As far as separation is concerned, the world is an attitude, an orientation, not a place. As long as we are in the flesh, we take some of the world with us wherever we go. Paradoxically, a holier-than-thou attitude is the essence of worldliness, because it is centered in pride. It is worldly attitudes and habits from which we are to separate ourselves. And we can participate in many worldly things just as easily with Christians as with non-Christians.

In His high priestly prayer, Jesus describes our proper relationship to the world. "I do not ask Thee to take them out of the world, but to keep them from the evil one. They are not of the world, even as I am not of the world. Sanctify them in the truth; Thy word is truth. As Thou didst send Me into the world, I also have sent them into the world" (John 17:15-18). God sends us into the physical world, the world *where* people live. What we are to be separate from is the world system, the *way* the world's people live (cf. 1 John 2:15-17).

You do not have to participate actively in the system to be a part of it. It is just as worldly to want to do the things of the world as to do them. To want worldly things is to have your heart in the world, no matter where your body is. If you are sitting in church thinking about the impression you are making on your fellow worshipers, at that moment and to that extent you are in the world—no matter how spiritual the worship service itself may be.

True separation is costly. "All who desire to live godly in Christ Jesus will be persecuted" (2 Tim. 3:12). The reason why more Christians are not persecuted is simply because so few are truly godly, truly living outside the camp of the world. Speaking sarcastically of some worldly Corinthian believers, Paul wrote, "We are fools for Christ's sake, but you are prudent in Christ; we are weak, but you are strong; you are distinguished, but we are without honor. To this present hour we are both hungry and thirsty, and are poorly clothed, and are roughly treated, and are homeless" (1 Cor. 4:10-11). It is easy to be distinguished in the eyes of the world if we compromise godly living. Paul preferred being hungry, poorly clothed, and mistreated with Christ above being distinguished and well off in the world.

SACRIFICE

Through Him then, let us continually offer up a sacrifice of praise to God, that is, the fruit of lips that give thanks to His name. And do not neglect doing good and sharing; for with such sacrifices God is pleased. (13:15-16)

Sacrifice was extremely important to the Jew. It was God's provision for cleansing of sin under the Old Covenant. Many Christian Jews were no doubt wondering if God required any kind of sacrifice under the New Covenant. They knew Christ offered the one and only sacrifice for sin. But they were used to many kinds of sacrifice, and perhaps God still demanded some offering, some sacrifice, even of Christians.

Yes, He does, they are told. He demands the sacrifice of our praise and of our good works in His name. He demands sacrifice not in the form of a ritual or ceremony, but in word and in deed—in our praise of Him and in our service to others.

IN WORD

God no longer wants sacrifices of grain or animals. He wants only the **sacrifice of praise to God, that is, the fruit of lips that give thanks to His name.** The psalmists knew a great deal about this sort of sacrifice. If their writings could be characterized by any single word it would be praise. "I will give thanks to the LORD according to His righteousness, and will sing praise to the name of the LORD Most High" (Ps. 7:17). "Why are you in despair, O my soul? And why are you disturbed within me? Hope in God, for I shall again praise Him" (43:5). "I will give thanks to Thee, O LORD, among the peoples; and I will sing praises to Thee among the nations" (108:3). All of the last five psalms begin with "Praise the LORD," which in Hebrew is *hallelujah*. The sacrifice God desires is the cry of our lips in praise to Him.

The Christian's sacrifice of praise is to be offered **continually.** It is not to be a fair-weather offering, but an offering in every circumstance. "In everything give thanks; for this is God's will for you in Christ Jesus" (1 Thess. 5:18).

IN DEED

John warns us that "the one who does not love his brother whom he has seen, cannot love God whom he has not seen" (1 John 4:20). In other words, if our praise of God in word is not accompanied by **doing good and sharing,** it is not acceptable to Him. Worship involves action that honors God.

443

Isaiah gave a similar warning to Israel. When the people asked God, "Why have we fasted and Thou dost not see?" the Lord replied, "Is this not the fast which I chose, to loosen the bonds of wickedness, to undo the bands of the yoke, and to let the oppressed go free, and break every yoke? Is it not to divide your bread with the hungry, and bring the homeless poor into the house; when you see the naked, to cover him; and not to hide yourself from your own flesh?" (Isa. 58:3, 6-7).

Praise of God in word and deed are inseparable. Lip service must be accompanied by life service. "This is pure and undefiled religion in the sight of our God and Father, to visit orphans and widows in their distress, and to keep oneself unstained by the world" (James 1:27). The only acceptable sacrifice we can offer to God with our hands is to do good to one another, to share, to minister in whatever ways we can to the needs of others in His name. "Little children," John says, "let us not love with word or with tongue, but in deed and truth" (1 John 3:18).

SUBMISSION

Obey your leaders, and submit to them; for they keep watch over your souls, as those who will give an account. Let them do this with joy and not with grief, for this would be unprofitable for you. (13:17)

The third standard of Christian behavior toward God is submission. The most obvious submission seen in this text is that given to church leaders. But God mediates his earthly rule, secular and spiritual, through various men. Even pagan rulers who have no use for God are nevertheless used by Him. "Let every person be in subjection to the governing authorities. For there is no authority except from God, and those which exist are established by God" (Rom. 13:1). But for believers, God's most important rule is through Spirit-controlled men. Someday God will rule all the earth through His Son, the King of kings, but in the meanwhile He rules His church through godly men. Submission to these men, therefore, is submission to God.

BECAUSE CHURCH LEADERS REPRESENT GOD

The leaders of the church are called elders (presbyters) or overseers (bishops), the titles being interchangeable. These mature men are ordered by the Spirit of God to rule over His church on earth until Christ returns.

As they traveled about, Paul and Barnabas appointed elders in every church they established (Acts 14:23). Paul directed Titus to "appoint elders in every city" (Titus 1:5). Every New Testament congregation had such men who ruled it. They fed and led the flock (cf. Acts 20:28).

In many churches today, the congregation rules the leaders. This sort of government is foreign to the New Testament. Church leaders are not to be tyrants, because they do not rule for themselves but for God. But the command is unqualified: **Obey your leaders, and submit to them.** It is the right of such men, under God and in meekness and humility, to determine the direction of the church, to preside over it, to teach the word in it, to reprove, rebuke, and exhort (Titus 2:15). They are to "shepherd the flock of God . . . exercising oversight not under compulsion, but voluntarily, according to the will of God; and not for sordid gain, but with eagerness; nor yet as lording it over those allotted to [their] charge, but proving to be examples to the flock" (1 Pet. 5:2-3). Pastors and elders are undershepherds, who serve under the "Chief Shepherd" (v. 4).

Just as church leaders are to rule in love and humility, those under their leadership are to submit in love and humility. "But we request of you, brethren, that you appreciate those who diligently labor among you, and have charge over you in the Lord and give you instruction, and that you esteem them very highly in love because of their work" (1 Thess. 5:12-13).

Jesus said, "He who receives whomever I send receives Me; and he who receives Me receives Him who sent Me" (John 13:20). When a man is placed in the rule of a local church, our submission and obedience to him is equivalent to submission and obedience to Christ.

When you do not have Spirit-filled leaders who rule well or submissive people who follow well, you have chaos and disunity in the church and open the doors to all sorts of spiritual problems.

BECAUSE CHURCH LEADERS ARE ACCOUNTABLE TO GOD

The priority of every pastor, every elder, every church leader, is to care for the spiritual welfare of the congregation, **for they keep watch over your souls, as those who will give an account.** It is a sobering responsibility to be a leader in Christ's church.

Paul had a pastor's heart, an abiding concern for the spiritual welfare of all those under his care. He could say to all his spiritual children what he said to the Corinthians: "I will most gladly spend and be expended for your souls" (2 Cor. 12:15). John too could say, "I have no greater joy than this, to hear of my children walking in the truth" (3 John 4). A pastor's sweetest joy is to see those in his church walking with the Lord and bearing fruit. And, contrarily, one of the saddest tragedies that can come to a pastor is that of spending years of his life working with those who do not grow, do not respond to spiritual leadership, and do not walk in the truth.

BECAUSE CHURCH LEADERS RECEIVE JOY

Let them do this with joy and not with grief is addressed to the people, not to the leaders. In other words, it is the responsibility of the church to help their leaders rule with joy and satisfaction. One way of doing this is through willing submission to their authority. The joy of our leaders in the Lord should be a motivation for submission. We are not to submit begrudgingly or out of a feeling of compulsion, but willingly, so that our elders and pastors may experience joy in their work with us.

It is a serious (and all too common) thing for stubborn, self-willed people in church congregations to rob their pastors of the joy God intends faithful pastors to have. Failure to properly submit brings **grief** rather than joy to pastors, and consequently brings grief and displeasure to God, who sends them to minister over us. **Grief** (*stenazontes*) means an inner, unexpressed groaning. It is a grief often known only to the pastor, his family, and to God. Because lack of submission is an expression of selfishness and self-will, unruly congregations are not likely to be aware of, or to care about, the sorrow they cause their pastor and other leaders.

Perhaps more than any other prophet, Jeremiah knew the grief caused by rebellious, stiff-necked people. He is called the weeping prophet for good reason. At his call God promised to make the prophet "as a fortified city, and as a pillar of iron and as walls of bronze against the whole land, to the kings of Judah, to its princes, to its priests and to the people of the land. And they will fight against you, but they will not overcome you, for I am with you to deliver you" (Jer. 1:18). All these opponents together could not silence Jeremiah or frustrate his ministry, for God was always with him. But even God could not prevent them from breaking the prophet's heart. "Oh, that my head were waters, and my eyes a fountain of tears, that I might weep day and night for the slain of the daughter of my people!" (9:1). They were slain because of their wickedness and rebelliousness, because "all of them are adulterers, an assembly of treacherous men. And they bend their tongue like their bow; lies and not truth prevail in the land; for they proceed from evil to evil" (9:2-3). Jeremiah spent a lifetime of anguish because of the self-willed, sinful people over whom God had given him spiritual leadership.

Even the Son of God was not spared grief. Satan could not conquer Him and the scribes and Pharisees could not confound Him, but the people could grieve Him. Their hardness of heart and rejection caused Him to cry out, "Jerusalem, Jerusalem, the city that kills the prophets and stones those sent to her! How often I wanted to gather your children together, just as a hen gathers her brood under her wings, and you would not have it!" (Luke 13:34).

In spite of Paul's straightforward exhortations and rebukes, most of the Corinthian believers apparently were little concerned about his authority or his feelings. There is no telling how many tears they caused him to shed.

But there is another type of response, the response that pleases God and pleases his leaders. To the Philippian Christians the apostle could say, "I thank my God in all my remembrance of you, always offering prayer with joy in my every prayer for you all" (Phil. 1:3-4). The reason was not that they were inherently a nicer group of people than the Corinthians (though they may have been) but that they held to sound doctrine and were submissive to their leaders. No doctrinal errors or rebelliousness is reflected in the Philippian letter. The squabble between Euodia and Syntyche is the only problem mentioned. The suffering Paul endured while serving them was not caused by them, but by critics outside the church. That sort of suffering simply added to his joy. "Even if I am being poured out as a drink offering upon the sacrifice and service of your faith, I rejoice and share my joy with you all. And you too, I urge you, rejoice in the same way and share your joy with me" (2:17-18).

The church at Thessalonica also brought a great deal of happiness to Paul. "For who is our hope or joy or crown of exultation? Is it not even you, in the presence of our Lord Jesus at His coming? For you are our glory and joy" (1 Thess. 2:19-20). Paul was so grateful for these dear believers that he hardly knew how to express his feelings. "For what thanks can we render to God for you in return for all the joy with which we rejoice before our God on your account" (3:9). These two churches were a pastor's delight.

Spiritual leaders, of course, are not infallible or perfect. There are times when a church member is justified in disagreeing with a pastor or elder, even in accusing such a leader of sin. But Scripture gives clear direction as to when and how this is to be done. "Do not receive an accusation against an elder except on the basis of two or three witnesses. Those who continue in sin, rebuke in the presence of all, so that the rest also may be fearful of sinning" (1 Tim. 5:19-20).

The attitude God wants His people to have toward their pastors and elders is, "that you appreciate those who diligently labor among you, and have charge over you in the Lord and give you instruction" (1 Thess. 5:12).

BECAUSE WE RECEIVE JOY

For members of the Body to be in constant rebellion against their pastors and elders prevents proper learning and proper growth. It brings spiritual barrenness and bitterness. A person who never brings joy will never have joy.

To cause our leaders grief is harmful to ourselves as well as to them and to the church as a whole. It is **unprofitable for you.** When we do not have a loving and obedient spirit, God is displeased, our leaders are grieved, and we lose our joy as well. Paul's joy in faithful believers was always related to their joy. "Rejoice in the same way and share your joy with me" (Phil. 2:18). You will never find a truly happy pastor apart from a happy congregation, or a happy congregation apart from a happy pastor.

SUPPLICATION

Pray for us, for we are sure that we have a good conscience, desiring to conduct ourselves honorably in all things. And I urge you all the more to do this, that I may be restored to you the sooner. (13:18-19)

Our fourth obligation to God is supplication. To pray for our leaders in the church is to serve and to please God. Prayer makes things possible; it moves the hand of God.

The writer of Hebrews apparently was a leader in the church, or churches, to whom he was writing, and here asks for the prayer support of those among whom he had ministered. Every servant of Christ needs the prayers of the believers he is called to work with. Church leaders are made of the same stuff as those they serve. They have sins, weaknesses, limitations, blind spots, and needs of all sorts, just as everyone else. They both need and deserve the prayers of God's people, without which they cannot be the most effective in His work (cf. James 3:1).

God's leaders face temptations that most other believers do not face to the same degree, because Satan knows that, if he can undermine the leaders, many others will go down with them. If he can get them to compromise, to weaken their stand, to lessen their efforts, to become dejected and hopeless, he has caused the work of Christ great damage.

Paul did not hesitate to ask for prayer. "Pray on my behalf, that utterance may be given to me in the opening of my mouth, to make known with boldness the mystery of the gospel" (Eph. 6:19). How much more do God's ordinary ministers need the prayer of their people.

IT IS DESERVED

The writer asks for prayer because **we are sure that we have a good conscience, desiring to conduct ourselves honorably in all things.** He was not being egotistical or arrogant, but simply saying that, to the best of his own knowledge, he had ministered to the people faithfully—not perfectly, but faithfully. He not only needed their prayers; he had earned their prayers. He had a right before God to expect them to pray for him.

He did not simply imagine or suppose that he had been faithful. He had a **good conscience** about it. Even the unsaved person has a conscience, a built-in sense of right and wrong, but his is defiled (Titus 1:15). As Christians, our consciences are cleansed, purified (Heb. 9:14). We do not become infallible or omniscient, but, under the Spirit's direction, we are able to distinguish right from wrong in a way we were never able to do before. A cleansed conscience not only enables us better to tell right from wrong but to be honest about it, with ourselves as well as with others. The writer of Hebrews could honestly say he had served well the people given into his care. He therefore had a right to expect their prayers.

I do not believe everyone deserves our prayer. Certainly not everything a person may ask us to pray about deserves our prayer. A man came to me once and asked that I pray for a ministry he had recently begun. It was a telephone ministry in which people would call up, leave a recorded message, and then be called on by this man or one of his workers. He had invested some $20,000 in electronic equipment and six months of time by himself and his co-workers. For this effort, they had seen two persons make "decisions" they "thought" were probably genuine. I suggested that, if he sold his equipment and began witnessing door-to-door, he and his workers could probably see more results in a week than they had seen in six months.

If a person asks for our prayer, we should want to know whether what they are asking prayer for deserves our effort. Prayer time is the most precious time we have, and it should be used wisely and carefully.

IT IS NEEDED

The writer was not asking for prayer only because he believed he deserved it. He had a need for it. The most urgent need on his mind when he wrote was that he might **be restored to you the sooner.** Whatever the reason had been for his leaving them, he was anxious to return.

Neither did Paul idly ask for prayer. Near the end of Romans he pleads with fellow believers, "strive together with me in your prayers to God for me, that I may be delivered from those who are disobedient in Judea, and that my service for Jerusalem may prove acceptable to the saints" (Rom. 15:30-31). He was asking a group of faithful believers to pray for his deliverance from a group of unfaithful believers.

God is sovereign, but prayer makes things possible that otherwise would not be possible.

CHRIST'S EXAMPLE

In all our behavior—in relation to others, to ourselves, and to God—Jesus Christ is our supreme example. If we want to see sustained love, where can we see it better than in Jesus, who, "knowing that His hour had come that He should depart out of this world to the Father, having loved His own who were in the world, He loved them to the end" (John 13:1)?

If we would learn sympathy, where better than from our Lord, who wept with Mary and Martha at the tomb of their brother Lazarus (John 11:35)?

If we want to know what sexual purity is like, who can show us better than Jesus, "who has been tempted in all things as we are, yet without sin" (Heb. 4:15)?

If we want to learn satisfaction, who was more content than Jesus, who said, "My food is to do the will of Him who sent Me, and to accomplish His work" (John 4:34) and, "The foxes have holes, and the birds of the air have nests; but the Son of Man has nowhere to lay His head" (Matt. 8:20)?

If it is steadfastness we need to appreciate, who was more steadfast than Jesus as He resisted Satan in the wilderness (Matt. 4:1-10)?

If we want to know how to be separate from the world, we should listen to Jesus' prayer, "I do not ask Thee to take them out of the world, but to keep them from the evil one. They are not of the world, even as I am not of the world" (John 17:15-16).

If we want to see sacrifice, Jesus not only made the perfect sacrifice, He *was* the perfect sacrifice, giving "Himself up for us, an offering and a sacrifice to God as a fragrant aroma" (Eph. 5:2).

If we would learn submission, who has ever submitted to the Father as Jesus did in the garden when He prayed, "Abba! Father! All things are possible for Thee; remove this cup from Me; yet not what I will, but what Thou wilt" (Mark 14:36)?

If we want to know what supplication is, we must listen to Jesus' great prayer on our behalf that constitutes the entire seventeenth chapter of John.

THE POWER OF GOD

Now the God of peace, who brought up from the dead the great Shepherd of the sheep through the blood of the eternal covenant, even Jesus our Lord, equip you in every good thing to do His will, working in us that which is pleasing in His sight, through Jesus Christ, to whom be the glory forever and ever. Amen. (13:20-21)

These verses are really a benediction and could stand without comment. Even Jesus' own examples, perfect and powerful as they are, cannot in themselves enable us to follow in His footsteps. We need more than example. The writer calls on God to make possible the out-working of this truth in the lives of His people. To attempt to live the Christian life with the purest doctrine and the finest examples, but without God's direct power, is to build with wood, hay, and straw (1 Cor. 3:12). We not only need to know God's will, we need to have His power. We need the **God of peace** to **equip** us **in every good thing to do His will.**

So God gives us His ethics and He gives us the power to follow them, to live them out. Christian growth and obedience have nothing to do with our own power. Christian growth and obedience are by God's power, **working in us that which is pleasing in His sight, through Jesus Christ.**

The greatest display of divine power in the history of the universe was at the resurrection of Jesus Christ, when God **brought up from the dead the great Shepherd of the sheep through the blood of the eternal covenant.** God is **the God of peace,** in that He has established peace with man through the blood of the cross (Col. 1:20). By that cross an eternal covenant was made (cf. Zech. 9:11; Ezek. 37:26). So the blood of **Jesus our Lord** is eternally powerful (unlike the repeated, temporary Old Covenant sacrifices) and satisfactory to God, thus He brought Him **up from the dead.** It is the God of this power and the power of this God that enable those who love Him to do His will. "Not that we are adequate in ourselves to consider anything as coming from ourselves, but our adequacy is from God" (2 Cor. 3:5).

The thing we must contribute to the Christian life is willing yieldedness. All we have to do is open the channel of our wills and let God's power work through us. "Now He who supplies seed to the sower and bread for food, will supply and multiply your seed for sowing and increase the harvest of your righteousness" (2 Cor. 9:10). We can work out our salvation because God is at work in us "both to will and to work for His good pleasure" (Phil. 2:12-13). Because Christ does the work, He deserves the credit and praise, **to whom be the glory forever and ever. Amen.**

A Short Postscript
(13:22-25)

But I urge you, brethren, bear with this word of exhortation, for I have written to you briefly. Take notice that our brother Timothy has been released, with whom, if he comes soon, I shall see you. Greet all of your leaders and all the saints. Those from Italy greet you. Grace be with you all. (13:22-25)

EXHORTATION

The writer gives a characterization to his epistle. He calls it **this word of exhortation.** (Cf. Acts 13:15 where this phrase is used as the designation for a sermon.) The book of Hebrews is a great treatise preached with a pen. It is an urgent call to the readers to come to single-minded devotion to the Lord Jesus Christ and to complete satisfaction with the New Covenant. The high and lofty doctrinal themes are the foundation for this primary exhortation.

Then, almost in an apologetic manner, he encourages the readers to **bear with** what he has written, to receive with receptive minds and warm hearts what he has said—in contrast to those in 2 Timothy 4:3

(whom Paul describes using the same verb, *anechō*) who do "not endure [bear with] sound doctrine."

The epistle has been straightforward, confrontive, uncompromising, somewhat complex, and taxing to mind, emotion, and will. Yet, even so, it is **written . . . briefly.**

Brachus (**briefly**) means short, or in a few words. The whole letter (under 10,000 words) is shorter than Romans or 1 Corinthians and can be read in less than an hour. If the writer had dealt fully with the great themes he discusses, the letter would have been inconceivably long. But it is amazingly short in comparison to the eternal and infinite truths it contains.

FOLLOW-UP

Take notice that our brother Timothy has been released, with whom, if he comes soon, I shall see you. (13:23)

They needed to know that one of God's choice servants, **our brother, Timothy** (who must have been well known to them) **has been released.** Although the term *apoluō* (**released**) has a variety of meanings, it is most frequently used in the New Testament in relation to releasing from custody prisoners who were under arrest or in prison. The historical detail of Timothy's imprisonment is unknown. We are not surprised that he, like his teacher, Paul, was put in jail for preaching Jesus. Timothy seemed to be faltering in his faithfulness when Paul wrote his second epistle to him. Thus, in 2 Timothy 1:6—2:12 and 3:12-14, the apostle encourages him to endure persecution and not to fear it. It is likely that Hebrews was penned soon after 2 Timothy, and we see that this man of God had responded well to Paul's previous exhortation.

The writer's hope was that Timothy would soon join him, and that together they would visit the readers. Here we see a clear illustration of the importance of following up with personal ministry those who are taught. Such ministry was an oft-expressed desire of the apostle Paul (see Rom. 15:28-29).

GREETING

Greet all of your leaders and all the saints. Those from Italy greet you. (13:24)

The readers had already been exhorted to obey their leaders (v. 17), and now they are asked to convey greetings to them and to **all the saints** who were part of that fellowship in Christ. The mention of **all of**

your leaders supports the other New Testament teachings of the plurality of elders (cf. Acts 20:17-38) who lead the people of God.

Those from Italy greet you may indicate that the group to which he wrote was in Italy, or simply that some Italian Christians were with him and sent their greetings.

BENEDICTION

Grace be with you all. (13:25)

The epistle ends with a simple, yet lovely conclusion in the form of a plea for God to grant **grace** to the readers (cf. Titus 3:15), as He does for all His children through the One who alone can give grace—the Lord Jesus Christ.

Bibliography

Barclay, William. *The Letter to the Hebrews*. Philadelphia: Westminster, 1957.

Bruce, F.F. *The Epistle to the Hebrews*. Grand Rapids: Eerdmans, 1964.

Griffith-Thomas, W.H. *Hebrews: A Devotional Commentary*. Grand Rapids: Eerdmans, 1970.

Hewitt, Thomas. *The Epistle to the Hebrews*. Tyndale New Testament Commentaries. Grand Rapids: Eerdmans, 1975.

Hughes, Philip Edgecumbe. *A Commentary on the Epistle to the Hebrews*. Grand Rapids: Eerdmans, 1977.

Kent, Homer A., Jr. *The Epistle to the Hebrews*. Grand Rapids: Baker, 1972.

Morris, Leon. *Hebrews: The Expositor's Bible Commentary*. vol. 12. Edited by Frank C. Gaebelein. Grand Rapids: Zondervan, 1981.

Murray, Andrew. *The Holiest of All*. Old Tappan, N.J.: Revell, 1969.

Newell, William R. *Hebrews: Verse by Verse*. Chicago: Moody, 1947.

Pink, Arthur W. *Exposition of Hebrews*. Grand Rapids: Baker, 1968.

Westcott, B.F. *The Epistle to the Hebrews*. Grand Rapids: Eerdmans, 1977.

Scripture Index

2:26	154, 317	1:21	5, 87	5	47, 94
3:1	448	2:5	322	6	23
3:13-18	405	2:20-21	143	11	300
4:4	329	3:4	36	13	48
4:13	142	3:9	86, 257, 280, 320, 404	14-15	313
5:1-3	352	3:10	35, 324, 418	24	201
5:5-6	352	3:12	418	24-25	18
5:7-8	330				
5:8	241	**1 John**		**Revelation**	
5:15	137	1:5	34	3:4	311
		1:6-7	312	3:21	55, 207
1 Peter		1:7	19	4:10-11	381
1:4	368	1:8	250	5:1	11
1:4-5	146	1:10	250	5:2	12, 26
1:10	248	2:2	223	5:3	12
1:10-11	10, 369	2:6	313, 405	5:4-5	12
1:10-12	4, 192	2:9	157	5:5	27
1:11	31	2:15	329, 350, 442	5:6	12, 172
1:12	31	2:17	350, 442	5:8	172
1:16	254, 396	2:18	241	5:9-10	59
1:18-19	19	2:19	83, 94, 270, 407	5:11	23, 415
1:19-20	235	3:2	140, 416	5:11-12	32
1:22-23	423	3:9	274	5:13-14	32
2:2	372	3:12	301	6	440
2:4-5	80	3:14	424	6:9-10	303
2:5	110, 372	3:16	425	6:12-14	417
2:9	110	3:17	425	6:14	35
2:15	420	3:18	444	7:4-8	213
2:17	98	3:18-19	425	9:11	48
2:21	66	4:8	157	11:7	48
3:1	430	4:10	65	11:15	12
3:1-2	404	4:20	443	12:4	23
3:6	430	5:1	157	13:8	235, 410
3:7	430	5:10	309	14:7	98
3:19-20	322	5:16	395	14:13	104
3:22	20	5:19	56, 160	19:10	415
4:7	241	5:20	34	19:11-16	242
4:10-11	156			19:15-16	37
4:13	368	**2 John**		19:20	48
4:14	354	6	312	20:4	59
5:2-3	445			20:11-15	141
5:4	445	**3 John**		20:12	410
5:5	425	4	313, 445	21:1-2	418
		7	155	21:3	415
2 Peter				21:27	415
1:3	423	**Jude**		22:18-19	7
1:3-4	254	3-4	302		
1:4	69, 311				

Moody Press, a ministry of the Moody Bible Institute, is designed for education, evangelization, and edification. If we may assist you in knowing more about Christ and the Christian life, please write us without obligation: Moody Press, c/o MLM, Chicago, Illinois 60610

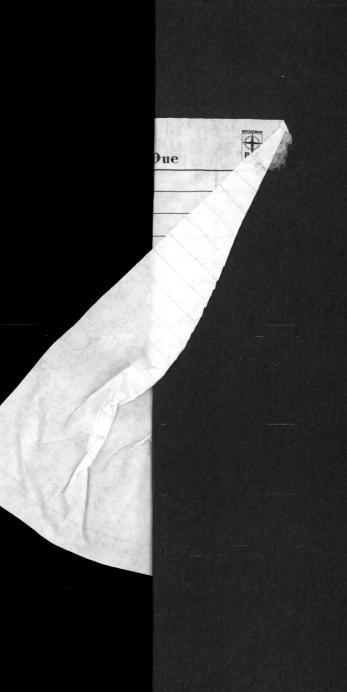

Due

BROADMAN

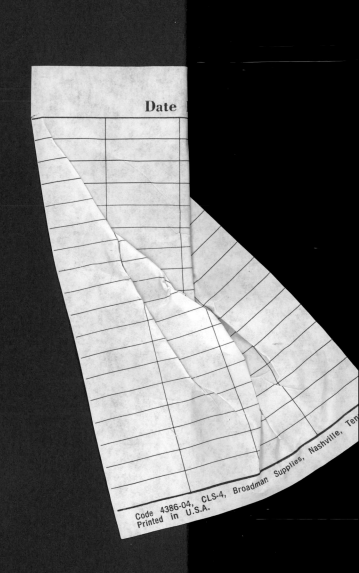

Date

Code 4386-04, CLS-4, Broadman Supplies, Nashville, Ten
Printed in U.S.A.

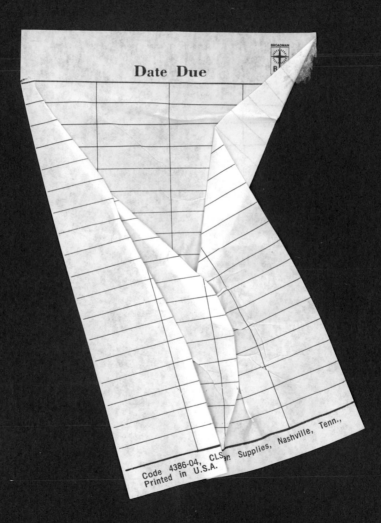

Date Due

Code 4386-04, CLS_n Supplies, Nashville, Tenn.,
Printed in U.S.A.